MW00855893

INTERNATIONAL TAXATION

IN A NUTSHELL®

TWELFTH EDITION

MINDY HERZFELD
Professor of Tax Practice
University of Florida,
Levin College of Law

WEST
ACADEMIC
PUBLISHING

The publisher is not engaged in rendering legal or other professional advice, and this publication is not a substitute for the advice of an attorney. If you require legal or other expert advice, you should seek the services of a competent attorney or other professional.

Nutshell Series, In a Nutshell and the Nutshell Logo are trademarks registered in the U.S. Patent and Trademark Office.

ISBN: 978-1-68467-346-9

*With thanks to Richard Doernberg,
author of the first 10 editions of
International Taxation in a Nutshell,
for entrusting me with his (25 year old)
baby and for serving as a role model
both professionally and personally.*

Mindy Herzfeld

PREFACE

The tax law that was enacted by Congress in December 2017 made major changes to the U.S. international tax rules, some of them the most significant since these rules were first established in the early decades of the 20th century. Over the past two years, Treasury and the IRS have engaged in the herculean tax of writing interpretive guidance for the new laws, issuing thousands of pages of regulations (proposed and final) in the process. This 12th edition of International Taxation in a Nutshell represents a significant revision from the 11th edition, which incorporated the statutory changes of TCJA but was published before any regulatory guidance had been released. There's no reason to think that Treasury and the IRS are done with this process, however. The upcoming years are sure to see finalization of proposed guidance as well as new and revised rules.

Those readers who are beginning their study of this subject for the first time are in some respects very fortunate: they are not burdened by expectations and old ways of thinking that ground those whose education was in a prior regime. New students of international taxation have the chance to become freshly minted experts in the post-TCJA tax rules, not far behind those who have decades of experience of practicing in this area. It's an exciting time to be studying this field.

The study of international taxation is not just relevant for law students who want to become expert in a highly technical area of the law. For anyone who is or will be involved in international business and cross-border investment transactions, it is important to have a basic understanding of the relevant tax laws. This book serves as an introduction to the U.S. law of international taxation for both law students interested in becoming tax experts and a broader audience of those engaged in cross-border business from a variety of backgrounds. It is a primer that can be useful for law and accounting students, foreign tax practitioners or scholars, U.S. tax practitioners seeking an introduction to the area or an overview of recent changes in the international tax rules, and others who might benefit from an overview of the U.S. tax laws governing international trade and investment. The book summarizes the law, offering some attention to the purposes of the various legal rules. However, it is beyond the scope of the book to offer a critical evaluation of the provisions summarized or to delve deeply into tax planning structures and techniques. Actually practicing international tax in reliance solely on this primer could be hazardous to your career.

It will come as no revelation that the U.S. income tax laws are wondrously complex, made even more so by recent changes ostensibly intended to "simplify" the law. Moreover, the student of U.S. international tax law should have some grounding in U.S. individual, partnership, state, employment and corporate tax principles. U.S. international tax does not exist in a vacuum. Knowledge of foreign tax systems is also useful. But realistically, many practitioners have their hands full trying to understand the U.S. system and collaborate with foreign colleagues on cross-border transactions. Ironically, it is because of the complexity that it is important to present a straight-forward conceptual framework of the U.S. international tax provisions. Even with a framework, the intricate rules governing U.S. taxation of international transactions can be mind-numbing. Without an understanding of the structure of the U.S. international tax provisions, the rules are all but incomprehensible. Unfortunately, that is all too often the case even with an understanding of the structure.

To use this book effectively, it is helpful to have the Internal Revenue Code open at all times. If you are truly ambidextrous, you should have the most updated version of the U.S. Income Tax Regulations at hand as well. Frequent references are made to both the Code and the regulations. There are some citations to caselaw and administrative rulings where they help illustrate the subject matter. However, the book is not a treatise, and so there is no attempt to treat comprehensively the caselaw and rulings.

To consider fully the international tax laws affecting international trade would require the study not only of U.S. international tax laws but also of foreign tax laws. However, such a study is beyond the scope of this book. So too is any consideration of the non-tax legal concerns affecting international transactions, including private international law, European Union law, the WTO, other free trade agreements, the internal laws of other nations, customs law, tariffs, and non-tax international treaties. The tax laws of the individual states of the United States are not discussed. The focus here is on U.S. international tax laws and U.S. income tax treaties.

The book is divided into three Parts. It begins with an introduction to the fundamentals of U.S. international taxation and the source rules. The second Part then addresses the U.S. activities of foreign taxpayers—that is, investment and business activities carried on by nonresident individuals and foreign corporations in the United States. After a consideration of what a nonresident is for U.S. tax purposes, the basic U.S. jurisdictional tax principles are considered in this Part, with some attention given to the branch profits tax and the provisions affecting foreign investment in U.S. real estate. Also included in this Part is a chapter on U.S. income tax treaties. The new U.S. tax act did not come about in a vacuum, and part of the context for these changes includes international developments in tax treaty principles. This chapter touches upon, but does not comprehensively address, those broader changes. The last chapter in this Part addresses filing, withholding, and reporting requirements.

The third Part of the book is directed at foreign activities of U.S. citizens and residents—that is, investment and business activities of U.S. citizens and residents, including domestic corporations that generate income outside the United States. Its these rules that underwent the most comprehensive revision in TCJA. The most important changes were in the treatment of controlled foreign corporations and the U.S. foreign tax credit, consideration of which topics forms the centerpiece of this Part. This Part also discusses passive foreign investment companies, intercompany pricing, rules governing the treatment of foreign currency, and international tax-free transactions. There is also a chapter on tax arbitrage—the heart of much international tax planning, including a discussion of how the parameters of such planning have shifted after passage of the TCJA and as a result of other global developments. The income tax provisions regulating the "ethics" of U.S. business behavior abroad are also briefly addressed.

Hopefully, this book kindles an interest in international taxation. If it does, the reader must move beyond this primer into the maw of the Internal Revenue Code, Regulations, rulings and caselaw that make up the substance of U.S. international taxation. In addition, there are ample secondary sources that explore the subject more comprehensively.

The material presented is current through August 14, 2019 with occasional attempts to gaze into the tax crystal ball in order to anticipate likely changes to the landscape of international tax rules in the short-term future.

With thanks to the many dedicated readers of the 11th edition whose comments and careful reading contributed to improvements to the 12th edition, especially including the students at University of Florida Levin College of Law's tax LL.M. program, the students in Reed Shuldiner's international tax class at University of Pennsylvania law school, the students in Steven Shay's class in U.S. international taxation at Leiden University, Aaron Hsu, summer associate at Ivins, Phillips & Barker, and Fernando Juarez of Stanford law school's 2019 LL.M. class, and Caroline Magdinec of Ivins, Phillips & Barker as well. Special thanks to 2019 UF Law LL.M. graduate Eric Monteerode Medeiros, to David Ernick of PwC for comments on the transfer pricing chapter, and to Richard Doernberg for his continued support and advice and tolerance for my mangling of his work.

Any errors are my own. Please send any comments, suggestions or corrections to herzfeld@law.ufl.edu.

MINDY HERZFELD

Washington, D.C.
August 14, 2019

OUTLINE

PART 1. OVERVIEW OF
FUNDAMENTAL CONCEPTS

PART 2. U.S. ACTIVITIES OF FOREIGN TAXPAYERS

Chapter 4. Taxing Rules for Non-U.S. Persons

PART 3. FOREIGN ACTIVITIES
OF U.S. TAXPAYERS

TABLE OF ABBREVIATIONS

TABLE OF CASES

References are to Pages

TABLE OF INTERNAL REVENUE CODE SECTIONS

References are to Pages

XXXI

TABLE OF TREASURY REGULATIONS AND REVENUE RULINGS

References are to Pages

INTERNATIONAL TAXATION

TAXATION

IN A NUTSHELL®

TWELFTH EDITION

PART 1

OVERVIEW OF FUNDAMENTAL CONCEPTS

CHAPTER 1
INTRODUCTION

§ 1.01   INTERNATIONAL TRADE AND INTERNATIONAL TAX

Over the past 70 years. technological improvements in communications and transportation have made the world smaller and contributed to the exponential growth of international trade. A comparison of Commerce Department data from 1960 to today shows just how much the world has changed in this regard. For all of 1960, the United States exported just under $26 billion and imported approximately $22 billion of goods and services, while in the single month of April 2019, exports of goods and services were more than $206 billion while imports were more than $257 billion. Recent backlashes against international trade and globalization notwithstanding, most of the factors that have contributed to the growth in international trade since the middle of the last century remain relevant. Global economic growth continues to depend on the cross-border trade in goods and services, albeit among shifting trends in global supply chains. International taxation of such cross-border trade is an important factor in the volume and flows of such trade.

§ 1.02   ECONOMICS OF INTERNATIONAL TRADE

Why do foreign taxpayers invest in the United States or U.S. taxpayers invest abroad? The following short excerpt from a venerable first-grade reader is instructive:

> Mr. Smith had a horse. He used to ride his horse to work. One day Mr. Smith said, "I want to get a car to go to work."

> Mr. Smith went to a place that sells cars. He asked, "Will you give me a car if I give you my horse?" The man who sells the cars wanted a horse. He took the horse and gave Mr. Smith a car. Both men were happy.*

In the aggregate, trade makes both parties better off. In this respect international trade is no different from domestic trade. (Note the key phrase here: "in the aggregate". An important issue in both domestic and global politics is how to address concerns of those on the margins of the aggregate.)

Despite pressures in some quarters on international trade, the relentless pressure for global trade likely will continue to grow. One can see how, also from Mr. Smith's example. If written in 1955, Mr. Smith probably was able to acquire a car that was designed and manufactured in the same country in which he was purchasing it. Most of the parts— from the steel body to the seat upholstery—were probably also made in a single country. Today's economy is vastly different, and the car that Mr. Smith acquires today is probably sourced from multiple countries and has crossed international borders many times in the process. The growth of

---

global supply chains—in both goods and services—has played a big role in contributing to the growth in international trade and the global economy as highlighted in the numbers above. Changes to cross-border trade, and to the taxation of cross-border transactions, have also been driven by the increasingly important role of intangibles in generating value and profits for businesses both domestically and globally.

§ 1.03   THE CENTRAL PROBLEM OF INTERNATIONAL TAXATION

When there is bilateral trade, the governments of both trading parties may want to collect a tax on any gains from the trade. To change slightly the example above, suppose that Mr. Smith exchanged cash instead of a horse for the car. Suppose further that the seller of the car is a U.S. citizen who resides in the United States, the car is manufactured in Canada, and Mr. Smith lives in Canada. The United States may claim the right to tax any gain on the sale of the car because of the seller's residence or citizenship, and Canada may claim taxing authority because the car was manufactured in Canada and sold in Canada to a Canadian resident. Overlapping claims of taxing authority—sometimes referred to as juridical double taxation—can create coordination difficulties.

To illustrate the necessity for coordination, suppose that Canada imposes a 50 percent tax on any gains occurring in Canada, and the United States imposes a 50 percent tax on any gains wherever they occur if earned by a U.S. resident (or citizen). Under these assumptions, the combined tax rate is 100 percent, the entire gain on the transaction would be taxed away, and it is likely that the transaction would never take place. The loss of the transaction would hurt both parties, others who would benefit from the trade (*e.g.*, employees of, and suppliers to, the manufacturer) as well as the treasuries of Canada and the United States. The study of international tax is the study of rules that attempt to address the overlapping tax authority of sovereign countries. It is also the story of taxpayers' attempts to exploit gaps in those rules to their benefit.

In the example just considered, potential double taxation arises because one country claims taxing authority based on the residence (or citizenship) of the taxpayer and another country claims taxing authority based on where the income arises. Juridical double taxation can also arise when each of two countries claims a taxpayer as a resident or where each of two countries claims that income arises in that country. Countries generally attempt to combat juridical double taxation both through unilateral domestic legislation and bilateral tax treaties with other countries. *See infra* Chapters 5 and 8.

§ 1.04 ECONOMICS OF JURIDICAL DOUBLE TAXATION

From an efficiency point of view, the aspirational goal for a tax system in general, or for the U.S. rules governing international transactions specifically, is the implementation of a tax-neutral set of rules that neither discourage nor encourage particular activity. The tax system should remain in the background, and business, investment and consumption decisions should be made for non-tax reasons. In the international tax context, the concept of tax neutrality has historically been measured against several standards.

One standard is capital-export neutrality. A tax system meets the standard of capital-export neutrality if a taxpayer's choice between investing capital at home or abroad is not affected by taxation. For example, if X Corp., a U.S. corporation, is subject to a 21 percent tax rate in the United States on its worldwide income, and the income from its Irish branch is also subject to a 12.5 percent Irish tax, a U.S. tax system with capital-export neutrality would credit the Irish tax against the potential U.S. tax liability and tax the Irish profits in the United States at a 8.5 percent residual tax rate. X Corp.'s tax rate is 21 percent regardless of the location of the investment. If the investment is located in the United States, taxes are paid to the U.S. treasury; if the investment is located in Ireland, the Irish treasury would collect as tax 12.5 percent of the income and the United States would collect as tax 8.5 percent of the income. With perfect competition, capital-export neutrality results in an efficient allocation of capital. X Corp. will make its investment decision based on business factors rather than tax rates.

The second neutrality standard is capital-import neutrality, sometimes referred to as foreign or competitive neutrality. This standard is satisfied when all firms doing business in a market are taxed at the same rate. For example, if the United States exempted X Corp.'s Irish income from U.S. taxation, there would be capital-import neutrality from an Irish perspective because X Corp. would be taxed at the same rate as a comparable Irish corporation doing business in Ireland. Compared with a tax crediting mechanism, this exemption method violates capital-export neutrality. A U.S. taxpayer will pay lower overall taxes if the investment is made in Ireland (12.5 percent rate) than if the investment is made in the United States (21 percent rate).

A third neutrality standard is national neutrality. Under this standard, the total U.S. returns on capital which are shared between the taxpayer and the U.S. Treasury are the same whether the capital is invested in the United States or abroad. That is, if the U.S. tax rate is 21 percent of a taxpayer's income (with the taxpayer keeping the other 79 percent of the income), the imposition of foreign taxes will not alter that rate. Applying the national neutrality principle to the example above, any taxes paid to Ireland by X Corp. would be deductible and not creditable against U.S. income tax liability; foreign income taxes would be treated in the same manner as any other domestic or international business expense. Notice the effect on the taxpayer is higher overall taxes because the deductibility of Irish income tax does not reduce U.S. tax dollar-for-dollar.

The U.S. tax system has elements of all three standards of neutrality. Historically, the tax credit mechanism, discussed *infra* in Chapters 8 and 10, allows U.S. taxpayers operating abroad to reduce U.S. taxes by an amount equal to any income taxes paid to other countries on foreign income (subject to limitation). This provision is driven by notions of capital-export neutrality. However, not all foreign taxes are creditable (*e.g.*, foreign property taxes, value added taxes, capital taxes), and allowance of the credit is limited in certain circumstances, most significantly by the 2017 U.S. tax reform. To the extent that a U.S. taxpayer incurs foreign taxes that are not creditable, those foreign taxes sometimes can be deducted for U.S. tax purposes. This treatment and other restrictions on the foreign tax credit mechanism are in keeping with the concept of national neutrality. To the extent that the United States exempts from U.S. taxation a portion of the earnings of foreign subsidiaries of U.S. corporations—another policy change introduced by the 2017 law—the capital-import neutrality principle is also advanced.

In recent years, tax scholars have suggested that tax systems should be based on different types of "neutralities." Some have developed a theory of capital ownership neutrality, which is based on a principle that taxes should not influence the decision of who owns assets. The theory of market neutrality would require that two firms competing in the same market should face the same overall effective tax rates on their investments. For example, if an American firm and a British firm compete with each other in Canada, the two firms should face the same effective tax rate.

As this book will demonstrate, the various principled theories upon which academics think international tax rules should be based sometimes (often) crash into the political realities of tax policy. The confluence of the desire to get the rules technically right from a theoretical perspective, combined with the political drivers of changing tax policies, contribute significantly to the complexity of the system.

§ 1.05 OVERVIEW OF WORLDWIDE INTERNATIONAL TAX SYSTEMS

Virtually every country has tax rules that govern the tax treatment of its residents operating abroad and foreign taxpayers operating in that country. While international taxing systems differ from country to country, there are some basic similarities and understandings. Sometimes these understandings are set forth in bilateral income tax treaties working in tandem with domestic tax laws; in other cases, it is the domestic tax laws of a country that determine the appropriate tax treatment.

In general, a country exercises jurisdiction for legal purposes based on either *nationality* or *territoriality*. With respect to taxation, a country may claim that all income earned by a citizen or a company incorporated in that country is subject to taxation because of the legal connection to that country. With limited exceptions, the United States exercises such jurisdiction over its citizens and companies incorporated in the United States regardless of where income is earned. Business profits earned directly by a U.S. corporation in Italy generally are subject to tax in the United States (and normally in Italy as well) unless a limited participation exemption applies. Salary earned by a U.S. citizen who is a resident of Switzerland from Swiss employment is subject to tax in the United States (and in Switzerland as well).

Basing tax jurisdiction on nationality can be justified by the benefits available to nationals. For example, in a very real sense U.S. citizens have an insurance policy; they can return to the United States whenever they want, and they have the protection of the U.S. government wherever they are abroad. Tax payments contribute to the availability of that "insurance." U.S. corporations, regardless of their physical presence in the United States, enjoy the benefits of U.S. laws that define corporate relationships. However, the United States is somewhat unusual in relying on citizenship or mere place of incorporation as a basis for jurisdiction.

In addition to nationality, countries often exercise jurisdiction based on *territoriality*. A territorial connection justifies the exercise of taxing jurisdiction because a taxpayer can be expected to share the costs of running a country which makes possible the production of income, its maintenance and investment, and its use through consumption. The principle of territoriality applies with respect to *persons* and *objects* (*i.e.*, income). Country A may claim taxing authority over a citizen of country B if that individual is considered a resident of country A. Similarly, a company incorporated in country B may be subject to tax in country A if there are sufficient connections. For example, many countries (not including the United States) find a sufficient territorial connection if the place of effective management of a corporation is situated within their boundaries.

Territorial jurisdiction over a *person* is analytically similar to jurisdiction based on *nationality*. In both cases it is the connection of the person to a country that justifies taxing jurisdiction. In the case of nationality, that connection is a legal one (*e.g.*, citizenship or incorporation). In the case of territorial jurisdiction over a person, the connection is factual (*e.g.*, whether that person is actually resident in a particular country). Either one may be referred as "residence" based jurisdiction.

Even if a person is not a citizen or resident of a country, that country may assert territorial tax jurisdiction over income deriving from within the territory of that country earned by a citizen or resident of another country. This is sometimes referred to as "source" jurisdiction because the source of the income is within a country. For example, a country may impose a tax on business profits of a nonresident earned within that country. Investment income, including dividends, interest, royalties, and rent, may also be subject to tax in the country in which such income arises. Typically, a country does not attempt to tax income with which it has no connection. For example, the United States normally does not tax income earned by a French corporation in France or in Germany. But even here there are significant exceptions. For example, under rules generally referred to as CFC (controlled foreign corporation rules) the income of a French company is taxable in the United States in cases where the U.S. tax laws deem it to be earned by its U.S. shareholder.

The potential for double taxation occurs when conflicting jurisdictional claims arise. For example, country A may claim the right to tax a person (including a corporation) based on that person's nationality or residence while country B stakes its claim of taxing authority because income is earned in country B. There is a norm of international taxation which the United States has generally followed that cedes the primary taxing authority to the country of territorial connection (*i.e.*, the "source" country where the income is earned) and the residual taxing authority to the country of nationality or residence (the "residence" country). Accordingly, the United States normally credits any income taxes paid in India on income earned in India by a U.S. citizen or resident against the income tax otherwise due in the United States, and only the excess, if any, of U.S. income tax on the foreign income over the foreign tax on such income is collected by the U.S. treasury. Many countries have adopted more of a territorial approach to jurisdiction and relieve any double taxation by exempting certain income (*e.g.*, business profits) earned in another country from the tax base, rather than including such income in the tax base and then granting a credit for foreign taxes paid as the United States does.

The taxation of income based on *territorial* jurisdiction generally takes one of two forms. A

country typically asserts full jurisdiction over
business profits generated within that country by a
nonresident (who in the case of the United States is
not a U.S. citizen), taxing those profits in the same
manner as if they were earned by a resident of that
country. Expenses associated with generating such
income are normally deductible. Non-business,
investment income, such as passive dividends,
interest, royalties and rent, typically is subject to
limited jurisdiction. Often such income is taxed by a
country in which the income arises on a gross basis
(*i.e.*, no deductions permitted) at rates ranging from
0 to 30 percent. The different rates that often apply
to such income when compared with business profits
reflect, in part, the fact that the territorial connection
for a full-blown business within a jurisdiction is often
more significant than the territorial connection for an
investment where the only connection may be the
payer's residence. It should also be noted that a low
tax rate on gross income may in fact result in a high
tax rate on net income. Suppose country A imposes a
30 percent tax on $100 of passive royalty income
earned by a resident of country B from a license with
a country A licensee. If the country B resident incurs
$60 of expenses to produce the $100 of gross income,
the effective tax rate in country A is 75 percent (*i.e.*,
a $30 tax on $40 of net income).

§ 1.06 RECENT CHANGES TO THE
INTERNATIONAL TAX SYSTEM

As the examples above demonstrate, without
concerted attempts by countries to address it, cross-
border trade could be negatively impacted by the

problem of double taxation. More recently, there has been a significant focus by governments and policy makers related to the opposite concern: the possibility of double non-taxation. In double non-taxation, taxpayers successfully exploit gaps or differences between individual countries' tax rules to generate income which is not subject to tax anywhere (so-called "stateless income"). The Paris-based OECD (Organization for Economic Cooperation and Development) has spent a lot of energy over the past several years marshalling countries to develop a coordinated approach to address concerns over double non-taxation. In 2013 it launched a Base Erosion and Profit Shifting Project, known as BEPS, with the intent of developing recommendations to combat these concerns. The 15 BEPS action items included a mix of recommendations for countries to change domestic laws, proposed changes to bilateral tax treaties, and a hodgepodge of other hot topics. You'll see mention of BEPS, and the BEPS action items, throughout this volume.

In order to accomplish the changes recommended as part of the BEPS project, the OECD also developed a Multilateral Instrument. This legal document was intended to implement BEPS changes to bilateral treaties without requiring countries to renegotiate the entire treaty. The complicated process by which countries could choose which changes to implement into which bilateral treaties is still unfolding.

In December 2017, the U.S. Congress adopted a different approach towards addressing some of the same concerns behind the OECD's BEPS project and other broader concerns over the out-datedness of the U.S. tax system and its international tax rules in particular. Public Law No. 115–97, informally known as the Tax Cuts & Jobs Act (TCJA) enacted the most sweeping changes to the U.S. international tax rules in the past century. Many of the changes were undertaken with the goal of making U.S. businesses more competitive in a global marketplace and ensuring that U.S. companies were incentivized to remain incorporated in the United States and keep operations and assets (especially high-value intangible assets) in the country. Two years later, the success of the law in achieving these goals remains unclear. Chapter 14 considers how the U.S. Congress, other countries and international organizations have responded to tax-motivated cross-border planning and how new rules may impact tax planning behaviors of businesses and individuals within the context of global tax developments.

The amendments to the Internal Revenue Code introduced by the TCJA are numerous and complex. Over the past two years, the IRS and Treasury have published thousands of pages of proposed, temporary and final rules that try to interpret and implement them in a sensible and administrable fashion. There are lots of uncertainties over how to apply these rules to specific facts. But two things are certain: the evolving story of U.S. international tax reforms is far from over, and the demand for expertise in understanding and applying the U.S. international tax rules has never been greater.

CHAPTER 2
BASIC U.S. JURISDICTIONAL TAX PRINCIPLES

§ 2.01 INTRODUCTION TO U.S. TAXING PROVISIONS

International transactions can be grouped into two broad categories: outbound and inbound. The term "outbound transactions" refers to U.S. residents and citizens doing business and investing abroad. The term "inbound transactions" refers to foreign taxpayers doing business and investing in the United States.

§ 2.02 OUTBOUND TRANSACTIONS

U.S. individual residents and citizens wherever residing are generally taxed on their worldwide income under the rates specified in I.R.C. § 1. However, there is an exclusion for certain income earned abroad by qualified individuals. *See* I.R.C. § 911 (discussed *infra* at § 7.02).

Historically, domestic corporations (*i.e.*, those created or organized in the United States, *see* I.R.C. § 7701(a)(4)) are also taxed on worldwide income under the rates specified in I.R.C. § 11. The TCJA in theory introduced a territorial system which would exempt foreign earned business income, but as will be discussed in greater detail, this territorial exemption applies only in limited circumstances. *See* Chapters 7 and 9. U.S. individuals or corporations that are partners in either a U.S. or foreign partnership are also taxable on worldwide income. U.S. taxpayers engaged in activities abroad generally compute taxable income in the same manner as U.S. taxpayers operating solely within the United States, although there are some differences with respect to foreign activities of U.S. taxpayers. For example, under I.R.C. § 168(g)(1)(A), there are limits on the method of depreciation available for property used outside the United States.

There are some important rules governing the U.S. taxation of foreign activities. These rules were substantially changed by the TCJA, and are treated in more detail in Chapters 7 and 9. Under these new rules, a U.S. corporate shareholder is generally entitled to a 100 percent dividend received deduction upon the distribution of a dividend from a 10 percent owned foreign subsidiary. I.R.C. § 245A. At the same time, the TCJA vastly expanded the circumstances under which the earnings of a foreign company with a U.S. shareholder will be taxed to the shareholder when earned. I.R.C. §§ 951–960; *infra* Chapter 9. Under the post-TCJA regime, a U.S. shareholder of a foreign company can be subject to very different rules, depending on whether the shareholder is an individual, a partnership, or a corporation for U.S. tax purposes (different rules also apply to shareholders that are S corporations).

For U.S. citizens and residents, including domestic corporations, among the most important international tax provisions are those dealing with the foreign tax credit. I.R.C. §§ 901–909. *See infra* Chapter 8. If a U.S. taxpayer earns income in

Germany, that income is taxable in the United States and may be taxable in Germany as well. In order to alleviate this double tax, the United States allows the taxpayer to offset taxes due in the United States with the income taxes paid in Germany. This foreign tax mechanism is full of twists and turns that are considered in more detail *infra*. For example, if Germany decides to tax income that the United States considers to be U.S. source income, no credit for German taxes paid is allowed to offset U.S. tax on that income. Also, if the German tax on the income earned in Germany is higher than the U.S. tax on that income, the U.S. taxpayer may not be able to credit the entire German tax against the U.S. tax liability. Essentially, the German tax can be used only to offset the U.S. tax on the German income (and in some cases other foreign source income), not the U.S. tax on U.S. source income. Otherwise the United States would cede to Germany the right to collect taxes on U.S. income.

Because the United States only provides a foreign tax credit for foreign income taxes imposed on income that the United States considers to be foreign source, the U.S. source rules, described *infra* in Chapter 3, play an important role in determining the total U.S. tax burden on U.S. persons' income earned overseas. U.S. taxpayers generally want to plan to maximize their foreign source income to allow a maximum foreign tax credit and thereby minimize any potential U.S. tax on the income. Whether a U.S. taxpayer earns foreign or U.S. source income, it will be taxable in the United States. But with foreign source income, the amount of U.S. tax may be lowered if foreign tax credits are available.

For example, suppose USCo currently earns $100 million of foreign source income from Country X, paying Country X income taxes of $42 million, and $100 million of U.S. source income. For U.S. tax purposes, USCo declares $200 million of taxable income and faces a potential U.S. tax (assuming a 21% tax rate) of $42 million. However, USCo may be able to take a credit for the foreign taxes paid, but only to the extent of the U.S. tax that would be imposed on the foreign source income. In this example, the credit would be limited to $21 million (*i.e.*, the potential U.S. tax on the foreign source income). In total, USCo would pay $21 million of U.S. tax and $42 million of foreign tax. Now suppose that USCo was able to change the source of what is now the $100 million of U.S. source income. If USCo can turn that income into foreign source income and not incur any additional foreign tax in doing so, then USCo may be able to use the full $42 million of foreign taxes paid to offset the $42 million potential U.S. tax on the total income. The result would be $0 U.S. tax liability and $42 million of foreign tax. By changing the source, the taxpayer in this example was able to save $21 million in U.S. tax. At the same time, the changes introduced by the TCJA have placed new limitations on U.S. shareholders' ability to utilize the foreign tax credit to offset U.S. tax otherwise owed on foreign earnings. These topics will be discussed in greater detail in Chapter 10 and 14.

§ 2.03 INBOUND TRANSACTIONS

The taxation of inbound transactions is not as all-encompassing as the taxation of outbound transactions. Nonresident aliens and foreign corporations are not subject to U.S. taxation on their worldwide income. While I.R.C. §§ 1 and 11 appear to apply to all taxpayers, I.R.C. §§ 2(d) and 11(d) apply the rates in a manner set forth in other specified provisions.

(A) INDIVIDUALS

For nonresident alien individuals, the basic taxing provisions are found in I.R.C. § 871. Under I.R.C. § 871(b), a nonresident alien individual engaged in a trade or business in the United States is taxed like a U.S. taxpayer under I.R.C. § 1 on taxable income which is effectively connected with the conduct of the trade or business. Broadly stated, nonresident alien individuals are taxed like U.S. taxpayers on most U.S. business income. Section 871(b) contains two important terms of art that are described in more detail *infra* at §§ 4.02–4.03: "engaged in a trade or business" and income "effectively connected" with the conduct of a trade or business within the United States (hereinafter sometimes referred to as "effectively connected income" or "ECI"). For a definition of these terms, *see* I.R.C. §§ 864(b) (engaged in a trade or business) and 864(c) (effectively connected income).

Nonresident alien individuals are also subject to U.S. taxation on some types of recurring investment income. Section 871(a) imposes a flat 30 percent tax on amounts received from sources within the United States which are "fixed or determinable annual or periodical gains, profits, and income" (hereinafter sometimes referred to as "FDAP" income). The most important categories of FDAP income are interest, dividends, rents, and royalties. These types of income generally are subject to a 30 percent tax on the gross amount of the distribution unless the distributions are income effectively connected with the conduct of a U.S. trade or business (*e.g.*, receipt of interest by a bank) in which case the income is subject to tax as business income on the net amount of income. (The rate may be reduced if there's a tax treaty in effect.) Although FDAP income includes "salaries, wages, . . . compensations, remunerations, [and] emoluments," virtually all income from services performed within the United States results in ECI that is taxed under I.R.C. §§ 871(b) or 882. *See* I.R.C. § 864(c)(2) and Reg. § 1.864–4(c)(6)(ii).

Generally, nonresident alien individuals are not taxable on capital gains transactions as such gains are not the recurring type of FDAP income addressed by I.R.C. § 871(a)(1). There are at least three exceptions to this rule. First, capital gains generated by the sale of U.S. real property or the stock of certain U.S. real property holding corporations are treated as ECI under I.R.C. § 897 and are therefore subject to tax in the same manner as other business income. *See infra* § 4.07.

Second, any capital gains transaction that is effectively connected with the conduct of a trade or business will be taxable under I.R.C. § 871(b) as business income. For example, suppose an Italian resident who is engaged in a paperback publishing business in the United States sells U.S. securities that were purchased with funds generated by the business and are managed by employees of the business who use the income generated by the securities to meet the current needs of the business. Gain from that sale would at first glance be taxable in the same manner as other business income. *See* I.R.C. § 864(c)(2). However, the regulations take the position that stock of a corporation is not treated as an asset held for use in a U.S. trade or business. Reg. § 1.864–4(c)(2)(iii). If the Italian resident sells assets used in the U.S. trade or business at a gain, the gain would probably be I.R.C. § 1231 gain that would be treated as capital gain. That capital gain would be taxable in the United States as income effectively connected with the conduct of the U.S. trade or business.

Under the third exception, which will almost never apply, capital gains for nonresident aliens present in the United States 183 days or more during the taxable year may be taxable in the United States. I.R.C. § 871(a)(2). Generally, a person present in the United States for more than 183 days will be a U.S. resident and will not be taxable under I.R.C. § 871(a)(2). *See* § 4.04(G) for a discussion of when I.R.C. § 871(a)(2) may apply.

(B) CORPORATIONS

The treatment of foreign corporations (*i.e.*, those incorporated abroad) parallels the treatment of nonresident alien individuals. A foreign corporation is taxed under I.R.C. § 11 on its taxable income effectively connected with the conduct of a U.S. trade or business. I.R.C. § 882. That is, a foreign corporation, like a domestic corporation, is taxed on business profits from the conduct of a trade or business in the United States. The fixed or determinable annual or periodical gains, profits, and income (*i.e.*, investment income) of a foreign corporation from U.S. sources is subject to a flat 30 percent gross basis tax under I.R.C. § 881 to the extent such income is not effectively connected with the conduct of a U.S. trade or business (again, subject to potential application of a treaty).

There is one other taxing provision affecting foreign corporations that must be considered—the branch profits tax under I.R.C. § 884. *See infra* § 4.05. Suppose a nonresident alien individual does business in the United States through a U.S. corporation. The corporation is taxed on its earnings under I.R.C. § 11 and the shareholder is subject to the 30 percent tax on any dividend paid in accordance with I.R.C. § 871(a). The two taxes comprise the double tax system that is a mainstay of U.S. corporate taxation in general. Suppose instead that the nonresident alien individual operates the U.S. business through a foreign corporation. The corporation's business income (the effectively connected income) is still taxable. I.R.C. § 882. Historically, when the foreign corporation distributed a dividend to its foreign shareholders, it was not difficult for the shareholder to avoid the imposition of the 30 percent tax under I.R.C. § 871(a).

In order to equalize the overall taxation of distributed corporate earnings regardless of whether the distributing corporation is a U.S. or foreign corporation, Congress enacted a branch profits tax. Under I.R.C. § 884, a foreign corporation must pay a 30 percent branch profits tax to the extent that its U.S. branch repatriates (or is deemed to repatriate) its earnings from the United States to the home country. The branch profits tax is levied in addition to the tax under I.R.C. § 882 on corporate income. Where the branch profits tax applies, there is no further tax when a foreign corporation makes a dividend distribution to its foreign shareholders.

(C) PARTNERSHIPS

A nonresident alien individual or nonresident corporation that is a partner in either a U.S. or foreign partnership is generally taxed as if the partner had earned the income directly. For example, a nonresident alien individual or foreign corporation is considered to be engaged in a trade or business within the United States if the partnership is so engaged. I.R.C. § 875. *See also Donroy, Ltd. v. United States*, 301 F.2d 200 (9th Cir. 1962). Ordinarily, a partnership is not a taxable entity for U.S. tax purposes.

§ 2.04   CITIZENSHIP AND RESIDENCY

(A) INDIVIDUALS

The United States is unusual among nations in taxing its citizens on their worldwide income regardless of their residence. In *Cook v. Tait*, 265 U.S. 47 (1924), plaintiff, a citizen of the United States, was a resident of Mexico. The Supreme Court held that U.S. taxation of the taxpayer's worldwide income violated neither the U.S. Constitution nor international law. The Court justified taxation on the theory that the benefits of citizenship extend beyond territorial boundaries. For example, the United States seeks to protect its citizens anywhere in the world. Also, citizens have the right to return to the United States whenever they want and participate in the economic system. In effect, a citizen of the United States has an insurance policy, and taxes are the cost of maintaining that policy.

Every person born or naturalized in the United States and subject to its jurisdiction is a citizen. Reg. § 1.1–1(c). A noncitizen who has filed a declaration of intention of becoming a citizen but who has not yet been granted citizenship by a final order of a naturalization court is an alien.

It is usually not difficult to determine whether a taxpayer is or is not a U.S. citizen for U.S. tax purposes. Determining residency can be more troublesome. Whether an individual is taxed on worldwide income under I.R.C. § 1 or essentially on U.S. business and investment income under I.R.C. § 871 often depends on the definition of residency. Prior to 1984, the definition evolved judicially, resulting in uncertainty in many situations. Now I.R.C. § 7701(b) provides a "bright line" test.

An individual is considered to be a resident of the United States if the individual meets any one of three tests: lawful admission to the United States (*i.e.*, "green card" test); "substantial presence" in the United States, or; a first year election to be treated as a resident. I.R.C. § 7701(b)(1)(A). An individual becomes a lawful permanent resident of the United States in accordance with the immigration laws. Once permanent residence is obtained, an individual remains a lawful permanent resident until the status is revoked or abandoned.

The heart of I.R.C. § 7701(b) is the "substantial presence" test. An individual meets this test if the individual is present in the United States for at least 31 days during the current year and at least 183 days for the three-year period ending on the last day of the current year using a weighted average. I.R.C. § 7701(b)(3). The weighted average works as follows: days present in the current year are multiplied by 1; days in the immediate preceding year are multiplied by $1/3$; days in the next preceding year are multiplied by $1/6$. For example, suppose an individual is present in the United States for 120 days in the current year and in each of the two preceding years. The individual does not satisfy the substantial presence test because the weighted average is only 180 days $((120 \times 1) + (120 \times 1/3) + (120 \times 1/6))$. If the individual was present in the United States 122 days each year, the individual would exactly meet the 183 day weighted average $((122 \times 1) + (122 \times 1/3) + (122 \times 1/6))$ and would be considered a U.S. resident.

An individual is present in the United States on any day the individual is physically present at any time during the day (except for commuters from

Mexico and Canada). I.R.C. § 7701(b)(7). For purposes of the residency test, individuals do not count days where the individual was unable to leave the United States because of a medical condition or days where the individual is a foreign government employee, a teacher, a student, or a professional athlete. I.R.C. § 7701(b)(3)(D).

Even if an alien satisfies the substantial presence test, the alien is not a resident if the individual is present in the United States on fewer than 183 days during the current year and has a tax home in a foreign country to which the individual has a closer connection than to the United States. I.R.C. § 7701(b)(3)(B). For this purpose, a tax home is considered to be located at a taxpayer's regular or principal place of business or if the taxpayer has no regular or principal place of business at his regular place of abode. I.R.C. § 911(d)(3); Reg. § 1.911–2(b).

A newly-arrived individual in the United States may be unable to satisfy the substantial presence test but may want to be considered a U.S. resident. For example, an individual present in the United States and earning a salary is fully taxable on the amount of salary income whether the individual is or is not a U.S. resident. However, if the individual is a U.S. resident, the overall tax burden may be less because of various personal deductions (*e.g.*, dependency deductions) that are not available to nonresidents. A special first-year election of residency is available for an alien if the individual is present in the United States for 31 consecutive days and at least 75 percent of the days in the part of the current year that begins with the first of the 31 consecutive days. I.R.C. § 7701(b)(4). In addition, the election may not be made before the individual meets the substantial presence test for the succeeding year (*i.e.*, the taxpayer either obtains a filing extension for the first year or files an amended return). If the election can be made, it is effective for the portion of the year beginning with the first of the 31 days.

(B) CORPORATIONS

The residency test for corporations is much simpler than the test for individuals. A U.S. corporation taxable on its worldwide income is a corporation created or organized in the United States. I.R.C. § 7701(a)(3) and (4). As a general rule, a foreign corporation (*i.e.*, a corporation not created or organized in the United States) is taxable under I.R.C. §§ 881 and 882 only on income effectively connected with the conduct of a trade or business in the United States or on specified U.S. investment income. I.R.C. § 7701(a)(5). However, in response to concerns that U.S. corporations were escaping U.S. taxation by re-incorporating overseas, Congress in 2004 enacted "anti-inversion" rules that treat some foreign corporations as U.S. corporations. I.R.C. § 7874. Treasury has been expanding the scope of this statutory rule since enactment. *See infra* § 13.02(G).

While the residence of a corporation may be easy to determine under U.S. law, it is not always easy to determine whether an entity is to be taxed as a corporation. Suppose entity E is formed in country X by US1 and US2, who are individual residents of the United States. Is the income earned by E, income earned by a nonresident corporation or is the income earned by a transparent partnership in which case individuals US1 and US2, U.S. residents, will be taxable? Historically, this has been a difficult problem compounded by the fact that country X might treat E as a corporation while the United States might treat E as a transparent partnership (or vice versa). "Check-the-box" regulations can provide taxpayers with flexibility in choosing whether they wish to be taxed as a pass-through or corporate entity for U.S. tax purposes—depending on how the entity is organized under local law. *See infra* § 14.02; Reg. § 301.7701–2 and –3. Under the regulations, the legal form matters in determining the extent of the taxpayer's flexibility to choose its taxable form. An entity with a single owner may be treated as disregarded unless an election is made to treat it as a corporation, while another entity may default to corporation status unless an election is made to treat it as a transparent entity. Entities that have more than one owner, unless they are "per se corporations," may be treated as partnerships or as corporations. (Per se corporations can't make an election to change their U.S. tax status). Reg. §§ 301.7701–1 *et seq.*

These "check-the-box" regulations govern the classification of an entity for U.S. tax purposes; another country may rely on its own domestic provisions in determining how it will treat the same entity for its tax purposes. While the ability to have an entity treated one way for U.S. tax purposes and another way for foreign tax purposes has been an important part of tax planning since promulgation of the check-the-box regulations, significant constraints were imposed on this type of planning with enactment by TCJA of "anti-hybrid rules." *See infra* at §§ 14.02, 14.03.

§ 2.05   EXPATRIATES

Suppose a citizen of the United States, fearing a high U.S. tax liability, renounces citizenship. First note that if the individual is a resident of the United States, the renunciation has no tax effect because U.S. residents are taxed in the same manner as U.S. citizens. If the individual is a nonresident, income from foreign sources (*e.g.*, interest or dividends from foreign investments) generally is not subject to U.S. taxation. However, under I.R.C. § 877A, if a citizen gives up U.S. citizenship, the taxpayer may be treated as if all property is sold for fair market value the day before expatriation. Accordingly, an "exit tax" would be imposed on any built-in gain.

For example, suppose a nonresident U.S. citizen owns shares of stock in a U.S. company. The shares have a basis of $1 million and a fair market value of $10 million. On the sale of the stock, the taxpayer faces $9 million of income for U.S. tax purposes. In order to avoid any U.S. tax, suppose the taxpayer renounces U.S. citizenship and then sells the stock. In the absence of a provision like I.R.C. § 877A, the taxpayer could avoid U.S. tax. However, I.R.C. § 877A would apply to immediately tax the gain (although in some cases, a taxpayer can elect to defer the tax).

Section 877A(a) generally imposes a "mark-to-market" regime on covered expatriates, providing that all property of a covered expatriate is treated as sold on the day before the expatriation date for its fair market value. The provision requires that any gain arising from the deemed sale is taken into account (subject to an exclusion amount which for 2018 was $725,000) for the taxable year of the deemed sale notwithstanding any other provisions of the Code. Any loss from the deemed sale generally is taken into account for the taxable year of the deemed sale to the extent otherwise provided in the Code. A taxpayer may elect to defer payment of tax attributable to property deemed sold. I.R.C. § 877A(b).

Generally, a covered expatriate is an expatriate (citizen or long-term resident) who: (1) has an average annual net income tax liability for the five preceding taxable years that exceeds a specified amount that is adjusted for inflation ($168,000 for 2018) (the "tax liability test"); (2) has a net worth of $2 million or more (the "net worth test"); or (3) fails to certify, under penalties of perjury, compliance with all U.S. Federal tax obligations for the five taxable years preceding the taxable year. I.R.C. § 877A(g).

Section 877A(b) provides that a covered expatriate may make an irrevocable election ("deferral election") with respect to any property deemed sold by reason of I.R.C. § 877A(a) to defer the payment of the additional tax attributable to any such property ("deferral assets"). The deferral election is made on an asset-by-asset basis. In order to make the election with respect to any asset, the covered expatriate must provide adequate security and must irrevocably waive any right under any U.S. treaty that would preclude assessment or collection of any tax imposed by reason of I.R.C. § 877A. Any deferred tax plus interest is due upon the earlier disposition of the asset (actually, when the tax return is due) or death of the expatriate (no tax planning opportunity here).

§ 2.06   INTRODUCTION TO U.S. INCOME TAX TREATIES

The basic ground rules governing the taxation of both nonresidents and residents often serve as a backdrop to a series of bilateral income tax treaties. *See infra* Chapter 5. These treaties typically allocate the taxing authority over specified types of income to the treaty partners. Once a treaty has allocated taxing authority to a treaty partner, the domestic tax laws of that partner govern the ultimate tax treatment. For example, the treaty between the United States and the Netherlands provides that business profits of a Dutch resident are exempt from U.S. taxation unless the profits are attributable to a permanent establishment (*e.g.*, a fixed place of business) in the United States. If the business profits are attributable to a U.S. permanent establishment, they are subject to taxation under either I.R.C. § 871(b) (individuals) or I.R.C. § 882 (corporations); if not, the profits are not taxable in the United States even if under purely domestic law principles the income would be considered income effectively connected with the conduct of a U.S. trade or business (*e.g.*, continuous sales of inventory to U.S.

purchasers through a U.S. independent agent). Treaties do not enlarge the taxing authority of the United States.

Treaties also typically reduce the rate of tax on certain "investment" income. While the U.S. domestic tax rate on this "investment" income is typically 30 percent (*see supra* § 2.03), treaties may reduce the applicable rate to 15, 5 or in some cases 0 percent. *See infra* Chapter 5.

A treaty may also determine residence where an individual under domestic law principles is a nontreaty resident of both the United States and its treaty partner. Many treaties contain residency tie-breaker provisions that may make an individual a nonresident of the United States even though that individual meets the substantial presence test of I.R.C. § 7701(b). *See infra* § 5.05(C).

CHAPTER 3
SOURCE RULES

§ 3.01 THE INCOME SOURCE RULES

The source rules are important both to: (1) U.S. citizens, residents, and domestic corporations; and (2) nonresident alien individuals and foreign corporations. For the former, the source rules matter because the foreign tax credit for income taxes paid to foreign countries is only available to offset U.S. income taxes on foreign source income. For example, if Japan taxes income of a U.S. corporation that under U.S. tax rules is U.S. source income, the income taxes paid to Japan may not be creditable as an offset against taxes payable to the United States on the income. I.R.C. § 904. *See infra* § 10.03.

For nonresident aliens and foreign corporations, the source rules are important for two reasons. In the case of income from a U.S. trade or business, it is generally the case that income must be from U.S. sources to be effectively connected income and therefore subject to taxation under I.R.C. §§ 871(b) (individuals) and 882 (corporations). *But see* I.R.C. § 864(c)(4). In the case of nonbusiness income (*i.e.*, FDAP income), the 30 percent withholding tax is applicable only to U.S. source income. For example, if a nonresident alien investor receives a dividend that is deemed not to be U.S. source income, there is no U.S. gross basis tax imposed. I.R.C. §§ 871(a) and 881. What follows is a summary of the source rules for particular types of income. *See* I.R.C. §§ 861–863, 865 and 884(f).

(A) INTEREST

(1) Domestic Payor

In general, interest is sourced by reference to the residence of the payor. Accordingly, interest paid by a domestic corporation, noncorporate resident of the United States, the federal government, or an agency or instrumentality of the federal government is U.S. source interest. A domestic partnership is considered a U.S. resident for purposes of the interest source rule only if the partnership is engaged in a trade or business in the United States at any time during the taxable year. Reg. § 1.861–2(a)(1). In determining the source of an interest payment, the place of payment, the place where the debt is located, the recipient's location, the currency used to make the payment all are irrelevant factors.

One exception to the residence-of-the-payor rule treats the payment of interest by a foreign branch of a U.S. bank on deposits as foreign source even though the juridical payor is a U.S. bank. I.R.C. § 861(a)(1)(A).

(2) Foreign Payor

In general, interest paid by a foreign corporation is foreign source income under I.R.C. § 862(a)(1). Accordingly a foreign lender is not subject to a 30 percent tax on the receipt of interest paid by a foreign corporation. However, where a foreign corporation is engaged in a trade or business in the United States through its U.S. branch, interest payments paid (or deemed to be paid) by the U.S. branch are treated as if paid by a domestic corporation. I.R.C. § 884(f). Accordingly, such interest is taxable under either I.R.C. §§ 871(a) or 881. *See* the discussion of the branch profits tax *infra* at § 4.05. Interest paid by a foreign partnership with a U.S. trade or business is treated in a similar manner to interest paid by a foreign corporation—the interest paid will be considered U.S. source income only if it is paid by a U.S. trade or business of the partnership (or allocable to income that is effectively connected or is treated as effectively connected with the conduct of a U.S. trade or business). I.R.C. § 861(a)(1)(B). However, to be eligible for this treatment, the foreign partnership must be predominantly engaged in the active conduct of a trade or business outside the United States. If the partnership is not predominantly engaged in the active conduct of a foreign trade or business, then *all* interest paid by the partnership will be treated as U.S. source income. Reg. § 1.861–2(a)(2).

Substitute interest payments (*e.g.*, payments made by a foreign borrower of securities to the foreign lender) are treated as U.S. source income if the interest accruing on the transferred security would have been U.S. source income. Reg. § 1.861–2(a)(7).

(B) DIVIDENDS

(1) Domestic Payor

Generally, a dividend paid by a domestic corporation is U.S. source income. I.R.C. § 861(a)(2)(A). It normally follows that such U.S. source income received by a nonresident alien or foreign corporation is subject to the 30 percent tax under I.R.C. §§ 871(a) or 881 (unless an applicable treaty reduces the tax rate). A dividend paid by a U.S. payor is taxable in the United States because the United States provides the economic environment in which the dividend-paying corporation conducts business. *But see* I.R.C. §§ 871(i) and 881(d) discussed *infra* at § 3.01(B)(2).

(2) Foreign Payor

Generally, a dividend paid by a foreign corporation to foreign shareholders is not U.S. source income and is not subject to a 30 percent tax in the United States. I.R.C. § 861(a)(2)(B). However, if the foreign corporation is engaged in a U.S. trade or business, a portion of any dividend payment may be treated as U.S. source income. If 25 percent or more of a foreign corporation's gross income for the three preceding years is U.S. business income, the portion of the dividend that is attributable to the corporation's U.S. business income is considered U.S. source income. Notwithstanding this rule, there will be no withholding tax on such a dividend because the foreign corporation will be subject to the branch profits tax instead. I.R.C. §§ 884(e)(3) and 871(i)(2)(D). *See infra* § 4.05.

A substitute dividend payment (*e.g.*, a payment made by a borrower of stock to the lender of stock which is equivalent to a dividend payment) is sourced in the same manner as the dividend payment itself. Reg. § 1.861–3(a)(6).

(C) PERSONAL SERVICES

The source rule for services is straightforward: compensation for services performed in the United States is U.S. source income subject to a *de minimis* exception. Typically, a nonresident alien performing services in the United States is deemed to be engaged in a trade or business in the United States, and the compensation is treated as effectively connected income which is taxable under I.R.C. § 871(b). However to the extent that compensation is paid for services performed outside the United States, generally the compensation is not subject to U.S. taxation. *See* Reg. § 1.861–4(b). If a corporation receives income in the nature of personal services performed by an employee or other agent, the corporation's compensation is sourced in the place where the employee or agent performs the services. *See, e.g., Bank of America v. United States*, 680 F.2d 142 (Ct.Cl. 1982). *See also Commissioner v. Hawaiian Philippine Co.*, 100 F.2d 988 (9th Cir. 1939) (corporations can generate "personal" services).

The *de minimis* exception to the place-of-performance rule provides that compensation for services performed by a nonresident alien individual temporarily present in the United States is foreign source income if the individual is not present in the United States for more than 90 days during the taxable year and the compensation does not exceed $3,000, a figure rendered virtually meaningless by the ravages of inflation since 1954, the year of enactment. Furthermore, the payments must be from a foreign employer not engaged in a trade or business in the United States or the foreign office of a U.S. employer. I.R.C. § 864(b)(1).

The payments covered by this place-of-performance rule include not only direct compensation but also fringe benefits (*e.g.*, pension payments), sales commissions, amounts received under a covenant not to compete, and even advertising income. *See Commissioner v. Piedras Negras Broadcasting Co.*, 127 F.2d 260 (5th Cir. 1942) (advertising revenues of Mexican radio station were foreign source income even though U.S. customers bought radio time to advertise to U.S. customers).

Not surprisingly, it is not always clear where services are performed. For example, suppose a Canadian hockey player is paid $1,000,000 a year by a U.S. hockey team. That portion of the salary attributable to games played in Canada is not taxed in the United States because it is foreign source income not effectively connected with the conduct of a U.S. trade or business. Should any portion of the $1,000,000 be allocable to pre-season activities? To post-season playoffs? To the off-season since the taxpayer was expected to report to his team in good shape? Since the taxpayer spent the off-season and much of the pre-season and play-offs in Canada, allocation of salary to those periods would lower the taxpayer's U.S. tax liability. *See Stemkowski v. Commissioner*, 690 F.2d 40 (2d Cir. 1982) (services include pre- and post-season but not off-season).

Questions also arise as to whether a particular payment is for services rendered or for something else. In *Karrer v. United States*, 152 F.Supp. 66 (Ct.Cl. 1957), a Swiss national, a scientist, maintained that he was compensated for services performed in Switzerland by a Swiss corporation for work culminating in several patents. The taxpayer maintained that the payments received were foreign source income not subject to U.S. taxation even though the payments were based on U.S. sales of the synthetic vitamins developed from his work. The IRS argued unsuccessfully that the appropriate source rule was the one dealing with royalties—I.R.C. § 861(a)(4)—and that the payments received for the use of a patent in the United States were U.S. source income. In *Cook v. United States*, 599 F.2d 400 (Ct.Cl. 1979), a sculptor's income on the sale of a sculpture was sourced in the country where the sculptor worked rather than in the country where the sculpture was sold.

In some cases, it may not be clear whether a payment is for services or the sale of property. For example, suppose that X Corp., a country X corporation, operates a server in country S from which customers for a fee can download financial reports. If USCo, a U.S. company, downloads a report, is the fee a payment for services or a payment for property? Generally, in situations where the supplier (*i.e.*, X Corp.) never owned the property but created it solely for the customer (*i.e.*, USCo), the payment is considered a payment for services performed rather than for the property. *See Boulez v. Commissioner*, 83 T.C. 584 (1984) (fee for services rather than a royalty for transfer of property because taxpayer created the property for the end-user).

In August 2019 the IRS proposed regulations on the classification of cloud transactions (REG–130700–14, 2019–36 I.R.B. 681), which also included proposed revisions to computer software regulations from 1998. The proposed rules would provide that when copyrighted articles are sold and transferred through an electronic medium, the sale is deemed to occur at the location of download or installation onto the end-user's device used to access the digital content for purposes of § 1.861–7(c) (addressing gains from the sale of personal property). Prop. Reg. § 1.861–18(f)(2)(ii). The IRS expects that vendors generally will be able to identify the location of downloads and installations. Under the proposed regulation, income from sales or exchanges of copyrighted articles is sourced under the rules for sourcing gains from the sale of property.

The Code provides specific source rules for certain types of services income. For example, one half of the income from furnishing transportation (*e.g.*, income of a shipping company or airline) is U.S. source if the trip begins or ends in the United States. I.R.C. § 863(c)(2)(A). If the trip begins and ends in the United States, all income is from U.S. sources even if some part of the trip is over international waters or a foreign country. A round trip is treated as two trips, an outbound and inbound trip. This special source rule for transportation income does not apply to salaries and wages of transportation employees.

International communications income of a U.S. taxpayer is treated as 50 percent from U.S. sources and 50 percent from foreign sources. I.R.C. § 863(e)(1)(A). International communications income of a foreign taxpayer is usually foreign source income unless the income is attributable to a U.S. office or other fixed place of business or to a controlled foreign corporation in which case 50 percent of the income is U.S. source income. Reg. § 1.863–9(b). Income from communications between two points in the United States is U.S. source income, even if routed through a satellite.

(D) RENTALS AND ROYALTIES

Rentals from the lease of tangible property are sourced where the property is located. I.R.C. §§ 861(a)(4) and 862(a)(4). For example, if a foreign corporation leases computer hardware to another foreign corporation which uses the hardware in the United States, rental payments are U.S. source income notwithstanding the residence of the lessor or lessee or where payments take place.

Royalties from the license of intangible property including patents, copyrights, know-how or other intellectual property are sourced according to where the intangibles are used. I.R.C. §§ 861(a)(4) and 862(a)(4). Essentially, the focus is on where the intangible is legally protected. If the intangible is legally protected in more than one jurisdiction (*e.g.*, a worldwide copyright license), the focus is on what legal protection the licensee is truly paying for. For example, if a U.S. taxpayer develops computer software abroad and licenses it to a foreign licensee who pays royalties under a contract signed abroad, the royalties are U.S. source income if the licensee uses the software in its U.S. trade or business. In this situation, it is the permission to use the copyright in the United States without infringing that justifies the royalty payments. If a patent, copyright, or other intangible is sold outright rather than licensed, but the sales proceeds are contingent on the productivity, use, or disposition of the intangible by the purchaser (*e.g.*, purchase price equal to 2 percent of gross sales), the source of the sales proceeds is determined as if such payments are royalties. I.R.C. § 865(d).

Suppose that a licensor from Bermuda licenses its worldwide rights in computer software to a Dutch licensee which sublicenses the intangible throughout the world including the U.S. rights to a U.S. sub-licensee. In the absence of a treaty between the United States and the Netherlands, the royalty paid by the U.S. sub-licensee to the Dutch sub-licensor for the right to exploit the U.S. rights in the software would be U.S. source FDAP income subject to U.S. withholding tax. I.R.C. §§ 881 and 1442. However, the applicable treaty does not permit U.S. withholding on such a payment. What about the royalty payment from the Dutch licensee (sub-licensor) to the Bermudan licensor? Should the portion of that payment attributable to royalties received from the U.S. sub-licensee be treated as U.S. source income even though paid by a non-U.S. payor to a non-U.S. payee? The possibility that the United States would collect multiple withholding taxes on royalties that are paid pursuant to sublicensing of an intangible (*e.g.*, X receives royalties from Y which receives royalties from Z which receives royalties from a U.S. sub-licensee) is referred to as the "cascading royalty" problem.

In *SDI Netherlands B.V. v. Commissioner*, 107 T.C. 161 (1996), the court rejected the cascading royalty approach, ruling that the payment from the Dutch licensee (sub-licensor) to the Bermudan licensor was not U.S. source income even to the extent the payment is attributable to royalties received by the sub-licensor from a U.S. sub-licensee exploiting the U.S. intangible rights. The court did not suggest how I.R.C. § 861(a)(4) applies to determine the source of the payment from the Dutch licensee in this situation. Note that in *SDI Netherlands*, the IRS did not argue that the Dutch licensee (sub-licensor) was merely a conduit so that the royalty was really being paid from the U.S. sub-licensee to the Bermudan licensor. If that were true, then both under the current treaty and under U.S. domestic law (*see e.g.*, I.R.C. § 7701(*l*) and Reg. § 1.881–3), the payment from the U.S. licensee would have been U.S. source income subject to a 30 percent tax under I.R.C. § 881.

Often it is not easy to determine the character of a particular payment that is received. Only after the character is determined can the appropriate source rule be applied. For example, suppose that a computer software company "licenses" computer software to customers in exchange for a royalty. A customer can acquire the software by downloading or by streaming. Conceivably, the payment might constitute a royalty, rental income from the lease of the application, sales proceeds from the sale of the copyright or sales proceeds from the sale of the application itself. Regulations from 1998 attempt to distinguish a copyright right from a copyrighted article with respect to computer software. A copyright right includes the right to make copies of a computer program for distribution to the public, the right to prepare derivative computer programs, the right to make a public performance or the right to publicly display the program. Reg. § 1.861–18(c)(2).

Once it is determined whether a copyright right or a copyrighted article has been transferred, then the issue is whether the entire copyright right or copyrighted article has been transferred or rather there has been a lease or license. In the example above, typically there is no transfer of a copyright right by the software provider, notwithstanding the license. Instead, a person who acquires the software is acquiring a copyrighted article. Because the acquirer obtains full rights in the software application, a sale has taken place and any proceeds are sales proceeds. On the other hand, if an acquirer were permitted to make copies of the software and distribute them to the public, the transfer would be the transfer of a copyright right and any proceeds received by the software provider would either constitute a royalty or sales proceeds from the sale of an intangible, depending on whether the acquirer has licensed the royalty (*e.g.*, the right to distribute for a limited period of time) or obtained full rights in the copyright.

Proposed regulations from August 2019 attempt to update the characterization rules for the vast changes to business transactions resulting from web-based services. These rules clarify the treatment of income from transactions involving on-demand network access to computing and other similar resources, and also extend the classification rules in existing Reg. § 1.861–18 to transfers of digital content other than computer programs. REG–130700–14, 2019–36 I.R.B. 681. Prop. Reg. § 1.861–19 provides rules for classifying a cloud transaction as either a provision of services or a lease of property for purposes of I.R.C. §§ 59A, 245A, 250, 267A, 367 and other Code sections, but doesn't provide sourcing rules for these transactions.

Under the proposed rules, a cloud transaction is defined as one through which a person obtains non-*de minimis* on-demand network access to computer hardware, digital content or other similar resources, a definition that also is intended to apply to other transactions that share characteristics of on-demand network access to technological resources, such as access to streaming digital content and access to information in certain databases. But it doesn't encompass every transaction executed or completed over the web; for example, the mere download or other electronic transfer of digital content for storage and use on a person's computer hardware or other electronic device doesn't constitute on-demand network access to the digital content and so isn't considered a cloud transaction for purposes of these rules.

The rules provide that a cloud transaction is classified solely as either a lease of property or the provision of services. Cloud transactions that have characteristics of both types of transactions generally are classified in their entirety as either a lease or a service, and not bifurcated into two. But in some cases, where the facts suggest that an arrangement involves multiple cloud transactions, the rules require a separate classification of each cloud transaction. The rules contain a list of factors for determining whether a cloud transaction is classified as the provision of services or a lease of property which generally result in transactions being characterized as a provision of services. Prop. Reg. § 1.861–19(c)(2).

The proposed regulations request comments on administrable rules for sourcing income from cloud transactions in a manner consistent with I.R.C. §§ 861 through 865.

For a discussion of whether a payment constitutes services or royalties, *see Sergio Garcia v. Commissioner*, 140 T.C. 141 (2013).

(E)   REAL PROPERTY

Gain or loss from the disposition of U.S. real property or stock of a U.S. real property holding corporation (as defined in I.R.C. § 897(c)) is U.S. source. Gain from the sale of real property located outside the United States is foreign source.

(F) PERSONAL PROPERTY

For purposes of determining source, the term "personal property" essentially includes all property (both tangible and intangible) that is not real property.

(1) Purchased Inventory

Gain from the sale of purchased inventory is sourced where the sale takes place—generally the place where title passes. I.R.C. §§ 865(b) and 861(a)(6). For example, gain from the sale of inventory purchased in France and sold in the United States is U.S. source income while gain from the sale of inventory purchased in the United States and sold in France is foreign source income.

The title passage rule for purchased inventory allows taxpayers great latitude. U.S. residents that sell inventory for use abroad can arrange for title to pass abroad creating foreign source income that enhances the ability to credit foreign income taxes. *See Liggett Group Inc. v. Commissioner*, T.C. Memo. 1990–18 (1990) (U.S. seller, purchasing goods from a foreign supplier, generated foreign source income on sales to U.S. purchaser where both the legal title and economic ownership (*e.g.*, benefits and burden of ownership) passed abroad).

But there are limits to acceptable title-passage manipulation. If a transaction is structured with the primary purpose of tax avoidance, the title-passage rule may not apply. Instead the risk of loss, location of negotiations, execution of the agreement, location of the property itself; and the place of payment may be relevant in determining source. Reg. § 1.861–7(c). If a nonresident maintains an office or other fixed place of business in the United States, income from the sale of inventory (and other personal property) attributable to such place of business is sourced in the United States regardless of where title passes. I.R.C. § 865(e)(2)(A). However, if the inventory is sold for use outside the United States and a foreign fixed place of business materially participates in the sale, gain on the sale is treated as foreign source income. I.R.C. § 865(e)(2)(B).

(2)   Produced Personal Property

The title-passage rule applies to personal property (including inventory) that is purchased and resold. The rule does not apply to personal property (including inventory) that is produced by the taxpayer. For example, suppose a foreign corporation has a Spanish factory that manufactures thermostats which are shipped to a U.S. warehouse where sales representatives sell the thermostats to U.S. purchasers. Such a transaction is referred to as a "Section 863 Sale" by the regulations. Reg. § 1.863–3. The TCJA amended the rule in I.R.C. § 863(b) that determines how to source the income from such a sale, so that it is now sourced solely to the country where production activities take place. Income derived from the sale of inventory property to a foreign jurisdiction is sourced entirely within the United States if the property was produced entirely in the United States; if the inventory property is produced partly within, and partly outside the

United States, the income derived from its sale is sourced partly to the United States. I.R.C. §§ 865(b) and 863(b)(2).

Once the income has been sourced under I.R.C. § 863(b), taxation in the United States depends on whether the income is effectively connected income under either I.R.C. §§ 864(c)(3) or (4). In the example above, the foreign source gain attributable to the production is not subject to U.S. taxation. If a portion of the production activities had taken place in the United States, the U.S. source sales portion of the gain would be taxable as income effectively connected with the conduct of a U.S. trade or business under I.R.C. §§ 864(c)(3) and 882.

The regulations under I.R.C. § 863 specify a multi-step process for sourcing income from manufactured inventory. These regulations fail to take account of the change to the sourcing rule made by the TCJA, and still incorporate the prior statutory rule which requires an allocation of source between location of production and sale. But aspects of the regulations remain relevant, such as the sourcing of production activity gross income according to the relative domestic and foreign production assets, and the allocation of expenses in accordance with regulations discussed *infra* in § 3.02 and § 10.04. Reg. § 1.863–3(c).

Under the regulations, production assets are tangible and intangible assets that are directly used to produce inventory. In the example above, if all the manufacturing assets are in Spain, 100 percent of the gross income is foreign source income not subject to

U.S. tax, regardless of where title to the thermostats is transferred. If the taxpayer had half of its manufacturing assets in Spain and half of its manufacturing assets in the U.S., then 50 percent of its income would be U.S. source.

The TCJA change to the source rule was intended to prevent planning opportunities available to U.S. taxpayers under prior law, which allowed taxpayers to generate untaxed, foreign source income that could absorb excess foreign tax credits generated from other business operations.

(3) Intangible Property

Gain from the sale of any patent, copyright, secret process or formula, goodwill, trademark, trade brand, or similar intangible is sourced in one of two ways depending on the nature of the sale. If the sales proceeds are contingent on the productivity, use, or disposition of the intangible, any gain is sourced as if the payments received were royalties (*i.e.*, source is determined by where the property is used). I.R.C. § 865(d). For example, if a nonresident alien sells a patent to a U.S. purchaser to be used in producing home security alarm systems in the United States in exchange for 5 percent of the gross sales proceeds of the systems, the gain from the patent sale is U.S. source income because the patent is used in the United States. I.R.C. § 861(a)(4).

If the sales proceeds are not contingent on the use of the intangible, any gain is sourced by reference to the residence of the seller. I.R.C. § 865(a) and (g). In the example above, if the nonresident alien sold the patent for a flat $800,000, any gain from the sale would be foreign source income. If the sales contract has both a non-contingent and contingent aspect (*e.g.*, sale for $800,000 plus 2 percent of gross sales proceeds), the amounts received will receive bifurcated treatment in accordance with the rules above.

There is a special source rule for goodwill. Noncontingent payments received for the transfer of goodwill are sourced in the country where the goodwill was generated. I.R.C. § 865(d)(3).

(4) Depreciable Personal Property

Gain from the sale of business equipment, automobiles, machinery and other depreciable personal property or from any amortizable intangible property (*e.g.*, patent, copyright, trademark, goodwill) may consist of two components for tax purposes: depreciation (or amortization) adjustments and appreciation (including inflationary gain). I.R.C. § 865(c). For example, suppose business machinery was purchased for $10,000 and that $3,000 of depreciation deductions were taken for U.S. tax purposes (reducing the machine's basis to $7,000) before the machinery was sold for $12,000. Of the $5,000 gain, $3,000 represents depreciation adjustments to the asset's basis for previous depreciation deductions and $2,000 represents capital appreciation (or inflation). To the extent that the previous depreciation deductions reduced U.S. source income, the depreciation adjustments are treated as U.S. source income regardless of the residence of the owner or the place where title passes. To the extent that previous depreciation deductions were taken against foreign source income, the depreciation adjustments are treated as foreign source income. Any other gain (*e.g.*, capital appreciation) is sourced like gains from inventory by determining where title passes. I.R.C. § 865(c)(2). TCJA, which allows (temporarily) for full expensing of certain qualified property, does not change these general rules but alters their impact. I.R.C. § 168(k).

(5) Other Personal Property

The general rule of I.R.C. § 865(a) which applies to nondepreciable personal property is essentially a residual rule although it does apply to sales of stock, securities, partnership interests and to the sale of intangibles where the sales proceeds are not contingent on the use of the intangible. Generally, income from the sale of nondepreciable personal property (*e.g.*, stock) by a U.S. resident is U.S. source income, while any gain from a sale by a nonresident produces foreign source income. For sales by a partnership, the rule is applied at the partner level. I.R.C. § 865(i)(5). If a U.S. resident maintains an office or other fixed place of business outside the United States, income from the sale of property attributable to that office is treated as foreign source income if the foreign country imposes at least a 10 percent tax on income from such a sale. I.R.C. § 865(e).

There is another exception to the residence-of-the-seller rule pertaining to stock dispositions. If a U.S.

resident sells stock of a foreign affiliate (as defined in I.R.C. § 1504(a)) in a foreign country where the affiliate derived more than 50 percent of its gross income from an active trade or business during the preceding three years, any gain is foreign source income. I.R.C. § 865(f). Even if a U.S. taxpayer sells stock of a foreign corporation which is not a foreign affiliate, any gain is foreign source income if a treaty between the purchaser's country and the United States so provides and the U.S. taxpayer chooses the benefits of the treaty. I.R.C. § 865(h). For a U.S. taxpayer, treating such gains as foreign source income may mean that any foreign taxes imposed on that gain are creditable against U.S. tax liability. In contrast, foreign taxes imposed on U.S. source income are not creditable against U.S. taxes on that income.

(6) Sales Through Offices or Fixed Places of Businesses in the United States

Notwithstanding the other source rules pertaining to the sale of personal property, if a nonresident maintains an office or other fixed place of business in the United States to which the gain from a sale is attributable, the gain is treated as U.S. source income. I.R.C. § 865(e)(2)(A). There is an exception for inventory property sold for use outside the United States through a foreign fixed place of business that materially participated in the sale. I.R.C. § 865(e)(2)(B).

The TCJA codified a long-standing position of the IRS that had been called into question by a 2017 Tax

Court case (*Grecian Magnesite Mining, Industrial & Shipping Co. v. Commissioner*, 149 T.C. No. 3 (2017)). I.R.C. § 864(c)(8). If a nonresident or foreign corporation sells an interest in a partnership that is engaged in a U.S. trade or business, gain or loss from the sale is considered effectively connected to the U.S. trade or business to the extent the sale of the assets of the partnership would have been treated as such. (*See* discussion *infra* at § 4.03.)

(G) OTHER GROSS INCOME

Scholarships, fellowship grants, prizes and awards are considered to be FDAP income subject to the 30 percent withholding tax if they are from U.S. sources and if the payment is included in gross income, *e.g.*, a prize, or a scholarship that does not satisfy the requirements of I.R.C. § 117. Reg. §§ 1.871–7(a)(2) and 1.1441–2. The source of a payment made to a nonresident as a scholarship etc. is the country of residence of the person making the payment. Reg. § 1.863–1(d)(2). For example, if a student from Hong Kong receives a scholarship from her government to study at a U.S. university, the payment would be foreign source income and would not be taxable by the United States. Conversely, a payment by a U.S. foundation for study at a U.S. university would be U.S. source income. If a nonresident conducts activities outside the United States, the scholarship has a foreign source regardless of the residence of the payor. For example, if a U.S. university grants a scholarship to a Hong Kong student for field work done abroad, the income will be foreign source income.

Suppose a foreign parent corporation guarantees a loan made by a bank to the foreign parent's U.S. subsidiary in order to reduce the interest rate on the loan. If the U.S. subsidiary pays a guarantee fee to its foreign parent to compensate for the guarantee, I.R.C. § 861(a)(9) provides that the payment generates U.S. income.

A "notional principal contract" is defined as a financial instrument that provides for the payment of amounts by one party to another at specified intervals calculated by reference to a specified rate on a notional principal amount in exchange for specified consideration. For example, suppose a nonresident enters into an exchange with a U.S. party to pay the U.S. party 10 percent annually on a $1 million notional principal amount in exchange for the U.S. party's payment on a $1 million notional principal amount of interest equal to the London Interbank Offered Rate (LIBOR) plus three percentage points. Note that the $1 million is notional because it is used merely as a reference; no $1 million payment is made by either party.

The nonresident might engage in this transaction because of an outstanding obligation to pay interest measured by LIBOR plus 3 percentage points owed to someone else which the nonresident wishes to transform from a risky payment (if LIBOR should rise unexpectedly) into a fixed 10 percent interest obligation. The U.S. party may be willing to undertake some risk, betting that the 10 percent payment received will exceed the LIBOR plus 3 percentage points paid. However, suppose that in Year 1, LIBOR is 9 percent. Therefore the net flow of income is $20,000 of income from the U.S. payor to the nonresident. Is that payment subject to taxation as FDAP income? Generally, income under a notional principal contract is sourced in the country of the recipient's residence. The income would be treated as foreign source income not subject to FDAP taxation under I.R.C. § 871(a) (or I.R.C. § 881). Reg. § 1.863–7(a).

However, I.R.C. § 871(m) treats certain notional principal contract payments as "dividend equivalents" which are treated as U.S. source income. For example, suppose the nonresident agrees to swap interest payments on a $10 million notional principal contract with a U.S. counterparty who agrees to swap a payment based on the dividends paid on $10 million of stock in a U.S. company. Any net amount paid to the nonresident will not be foreign source income under Reg. § 1.863–7(a), but instead will be U.S. income. Similar treatment results for other substitute dividend transactions.

What is the source rule for items where there are no specific source rules? Where an item of income is not characterized by statute or regulation, courts have sourced the item by comparison and analogy with the most closely related items of income specified within the statutes. *Bank of America v. United States*, 680 F.2d 142, 147 (Ct.Cl. 1982).

(H) RESIDENCE FOR SOURCE
RULE PURPOSES

There is a special definition of "residence" for purposes of determining the source of income that is different from the definition of "residence" under I.R.C. § 7701(b) for overall taxing purposes. For source purposes, a U.S. citizen or resident alien under I.R.C. § 7701(b) who does not have a "tax home" (*see* Reg. § 1.911–2(b) and I.R.C. § 162(a)(2)) in the United States is a nonresident. I.R.C. § 865(g). Conversely, a nonresident alien who has a tax home in the United States is a U.S. resident for purposes of the source rule under I.R.C. § 865. Generally, a taxpayer's "tax home" is located at the taxpayer's regular or principal place of business.

§ 3.02   DEDUCTION ALLOCATION RULES

(A) IN GENERAL

The 30 percent tax on FDAP income of a nonresident is imposed on gross income; no deductions are allowed. However, the tax on a nonresident's income that is effectively connected with the conduct of a trade or business is imposed on taxable income. I.R.C. §§ 861(b), 871(b), 882, and 873. As a result, the allocation and apportionment of expenses serves an important function for foreign taxpayers engaged in a U.S. trade or business. To the extent that expenses are allocated and apportioned against income effectively connected to the conduct of a U.S. trade or business, a foreign taxpayer's income subject to U.S. tax liability is reduced. Keep in mind that what the United States does under its domestic law has no necessary effect on how expenses will be treated by the nonresident's home country.

Allocation and apportionment of deductions also plays an important role for U.S. residents and citizens doing business or investing abroad. These taxpayers are taxable on worldwide income earned directly or through a branch, so that all deductible expenses potentially reduce U.S. tax liability. Furthermore, these taxpayers can offset their U.S. tax liability with foreign income taxes paid on their foreign source taxable income (*i.e.*, taking deductions into account) if those foreign taxes do not exceed the U.S. tax potentially imposed on that income. To the extent expenses are allocated and apportioned against foreign source income, a U.S. taxpayer may have a smaller foreign tax credit. For this reason, U.S. taxpayers generally prefer expenses to be allocated and apportioned against U.S. source income.

The rules for allocating expenses for purposes of the foreign tax credit calculation are complex and have been extensively modified by the IRS as a result of changes made to the taxation of U.S. persons' foreign income by the TCJA. They are discussed in greater detail in Chapter 10, *infra*, which covers the limitation on the foreign tax credit. The Code does not, for the most part, specify with precision how expenses should be allocated between U.S. and foreign sources. But in general a taxpayer is required to: (1) allocate deductions to a class of gross income; and then, if a statutory provision requires, (2) apportion deductions within the class of gross income between the statutory grouping (*e.g.*, effectively connected income for a nonresident taxpayer and foreign source income for a U.S. taxpayer) and the residual grouping (*i.e.*, everything else). Reg. § 1.861–8(a)(2). Often expenses bear a definite relationship to a class of gross income in which case no further allocation is necessary although it may be necessary to apportion the income between U.S. and foreign sources (or for a nonresident, between effectively connected income and all other income). For example, direct business expenses deductible under I.R.C. § 162 can often be allocated to specific income.

To illustrate the operation of these rules to a foreign person: suppose that ForCo, a foreign corporation, purchases and sells computer hardware in the United States through a U.S. branch and in foreign markets through foreign branches. ForCo also sells computer books exclusively in foreign countries. For the taxable year, ForCo has gross income of $2,000,000 of which $800,000 is from the sale of computer equipment and is effectively connected to the conduct of a trade or business in the United States, $700,000 is from sales of computer equipment outside the United States, and $500,000 is from sales of computer books outside the United States. ForCo's marketing department incurs deductible expenses of $400,000 with respect to all of ForCo's products and $100,000 for advertising relating only to ForCo's books.

Under these facts, the general marketing expense of $400,000 is allocated to the class of gross income from sales of all of ForCo's products, and the $100,000 advertising expense is allocated to gross income from the sale of books. For purposes of determining the amount of effectively connected income under I.R.C. § 882(c) with respect to the sale of computer equipment, it is necessary to apportion the $400,000 marketing expense between the gross income in the statutory grouping of effectively connected income and the residual grouping of non-effectively connected income. In this instance the amount apportioned to U.S. effectively connected sales is based on gross income from sales as follows:

$$\$400,000 \ \times \ \frac{\$800,000}{\$2,000,000} \ = \ \$160,000$$

The remaining $240,000 of general marketing expense is apportioned to the residual grouping of sales of computer equipment and books outside the United States. Because the $100,000 advertising expense is definitely related to a class of income (*i.e.*, book sales) that is in the residual grouping, there is no apportionment. Consequently, the net effectively connected income equals $800,000 minus $160,000, or $640,000.

In the example, just considered, if the taxpayer was a U.S. corporation the same process would be necessary but for a different purpose, *i.e.*, in order to determine the foreign tax credit. For U.S. taxpayers, the foreign source income is the statutory grouping

and the U.S. source income is the residual grouping.
But *see* the discussion in Chapter 10.

(B) INTEREST

(1) U.S. Corporations

The allocation and apportionment of interest
expense often plays a significant role in determining
a taxpayer's tax posture. Some interest is directly
allocated to a specific class of income if the loan
proceeds are applied to purchase and improve real
property or depreciable personal property and the
creditor can look only to the identified property for
security. Reg. § 1.861–10T(b). But if money is
borrowed for general business purposes, the interest
accrued or paid (depending on method of accounting)
is first allocated against all of the taxpayer's gross
income and then is apportioned under I.R.C. § 864(e)
between U.S. and foreign sources generally according
to the basis of all of the taxpayer's assets. *See*
Chapter 10 for a more detailed discussion of interest
expense allocation and apportionment.

(2) Foreign Corporations Engaged in a U.S. Trade or Business

Foreign corporations engaged in a U.S. trade or
business, particularly foreign banks, benefit from
allocation rules under Reg. § 1.882–5. These rules
generally have the effect of apportioning a larger
interest deduction against U.S. source income than
the asset allocation method of Reg. §§ 1.861–8 *et seq.*,
and are discussed in greater detail in § 4.06, *infra*.

(C) RESEARCH AND EXPERIMENTAL EXPENDITURES

The allocation of research and experimental expenditures (often referred to as R&E, R&D or research and development expenditures) is an issue of great importance to U.S. corporations and great difficulty for the IRS. To the extent that research and experimental expenditures are allocated and apportioned against foreign source income, foreign source taxable income is reduced and so might the foreign tax credit be reduced for income taxes paid abroad. U.S. taxpayers normally want to allocate and apportion as much of these expenses as possible to U.S. source income to maximize the foreign tax credit. *See infra* § 10.04(C). It is often not possible to allocate and apportion research and experimental expenditures with precision. By allocating a specified percentage of the research and experimental expenditures on the basis of where the research activities take place, Congress recognized that research and experimental expenditures do not always result in the direct production of income.

Under I.R.C. § 864(g), taxpayers are required to allocate research and experimentation expenses undertaken solely to meet legal requirements imposed by a government to the jurisdiction of that government (assuming the expenditures are not expected to generate income outside the jurisdiction). For example, where a taxpayer performs tests on a product in response to a requirement of the U.S. Food and Drug Administration, the costs of testing are allocated solely to gross income from U.S. sources.

After accounting for such legal requirements, a taxpayer is required to allocate the remaining expenses either using the sales or the gross income method. Under the sales method, 50 percent of the deduction for research and experimentation shall be apportioned exclusively to the geographic location where the activities accounting for more than half the deduction were performed. The remainder is apportioned on the basis of where the sales resulting from the research take place. Reg. § 1.861–17.

The IRS and Treasury have said that they are revisiting the rules for allocation and apportionment of R&D expenses. It is possible that by the time you are reading this, there will be new rules governing how to do so.

(D) LOSSES

Suppose that USCo, which has foreign operations, suffers a loss in the conduct of its business. The source of that loss is important in determining USCo's foreign tax credit. For example, suppose that USCo has $100 of U.S. source income and $100 of foreign source income on which a $21 foreign tax is imposed. If USCo also has a $60 loss which is treated as U.S. source loss, then USCo will face a U.S. tax on the $40 of net U.S. source income. The potential $21 U.S. tax on the $100 of foreign source income may be offset by the $21 foreign tax credit. On the other hand, if the $60 loss is allocated against foreign source income, then USCo faces a U.S. tax on $100, rather than $40, of U.S. source income. (Again, the potential U.S. tax on the foreign source income will be offset by the foreign taxes paid.) If income from the activity that produced a loss would have been foreign source income, then the loss generally is allocated and apportioned against foreign source income. I.R.C. § 865(j); Reg. § 1.865–1. While this rule applies to the sale of personal property (with some exceptions including inventory) at a loss, the allocation and apportionment of losses from the sale of inventory is sourced in the same manner, albeit under different authority. Reg. § 1.861–8.

Suppose that USCo disposes of stock in a foreign corporation at a loss. Income generated by the stock would have been treated as foreign source income. I.R.C. § 861(a)(2). On the other hand, if the stock had been sold at a gain, the gain might have been U.S. source income. I.R.C. § 865(a). If the stock sold were stock of an affiliate that conducted a trade or business in a foreign country, any gain might have been treated as foreign source income. Given these possible treatments for income or gain associated with the stock, how should a loss be allocated and apportioned?

In general, loss from the sale of stock is sourced in the same manner as gain (*i.e.*, residence of the seller) ignoring whether the stock sold is stock of an affiliate (I.R.C. § 865(f)) or would have been treated as a foreign source dividend if sold at a gain (I.R.C. § 1248). Reg. § 1.865–2. However, if the stock sale is attributable to an office or other fixed place of business in a foreign country, the loss is allocated against foreign source income if a gain on the sale of stock would have been taxable by the foreign country at a 10 percent or greater rate. Reg. § 1.865–2(a)(2). Also, a loss on the sale of stock in a foreign corporation is allocated against foreign source income to the extent that dividends paid during the previous 24 months were treated as foreign source income. Reg. § 1.865–2(b)(1).

PART 2

U.S. ACTIVITIES OF
FOREIGN TAXPAYERS

CHAPTER 4

TAXING RULES FOR NON-U.S. PERSONS

§ 4.01 OVERVIEW

Income earned by nonresidents generally falls under one of two taxing regimes. For a nonresident (individual or corporation) "engaged in a trade or business" in the United States, the net income that is "effectively connected" with the conduct of that trade or business is taxed in the same manner as net income earned by a U.S. resident (individual or corporation). I.R.C. § 871(b) (individuals) and I.R.C. § 882 (corporations). Fixed or Determinable Annual or Periodical gains, profits, and income (*i.e.*, basically investment income often referred to as FDAP income) from U.S. sources earned by a nonresident is typically taxed on a gross basis at a flat 30 percent statutory rate (or lower treaty rate). I.R.C. §§ 871(a) (individuals) and 881 (corporations).

What follows is a consideration of these two taxing regimes as well as other taxing provisions affecting nonresidents. Then the administrative provisions that enforce this taxing framework are addressed. *See supra* Chapter 3 for a discussion of the source rules which play an important role in the taxing regimes discussed in this chapter. We conclude the chapter with an overview of some of the measures Congress has enacted to try and prevent non-U.S. persons from stripping out the U.S. tax base (often referred to as "base erosion").

§ 4.02   "ENGAGED IN A TRADE OR BUSINESS" IN THE UNITED STATES

If a nonresident conducts a U.S. trade or business (USTB), the income effectively connected with the conduct of the trade or business is taxed in the same manner as business income of a U.S. resident. I.R.C. §§ 871(b) (individuals) and 882 (corporations). Partners in a partnership are considered to be engaged in a trade or business in the United States if the partnership is engaged in a trade or business in the United States. I.R.C. § 875(1). A partnership is considered to be engaged in a trade or business in the United States if a partner is so engaged and is acting as an agent of the partnership. *See, e.g., Donroy, Ltd. v. United States*, 301 F.2d 200 (9th Cir. 1962).

The international tax provisions of the Code provide little guidance as to what constitutes a USTB. *See* I.R.C. § 864(b). Certainly, passive investment activity does not rise to the level of a trade or business. For example, a nonresident individual or foreign corporation merely collecting interest or dividends from a U.S. payer is not engaged in a trade or business in the United States. The gross interest or dividend income (with no deductions permitted) normally would be subject to tax at a 30 percent statutory (or lower treaty) rate. I.R.C. §§ 871(a) or 881. Similarly, a foreign investor that merely collects rental income on U.S. property from a tenant under a net lease (*i.e.*, where the tenant is responsible for maintenance, taxes, and insurance) is not considered engaged in a USTB and would normally be subject to the 30 percent tax. *But see* I.R.C. §§ 871(d), 882(d).

In the absence of statutory or regulatory guidance, the standard for when a non-resident is considered to be engaged in a USTB has been developed by the courts over decades. In 1940, the Second Circuit held that a nonresident is considered to be engaged in a USTB if its activities in the United States are "considerable . . . as well as continuous and regular." *Pinchot v. Commissioner*, 113 F.2d 718, 719 (2d Cir. 1940). The standard for determining the existence of a USTB articulated by the courts is both qualitative and quantitative. *See Scottish American Investment Co. v. Commissioner*, 12 T.C. 49, 59 (1949) ("[I]t is a matter of degree, based upon both a quantitative and a qualitative analysis of the services performed, as to where the line of demarcation should be drawn."). Note that under treaties, a different standard, the permanent establishment (PE) standard, generally applies. *See* discussion in § 5.05(D)(1).

Activities conducted by a nonresident alien or a foreign corporation in the United States through an agent pose the most difficult questions concerning what constitutes a USTB. For example, in *Lewenhaupt v. Commissioner*, 20 T.C. 151 (1953), the taxpayer, a resident of Sweden, was the owner of U.S. real property which was managed by a U.S. agent. The agent was given power of attorney and used the power to buy and sell real property, execute leases, collect rents, arrange for repairs, pay taxes and mortgage interest, and arrange for insurance. The court found that these activities were "considerable, continuous, and regular" and constituted the conduct of a USTB by the principal, even where the agent was an independent agent.

There are special agency rules for nonresidents trading in stocks, securities or commodities. If a foreign taxpayer actively trades stocks, securities or commodities, the activity can rise to the level of a trade or business when made through a resident independent broker if the transactions are directed through an office of the taxpayer located in the United States. I.R.C. § 864(b)(2)(C). However, in the absence of a U.S. office, nonresidents, including dealers, may trade in stocks, securities or commodities through a resident broker or other independent agent without establishing a USTB. I.R.C. § 864(b)(2)(A)(i) and (B)(i). A nonresident who is not a dealer may trade for the investor's own account through an employee or other dependent agent without having a USTB even if the nonresident operates through a U.S. office. I.R.C. § 864(b)(2)(A)(ii) and (B)(ii). *See InverWorld, Inc. v. Commissioner*, T.C. Memo. 1996–301 (1996) for a thorough analysis of the "engaged in a trade or business" requirement.

The threshold for business activities in the United States to constitute a USTB is low. Certainly the sale of inventory on a regular basis resulting from activities in the United States constitutes a USTB. *See, e.g., Handfield v. Commissioner*, 23 T.C. 633 (1955). The IRS has taken the position that a foreign taxpayer present in the United States to demonstrate its product and solicit orders was engaged in a trade or business in the United States even in the absence of a U.S. office. Rev. Rul. 56–165, 1956–1 C.B. 849.

In some instances, it is clear that the taxpayer is engaged in a trade or business, but it is not clear whether the trade or business is in the United States. In *United States v. Balanovski*, 236 F.2d 298 (2d Cir. 1956), a taxpayer came to the United States to purchase trucks and other equipment. The trucks and equipment purchased were then sold to the Argentine government. Upon receiving bids from American suppliers, the taxpayer would submit the bids at a markup to the Argentine government. If the government approved the price, the taxpayer would purchase the equipment with funds that were wired to the United States by the Argentine government. Taxpayer operated out of a hotel room with the help of a secretary. The level of taxpayer's activities, including the solicitation of orders, the inspection of merchandise, and the purchase and sale of the merchandise convinced the court that the taxpayer was engaged in a trade or business and that the trade or business was conducted in the United States rather than in Argentina. Accordingly, the taxpayer was taxed on income arising from the sales to the Argentine government.

In contrast, in *Commissioner v. Spermacet Whaling & Shipping Co.*, 281 F.2d 646 (6th Cir. 1960), *aff'g* 30 T.C. 618 (1958), the court concluded that there was no USTB where the taxpayer, a foreign corporation, was collecting sperm oil from whales caught on high seas and selling it in the United States through a U.S. middleman. All activities for the collection and production of such oil were performed entirely outside of United States including reconditioning and equipping a ship for an expedition, employing 300 people out of Norway, fishing for whales and executing all contracts. The only activities that took place in the United States were maintenance of a bank account, purchases of fuel oil, meeting of the board of directors of a foreign corporation and passage of title to the oil.

The performance of personal services in the United States by a nonresident is a USTB. I.R.C. § 864(b). For example, a single performance by a visiting entertainer or athlete in the United States constitutes a USTB. *See e.g.*, Rev. Rul. 70–543, 1970–2 C.B. 172. Rendering a *de minimis* level of services does not constitute a trade or business if: (1) the services are performed while the taxpayer is temporarily present in the United States; (2) the taxpayer is present in the United States for no more than 90 days during the taxable year; (3) the compensation for the services in the United States does not exceed $3,000; and (4) the employer is not engaged in a trade or business in the United States or a foreign office of a U.S. person. Treaties often broaden this *de minimis* rule. *See infra* Chapter 5.

Hedge funds (which are generally organized as partnerships often with foreign investors), often purchase debt instruments in the United States (including mortgages, distressed business loans, etc.), sometimes with the goal of buying loans at a discount and then selling or settling them at or near the face value. This type of activity raises many issues that have not yet been fully resolved. Arguably, the mere purchase and sale of debt instruments should fall into the I.R.C. § 864(b)(2) securities trading exception. However, if the fund originates loans directly or indirectly through a pre-wired arrangement to buy loans originated by a related or unrelated lender, that activity if considerable, continuous and regular is likely a trade or business whether done directly or through a dependent or independent agent. *See* GLAM 2009–010. In ILM 201501013, the IRS concluded that a fund organized as a partnership in the Cayman Islands was engaged in a USTB through the activities of its U.S. fund manager, which conducted extensive lending and stock distribution activities on behalf of the fund through a U.S. office. The taxpayer that was the subject of the ILM filed a petition in 2015 with the Tax Court. *YA Global Investments LP et al. v. Comm'r*, No. 14546–15. The case remains ongoing.

The law is evolving—very slowly—to address the taxation of investments in and trading in cryptocurrencies. In the only guidance issued to date, the IRS determined that for federal tax purposes, "virtual currency is treated as property" to which general tax principles applicable to property transactions apply. Notice 2014–21, 2014–16 I.R.B. 938. The characterization of the asset will ultimately determine the tax treatment. Not just taxpayers, but members of Congress have requested that the IRS provide additional guidance as to the taxation of cryptocurrencies. Stay tuned.

§ 4.03 "EFFECTIVELY CONNECTED" INCOME

(A) U.S. SOURCE INCOME

If a nonresident alien or foreign corporation is engaged in a trade or business in the United States, the taxpayer is taxable at rates generally applicable to U.S. residents (or citizens) on income that is "effectively connected" with the conduct of the USTB. The term "effectively connected" is defined in I.R.C. § 864(c). If a taxpayer is engaged in a trade or business in the United States, generally, all sales, services, or manufacturing income from U.S. sources is effectively connected income (ECI). I.R.C. § 864(c)(3) and (2). For example, suppose that a foreign corporation is engaged in a trade or business in the United States of selling electronic equipment to U.S. customers through its U.S. branch. Any income generated by the U.S. branch is clearly ECI. In addition, any income generated from the sale of equipment (or any other inventory in the United States) by the home office without any involvement of the U.S. branch may be ECI if title to the inventory passes in the United States. Reg. § 1.864–4(b). Income from the performance of services in the United States is ECI. *See* I.R.C. § 864(c)(2) and Reg. § 1.864–4(c)(3).

Income that would normally be U.S. source investment income (that is, FDAP income) is ECI if either: (1) the income is derived from assets used in the conduct of the USTB ("asset use"); or (2) the activities of the trade or business are a material factor in the realization of the income ("business activities"). I.R.C. § 864(c)(2). For example, the "asset-use" test is satisfied if a taxpayer receives interest from an account receivable arising in the trade or business. The "business-activities" test determines if dividends derived by dealers in securities or royalties derived from a patent licensing business or service fees derived from a services business are considered effectively connected income. Reg. § 1.864–4(c)(3). For a thorough analysis of the "effectively connected" requirement, *see InverWorld, Inc. v. Comm'r*, T.C. Memo. 1996–301 (1996).

Under I.R.C. § 864(c)(8), enacted as part of the TCJA, a nonresident who disposes of an interest in a partnership that is engaged in a USTB is subject to U.S. tax on any gain or loss from such sale as effectively connected income to the same extent as if the partnership sold all of its assets at fair market value as of the date of the sale or exchange. Section 864(c)(8) overturns a Tax Court decision, that itself had reversed the IRS' long-standing position on this issue. *Grecian Magnesite Mining v. Comm'r*, 149 T.C. No. 63 (2017), *aff'd* No. 17–1268 (D.C. Cir. 2019). New I.R.C. § 1446(f) provides withholding rules to enforce this provision, requiring the transferee to withhold 10 percent of the amount realized. If the transferee fails to withhold, the partnership is obligated to do so. Withholding is generally required unless the transferor gives the transferee an affidavit stating that they are not a foreign person and provides a U.S. taxpayer identification number. Proposed regulations provide other exceptions to the general withholding obligation and rules to determine the amount to be withheld. REG–105476–18, 2019–27 I.R.B. 63.

(B)   FOREIGN SOURCE INCOME

Generally, income from foreign sources is not treated as ECI and is therefore not taxable in the United States. I.R.C. § 864(c)(4)(A). However, there are exceptions for certain income from foreign sources that is "attributable to" a U.S. "office or fixed place of business." The foreign source income that is swept into the U.S. taxing net is generally the type of income the source of which could be easily manipulated to avoid U.S. taxation.

Rents or royalties from intangible property located or used outside the United States which are derived in the active conduct of a USTB can be effectively connected income. I.R.C. § 864(c)(4)(B)(i). For example, if a foreign corporation engaged in a USTB of licensing patents licenses Mexican patents or trademarks through its U.S. office, income generated by the licensing of those intangibles to unrelated parties may be ECI if the income is attributable to the U.S. office. Note that if the royalties are from related parties, the income is not treated as ECI. I.R.C. § 864(c)(4)(D).

Dividends or interest from stock or securities derived from a USTB by banks or other financial institutions or by a corporation whose principal business is trading stock or securities for its own account are ECI even if the income is from foreign sources. I.R.C. § 864(c)(4)(B)(ii). For example, a Japanese bank with a U.S. branch which earns interest from loans to Canadian borrowers has ECI if the income is attributable to the U.S. branch (*i.e.*, the loans are made by the U.S. branch). Note that if the interest is from related parties, the income is not treated as ECI. I.R.C. § 864(c)(4)(D).

Suppose that a nonresident is engaged in a trade or business in the United States through a U.S. branch but arranges to sell inventory with title passing abroad even though the inventory is intended for use in the United States. Under I.R.C. § 864(c)(4)(B)(iii), any foreign source gain from the inventory sale is treated as ECI which is taxable in the United States. However, if a foreign office of the taxpayer materially participates in the sale and the inventory is not used in the United States, gain is not considered ECI. While this provision applies to foreign source income, in most situations of the type described, the income produced will be treated as U.S. source income under I.R.C. § 865(e)(2) and, therefore, treated as ECI under I.R.C. § 864(c)(3). That is, the more recent source rule in I.R.C. § 865(e)(2) has made I.R.C. § 864(c)(4)(B)(iii) largely irrelevant.

The foreign source income described above is treated as U.S. source ECI under I.R.C. § 865(e)(2) if it is attributable to an "office or other fixed place of business" in the United States. Generally, a foreign taxpayer is deemed to have an "office or other fixed place of business" in the United States if it has a store or plant or an office where the taxpayer engages in a trade or business. Reg. § 1.864–7. An office or fixed place of business of an agent does not satisfy this requirement unless the agent: (1) possesses and regularly exercises the authority to negotiate and conclude contracts for the principal or maintains a stock of merchandise from which he regularly fills orders on behalf of the principal; and (2) is not an independent agent. I.R.C. § 864(c)(5)(A).

For purposes of I.R.C. § 864(c)(4)(B), income is "attributable to" a U.S. office if: (1) the office is a material factor in the production of income; and (2) the income is realized in the ordinary course of the trade or business of the office. I.R.C. § 864(c)(5)(B). For example, an office would be considered to be a material factor in the production of income if it participated in soliciting an order, negotiating a contract, or performing other significant services for the consummation of the sale. Reg. § 1.864–6(b)(2).

Each category of income that is treated as effectively connected with a USTB is expanded to include economic equivalents of such income (*i.e.*, economic equivalents of certain foreign-source: (1) rents and royalties; (2) dividends and interest; and (3) income on sales or exchanges of goods in the ordinary course of business). Thus, such economic equivalents are treated as ECI in the same circumstances that foreign-source rents, royalties, dividends, interest, or certain inventory sales are treated as U.S.-ECI. I.R.C. § 864(c)(4)(B). For example, foreign-source interest and dividend equivalents (*e.g.*, a swap) are treated as U.S.-ECI if the income is attributable to a U.S. office of the foreign person, and such income is derived by such foreign person in the active conduct of a banking, financing, or similar business within the United States, or the foreign person is a corporation whose principal business is trading in stocks or securities for its own account. Treaties generally apply a different standard for determining the profits that are taxable in the United States. *See* § 5.05(D)(1).

(C) INCOME EFFECTIVELY CONNECTED TO A PRE-EXISTING TRADE OR BUSINESS

The preceding discussion focuses on whether U.S. and foreign source income from a *current* trade or business is ECI. But suppose a foreign taxpayer in its last year of conducting a trade or business in the United States sells its inventory or performs services with payments to accrue and be due over the next ten years. As the payments accrue or are received, the foreign taxpayer is no longer engaged in a trade or business in the United States. Nevertheless, under I.R.C. § 864(c)(6), the payments are characterized as they would have been taken into account in the year in which the sale took place or the services were performed. If the income would have been ECI in the year of sale (or performance) had the entire purchase price been received, the income will be ECI even if received after the year of sale.

A related provision addresses the situation where a foreign taxpayer ceases to conduct a trade or business in the United States and then disposes of property used in that trade or business, such as plant or equipment. If the property had been sold while the foreign taxpayer was engaged in a trade or business in the United States, the income would have been

ECI. But once the foreign taxpayer has ceased to conduct the trade or business, in the absence of a corrective provision, the income from the sale would not be ECI, nor would it be subject to a gross base tax under I.R.C. § 871(a) (individuals) or I.R.C. § 881 (corporations). However, under I.R.C. § 864(c)(7), property that is business property retains its character for ten years after business use ceases; any gain from its sale will be ECI.

(D) EFFECTIVELY CONNECTED INCOME ELECTION

There are some situations where a foreign taxpayer may prefer to have income treated as if it were effectively connected to the conduct of a USTB even though it is not. Nonresident alien individuals and foreign corporations that own U.S. real property as an investment can elect to treat the rental income as ECI. I.R.C. §§ 871(d) and 882(d). This "net basis" election allows a holder of U.S. real property held as an investment the benefit of business deductions for depreciation and interest expense rather than being taxed at a flat 30 percent rate on gross rental income. A higher nominal tax rate applied to net income can be more favorable to a taxpayer than a lower rate applied to gross income. The reduction in corporate rates in the 2017 tax act—with no corresponding decrease in statutory withholding rates—makes the net basis election even more attractive. In addition, I.R.C. § 199A (enacted as part of TCJA) entitles pass-through income earned by nonresident aliens to an even lower rate if the income constitutes as "qualified business income." Whether or not a nonresident makes a net basis election, any gain or loss on the sale of U.S. real property is taxed as if the taxpayer was engaged in a USTB and as if any gain or loss on the sale was effectively connected with such trade or business even if the nonresident was a passive investor. I.R.C. § 897.

(E) DIGITAL BUSINESSES

The U.S. rules for sourcing and taxing effectively connected income haven't changed much to reflect the realities of doing business in the 21st century, including the ease with which it's now possible for merchants to sell goods remotely via the internet and the extent to which consumption that formerly required purchasing a good in a physical location often now takes place as a remote service (think streaming movies and music, and gaming). Other economic trends that haven't been reflected in U.S. tax rules include the growth of global supply chains.

In August 2019, the IRS issued proposed regulations providing guidance on how to characterize cloud computing transactions. These proposed rules leave many questions unanswered and only apply once finalized. In the meantime, the OECD is moving ahead with a separate plan to figure out how to tax what it refers to as "digitalized" income. *See* discussion *infra* Chapter 14.

§ 4.04   NONBUSINESS INCOME
FROM U.S. SOURCES

Under I.R.C. §§ 871(a) and 881(a) nonresident aliens and foreign corporations are subject to a 30 percent tax (or lower treaty rate) on several types of nonbusiness income. The tax is imposed at a flat 30 percent rate without any deductions or other allowances for costs incurred in producing the income and is typically collected through withholding. The tax applies to interest, dividends, rents, royalties, and other "**F**ixed or **D**eterminable **A**nnual or **P**eriodical" income (FDAP income) if the income is: (1) includible in gross income; (2) from U.S. sources; and (3) not effectively connected with the conduct of a U.S. trade or business. Accordingly, tax-exempt interest from state and municipal obligations generally is not taxable when received by nonresidents. Similarly, FDAP income from sources outside the United States is not taxable when received by a nonresident. FDAP income from sources within the United States that is effectively connected with the conduct of a U.S. trade or business is taxable on a net basis in the manner described *supra* in § 4.03. *See* the final clause of I.R.C. §§ 871(a), 881. Actual payment is not necessarily a prerequisite to taxation of FDAP income. *See Central Gas de Chihuahua, S.A. v. Comm'r*, 102 T.C. 515 (1994) (U.S. source rental income reallocated from a related corporation was subject to tax under I.R.C. § 881 even though no actual payment was received).

The 30 percent tax on gross FDAP income should be contrasted with the tax on net business income that applies to income effectively connected to the conduct of a U.S. trade or business. The decision to tax FDAP income on a gross basis, generally through a flat 30 percent withholding tax, is more a concession to economic reality than it is a policy decision. While a nonresident engaged in a trade or business in the United States often has assets (*e.g.*, factory, office, machinery) that may be seized if the nonresident fails to pay the required tax, the nonresident with FDAP income may escape U.S. tax jurisdiction if no withholding tax is collected before payment is received.

While the TCJA lowered the U.S. corporate rate and generally provided individual taxpayers with a deduction for qualified business income earned through a pass-through entity (I.R.C. § 199A), the statutory withholding rate on FDAP income has remained the same. This increases the importance of proper planning for the structuring of U.S. investments made by foreign investors.

A brief consideration of various categories of FDAP income follows. Note that treaties generally reduce withholding rates imposed on FDAP income. *See* § 5.05(D)(3).

(A) INTEREST

The term "interest" includes both original issue discount as well as unstated interest (*i.e.*, the portion of a deferred payment under a contract of sale that is treated as interest). Notwithstanding these inclusions, interest received by nonresident investors from unrelated borrowers often is not subject to the 30 percent tax because of the "portfolio interest" exception discussed *infra*.

(1) Original Issue Discount

An original issue discount obligation is one where the face value exceeds the issue price. For example, suppose that a foreign corporation makes a $6 million loan to a U.S. corporation and receives in exchange a debt instrument which provides for no stated interest but rather the payment of $9 million in 5 years from the date the loan was made. The $3 million difference between the issue price and the redemption price is treated as interest which must be accrued for tax purposes by both the lender and the borrower regardless of their methods of accounting. I.R.C. § 1273. This rule does not apply to short-term OID instruments. I.R.C. § 871(g)(1)(B). The original issue discount is treated as if interest payments were actually paid by the borrower to the lender which in turn are loaned back to the borrower. However, the original issue discount accrued by a nonresident lender is not subject to the 30 percent tax on investment income until the debt instrument is sold, exchanged or retired. I.R.C. §§ 871(a)(1)(C) and 881(a)(3).

(2) Portfolio Interest

U.S. source interest received by a nonresident is not subject to a 30 percent tax if the interest paid is "portfolio interest." I.R.C. §§ 871(h) and 881(c). The purpose of this exemption is to allow U.S. borrowers to compete for loans with borrowers from other countries which often do not tax interest payments made to foreign lenders. For example, suppose a U.K. lender is considering a $100 million loan to USCo, a

U.S. corporation, or ForCo, a comparable Swiss corporation. If the interest payable by USCo would be subject to a 30 percent U.S. withholding tax under I.R.C. §§ 881 and 1442 (assuming the U.K. lender would not qualify for benefits under the U.S.-U.K. treaty) but interest payable by ForCo would not be subject to a withholding tax in Switzerland, the loan to ForCo may become relatively more attractive assuming comparable interest rates and levels of risk.

In enacting the portfolio interest exemption, Congress sought to restrict its benefits to the intended beneficiaries (*i.e.*, U.S. borrowers and unrelated foreign lenders) rather than unintended beneficiaries such as foreign lenders related to the U.S. borrower or any U.S. lenders (or subsequent U.S. purchasers of the debt instruments). To protect against the use of the portfolio exemption by related foreign lenders, the exemption does not apply to interest payments made to a foreign lender who owns (directly or indirectly) 10 percent or more of the voting power of the stock of the borrower. I.R.C. § 871(h)(3). For purposes of the 10 percent test, evaluation of a partnership which owns 10 percent or more of a U.S. payor of interest takes place at the partner level. Accordingly, if 100 unrelated partners each owns 1 percent of a partnership which owns 100 percent of a U.S. interest payor, the portfolio interest exemption should be available with respect to interest paid on a loan from the partnership to the U.S. borrower. Reg. § 1.871–14(g). A change made to the definition of constructive ownership in I.R.C. § 958(b) by the TCJA has (likely inadvertently) expanded the definition of related party for purposes of applying the portfolio interest exemption.

To protect against the use of the portfolio exemption by any U.S. lenders, to qualify for the portfolio interest exemption interest must be paid on registered obligations (*i.e.*, where the issuer records the owner of the instrument and surrender of the old instrument or a book entry is required for any transfer) and the issuer needs to obtain a statement that the beneficial owner is not a U.S. person. I.R.C. § 871(h)(2)(B). Interest on bearer obligations (*i.e.*, where no book entry is made) generally does not qualify for the portfolio interest exemption. In 2017 the IRS issued proposed regulations that provide for an exception in certain cases when a physical certificate issued in bearer form may be considered to be in registered form. REG–125374–16, 2017–41 I.R.B. 300.

Because portfolio interest can escape U.S. withholding, but dividends paid by U.S. corporations are subject to a 30 percent gross basis withholding tax, foreign investors might seek to disguise a dividend payment as an interest payment. Conceptually, a dividend is more dependent on the ups-and-downs of the dividend-paying corporation than interest paid by the same corporation. That is, loans are generally less risky than equity investments in part because lenders have a higher priority as a creditor than the shareholders. To prevent the unintended use of the portfolio interest exemption for more speculative income flows— "contingent interest"—I.R.C. § 871(h)(4) denies the portfolio interest exemption for any interest determined by reference to the receipts, sales, income, or asset appreciation of the debtor (or a related person). Moreover, if the interest rate is tied to the dividend rate of the payor, the portfolio interest exemption is not available. For example, if a nonresident corporation makes a $1,000,000 loan to an unrelated U.S. borrower with interest in the amount of 5 percent a year, plus 1 percent of the borrower's gross sales, the noncontingent $50,000 interest payment may qualify for the portfolio interest exemption. The interest tied to the borrower's sales, while still treated as interest (assuming the "loan" is treated as debt for U.S. tax purposes), would be subject to the 30 percent rate specified in I.R.C. § 881 (unless a lower treaty rate applies).

(3) Conduit Financing

Suppose that a foreign corporation is contemplating a loan to its U.S. subsidiary. Interest paid by the subsidiary will not qualify for the portfolio interest exemption because the parties are related. I.R.C. § 881(c)(3). Suppose instead that the foreign parent makes a loan to an unrelated foreign borrower (intermediate entity) who on-lends the funds to the U.S. subsidiary. Taken at face value, the interest payment from the U.S. subsidiary to the foreign unrelated party could qualify for the portfolio interest exemption. The interest paid from the unrelated intermediate entity to the foreign parent would normally not be subject to a U.S. withholding tax. To counteract this type of arrangement,

Congress authorized Treasury to promulgate multiparty financing (*i.e.*, conduit financing) regulations under I.R.C. § 7701(*l*).

The purpose of these Regulations (found in Reg. § 1.881–3) is to prevent foreign taxpayers from using intermediate entities to obtain the unintended benefit of reduced withholding (*e.g.*, through the portfolio exemption or through treaty reduction of withholding tax). The IRS has the authority to disregard, for purposes of I.R.C. § 881, the participation of one or more intermediate entities in a "financing arrangement" where such entities are acting as "conduit entities." Reg. § 1.881–3. A "financing arrangement" is a series of two or more financing transactions (*e.g.*, lending money, leasing or licensing property), whereby one party (financing entity) loans money or other property through one or more parties (intermediate entities) to another party (financed entity).

An intermediate entity will be considered a "conduit entity" if certain conditions exist. First, the participation of the intermediate entity in the financing arrangement must reduce the tax imposed by I.R.C. § 881. Second, the participation of the intermediate entity is pursuant to a tax avoidance plan. Finally, the intermediate entity is either: (1) related to the financing entity or the financed entity; or (2) unrelated, but "would not have participated in the financing arrangement on substantially the same terms *but* for the fact that the financing entity engaged in the financing transaction with the intermediate entity."

If a financing arrangement is found to be a conduit financing arrangement, payments from the financed entity to the intermediate entity will be recharacterized as if the payments were made directly to the financing entity. To return to the example above, interest payments from the U.S. subsidiary would be treated as if they were made to the foreign parent corporation so that the portfolio interest exemption would not be available if the intermediate entity would not normally have participated in such a transaction on substantially the same terms.

The conduit financing regulations also come into play where a non-treaty lender facing a 30 percent U.S. withholding tax on interest paid by a U.S. borrower arranges a back-to-back loan arrangement through a treaty resident that qualifies for a favorable withholding rate on interest under the applicable treaty with the United States. It is likely in this situation that the conduit financing regulations will treat this arrangement as a direct loan from the non-treaty lender that is subject to 30 percent withholding tax.

(4) Bank Deposits

Interest earned by a nonresident investor on U.S. bank deposits is not subject to the 30 percent tax on FDAP income even though the income is U.S. source income. I.R.C. §§ 871(i) and 881(d). Deposit interest that is effectively connected with the conduct of a U.S. trade or business is taxable as business income. *See supra* § 4.03(A).

(5) Interest Substitutes

Suppose that ForCo, a foreign corporation, makes a loan to SubCo, a U.S. subsidiary. Interest payments are subject to a 30 percent withholding tax under I.R.C. § 881. Now suppose that ForCo lends the SubCo note to PF, a U.S. tax-exempt pension fund, for a two-year period. Pursuant to the loan agreement, PF agrees to make a substitute payment to ForCo in the amount of any interest payment PF receives from SubCo. Is the substitute payment subject to I.R.C. § 881 even though it is not an interest payment? Regulations clarify that the substitute payment will have the same character as the underlying interest payment and will be subject to I.R.C. § 882 whether the borrower is a U.S. or foreign borrower. Reg. § 1.881–7(b). The same treatment applies if ForCo sells the debt instrument under a contract that entitles it to repurchase or repossess the debt instrument after two years (*i.e.*, a "repo"). If ForCo could have qualified for the portfolio interest exemption (*i.e.*, 0 percent withholding) had the interest payment been paid directly to it, then the substitute payment can qualify for the portfolio interest exemption as well.

(B) DIVIDENDS

Dividends from U.S. sources (*e.g.*, from a U.S. payor) are generally subject to the 30 percent withholding tax.

Dividends paid by a foreign corporation with substantial U.S. earnings can result in U.S. source income under I.R.C. § 861(a)(2)(B). However, the 30 percent withholding tax does not apply because of the operation of the branch profits tax. *See infra* § 4.05. Congress has explicitly clarified that FDAP taxation does not apply to dividends paid by a foreign corporation. I.R.C. § 871(i)(2)(D).

Just as there can be substitute interest payments where a foreign taxpayer lends a debt instrument, there can be substitute dividend payments where a foreign owner of stock lends the stock to a person and receives a substitute payment equivalent to a dividend distribution on the loaned stock. *See supra* § 4.04(A). Substitute dividend payments are treated as FDAP income in the same manner as an actual dividend. *See* I.R.C. § 871(m) as well as Reg. §§ 1.871–7(b)(2) and 1.881–2(b)(2). If the actual dividend paid to a foreign stock borrower is subject to U.S. FDAP taxation, the tax on the foreign-to-foreign substitute dividend is equal to the tax that would have been imposed if the dividend was paid directly to the lender minus any U.S. tax paid by the borrower. For example, if the borrower was subject to a 5 percent U.S. withholding tax because of the application of a treaty between the borrower's country and the United States, the substitute payment would be subject to a 25 percent U.S. withholding tax (*i.e.*, 30 percent minus 5 percent) if the lender was a resident of a country that did not have a treaty with the United States. But *see* Notice 2018–5, 2018–3 I.R.B. 341 (2018) (allowing withholding agents to apply transition rules outlined in Notice 2010–46, to addresses potential over-withholding for securities lending and sale repurchase agreements).

(C) RENTS AND ROYALTIES

Rental income received by a nonresident is subject to the 30 percent withholding tax if the activities of the nonresident (or agent) in managing the property do not amount to the conduct of a trade or business in the United States. If the activities do amount to a USTB, the income from such activities is taxable as business income. *See supra* § 4.02. For an election to treat FDAP rental income as ECI, *see supra* § 4.03(D).

Although not specifically listed in I.R.C. §§ 871(a) or 881, royalty payments are subject to the 30 percent withholding tax if the royalty income is not effectively connected with the conduct of a U.S. trade or business. Reg. §§ 1.861–5 and 1.871–7(b). Royalties are taxable whether received in installments or in a lump sum. *See Commissioner v. Wodehouse*, 337 U.S. 369 (1949). Moreover, gain from a sale of royalty-producing property is treated as a royalty if payments are contingent on the property's productivity, use, or disposition. I.R.C. § 871(a)(1)(D).

(D) INCOME FROM SERVICES

Although salaries and wages are listed as FDAP income (largely for historical reasons), they are almost never subject to the 30 percent tax. Instead, a taxpayer rendering services in the United States is considered to be in a trade or business so that services income is taxable as ECI. *See supra* § 4.02.

Pensions and other distributions from retirement plans are potentially subject to the 30 percent withholding tax. I.R.C. § 871(a)(1)(B). However, a nonresident does not have gross income for annuity payments received under a qualified retirement plan. I.R.C. § 871(f). The exclusion applies if all of the personal services giving rise to the annuity were either: (1) performed outside the United States while the taxpayer was a nonresident; or (2) within the United States while the taxpayer was temporarily present (*i.e.*, 90 days or less) earning a *de minimis* amount of income (*i.e.*, $3,000 or less). Furthermore, if fewer than 90 percent of the participants in the retirement plan are citizens or residents of the United States when the nonresident's annuity begins, there is no exclusion unless the nonresident's country of residence either: (1) grants a substantially equivalent exclusion to U.S. residents and citizens; or is a beneficiary developing country under the Trade Act of 1974.

(E) SOCIAL SECURITY BENEFITS

Eighty-five percent of any monthly old age, survivors, and disability benefits or railroad retirement benefits received by a nonresident is subject to a 30 percent tax under I.R.C. § 871(a)(3).

(F) OTHER FDAP INCOME

Other FDAP income subject to the 30 percent withholding tax includes alimony, commissions, prizes, and gambling winnings. Guarantee fees paid by a U.S. borrower to a related foreign company which guarantees a bank loan can constitute FDAP income. I.R.C. § 861(a)(9).

(G) CAPITAL GAINS

Capital gains received by a nonresident from the sale of property are almost never subject to the 30 percent withholding tax—with one significant exception for U.S. real property interests. For example, if a nonresident sells stock in a U.S. corporation at a gain, typically the United States cannot tax the gain. However, gains from the sale of property that are effectively connected (or are deemed to be effectively connected) with the conduct of a U.S. trade or business are taxable as business income. *See infra* § 4.07(B) for a discussion of gains from the disposition of U.S. real property interests. Section 871(a)(2) does tax all U.S. capital gains for nonresidents that are present in the United States for 183 days or more during a taxable year. However, the provision predates changes in the residency rules. It is now the case that an individual who is present in the United States for 183 days or more during the taxable year often will be considered a U.S. resident taxable on worldwide income (including capital gains) and so I.R.C. § 871(a)(2) will not apply. *See* I.R.C. § 7701(b). It is possible that a person might not satisfy the 183-day test under I.R.C. § 7701(b) (certain days where the taxpayer is present in the United States may not count (*e.g.*, taxpayer is a foreign government diplomat)) but might satisfy the 183-day test under I.R.C. § 871(a)(2) which does not refer to the method of counting days under I.R.C. § 7701(b).

§ 4.05   THE BRANCH PROFITS TAX

(A) THE BRANCH PROFITS TAX
ON BRANCH EARNINGS

Prior to the enactment of the branch profits tax in 1986, a foreign corporation owned by foreign investors and doing business in the United States was taxed at the corporate level under the regular corporate graduated rates on its income effectively connected with a U.S. trade or business. I.R.C. §§ 882 and 11. If the foreign investors operated in the United States through a domestic corporation, the outcome was the same. However, differences in treatment arose when the corporation distributed the corporate earnings to the foreign owners.

For a domestic corporation, the dividend was subject to a 30 percent tax rate (or reduced treaty rate) under I.R.C. § 881 with the tax collected through withholding. I.R.C. § 1442. For a foreign corporation, prior to the Tax Reform Act of 1986, it was much less likely that a dividend paid to foreign investors would be subject to any U.S. tax either because of a favorable income tax treaty or because the dividend would be foreign source income not subject to the 30 percent tax under I.R.C. §§ 871(a) or 881 due to the distributing corporation's mix of foreign and U.S. income. *See* I.R.C. § 861(a)(2).

The purpose of the branch profits tax is to subject the income earned by foreign corporations operating in the United States to two levels of taxation like income earned and distributed by U.S. corporations operating in the United States. In the latter case, the income is taxed at a rate of 21 percent when earned by a U.S. corporation and is subject to a maximum 30 percent tax when the corporation makes a dividend payment. I.R.C. § 881(a). In the case of a foreign corporation, under the branch profits regime, income is taxed at a rate of 21 percent when it is earned, and an additional 30 percent branch profits tax is imposed when the income is repatriated from the U.S. branch to the foreign home office by the foreign corporation (or deemed to be repatriated because it is not reinvested in "U.S. assets"). In effect, the branch profits tax provision treats the U.S. branch as if it were a U.S. subsidiary of the foreign corporation.

Note that the branch profits tax results in two taxes on the foreign corporation with the U.S. branch—one tax when the income is earned and one tax when the earnings are repatriated or deemed repatriated. In the case of a U.S. corporation, there is only one tax imposed on the corporation that earns the income. The second tax in this case is imposed on the shareholder when the earnings are distributed as a dividend. The branch profits tax is a proxy for this second level of tax that would be imposed on a dividend from a U.S. corporation to a foreign shareholder.

The 30 percent branch profits tax is levied on the "dividend equivalent amount" in lieu of a secondary withholding tax on dividends paid by the foreign corporation to its shareholders. I.R.C. § 884(e)(3). The "dividend equivalent amount" equals the foreign corporation's earnings and profits that are effectively connected with the conduct of a trade or business in the United States subject to certain specified adjustments. I.R.C. § 884(b). To the extent that the effectively connected earnings and profits are invested in qualifying U.S. assets, the dividend equivalent amount (DEA) is decreased. This DEA base to which the branch profits tax applies is decreased because the branch is deemed not to have repatriated the earnings to the corporation's home country. Conversely, to the extent that a foreign corporation's investment in qualifying U.S. assets decreases (because of an actual repatriation of assets or because U.S. property of the branch which previously was invested in qualifying U.S. assets is converted into other nonqualifying assets), the DEA increases. The increase in the DEA reflects the fact that effectively connected earnings of a previous year are being repatriated or are treated as having been repatriated. Generally, qualifying U.S. assets consist of money and property used by the foreign corporation to conduct a trade or business in the United States. I.R.C. § 884(c)(2).

To illustrate how the branch profits tax might operate, suppose that ForCo is incorporated in a foreign country which does not have a treaty with the United States. In Year 1, ForCo earns $4 million of net income from business operations conducted by its U.S. branch. At a flat 21 percent tax rate, ForCo will pay $840,000 in U.S. income tax on its effectively connected income. I.R.C. § 882. If the remaining $3.16 million is repatriated to ForCo's home office (or is invested in nonqualifying U.S. assets), the branch profits tax provision imposes an additional 30 percent tax, or $948,000. However, if ForCo reinvests the $3.16 million in its U.S. business, there is no immediate branch profits tax liability.

Suppose that ForCo does reinvest the proceeds in its U.S. trade or business in Year 1 so that the branch profits tax does not apply. In Year 2, ForCo earns no net income but transfers $300,000 from the U.S. business to the home office. The $300,000 repatriation is subject to the 30 percent branch profits tax because ForCo's dividend equivalent amount is increased by the disinvestment in qualifying U.S. assets.

(B) THE BRANCH PROFITS TAX ON INTEREST

Along with the branch profits tax on repatriated earnings, the Code imposes a 30 percent tax on interest paid (or deemed paid) by a branch of a foreign corporation engaged in a USTB. In the absence of I.R.C. § 884(f) which imposes this branch level tax on interest, it would be possible for a foreign corporation to decrease or even avoid the branch profits tax by making interest payments to its foreign investors. To the extent that the deductible interest payments are allocable to the branch's earnings, the interest payments would decrease taxable income, effectively connected earnings and profits and, ultimately, the DEA on which the branch profits tax is based. In the example above, if ForCo distributed all of its $4 million of net income to its foreign investors in the form of deductible interest, ForCo would have no taxable income, no effectively connected earnings and profits, and no DEA for branch profits tax purposes.

ForCo would also not have any effectively connected income for regular tax liability purposes but that would be true whether ForCo was a foreign or domestic corporation. However, if ForCo were a domestic corporation, the U.S. source interest payments would be subject to the 30 percent tax under I.R.C. §§ 871(a) or 881. In the absence of I.R.C. § 884(f), interest payments by a foreign corporation would often be foreign source income not subject to a 30 percent tax. I.R.C. § 884(f) seeks to remove this difference.

Section 884(f) contains two rules for taxing interest paid by the U.S. branch of a foreign corporation. Section 884(f)(1)(A) provides that, for a foreign corporation engaged in a USTB, interest paid by the U.S. trade or business (*i.e.*, where the loan is on the books of the branch) is treated as if paid by a domestic corporation. Consequently, under I.R.C. § 861(a)(1), the interest is U.S. source income generally subject to a flat 30 percent tax under I.R.C. §§ 871(a) or 881. However, if the interest payment qualifies as portfolio interest, there is no U.S. taxation. *See supra* § 4.04(A)(2).

Section 884(f)(1)(B) provides that, to the extent that the amount of interest allowable as a deduction under Reg. § 1.882–5 in computing taxable income of the U.S. branch exceeds the interest actually paid by the branch, the excess shall be treated as interest paid by a fictional U.S. subsidiary (the branch) to the parent, thereby subjecting the notional interest payment to a 30 percent tax under I.R.C. § 881. *See* discussion in § 4.06. The portfolio interest exemption will not apply to this excess interest because it is deemed to be paid to a related entity (*i.e.*, the home office). I.R.C. § 871(h)(3).

(C) THE BRANCH PROFITS TAX AND SECONDARY WITHHOLDING ON DIVIDENDS

A foreign corporation with a U.S. branch is subject to the regular U.S. corporate income tax under I.R.C. § 882 on income which is effectively connected with a USTB. Such income is also subject to the branch profits tax to the extent the income is not reinvested in qualifying U.S. assets, as defined in I.R.C. § 884(c)(2). There is no further tax when the foreign corporation makes a dividend distribution to its foreign investors. I.R.C. §§ 884(e)(3)(A) and 871(i)(2)(D).

(D) THE BRANCH PROFITS TAX AND INCOME TAX TREATIES

The statutory rate for both the branch profits tax and the branch profits tax on interest is 30 percent. However, as explained in Chapter 5, the dividend article (or branch profits tax article) of an applicable treaty may reduce the rate of tax on repatriated branch profits to 5 percent or even eliminate the branch profits tax. Similarly, the rate of withholding tax on interest paid by a branch or treated as paid by a branch often is reduced under the applicable treaty interest article often to 10 percent or 0 percent.

§ 4.06   SPECIAL INTEREST EXPENSE ALLOCATION RULES FOR FOREIGN CORPORATIONS

As noted in Chapter 3, special interest expense allocation rules apply for foreign corporations (particularly banks). In a 3-step process under Reg. § 1.882–5, a foreign corporation first determines the value of U.S. assets (typically adjusted basis) that generate U.S. effectively connected income. Next the foreign corporation determines its U.S. connected liabilities by multiplying those U.S. assets by a specified fixed ratio of 50 percent (95 percent for a bank) or by the actual ratio of worldwide liabilities to worldwide assets. In the third step, the foreign corporation determines the interest allocable to the U.S. connected liabilities under the adjusted U.S.-booked liabilities method (ABLM) or the separate currency pools method (SCPM), which is more sensitive to currency fluctuation.

To illustrate at a high level, suppose that ForCo, a foreign corporation, has a U.S. branch. For the taxable year, ForCo has $500 of assets used to generate U.S. effectively connected income and $3,000 of worldwide assets. ForCo's worldwide liabilities are $2,400 of which $300 appear on the books of the U.S. branch. The branch shows a $30 interest payment. The interest rate on ForCo's U.S. dollar liabilities booked outside the United States (*e.g.*, dollar denominated loans made by ForCo's home office) as well as its foreign currency denominated loans is 8 percent. ForCo's worldwide interest payment is $198 ($30 in the United States plus 8 percent × $2,100, or $168 on loans outside the United States). Assume that ForCo will use ABLM in the third step.

The U.S. connected liabilities of ForCo under the actual ratio method is $2,400/$3,000 × $500, or $400. The interest apportioned against the U.S. connected liabilities under the ABLM method is equal to the $30 of interest shown on the books of the branch plus the U.S. connected liabilities in excess of those shown on the U.S. books (*i.e.*, $100) multiplied by the interest rate on U.S. dollar liabilities booked outside the United States (*i.e.*, 8 percent). In sum, ForCo can apportion $38.00 of interest expense against U.S. source effectively connected income. If interest expense for ForCo were allocated under the asset method applicable to U.S. taxpayers, only $33 of interest ($500/$3,000 × $198) would have been allocated and apportioned to its income effectively connected with the conduct of a U.S. trade or business.

§ 4.07   FOREIGN INVESTMENT IN U.S. REAL PROPERTY

(A) OPERATIONAL INCOME

Suppose a foreign investor owns U.S. real property that produces rental income. If the foreign investor is considered to be engaged in a USTB, the net rental income (gross rental income minus deductions for depreciation, maintenance, mortgage interest etc.) is effectively connected income taxable in the same manner as other business income of a U.S. taxpayer.

I.R.C. §§ 871(b) and 882. If a foreign investor is not engaged in a trade or business in the United States, the gross rental income is taxed at a 30 percent rate under I.R.C. §§ 871(a) or 881. Normally, a foreign investor prefers the benefit of offsetting deductions, including depreciation and interest expense, compared with a tax on gross income; this preference is made even stronger by the large differential between the U.S. corporate tax rate (21 percent) and the gross basis statutory withholding rate (30 percent) post-2017. Under I.R.C. §§ 871(d) and 881(d), a foreign investor not engaged in a trade or business in the United States can elect to treat the rental income as effectively connected income which can be offset by any appropriate deductions before applying the tax rates under I.R.C. §§ 1 and 11. This "net basis" election generally is revocable only with the consent of the Commissioner.

To illustrate, suppose that ForCo, a foreign corporation, owns an apartment building in the United States that produces $2 million of rental income. To avoid the 30 percent withholding tax on the rental income, ForCo might prefer to make the net basis election and face a 21 percent tax on net income. If ForCo has $1.5 million of expenses (*e.g.*, depreciation, interest expense, maintenance) in connection with the apartment building, a 21 percent corporate tax rate applied to $500,000 of net income produces a much lower U.S. tax bill ($500,000 × 21% = $105,000) than the 30 percent withholding rate applied to $2 million of gross income ($2 million × 30% = $600,000). Note that if ForCo's business could qualify for the I.R.C. § 199A deduction, the rate could be even lower than 21 percent. Also note that the I.R.C. § 163(j) limitations generally don't apply to real estate businesses. For the I.R.C. § 163(j) interest expense limitation, *see* § 4.09(A).

Suppose that a nonresident alien or foreign corporation with U.S. real property derives no gross income but incurs expenses in connection with the property. Can the taxpayer make a net basis election in order to use the deductions to offset other income the taxpayer may have from activities that are effectively connected with the conduct of a U.S. trade or business? In Revenue Ruling 91–7, 1991–1 C.B. 110, the IRS ruled that a nonresident may not make a net basis election with respect to U.S. real property for a taxable year in which the taxpayer does not derive any income from such property. However, it should not be difficult for a nonresident with U.S. real property to generate some gross income from the property in order to make the net basis election. In Revenue Ruling 92–74, 1992–2 C.B. 156, the IRS ruled that the excess of deductions attributable to U.S. real property over income from the property may be used to offset income from the conduct of a USTB, and, if necessary, may be carried forward to other years as a net operating loss. The ruling applies to a foreign corporation but logically should be extended to nonresident aliens as well.

(B)   DISPOSITIONAL INCOME

Gain from the sale of U.S. real property by a nonresident engaged in a trade or business of buying and selling real property is treated as effectively connected income taxable in the United States even in the absence of a special provision. However, a foreign investor not engaged in a trade or business normally—absent a special provision—would not have U.S. taxable gain (or loss) on the sale of a capital asset (*e.g.*, real property) because capital gain of a nonresident is not normally subject to the 30 percent withholding tax. I.R.C. §§ 871(a) and 881.

Concerned with increasing foreign ownership of U.S. real property, in 1980 Congress enacted I.R.C. § 897 (the Foreign Investment in Real Property Tax Act, or FIRPTA) which treats gain from the sale of a "United States real property interest" as if the taxpayer is engaged in a trade or business in the United States, and as if the gain is effectively connected income. I.R.C. § 897(a). But tension between ensuring appropriate taxation of foreign investors in U.S. real property and limiting foreign investment in U.S. real estate, and the need to encourage foreign investment is ongoing and after extensive lobbying efforts, a law change in 2015 granted a special exception to the general rule for foreign owners of U.S. real property interests that are qualified foreign pension funds, or entities all of the interests in which are held by a qualified foreign pension fund. I.R.C. § 897(*l*). Proposed regulations issued in 2019 provide taxpayers with guidance as to what constitutes a qualified pension fund for this purpose. *See* REG–109826–17, 2019–26 I.R.B. 1349.

A U.S. real property interest can include not only a fee interest in U.S. real property but leaseholds, options, and natural resources. If a nonresident holds

U.S. real property through a partnership or trust, the sale by the entity of U.S. real property or the sale by the nonresident of the interest in the entity may produce effectively connected income. I.R.C. §§ 875 and 897(g). The Code "looks through" the entity and attributes the sale by the entity to the participants or treats the sale of the entity interest partially as a sale of the U.S. real property held by the entity.

The look-through paradigm does not apply to a corporate entity which is treated instead as a separate taxpaying entity. A sale by a foreign corporation of U.S. real property is not attributed to the shareholder. Instead, the foreign corporation is taxed on any gain as if the gain were ECI. I.R.C. § 897. Because the foreign corporation is taxed on gain from the sale of U.S. real property under I.R.C. § 897, a foreign shareholder who sells appreciated stock in the foreign corporation is not taxable on the sale. If a U.S. corporation sells U.S. real property, the corporation is, of course, taxable under I.R.C. § 11. If a foreign shareholder sells appreciated stock of a U.S. corporation most of the assets of which are U.S. real property, the shareholder may be taxed on any gain (which is treated as ECI).

An equity interest in a U.S. corporation is a "U.S. real property interest" (USRPI) and therefore subject to I.R.C. § 897 if the corporation is a "U.S. real property holding corporation" (USRPHC). I.R.C. § 897(c)(2). A U.S. corporation is a USRPHC if on any "determination date" (see below) during the previous five years the fair market value of the corporation's USRPIs equaled at least 50 percent of the sum of the fair market value of the corporation's total worldwide real property interests plus business assets. For example, if on a determination date during the applicable period, a domestic corporation owns U.S. real property with a fair market value of $100,000, foreign real property with a fair market value of $75,000 and business assets with a fair market value of $50,000, it is not a USRPHC and the stock is not a USRPI ($100,000/$225,000). If the corporation disposes of $25,000 of business assets (*e.g.*, distribution to its shareholders), it would become a USRPHC ($100,000/$200,000), and any subsequent sale of the corporation's stock at a gain would be taxable in the United States.

A domestic corporation is a USRPHC during the five-year test period if it is a USRPHC on any "determination date." Generally, those dates are: (a) the last day of a corporation's tax year, and (b) the date of each transaction that might cause a corporation to become a USRPHC. Such transactions include either the acquisition of a USRPI or the disposition of foreign real property or assets used in a trade or business. Reg. § 1.897–2(c). In the example above, the disposition of the $25,000 of business assets would trigger a determination date thereby rendering the corporation a USRPHC.

A look-through rule applies to determine whether a U.S. corporation is a U.S. real property holding corporation. If the U.S. corporation owns an interest in a transparent entity (*e.g.*, a partnership) or at least 50 percent (by value) of the stock of a U.S. or foreign corporation, a pro rata portion of the entity's assets is considered to be owned by the parent corporation. I.R.C. § 897(c)(5). If USCo, a U.S. corporation, owns less than 50 percent (by value) of the stock of a second corporation, there is no "look-through." An "all-or-nothing" rule applies instead. If the second corporation is a USRPHC (or would be if it were a U.S. corporation), then the entire stock interest is treated as a USRPI in calculating whether USCo is a USRPHC. Note that while a foreign corporation can be a USRPHC for purposes of testing whether a U.S. corporation as a shareholder is a USRPHC (*see* I.R.C. § 897(c)(4)), stock of a foreign corporation is not a USRPI (*i.e.*, sale of stock of a foreign corporation by a foreign taxpayer is never taxable under I.R.C. § 897(a)).

If a class of stock is regularly traded on an established securities market, the stock will be a USRPI in the case of a more than 5 percent holder (*i.e.*, a holder that owned more than a 5 percent interest during a 5-year look-back period). I.R.C. § 897(c)(3). If a seller is not a more than 5-percent shareholder, gain on the sale of the stock should not be subject to U.S. tax.

For example, suppose a foreign individual holds a 1 percent interest in the publicly-traded stock of a United States real estate investment trust (*i.e.*, a REIT). A REIT is a U.S. corporation having at least 100 shareholders that is treated as a pass-through entity (*i.e.*, not entity-level tax) essentially if almost all of its income is real estate related income and it distributes 90 percent or more of its taxable income each year. Gain on the sale of the REIT stock is not taxable in the United States because the stock is publicly traded and the seller is not a more than 5-percent shareholder. Moreover, even if the stock of the REIT were not publicly traded, if foreign investors own less than 50 percent of the value of the REIT stock during the previous 5-year period (*i.e.*, the REIT is "domestically controlled"), gain on the sale of shares by any foreign investor—regardless of ownership level—is not taxable under I.R.C. § 897. I.R.C. § 897(h)(2). Changes to the law in 2015 relaxed the rules as applied to REITs, making it easier for foreign persons to invest in REITs without incurring U.S. tax on the disposition of such interests. *See* Prop. Reg. § 1.897(*l*)–1. REG–109826–17, 2019–26 I.R.B. 1349.

If a U.S. corporation is a USRPHC, a disposition by a nonresident of any interest (other than an interest solely as a creditor) at a gain is subject to U.S. taxation. I.R.C. § 897(a). Hybrid securities as well as stock interests are covered. The tax is enforced by means of a withholding obligation imposed on the transferee, who is required to withhold 15 percent of the amount realized by a transferor that is a foreign person (the withholding amount is 10 percent in the case of property acquired for use as a residence when the amount realized does not exceed $1 million). As a result of the 2017 reduction in the corporate tax rate, the withholding rate applied to partnerships on FIRPTA gain allocated to a non-U.S. corporate partner is 21 percent. I.R.C. §§ 1445(e), 1446(b). A transferee that is required to withhold but fails to do so is required to pay the assessed amounts, plus penalties and interest, and may also be subject to civil and criminal penalties.

Dispositions other than sales can trigger U.S. taxation. Suppose that a nonresident holding U.S. real property exchanges the property for stock of a foreign corporation in a nonrecognition exchange qualifying under I.R.C. § 351. If there is no recognition on the exchange, the foreign taxpayer would then be free to sell the stock in a foreign corporation free of U.S. taxation. However, I.R.C. § 897(e) overrides all statutory nonrecognition provisions unless the property received in the transaction would be taxable in the United States if sold (*e.g.*, if the foreign owner gives up a USRPI interest and receives a USRPI interest in return—a "USRPI for USRPI" exchange). In the example, the foreign taxpayer may not be able to rely on I.R.C. § 351 because gain from the sale of stock in a foreign corporation by a nonresident is not taxable in the United States. However, even foreign-to-foreign exchanges can sometimes qualify for nonrecognition. *See* Reg. § 1.897–6T(b) and Notice 2006–46, 2006–1 C.B. 1044.

A number of the FIRPTA provisions address a variety of corporate and partnership transactions. *See* I.R.C. § 897(d) and (e). The detailed interplay of FIRPTA with corporate and partnership provisions is beyond the scope of this book. However, the thrust of these provisions is to ensure that if a transferor of a USRPI in what would otherwise be a tax-free transaction does not get back a USRPI (*i.e.*, a USRPI interest for a USRPI interest), then the transfer is taxable or the gain can be preserved.

§ 4.08   TRANSPORTATION INCOME

If a foreign corporation is engaged in a U.S. trade or business that generates transportation income and the income is effectively connected with the trade or business, it is subject to the regular U.S. corporate income tax. I.R.C. § 882. Transportation income is treated as effectively connected if the foreign corporation has a fixed place of business within the United States that is involved in the earning of the income, and if substantially all (at least 90 percent) of the U.S. gross transportation income of the foreign corporation for the tax year is attributable to regularly scheduled transportation (or, for income from the leasing of a vessel or aircraft, is attributable to a fixed place of business in the United States).

However, if a foreign corporation has U.S.-source transportation income that is not effectively connected with a USTB, then that income is subject to a 4 percent gross withholding tax under I.R.C. § 887(a). The 4 percent tax applies only to the extent that the foreign corporation's transportation income is derived from U.S. sources as determined in accordance with I.R.C. § 863(c)(2). Under those sourcing rules, transportation income is foreign sourced if it is derived from transportation between two non-U.S. locations, and as such, that income would not be subject to U.S. taxation. If the income is derived from transportation that either begins or ends in the United States, the transportation income is considered to be 50 percent U.S.-source and 50 percent foreign-source, with the U.S.-source portion being subject to the 4 percent withholding tax under I.R.C. § 887.

There are two exceptions under which income from the international operation of ships and aircraft can be exempted from gross and net-based U.S. taxes. First, most U.S. tax treaties contain a shipping and air transport article that generally provides that income derived by a corporation from the operation of ships or aircraft in international traffic is taxable only in the country in which the corporation is a resident. *See* Art. 8 of the U.S. Model Treaty discussed *infra* in § 5.05. Thus, foreign corporations that are resident in a U.S. treaty partner country whose treaty provides for that exemption can avoid U.S. tax on transportation income imposed by I.R.C. § 887.

Second, a statutory exemption exists in I.R.C. § 883 that provides that gross transportation income derived by a foreign corporation from the international operation of ships or aircraft is exempt from U.S. taxation if the corporation's country of residence provides for a reciprocal exemption. A corresponding exemption from the 4 percent withholding tax under I.R.C. § 887 also exists under I.R.C. § 883. Thus, if the country where the foreign company is incorporated does not impose an income tax, or if it grants an equivalent exemption from its income tax for transportation income earned by U.S. corporations (either via domestic law or by an exchange of diplomatic notes), the foreign corporation will not be subject to U.S. taxation (either gross-or net-based) on its U.S.-source transportation income.

§ 4.09   ANTI-BASE EROSION MEASURES

Over the years, Congress' concern about non-U.S. persons' ability to reduce their U.S. taxes by artificially decreasing their U.S. taxable income, often through deductible payments to foreign related parties, has led it to enact increasingly punitive measures to combat this problem. Most recently, a number of provisions were enacted or amended in the TCJA with the goal of preventing such base erosion activities. But at the same time, Congress has had to balance these concerns with the desire to attract foreign investment. This dynamic and balancing act continues to play out. We consider some of these measures below. Although enacted ostensibly to prevent foreigners from stripping out the U.S. tax base, these provisions are not limited to these types of taxpayers but often have adverse—perhaps unintended—effects on U.S. taxpayers as well.

(A) INTEREST STRIPPING

In general, I.R.C. § 163 provides for the deduction of interest expense. However, under I.R.C. § 163(j) as amended by the TCJA, interest deductions may be disallowed to the extent that the interest paid exceeds 30 percent of the taxpayer's adjusted taxable income for the year, with certain narrow exceptions. Prior to TCJA, I.R.C. § 163(j) primarily impacted interest payments made to related foreign parties; as amended, it applies to practically all taxpayers with certain limited expenses. But it still has an especially perverse effect on the financing practices of foreign-parented multinationals with U.S. subsidiaries. That's because previously, the U.S. operations could be highly leveraged with the lender being a related party without any adverse financial statement impact. Amended I.R.C. § 163(j) diminishes the benefits from this type of planning.

Even in situations where I.R.C. § 163(j) does not pose a problem, an interest expense deduction may be disallowed to a U.S. accrual basis taxpayer if the interest is payable to a related party. Under I.R.C. § 267(a)(3), a U.S. taxpayer is essentially put on the cash method of accounting for purposes of deducting interest paid to a related foreign party unless the foreign related party's accrued income is taxable in the United States. Similar rules apply to other deductible payments made to related foreign parties (*e.g.*, royalties). Any deductible expense that has accrued will be deductible when payment is made or is considered to be made.

Section 163(j) prior to enactment of the TCJA restricted the deductibility of interest expense in the case of payments to foreign related parties that met certain threshold requirements (*i.e.*, a sufficiently high debt: equity ratio and a threshold of interest expense as a percentage of adjusted taxable income). The rule was intended to protect the U.S. tax base in cases when, for example, the recipient of the payment resided in a treaty jurisdiction and where under the applicable treaty, the United States was not allowed to tax the payment under I.R.C. § 881. In such a situation, the deduction for interest expense could reduce the U.S. tax base without an offsetting inclusion in the U.S. tax base.

The TCJA significantly enlarged the scope and application of the limitation on deductibility of interest expense. New I.R.C. § 163(j) doesn't just apply to related party payments, but limits deductibility of any 'business interest' paid or accrued by a taxpayer, according to a formula based on the taxpayer's total interest income plus 30 percent of "adjusted taxable income," roughly equivalent to earnings before interest, depreciation and amortization.

The new I.R.C. § 163(j) limitation applies to taxable periods starting after December 31, 2017. Taxpayers with gross receipts of less than $25 million are excluded from its application, as are some real estate businesses. Generally, amounts disallowed can be carried forward indefinitely. In the case of interest paid by a partnership, the limitation is applied at the partnership level. Complex rules apply to ensure that partners in a partnership are not able to double count the partnership income for purposes of applying the limitation at the partner level, and to allow excess limitation at the partnership level to be used by the partners.

Unlike under prior law, whether the 30 percent withholding tax rate on interest is reduced under a tax treaty is irrelevant for purposes of determining whether the limitation applies.

Proposed regulations issued in 2018 provide that amounts carried forward under old I.R.C. § 163(j) as disallowed disqualified interest are included as disallowed business interest expense carryforwards to the extent that the amounts otherwise qualify as business interest expense of the taxpayer under the proposed rules. REG–106089–18, 2019–05 I.R.B. 431. The disallowance under I.R.C. § 163(j) not only applies to U.S. subsidiaries of foreign parents, but can also apply to limit the deduction of interest otherwise permitted to the U.S. branch of a foreign corporation under Reg. § 1.882–5. *See* § 4.06.

Prior to the changes made to I.R.C. § 163(j) by the TCJA, Treasury tried to address base erosion concerns from earnings stripping (and related concerns about inversion transactions, *see* § 13.02(G)) with regulations under I.R.C. § 385. That statute grants Treasury broad authority to prescribe regulations to determine when an interest in a corporation is to be treated as stock or debt. Treasury utilized that authority to write rules that recharacterize debt instruments as equity (thus effectively but indirectly denying an interest expense deduction) if issued pursuant to certain transactions. Note that these regulations have been identified as potentially overly burdensome under Executive Order 13789 (2017) and may be withdrawn or otherwise modified. The IRS has already proposed to withdraw the documentation requirements imposed by the rules. *See* Notice 2017–38; 2017–30 I.R.B. 147; REG–130244–17, 2018–41 I.R.B. 591.

(B) THE BASE-EROSION AND
ANTI-ABUSE TAX

An even more radical measure enacted by Congress in the TCJA to address base erosion concerns is new I.R.C. § 59A, known as the base erosion and anti-abuse tax (BEAT). That provision operates as an alternative minimum tax on U.S. corporations (that exceed a minimum threshold in size) that make large amounts of "base eroding" payments that are not fully subject to U.S. withholding tax to related foreign entities. For an example of the type of perceived abuse that I.R.C. § 59A was intended to address, consider the following example. Suppose that ForCo has a U.S. subsidiary (USSub) that earns $100 of net income. The U.S. tax base is $100, and under I.R.C. § 11 would generally be subject to $21 of corporate tax. Now suppose that ForCo and USSub arranged their affairs so that USSub pays a $40 deductible expense to ForCo. As a result, the U.S. tax base is only $60 ($100 − $40). If the deductible expense is not subject to U.S. withholding tax under a treaty or otherwise, then the U.S. Treasury's tax collection would be reduced from $21 to $12.60. Yet the total income generated be ForCo and USSub combined has not been reduced by the deductible payment.

The BEAT tax is imposed on an alternative base that excludes base eroding payments and the "base erosion percentage" of any net operating loss ("NOL") for the tax year, and doesn't take into account most tax credits. If there is a 30 percent withholding tax imposed, then there is no need to apply the tax. If

I.R.C. § 59A applies, the rate of tax is 5 percent for tax years beginning in calendar year 2018, 10 percent for tax years beginning in 2019 through 2025, and 12.5 percent for tax years beginning after December 31, 2025. Some banks and securities dealers are subject to a rate 1 point higher than the regular rate. Section 59A applies only to corporations (other than regulated investment companies (RICs), REITs, or S corporations) that have average annual gross receipts for the three-year period ending with the preceding tax year of at least $500 million and that make base erosion payments to related foreign persons of 3 percent (2 percent for certain banks and securities dealers) or more (during the tax year) of all their deductible expenses and base erosion tax benefits.

Base erosion payments generally include deductible payments to related foreign parties, the purchase of depreciable or amortizable property from related parties, certain reinsurance payments, and payments to foreign members of an affiliated group that inverted after November 9, 2017 (*see* § 13.02(G) for a definition of an inversion). Base erosion payments do not include payments for cost of goods sold. They also don't include qualified derivative payments, or payments for the cost of services if they meet the requirements for the services cost method under the transfer pricing rules in I.R.C. § 482. (*See infra* Chapter 11 for a discussion of I.R.C. § 482). A related person generally is a person who owns at least 25 percent of the taxpayer; constructive ownership rules apply. A taxpayer is allowed to offset the BEAT tax with the research credit and 20 percent of three other credits (including the low income housing credit and certain energy credits) but not the foreign tax credit.

To illustrate how the BEAT works, suppose that in 2019 USCo, an applicable taxpayer (within the meaning of the statute) provides services to U.S. customers worth $300. To provide those services, USCo subcontracts with its parent company (ForCo) to provide the services, deducting $200 it pays to ForCo. The $200 payment is not subject to U.S. withholding tax. In addition, USCo incurs $20 of other deductible expenses paid to unrelated parties in connection with the services performed.

The base erosion tax benefit is the $200 not subject to full U.S. withholding tax that is paid to a related party. It does not qualify for the under 3 percent safe harbor because USCo's base erosion percentage is: $200/$220, or almost 91 percent. USCo's base-erosion minimum tax amount ("BEMTA") is equal to the excess of 10 percent multiplied by USCo's modified taxable income minus the regular tax liability. For USCo, modified taxable income is $300 of gross income minus $20 of non-base eroding payments, or $280. BEMTA equals: (.10 × $280) minus the regular tax liability on USCo's taxable income. USCo's taxable income is $80 ($300 − $200 − $20) and its regular tax liability is .21 × 80, or $16.80. So BEMTA equals $28 minus $16.80, or $11.20. The total U.S. tax is the $16.80 plus $11.20 or $28 on a tax base of $280, ignoring the base erosion payments.

In proposed regulations, the IRS has determined that non-cash consideration such as stock or property is considered amounts paid for purposes of BEAT. This means that non-recognition transactions (such as an inbound I.R.C. § 332 transaction) can be implicated as base erosion payments, a potential trap for the unwary.

BEAT is an anti-abuse tax that operates according to what's known as a "cliff-effect": if taxpayers meet the criteria for applicability, they are fully subject to the BEAT. This provides strong incentives for taxpayers to structure their affairs to avoid falling off this cliff, such as by ensuring that global contracts don't require a U.S. affiliate to make payments to a related foreign party. As a result, it's not clear that the BEAT is having its full desired effect on the taxpayers it presumably intended to target. There also have been questions raised as to whether its compatible with U.S. treaty obligations. *See* Chapter 5. For a variety of reasons, one can expect changes to this provision in the years ahead.

§ 4.10   TAXATION OF FOREIGN GOVERNMENTS

Historically, the United States has exempted from U.S. federal income tax certain types of U.S. source investment income derived by foreign governments. I.R.C. § 892. However, income which foreign governments derived from "commercial activities" has generally been taxable as if the income was earned by a foreign private corporation.

A foreign government (or subdivision) or its agent seeking exemption from U.S. taxation must satisfy two basic requirements: a status requirement and an income requirement. The foreign government must qualify as a "foreign government" for purposes of the provision, and the income it receives must be the type eligible for exemption under I.R.C. § 892. The term "foreign government" includes "a controlled entity" of a "foreign sovereign." A "controlled entity" is an entity (*e.g.*, a corporation) that essentially is wholly-owned by a single foreign sovereign, the earnings of which do not inure to the benefit of any individual, and whose assets would vest in the foreign sovereign upon dissolution. Reg. § 1.892–2T(a)(3). A pension trust for the benefit of foreign government employees can qualify as a "controlled entity." Reg. § 1.892–2T(c).

A foreign government (or controlled entity) is exempt from U.S. taxation on income from stocks, bonds or other securities and interest on bank deposits. I.R.C. § 892(a)(1). The exemption does not cover rental income from U.S. real property or any gain from the disposition of such property. However, gain from the sale of stock of a corporation owning U.S. real property can be exempt from U.S. taxation unless the foreign government holds a controlling interest in the corporation. Like rental income, income derived by a foreign government (or controlled entity) from the conduct of commercial activity is subject to U.S. taxation. I.R.C. § 892(a)(2).

Moreover, income received from or by a "controlled commercial entity" is subject to U.S. taxation. I.R.C. § 892(a)(2). A "controlled commercial entity" is an entity engaged in commercial activities anywhere in the world if the government holds (by value or voting interest) 50 percent or more of the total of such interests or a lesser amount if it holds effective control. For example, if the government of India owns a corporation that is engaged in commercial activities anywhere in the world, any income received by that corporation may be subject to U.S. taxation under normal U.S. taxing rules. Thus, if the corporation receives dividends or interest from a U.S. payor, the corporation may be taxable under I.R.C. § 881. A corporation is deemed to be engaged in commercial activities if it is a U.S. real property holding corporation or in the case of a foreign corporation would be a U.S. real property holding corporation if it were a U.S. corporation.

Proposed regulations under I.R.C. § 892 provide that an entity not otherwise engaged in commercial activities will not be deemed to be engaged in commercial activities solely because it holds an interest as a limited partner in a limited partnership, as defined in the Prop. Reg. § 1.892–5(d)(5)(iii)(B). In general, the partnership interest should not give any rights to participate in the management and conduct of the partnership's business at any time during the tax year. Even in proposed form, these regulations can be relied on. Although the commercial activity of a limited partnership will not cause a controlled entity of a foreign sovereign limited partner meeting the requirements of the exception for limited partnerships to be engaged in commercial activities, the controlled entity partner's distributive share of partnership income attributable to such commercial activity will be considered to be derived from the conduct of commercial activity, and therefore will not be exempt from taxation under I.R.C. § 892.

If a foreign government has income that is not exempt from U.S. taxation under I.R.C. § 892, the foreign government is treated as a foreign corporation for purposes of applying the U.S. domestic tax rules. Furthermore, the foreign government is treated as a corporate resident of its country, allowing the foreign government to qualify for tax benefits provided by an applicable income tax treaty with the United States. I.R.C. § 892(a)(3).

CHAPTER 5

THE ROLE OF INCOME TAX TREATIES

§ 5.01 THE BILATERAL INCOME TAX TREATY NETWORK

Many of the Code ground rules discussed in the previous Chapters (and in the following Chapters dealing with U.S. taxpayers) are altered by more than 50 bilateral income tax treaties between the United States and its trading partners (referred to in tax treaties as "contracting states" rather than "countries"). The principal purpose of this income tax treaty network is to facilitate international trade and investment by lowering tax barriers to the international flow of goods and services. Lower overall taxation encourages trade and investment. Every contracting state involved in international commerce acts in two capacities for tax purposes. In some situations a contracting state claims the right to tax as the residence state of a taxpayer. In other situations a contracting state asserts tax jurisdiction based on the source of income earned by a nonresident.

While most contracting states have enacted domestic laws governing international transactions and providing unilateral relief from juridical double taxation, these unilateral efforts do not always eliminate jurisdictional overlaps. For example, if Canada under its domestic rules considers a taxpayer to be a resident of Canada while the United States under its rules considers the taxpayer to be a resident of the United States, there is likely to be double taxation of the income earned by that taxpayer. One purpose of an income tax treaty is to resolve such residence-residence conflicts.

Similarly, if a resident of the United States earns income in Germany, a tax treaty typically alleviates potential double taxation either by granting exclusive tax jurisdiction to the residence state (*e.g.*, under many U.S. treaties, only the residence state can tax interest income paid by a payor in the other contracting state) or providing for shared tax jurisdiction with the residence state entitled to residual taxation after taking source state taxation into account (*e.g.*, business profits attributable to a permanent establishment in the other contracting state).

Treaties also provide a degree of certainty and predictability so that taxpayers can arrange their affairs. The clarification of tax jurisdiction and the mutual agreement procedures for resolving treaty problems contained in a tax treaty help smooth out some of the rough edges for a taxpayer dealing with different states with different laws. Also, the provisions in a treaty for the exchange of information between states help contracting states enforce their domestic tax provisions.

While the discussion of treaties has been placed in Part II dealing with U.S. activities of foreign taxpayers, treaties also address the tax treatment of U.S. taxpayers by the other contracting state and how that tax treatment is recognized for U.S. tax purposes.

§ 5.02 THE TREATY MAKING PROCESS IN THE UNITED STATES

The Executive Branch of the United States, as part of its authority to conduct the foreign relations of the United States has the exclusive authority to negotiate income tax treaties. The Department of Treasury, through the Assistant Secretary for Tax Policy and the International Tax Counsel does the actual negotiation. Once a treaty is signed by the President or the President's delegate, the treaty is transmitted to the Senate for its advice and consent. Typically the Senate Foreign Relations Committee conducts hearings before approving or rejecting a treaty. If a treaty is approved by the Committee, the full Senate votes on the treaty. Occasionally, the Senate will approve a treaty subject to a reservation in respect of a particular provision. In such a case, from the U.S. perspective the treaty may enter into force except in respect of such a provision. Once the Senate approves a treaty, it enters into force upon the exchange of instruments of ratification by the Executive Branch. From time to time, treaties are amended through bilateral Protocols which must also undergo the ratification process as described above. The United States and a treaty partner can enter into an agreement that interprets or clarifies an existing treaty, known as a Competent Authority Agreement, without requiring Senate ratification.

For almost 10 years, a single U.S. Senator held up ratification of a growing number of pending and signed U.S. tax treaties and protocols. In July 2019, the Senate ratified 4 protocols to existing treaties with Spain, Luxembourg, Japan and Switzerland. But three treaties—those with Poland, Hungary and Chile—remain pending awaiting resolution of a treaty override question that has arisen as a result of TCJA (*see* discussion below).

§ 5.03   THE RELATIONSHIP OF INCOME TAX TREATIES AND THE CODE

Income tax treaties exist to limit a contracting state's tax jurisdiction in order to avoid international double taxation. To that end, a treaty provision should not be construed to restrict in any manner any exclusion, exemption, deduction or credit, or any allowance accorded by the domestic laws of the treaty partners. Stated differently, income tax treaties can reduce a taxpayer's U.S. tax liability but cannot generally increase it.

U.S. income tax treaties have the same force as domestic law (*i.e.*, both are the "supreme Law of the Land"). U.S. Const. art. VI, cl. 2. If a treaty conflicts with federal law (*e.g.*, a tax provision), generally, for domestic law purposes, the later-in-time rule prevails. *Whitney v. Robertson*, 124 U.S. 190 (1888). Whenever possible, courts try to construe treaty provisions and domestic tax laws harmoniously. If a taxpayer claims that a statutory provision is affected by a tax treaty, the taxpayer must disclose reliance

on a treaty to modify application of a Code provision.
I.R.C. § 6114.

The domestic later-in-time rule sometimes leads to
a violation of international law. When Congress
enacts a statutory provision that directly overrides a
pre-existing treaty provision, the later enacted
statute prevails for domestic law purposes. However,
the United States is not relieved of its treaty
obligations and failure to comply with a treaty
results in a violation of international law. *See* Vienna
Convention on the Law of Treaties, Art. 27 (signed
but not ratified by the United States); Restatement
of Foreign Relations Law of the United States,
§ 135(1)(b). There are no practical remedies for such
a violation of international law, except that the
contracting state against which the breach was
committed can terminate or partially terminate the
treaty.

Notwithstanding the international law
implications, I.R.C. § 7852(d) clearly states that
neither a treaty provision nor a tax provision has
preferential status (so that the domestic later-in-time
rule applies). The uneasy relationship between U.S.
treaties and domestic law is expressed in I.R.C.
§ 894(a) which provides that Code provisions should
be applied "with due regard to any treaty obligation
of the United States."

The United States is fairly unique in this
approach. Many other countries pay much greater
deference to treaty obligations when enacting
changes to domestic tax laws. A number of provisions
of the TCJA, notably the BEAT (discussed *supra* in

§ 4.09(B)) have raised these types of treaty override concerns, and three treaties currently pending in the Senate (with Poland, Hungary and Chile) are being held up because of Treasury's concern to include a reservation for BEAT.

§ 5.04   DEVELOPMENT OF MODEL INCOME TAX TREATIES

The United States has had a dual purpose in treaty design: to harmonize its domestic tax rules with the rules of other states and at the same time to preserve domestic tax jurisdiction over its citizens and residents. Historically, the United States has followed a series of model income tax treaties in negotiating its income tax treaties with other nations. The starting point for U.S. treaty negotiations was a U.S. model income tax treaty first developed in 1977 and revised most recently in 2016 ("2016 U.S. Model"). No treaty based on the 2016 U.S. Model has yet been ratified.

Many of the European and other trading partners of the United States use a model treaty developed by the Organization for Economic Cooperation and Development ("OECD Model"). The United States is also a member of the OECD. The member states of the OECD also have agreed to Commentaries on the OECD Model treaty. The OECD Model and Commentaries provide useful explanations of treaty provisions and are often cited by U.S. courts. *See e.g.*, *National Westminster Bank, PLC v. United States*, 512 F.3d 1347 (Fed. Cir. 2008); *Taisei Fire & Marine Insurance Co. v. Commissioner*, 104 T.C. 535 (1995).

While the two models are far more alike than different, there are some fundamental differences. Under the 2016 U.S. Model, a dual resident company is not considered a resident in either country and thus is ineligible for treaty benefits. The OECD Model leaves the tie-breaker decision in the hands of the competent authority. Where there is potential double taxation, the U.S. Model has historically relied on the credit method (*i.e.*, a contracting state credits the taxes paid to the other contracting state on income earned in the other contracting state) for relief while the OECD Model recognizes the exemption method (*i.e.*, a contracting state exempts income earned in the other contracting state) as well as the credit method.

Still another difference between the two models lies in the treatment of interest income. The U.S. Model has generally assigned exclusive tax jurisdiction to the state where the recipient resides while the OECD Model permits the source state (*i.e.*, where the payor resides) a limited right to tax interest paid to a resident of the other state. There are other important structural differences between the two Models as well. For example, the U.S. Model has not generally extended to state and local income tax laws while the OECD Model does. Finally, the U.S. Model has since 1977 incorporated some version of a bright-line approach to address the problem of treaty shopping, a term that describes taxpayers' attempts to use a treaty for tax avoidance reasons (a detailed Limitation on Benefits provision) while the 2017 OECD Model adopted for the first time a more general anti-abuse test (the "principal purpose test"). *See* 2016 U.S. Model Art. 22.

Changes to the OECD Model Treaty made as a result of the BEPS Project (discussed *supra* in Chapter 1) widened the gap between the U.S. Model Treaty and the OECD Model in a number of important ways, as discussed further below.

In addition to the U.S. and OECD Models, the United Nations tax committee (officially known as the Committee of Experts on International Cooperation in Tax Matters) has produced a UN Model (updated in 2017) intended as a guide for treaties between developed and developing states. While the U.S. and OECD Models have tended to favor capital exporters (*i.e.*, the residence state), the UN Model favors capital importing states (*i.e.*, the source state) by assigning greater taxing authority to the source state with respect to both investment and business income. In negotiating with the United States, a developing state may rely on the UN Model as its starting point, but the UN Model has not reached the same level of acceptance as the OECD Model.

While the U.S. Model has served as a starting point for U.S. treaty negotiation, U.S. bilateral income tax treaties show a remarkable degree of individuality.

§ 5.05   INCOME TAX TREATY PROVISIONS

Although there is some variation in income tax treaty provisions between the United States and its trading partners, there are a number of typical provisions that are found in virtually all U.S. income tax treaties. As indicated above, all U.S. tax treaties in effect today rely on an earlier version of the U.S. Model than the 2016 version.

(A) INTERPRETATION OF U.S. INCOME TAX TREATIES

All modern U.S. treaties contain a provision that establishes a hierarchy of interpretation rules that apply to treaty terms. *See* 2016 U.S. Model, Art. 3(2). First, many treaty terms are specifically defined in the treaty (*e.g.*, the definition of "interest"). If a term is not specifically defined, the context of the treaty, including all relevant background material involving the treaty, may require a particular definition. If the context of a treaty does not require a particular definition, the contracting state applying the treaty applies its own domestic tax law. Even if the other contracting state might reach a different conclusion with respect to a definition, it is obligated to honor the conclusion reached by the contracting state applying the treaty if under Article 3(2) that state acted in accordance with the treaty.

It is generally accepted that any reference to domestic law of a contracting state refers to that law as it may change from time to time that is, a dynamic rather than a static interpretation. Dynamic interpretation does not mean that a state is free unilaterally to amend its domestic law for the exclusive purpose of altering the application of a treaty provision.

(B) SCOPE OF THE TREATY

Articles 1, 2, and 29 of the U.S. Model address the coverage of the treaty in respect of persons, taxes, territory and time. Generally, the treaty applies to residents of a contracting state. However, it is U.S. policy that a tax treaty can limit the ability of the United States to tax the residents of other states but should "save" for the United States the right to tax U.S. citizens and residents on their worldwide income. 2016 U.S. Model, Art. 1(4). For example, under this "saving clause," a resident of the United Kingdom who is not a U.S. citizen can rely on Article 11 of the U.S.-United Kingdom treaty (signed in 2011) to avoid U.S. taxation of interest paid by a U.S. borrower. However if that U.K. resident was also a U.S. citizen, the United States reserves the right under Article 1(4) to tax fully the interest income, as if the treaty were not in effect. Even if the interest is paid by a U.K. borrower to a resident of the United Kingdom, the United States will tax the interest if the U.K. resident is also a U.S. citizen, although the responsibility for avoiding double taxation in this situation lies with the United States. *See* 2016 U.S. Model, Art. 23(4).

Turning to the scope of coverage in respect of taxes, territory, and time, not surprisingly U.S. income tax treaties address federal income taxes. State and local income taxes are not covered much to the disappointment of U.S. treaty partners who would like protection from what they regard as unfair state taxation by some U.S. states which, using a formulary approach, sometimes tax income not related to activities in the state. Treaties have no fixed duration and generally provide for termination by a contracting state with six months' notice. 2016 U.S. Model, Art. 30. Reflecting a shift towards protecting treaties from being used by taxpayers to engage in base erosion activities, the 2016 U.S. Model introduced a new Article 28 allowing for a process of partial termination of a treaty in cases where the country's law has changed in certain circumstances (such as a significant reduction in the tax rate or an exemption). No treaties have yet been ratified that include such a provision, and the United States is the only country that has proposed such a mechanism.

Under Article 1(2), a treaty should not be applied in a way that would deprive the taxpayer a benefit which would be available if the treaty had not come into effect. That is, a treaty cannot increase a taxpayer's U.S. tax liability compared to the tax consequences in the absence of a treaty. For example, if a resident of the other contracting state has business income and business losses from two different activities conducted in the United States, the taxpayer can elect to be taxed under the U.S. domestic tax rules if those rules produce a more favorable outcome (*e.g.*, the ability to offset the business income with the business losses) for the taxpayer than taxation under the applicable treaty. However, the taxpayer must behave consistently with respect to any single category of income (*e.g.*, the taxpayer cannot choose treaty benefits with respect to the business income and statutory treatment of the business losses). Rev. Rul. 84–17, 1984–1 C.B. 10. If different categories of income are unrelated (*e.g.*, business income and dividends), a taxpayer can claim statutory treatment with respect to one category and treaty benefits with respect to the other category.

Another new provision of the 2016 U.S. Model also reflects Treasury's focus on preventing base erosion. Article 1(8) contains what is known as a "triangular rule," which denies treaty benefits to items of income derived by one of the parties to the treaty, if they are attributable to a permanent establishment in another country taxable at a low rate (and not taxed in the country that legally derives the income). Like some of the other provisions included in the 2016 U.S. Model, this rule provides an indication of the U.S. Treasury's focus in treaty negotiations going forward.

(C) DEFINITIONS

Articles 3–5 of the U.S. Model contain definitions of key terms used throughout the treaty. The definition of the term "resident" is central to the application of a treaty because treaties often assign taxing authority to the state of residence. Each contracting state defines residence for individuals and companies under its domestic law. A partnership typically is not a resident of a contracting state unless it is taxed as an entity. However, partners of a contracting state may be residents entitled to the application of a treaty to partnership income.

Because a contracting state applies its own domestic definition of the term "resident," an individual taxpayer may be a resident of both states. For example, T might be a U.S. resident by virtue of I.R.C. § 7701(b) and a French resident under French domestic law. Under the residency tie-breaker provision in Article 3(3) of the U.S.-France treaty (or Article 4(3)(a) of the 2016 U.S. Model), T is a resident of the State in which T has a permanent home. If T has a home available in both states, T is a resident of the state where his personal and economic relations (center of vital interests) are closer. If the center of vital interests cannot be determined, a "habitual abode" test is applied. In the absence of a habitual abode, citizenship will be the determining factor. If T is a citizen of both states or neither state, the contracting states promise to try to settle the question by mutual consent.

Suppose USCo is incorporated in the United States but its place of effective management is in a foreign state so that it is considered a resident by both states under their domestic laws. *See e.g.*, Art. 4(1) of the U.S.-UK income tax treaty. The 2016 U.S. Model contains a new residency tie-breaker provision (Art. 4(4)) that penalizes such companies, providing that if a company is considered to be a resident of both countries, it is not treated as a resident of either one for purposes of obtaining treaty benefits. In other words, the 2016 U.S. Model would exclude without recourse dual resident companies from obtaining the benefits of a tax treaty.

One of the more challenging treaty issues is to determine the treaty residence of hybrid entities (*i.e.*, a flow-through or transparent entity for U.S. tax purposes but a corporation for foreign tax purposes) and reverse hybrid entities (*i.e.*, a corporation for U.S. tax purposes but a flow-through for foreign tax purposes). Hybrids and reverse hybrids became prevalent as a result of the check-the-box rules in Reg. §§ 301.7701–2 and –3. (*See* discussion *infra* § 14.02.) Essentially, the rule under U.S. domestic law and U.S. treaties is that the residence state determines residence and the source state follows the residence state determination. *See* I.R.C. § 894(c), Reg. § 1.894–1(d) and Art. 1(6) of the U.S. Model.

For example, suppose that Canadian investors own 100 percent of the interest in a Cayman Islands entity that is reverse hybrid. The Cayman Islands entity receives interest from a U.S. payor. In deciding whether the treaty with Canada applies (there is no U.S. treaty with the Cayman Islands), the United States will look to how Canada treats the U.S. income earned by the Cayman entity. If the United States followed its own view, it would not apply the treaty because the income is earned by a Cayman Islands corporation, but if Canada taxes the income earned by the Cayman entity directly to the Canadian investors, the United States will apply the treaty with Canada. Reg. § 1.894–1(d)(1).

Now suppose that the Cayman Islands entity was a hybrid entity (*i.e.*, a flow-through entity for U.S. tax purposes but a corporation for Canadian tax purposes). If the United States followed its own view, it would apply the treaty with Canada because the United States sees the Cayman Islands entity as a flow-through. But Canada does not tax the investors on the income from the United States because Canada thinks the income was earned by a Cayman Islands corporation. Therefore, the United States would not apply the treaty with Canada in this situation. The same situation would apply if the hybrid were a U.S. Limited Liability Company (LLC) (rather than a Cayman Islands entity) which was treated as a corporation for Canadian purposes, but was transparent for U.S. tax purposes. The U.S. generally would not apply the Canadian treaty with respect to income earned in the United States where that income is not taxable in the hands of a Canadian resident. *See* Art. 1(7) of the U.S.-Canada treaty.

Sometimes more than one treaty may apply at the same time. Suppose that Canadian investors own 100 percent of the interest in a U.K. entity that is treated as a flow-through entity by Canada and as a corporation by the U.K. Income earned in the U.S. will be subject to taxation in the hands of a resident in both the U.K. and in Canada. In this situation, the United States is obligated to apply both the treaty with the U.K. and the treaty with Canada. For example, if the U.K. treaty provided a maximum U.S. withholding rate of 0 percent and the Canadian treaty provided a maximum withholding rate of 10 percent, the United States should honor both treaties by withholding at 0 percent.

Suppose ForCo, a resident of both Country X and Country Y under the laws of each country, is treated as a resident of Country Y and not of Country X for purposes of the X-Y treaty and, as a result, is not liable to tax in Country X by reason of its residence. Is it entitled to claim the benefits of the U.S.-X Convention as a resident of Country X or of the U.S.-Y Convention as a resident of Country Y?

Revenue Ruling 2004–76, 2004–2 C.B. 111, determines that if ForCo is treated as a resident of Country Y and not of Country X for purposes of the X-Y treaty and, as a result, is not liable to tax in Country X by reason of its residence, it is not entitled to claim benefits under the U.S.-X treaty, because it is not a resident of Country X under the relevant article of the U.S.-X treaty. However, ForCo is entitled to claim benefits under the U.S.-Y treaty as a resident of Country Y, if it satisfies the requirements of the applicable limitation on benefits article, if any, and other applicable requirements in order to receive benefits under the U.S.-Y treaty.

The approach described above where the U.S. looks to the treatment of the taxpayer in the residence country clearly applies to FDAP income. Section 894(c) does not apply to business profits or to the branch profits tax. However, in more recent treaties and protocols including those with Belgium, Canada, Japan and the United Kingdom, the treaties clarify that all income whether FDAP or otherwise will be entitled to treaty benefits if taxed in the hands of a qualifying treaty resident.

(D) CLASSIFICATION AND ASSIGNMENT RULES

Articles 6–21 of the U.S. Model provide the classification and assignment rules that classify types of income and assign taxing authority over that income to one or both contracting states.

(1) Business Income

Generally, a resident of a contracting state is not taxed on business income derived in the other contracting state unless the business income is "attributable to" a "permanent establishment" (PE) located in the other contracting state. If there is no permanent establishment, income that would otherwise be taxable in the state in which such income is earned in the absence of a treaty is not taxable in that state. For example, a foreign corporation engaged in a trade or business in the United States but not through a PE (*e.g.*, regularly selling inventory in the United States from a foreign business office using local independent sales agents) generally would not be taxable in the United States under an applicable treaty.

The definition of the term "permanent establishment" varies from treaty to treaty but in general a permanent establishment takes the form of either a physical PE or an agency PE. A third PE category—a construction site PE—may exist where a building site or construction or installation project or drilling rig used for the exploration of natural resources lasts more than twelve months.

The physical PE refers to a fixed place of business (*e.g.*, a factory or office) through which the business of an enterprise is carried on. A presence in the United States which might rise to the level of a "trade or business" under U.S. domestic tax law may not constitute a permanent establishment under treaty principles. *See e.g.*, *De Amodio v. Commissioner*, 34 T.C. 894 (1960) (taxpayer's business activities in the

U.S. conducted by independent agents). Note that whether a resident of a contracting state has a PE in the other contracting state is not a function of ownership. The issue is whether the taxpayer has the premises "at its constant disposal." OECD Commentary, Art. 5, ¶ 10. Accordingly, a leased premises can be a permanent establishment.

Suppose that a foreign corporation conducts its business activities in the United States, not through its own employees, but rather through an agent that is paid a fee. To determine whether the foreign corporation has a U.S. permanent establishment is a two-step process. First, it might be the case that the agent's physical premises is "at the constant disposal" of the foreign principal (*e.g.*, employees of the foreign corporation use the premises as they please). If so, then the foreign corporation would have a physical PE in the United States. But suppose that the foreign corporation did not have the premises of the agent at its constant disposal. In some cases, the activities of the agent, as opposed to the physical location, may create a PE.

A dependent agent of the taxpayer with authority to conclude contracts in the name of the principal and which habitually exercises that authority may constitute a PE of the principal. However, an independent agent acting in the ordinary course of the agent's business does not constitute a PE of the principal. An agency PE is based on the activities of the agent, not the agent's physical location. For example, a traveling employee with no fixed base might constitute a permanent establishment for the employer if the employee habitually concludes contracts binding the employer.

In *Taisei Fire & Marine Insurance Co. v. Commissioner*, 104 T.C. 535 (1995), four Japanese property and casualty insurance companies (insurance companies) executed management agreements with Fortress Re Inc., a North Carolina corporation. The management agreements authorized Fortress to act as the agent for each company to underwrite insurance on behalf of each company. Either party could terminate the agreement by giving six months' notice. Fortress retained "total control over the handling and disposition of claims on behalf of [the Japanese insurance companies]," and remained free to enter into other management agreements with other companies.

Although representatives of the insurance companies met on occasion in Japan for business reasons, they did not discuss their individual relationships with Fortress. Each year, a Fortress representative visited the offices of each of the insurance companies in Tokyo; other communications occurred via letter or telex, but not telephone. A representative of each of the four companies visited Fortress's offices one or two times each year.

The IRS asserted that these Japanese companies were not exempt from U.S. income tax, because their profits were attributable to a U.S. permanent establishment of Fortress, which exercised on a regular basis its authority to bind its principals. The

Tax Court held that Fortress was not a "permanent establishment" of the insurance companies. The court concluded that, during the years at issue, Fortress was legally and economically independent of the four companies and therefore even if Fortress concluded contracts, doing so as an independent agent did not create a PE.

Examining the question of legal independence, the court noted that, under the management agreements, Fortress had complete discretion to conduct reinsurance business on behalf of the petitioners. The court also pointed out that the petitioners held no interest in Fortress and rejected the IRS's contention that the petitioners "exercised 'comprehensive control' over Fortress by acting as a 'pool.'"

Turning to economic independence, the court noted that parties to the management agreements could terminate their contractual relationship on six months' notice. The court rejected the IRS's assertion that Fortress bore no entrepreneurial risk because its operating expenses were covered by management fees and because it was guaranteed business on behalf of the petitioners' creditworthiness. Analogizing the instant facts to the case of a large mutual fund that charges an annual fee to cover operating expenses, the court wrote: "Clearly, the mutual fund company would not be considered dependent on its thousands of investors."

If a parent corporation in state A has a subsidiary in state B, the subsidiary does not automatically constitute a PE of the parent merely because of the parent's ownership, enabling state B to tax some of the parent's profit. However, if the subsidiary acts as an agent of the parent with authority to conclude contracts in the name of the parent which is habitually exercised, then the subsidiary may constitute a PE of the parent (or if employees of the parent have the premises of the subsidiary at their constant disposal, there may be a physical PE). In a partnership context, the permanent establishment of a partnership or of any partner is attributed to all of the partners.

Article 5(4) of the U.S. Model specifically provides that a PE does not include: (1) the use of facilities or the maintenance of a stock of goods or merchandise in a contracting state for storage, display, delivery; (2) the maintenance of a stock of goods or merchandise solely for processing by another enterprise; (3) the maintenance of a fixed place of business for the purpose of purchasing goods or merchandise or collecting information; or (4) the maintenance of a fixed place of business solely for engaging in any other activity of a preparatory or auxiliary character. But once a taxpayer crosses the line from preparatory or auxiliary activities into a full-fledged set of business activities, a PE would exist and all business profits (including those attributable to the preparatory or auxiliary activities) attributable to the PE may be taxed in the source state (*i.e.*, the state where the PE is located).

The U.S. Model historically has been fairly closely aligned with the OECD Model with regard to what constitutes a PE. But changes to the OECD Model introduced by the BEPS Project (discussed in Chapter 1) modified the PE definition in important ways that the United States has declined to adopt. For example, under the OECD BEPS recommendations, the activities conducted by two related parties may be combined to create a permanent establishment. The OECD Model now also contains a broader definition of when a dependent agent's activities can create a PE for the principal than the U.S. Model does. Because some countries have already incorporated at least some of the recommended OECD Model changes into their existing treaties via the OECD Multilateral Instrument (*see* discussion in Chapter 1), U.S. taxpayers engaged in business overseas may find that that cross-border activities between two countries (neither of which is the United States) are governed by much different rules than would apply if a U.S. person was a party to the transaction. The 2016 U.S. Model did, however, include one change to the PE definition recommended by the OECD BEPS project, namely a rule intended to protect against contract-splitting abuses of the 12-month PE threshold for building sites or construction or installation projects.

Suppose that ResCo, a state R corporation, maintains a server in state S which is engaged in electronic commerce (*e.g.*, provides financial information on a web site for a fee). Can the server constitute a PE in state S, thereby permitting source state taxation of business profits attributable to the PE? Under most treaty language, neither the server (*i.e.*, the computer itself) nor the web site can constitute a PE. However, the Commentaries to the OECD Model suggest that the premises where the server is located can constitute a PE if ResCo has those premises at its disposal. OECD Commentary, Art. 5, ¶ 123–131. There may be a PE whether ResCo owns the premises or leases it in a manner where ResCo controls the premises. Mere use of space on a third party's server (*e.g.*, a hosted web site) should not constitute a PE under current guidelines.

Readers who are used to conducting much of their personal and business lives in a virtual space may find the OECD definition of a PE as based on a physical presence to be hopelessly outdated. It will be no surprise that many government officials share this view. As a result, there is consideration underway to move towards a concept of a "virtual PE" as part of the OECD's project to update international tax rules for a digitalized economy. Proposals for changes in that regard are expected in 2020. *See* § 14.06.

Generally the term "business profits" means income derived from the active conduct of a trade or business, including the performance of personal services and the rental of tangible personal property. The term "attributable to" generally refers to net income that is produced by the permanent establishment as if it were an independent entity operating at arm's-length. For a discussion of arm's length principles, *see infra* Chapter 11. Accordingly, the deductions reasonably connected with the production of income by the permanent establishment, including an appropriate amount of overhead, reduce the amount of income that is taxable by the state in which the permanent establishment is situated. Questions over how to allocate income (and deductions) between a PE and its home office have been highly controversial. The OECD has attempted to develop principles in this area, referred to as the "Authorized OECD Approach." Many countries, including the United States, have declined to accept this approach in whole or in part.

In *National Westminster Bank v. United States*, 512 F.3d 1347 (Fed. Cir. 2008) the Court of Federal Claims held that the interest expense regulations under Reg. § 1.882–5 (*see supra* § 4.06) are inconsistent with the "separate enterprise" requirements of Art. 7 of the U.S.-U.K. income tax treaty because the regulations rely on a formula and are not based on a deemed arm's length relationship between the U.S. branch and the U.K. home office.

Treaties sometimes deal separately with specific types of business income. For example, Art. 8 of the U.S. Model provides that income (from direct operation or from rental activities) from shipping and air transport in international traffic is generally taxable in the state of residence of the entrepreneur rather than in the state in which the income is produced, even if the income is attributable to a permanent establishment in that state. (*See also* Art. 8 of the OECD Model). This rule reflects a concern that difficulties in allocation may otherwise result in multiple taxation of shipping profits. Article 6 of the U.S. Model provides that income from real property may be taxed in the state where the property is located. The income may also be taxed in the owner's state of residence if relief from double taxation is allowed for any situs state taxation. The real property article applies both to business and investment income from real property.

Articles 6, 7 and 8 of the U.S. Model deal with allocation of business profits within an enterprise. Article 9 of the U.S. Model allows business profits (and other income) to be allocated between associated enterprises to reflect an arm's-length relationship. Article 9 makes possible the application of the principles of I.R.C. § 482 and related provisions. *See infra* Chapter 11.

(2) Personal Services Income

Under the 2016 U.S. Model and newer treaties, where a taxpayer resident in contracting state R performs independent personal services (*e.g.*, consulting not as an employee) in contracting state S, the income generated by the services performed is taxable in contracting state S only to the extent that the income is attributable to a permanent establishment in contracting state S. *See* 2016 U.S. Model Art. 21. In older treaties, a separate article dealing with independent personal services essentially reached the same result.

Under Article 14 of the U.S. Model, if an individual resident of a contracting state performs dependent personal services (*i.e.*, services as an employee) in the other contracting state, the state in which such services are performed has taxing authority over any remuneration paid if any one of the following three conditions is satisfied: (1) the recipient is present in the state where services are performed for more than 183 days during the taxable year; (2) the remuneration is paid by, or on behalf of, a resident of that state; or (3) the remuneration is borne by (*i.e.*, is deducted by) a permanent establishment or fixed base that the employer maintains in that state. 2016 U.S. Model, Art. 14.

Pensions derived by an employee are taxable exclusively in the employee's state of residence. 2016 U.S. Model, Art. 17(1). *See also* Art. 18. The IRS takes the position that to qualify as a pension, payments must meet the following cumulative requirements: (i) the recipient has been employed for at least 5 years or he/she was 62 or older at the time the payment was made; (ii) the payment is made (a) on account of the employee's death or disability, (b) as part of a series of substantially equal payments over the employee's life expectancy (or over the life expectancy of the employee and his beneficiary), or (c) paid on account of the employee's retirement after 55; and (iii) all payments are made after the employee has separated from service or on or after the date at which the employee reached the age of 70.5. Deferred bonuses paid by the employer to the individual after retirement do not constitute 'pensions or other similar remuneration' under Art. 17 but are covered by Article 14. Rev. Rul. 71–478, 1971–2 C.B. 490.

While Article 14 of the U.S. Model is the major provision addressing income from the performance of personal services, particular types of income from services are addressed elsewhere. For example, income earned by artistes and sportsmen because of their high earning capacity is generally taxable in the state of performance even if the income earned is not attributable to a fixed base (*e.g.*, income from a 2 week musical tour). 2016 U.S. Model, Art. 16. Directors' fees and other compensation derived by a resident of a contracting state for services rendered in the other contracting state in the capacity as a member of the board of directors of a company in that other state may be taxed in the company's state even if the director does not have a fixed base in that state. 2016 U.S. Model, Art. 15. There are special rules for government employees (Art. 19) and students and trainees (Art. 20) as well.

(3) Investment Income

The U.S. Model contains specific provisions addressing the taxation of dividends, interest, royalties, rental income from real property, and capital gains. In the absence of a treaty, dividends from U.S. sources paid to a nonresident of the United States are normally subject to a 30 percent withholding tax on the gross amount paid. I.R.C. §§ 871(a) and 881. U.S. income tax treaties generally modify these rates through a reciprocal reduction of rates that the payor's state (*i.e.*, the source state) can impose on dividends distributed to a resident of the other contracting state. Under Article 10 of the 2016 U.S. Model, the maximum source state treaty tax rate on dividends is 15 percent. The 2016 U.S. Model reduces the maximum rate to 5 percent in some cases for dividends paid to a corporation owning as little as

10 percent of the aggregate voting power and value of the stock of the dividend-paying corporation, provided a holding period of 12 months has been met. *See* 2016 U.S. Model, Art 10(2). By limiting the source state rate of taxation, treaties reduce the incidence of double taxation. However, to the extent that a dividend recipient is taxed both by the source state and the residence state, the residence state must relieve any double taxation. 2016 U.S. Model, Art. 23. More recent treaties and Protocols (*e.g.*, with the United Kingdom, Belgium, Denmark, Germany, the Netherlands, Mexico, Japan, Australia and most recently Spain) eliminate the withholding on direct dividends from a subsidiary to a parent corporation in some cases so that dividends from a subsidiary can be paid to the parent corporation free of any source state withholding tax.

New to the 2016 U.S. Model is a restriction on eligibility for treaty benefits for dividends paid by an expatriated entity within ten years from the date of the inversion transaction. 2016 U.S. Model, Art. 10(5). These restrictions also apply to payments of interest and royalties by expatriated entities. 2016 U.S. Model, Art. 11(2), Art. 12(2)(b). The U.S. branch profits tax was enacted as a substitute tax for any tax that might be payable on dividends paid by a foreign corporation out of U.S. earnings and profits. *See supra* at § 4.05. The 2016 U.S. Model clarifies that the United States may impose its branch profits tax on income repatriated from a U.S. branch to a foreign corporation's home office. The tax on that repatriation is the same as that which would be imposed on a U.S. corporation making a dividend payment to its foreign parent corporation; the applicable tax rate generally is 5 percent, but in some treaties with no withholding tax on dividends paid to certain qualified persons (*e.g.*, publicly-traded parent corporation), the branch profits tax may also not be imposed. 2016 U.S. Model, Art. 10(10).

The U.S. Model treats interest in a manner similar to dividends, limiting source state taxation, but there are important differences. Article 11 does not permit any taxation of interest by the source state (*i.e.*, the state where the payor resides) although there are U.S. treaties based on the OECD Model that do permit the source state to tax interest at a rate not exceeding 10 percent (*e.g.*, the treaty with Spain).

The 2016 U.S. Model introduced new restrictions on eligibility for the lower rate on interest and royalties (and guarantee fees), for payments made to a "special tax regime". 2016 U.S. Model, Art. 3(1)(*l*). The goal of these new provisions is to deny treaty benefits when an amount that would otherwise be subject to U.S. withholding tax is not taxed or is taxed at a preferential rate in the jurisdiction of its beneficial owner. In furtherance of this goal, the 2016 U.S. Model denies treaty benefits if the beneficial owner of the payment benefits from a special tax regime, which generally means that the amounts are subject to a preferential tax rate (relative to other types of income), or that is excluded from the tax base through one or another specified mechanisms, so long as its then subject to an effective tax rate less than either 15 percent or 60 percent of the general statutory rate in the recipient jurisdiction. But the

2016 U.S. Model also says that a special tax regime won't be considered as such until the countries have consulted, and there's been a 30 day waiting period after a public consultation.

As with other more radical provisions of the 2016 U.S. Model, this provision does not exist in any treaties currently in effect.

Like interest, royalties (*e.g.*, amounts paid for the use of copyrights, artistic or scientific works, patents, secret formulae, trademarks, know-how) derived and beneficially owned by a resident of a contracting state are taxable only in that state under Art. 12 of the U.S. Model. However, many developing states, following the UN Model, do permit limited source state taxation typically at rates not exceeding 15–20 percent of the royalty. The United States has entered into treaties with many developing states (*e.g.*, India), permitting source state taxation of royalties.

Under those treaties that permit source state taxation, it can be very important to determine whether a particular payment is a royalty or constitutes business profits. For example, suppose that ResCo, a state R resident, is engaged in electronic commerce through a server located in state R. An unrelated customer, SourceCo, located in state S, acquires some type of digital output (*e.g.*, a report, software) for a fee. If state S regards the fee as a royalty, state S may withhold on the royalty. If state R regards the fee as business profits, then in its view state S has no right to tax because there is no permanent establishment in state S. Generally, in order to constitute a royalty in this context, a payment must be for the right to acquire an interest in the copyright that can then be exploited rather than the output of ResCo exploiting the copyright. *See* OECD Commentary, Art. 12, ¶¶ 12–17.

If interest, dividend, or royalty income derived by a recipient is attributable to a PE the recipient maintains in the other contracting state, then the income is treated as business profits fully taxable in the state where the PE is situated under the business profits article rather than being subject to a withholding tax. *See* 2016 U.S. Model, Arts. 10(8) (dividends), 11(5) (interest), and 12(5) (royalties).

While source state taxation of income from dividends, interest, and royalties is generally limited by a treaty, income derived by a resident of a contracting state from real property situated in the other contracting state may be fully taxed under Article 6 of the U.S. Model in the state where the property is situated. If that state under its domestic provisions would tax income from real property on a gross income basis, Article 6(5) allows the recipient an election to tax such income on a net basis.

Taxing jurisdiction over gains from the disposition of investment property depends on the nature of the property. Gain from the disposition of real property or an interest in an entity whose property consists primarily of real property is subject to tax in the contracting state in which the property is situated under its domestic law. *See* 2016 U.S. Model, Art. 13. Gain from the alienation of personal property (*e.g.*, machinery and equipment) attributable to a PE is taxable in the contracting state where the PE is situated. There are special rules for gains from the disposition of ships or aircraft or containers. 2016 U.S. Model Art. 13(4), (5). Gain from the disposition of stock or securities is normally taxable exclusively in the state of the seller's residence. 2016 U.S. Model Art. 13(6).

(4) Other Income

Any income that is not specifically covered in a treaty generally is subject to taxing authority exclusively in the residence state of the recipient. 2016 U.S. Model, Art. 21. For example, a contracting state is not free under its domestic law to tax guarantee fees paid by a U.S. subsidiary to its foreign parent corporation for a parent guarantee that helps the U.S. subsidiary secure a beneficial bank loan. It should be noted, however, that some U.S. treaties (*e.g.*, the treaty with Canada) do permit source state taxation of Other Income. Under those treaties, the United States would be able to collect a 30 percent withholding tax under its view that such guarantee fees are Other Income and not business profits. *See* I.R.C. §§ 861(a)(9) and 881.

The 2017 UN Model Treaty introduces a new provision that permits source country withholding on fees for "technical services." UN Model Art. 12A. (Some existing treaties to which the United States is a party contain a similar provision, *see*, *e.g.*, U.S.-India Treaty Art. 12). Fees for technical services is a term that's broadly defined, as any payment received in consideration of technical, managerial and consultancy services.

(E) AVOIDANCE OF DOUBLE TAXATION

A major purpose of the U.S. bilateral income tax treaty network is to eliminate international double taxation. U.S. income tax treaties contain reciprocal commitments by each state when acting as a residence state to provide either a foreign tax credit for taxes paid in the source state or to exempt income earned in the other contracting state. For example, the United States grants a credit for any foreign income taxes paid on foreign source income while often the other contracting state exempts from its taxation U.S. source business income (and grants a credit for source state taxation of investment income). 2016 U.S. Model, Art. 23.

(F) LIMITATION ON BENEFITS

Not surprisingly, foreign taxpayers investing or doing business in the United States often will try to structure their affairs to take advantage of a favorable income tax treaty. This is sometimes referred to as "treaty shopping." Historically, the United States—more than any other country—has been preoccupied with the perceived treaty shopping problem; the OECD's BEPS Project reflected a shift among other countries' to also focus on ensuring that their treaties could not be utilized for treaty shopping and base erosion. (*See* discussion *infra*).

Treaty shopping generally takes one of two forms: a taxpayer of a state that has no treaty with the United States seeks the coverage of a favorable treaty, or a taxpayer of a U.S. treaty partner prefers the treaty of another state. Often, a foreign taxpayer investing in the United States may seek out a treaty that provides for a low rate of taxation by the United States on investment income generated in the United States.

Absent some restrictions on treaty shopping, a treaty with one state could become a treaty with the world. With increasing determination, the United States has sought to curtail treaty shopping on many fronts. In *Aiken Indus., Inc. v. Commissioner*, 56 T.C. 925 (1971), a Bahamian company that loaned money to a U.S. subsidiary assigned the obligation to a Honduran subsidiary under the same terms (*i.e.*, payment schedule and interest rate) as the obligation from the U.S. subsidiary. The Honduran subsidiary realized no profit from the transaction since the interest it received from the U.S. corporation was immediately payable to the Bahamian corporation. The U.S. subsidiary claimed that no U.S. withholding tax was required under I.R.C. §§ 881 and 1442 in respect of the interest payments made to the Honduran company under the applicable treaty. There was no treaty between the United States and the Bahamas.

The tax court ruled that the Honduran corporation never "received" the interest payments as required under the U.S.-Honduras tax treaty because the receipt of the interest and the obligation to transmit the interest to the Bahamian corporation were inseparable. The tax court found that the treaty provision required more than temporary physical possession; the Honduran corporation was required to have complete dominion and control in order for the treaty to apply. Characterizing the Honduran corporation as a mere "conduit," the Tax Court noted that the transaction had no economic or business purpose but existed only to avoid U.S. taxation through the treaty benefits. *See also* Rev. Ruls. 84–152, 1984–2 C.B. 381 and 84–153, 1984–2 C.B. 183.

In its treaty negotiations, the United States has generally insisted on the insertion of a limitations on benefits (LOB) provision, and almost all U.S. treaties in effect today have such a provision. 2016 U.S. Model, Art. 22. A treaty LOB provision determines whether a treaty resident under Article 4 is a "qualified person" permitted to receive treaty benefits. The LOB provision functions as a supplement to a treaty residence article. The focus of the treaty LOB provisions is on corporate taxpayers. Individual taxpayers who are residents of a contracting state will be qualified persons. But for business entities, the LOB provisions are more involved.

While there is much variation in the nature of these provisions, a typical treaty might provide that certain treaty benefits are not available to a foreign corporation unless one of several tests is met. For example, if the stock of a corporation is publicly traded on a recognized stock exchange of either contracting state or a foreign corporation is owned by such a publicly-traded entity in the same country of residence, it may typically qualify for treaty benefits. 2016 U.S. Model, Art. 22(2)(c).

A corporation that cannot qualify under the publicly-traded test may qualify under an ownership/

base erosion test. *See* 2016 U.S. Model, Art. 22(2)(f). If no more than 50 percent of a corporation's stock is held by third-country taxpayers, the ownership test may be satisfied. For example, if Saudi Arabian investors form a Dutch company solely to invest in U.S. stock and securities, the company does not qualify for reduced U.S. tax rates under the Dutch treaty on interest and dividends paid by a U.S. payor.

Suppose the Saudi Arabian investors arrange for Dutch individuals to hold 51 percent of the Dutch company's stock while the Saudi investors hold the other 49 percent and capitalize the company with as much debt as possible. While this arrangement satisfies the stock ownership requirement, it may not satisfy the base erosion test which denies treaty benefits if a company's income is syphoned off in substantial part to meet deductible liabilities owed to nonresidents (or to persons that benefit from a "special tax regime"), thereby eroding the tax base of the residence state.

Even if a company does not satisfy both the stock ownership and base erosion tests, treaty benefits may be available under a "derivative benefits" provision in some existing treaties (*e.g.*, those with EU members); the 2016 U.S. Model (Art. 22(4)) includes a derivative benefits test for the first time. For example, suppose that a German corporation (publicly-traded on a German stock exchange) owns all of the stock of a Dutch corporation which receives a royalty payment from a U.S. licensee. The Dutch corporation could not satisfy either the publicly-traded (*i.e.*, not owned by a publicly-traded Dutch corporation) or ownership/base erosion tests, but there really is no treaty shopping in this situation because had the German corporation received the royalty, it would have received the same treaty benefits under the U.S.-Germany treaty. Under the derivative benefits test, the treaty between the U.S. and the Netherlands will apply (the treaty "derives" its application from the fact that the benefits would have been available under the U.S.-Germany treaty) if the ultimate owners of the Dutch entity are qualified treaty residents of certain countries (*e.g.*, the EU, European Economic Area or NAFTA) and if the tax consequences under the treaty with the Netherlands are no more favorable than would have been the case under the treaty with Germany; the 2016 U.S. Model also includes a base erosion test that must be satisfied for the derivative benefits test to be met but current, in-force treaties do not.

Even if none of these tests is satisfied, a corporation may enjoy treaty benefits under an active trade or business test, although the corporation is not a qualified resident. For example, suppose that Taiwanese shareholders own all of the stock of a Japanese corporation which earns income in the United States. If the Japanese corporation conducts a trade or business in Japan and the income received from the United States is derived in connection with (or is incidental to) the Japanese business, the income may qualify for treaty benefits. If income is received from a related U.S. payor, the business activities in Japan must be substantial when compared with the business activities in the United States. The 2016 U.S. Model introduced significant changes to the actively traded test, including the requirement that the item of income must "emanate from" the qualifying trade or business in order to satisfy the test. 2016 U.S. Model, Art. 22(3). The term "emanate from" is supposed to be explained in a Technical Explanation to the 2016 U.S. Model, but no explanation has yet been published by the Treasury. The 2016 U.S. Model also provides that an active trade or business cannot include operating as a holding company or providing group financing, or making or managing investments.

The 2016 U.S. Model contains a headquarters test that allows a holding company to qualify for treaty benefits if it functions as the headquarters for a corporate group operating in at least 4 countries and meets other requirements, such as if the company's primary place of management and control is in the country in which it's resident. Not very many companies can satisfy this test. 2016 U.S. Model, Art. 22(5).

Finally, the Competent Authority of the contracting state in which income is earned can grant treaty benefits if a taxpayer doesn't otherwise qualify. But practically speaking, this is not something taxpayers can rely on when structuring an investment.

The OECD's BEPS Project reflected a shift in other countries' focus on treaty shopping as an area of concern. As a result, the project made inclusion of an anti-abuse rule in treaties a "minimum standard." Although the LOB can satisfy the anti-abuse rule requirement, most countries have instead opted for a different type of anti-abuse rule: a "principal purpose test" (PPT). The 2017 OECD Model (Art. 29(9)) states that treaty benefits won't be granted if it is reasonable to conclude that obtaining that benefit was one of the principal purposes of any arrangement or transaction that resulted in that benefit. How this test will be applied by different jurisdictions will remain to be seen in the years ahead.

(G) NONDISCRIMINATION

Because the fundamental purpose of an income tax treaty is to minimize the impact taxes have on the free flow of international trade, treaties typically contain mutual assurances that each treaty partner will not use excessive taxation as a protectionist device. In general, nationals and residents of each treaty state should play on a level playing field with nationals and residents of the other treaty state in the same circumstances. This nondiscrimination commitment takes the form of a promise by each partner in exercising its source-based and residence-based jurisdiction not to tax nationals and residents of the other contracting state more heavily than its own similarly situated nationals and residents. *See* 2016 U.S. Model, Art. 24.

A nondiscrimination article typically provides that a citizen of one contracting state that is resident in the other contracting state may not be treated less favorably than a citizen of the other contracting state in the same circumstances. Similarly a corporate resident of one contracting state doing business through a permanent establishment in the other contracting state cannot be treated less favorably than a corporation resident in the other contracting state. For example, if the United States imposed a higher tax on the business profits of a U.S. PE than on similar profits earned by a U.S. corporation, the provision would violate the nondiscrimination article.

Nondiscrimination articles also typically prevent a contracting state from denying a deduction for interest, royalties, or other disbursements paid to a resident of the other contracting state if those same payments would be deductible if paid to a resident of the state of the payor. Similarly, some might argue that the branch profits tax being a second tax on a foreign corporation in addition to the regular tax violates nondiscrimination articles. Most recent U.S. treaties eliminate the problem by specifically providing that the imposition of the branch profits tax does not violate the treaty.

The presence of a nondiscrimination article in a treaty does not mean that all nonresidents must be taxed in the same manner as residents. The concept of discrimination implies a comparison of similarly situated persons. For example, nonresidents and foreign corporations may be subject to a 30 percent gross basis tax on FDAP income paid by a U.S. payor while U.S. individuals and corporations are taxed on similar income on a net basis under I.R.C. §§ 1 or 11. However, the 30 percent withholding tax is not considered discriminatory because nonresidents are not "similarly situated" to U.S. residents U.S. residents are taxed on worldwide income while nonresidents are generally taxed only on income that is connected to the United States through the source rules. The same reasoning allows different rules for exemptions, filing status, etc. to apply to nonresidents. To determine whether a contracting state is discriminating in violation of a treaty, no comparison can be made between a nonresident noncitizen of the United States and a nonresident citizen of the United States because they are not in the same circumstances: the U.S. citizen is taxable on worldwide income while the non-U.S. citizen is not subject to worldwide taxation in the United States.

Unlike most other provisions in the treaty, the nondiscrimination article applies to taxes of every kind, including those imposed by states and other local authorities. That is, a state is not permitted to discriminate against nonresidents in a manner that violates Art. 24. 2016 U.S. Model, Art. 24(7).

(H) MUTUAL AGREEMENT PROCEDURE

U.S. income tax treaties typically contain a mutual agreement procedure provision for resolving treaty disputes. *See* 2016 U.S. Model, Art. 25. Under such a provision, if a taxpayer claims that the action of the tax authorities of a contracting state has resulted, or will result, in taxation that violates the treaty, the competent authorities of both contracting states seek to reach an agreement to avoid double taxation. Under a mutual agreement article, the competent authorities of the contracting states can enter into a mutual agreement (which may modify domestic law) in order: (i) to resolve specific cases in which a taxpayer alleges violation of a treaty; (ii) to agree upon interpretation and application of a treaty provision; and (iii) to eliminate double taxation in cases not expressly provided for in the treaty. In the United States, the competent authority is the Secretary of the Treasury or his delegate, which is the IRS Commissioner, Large Business & International Division.

Typical issues that may be resolved by mutual agreement include: the attribution of income to a permanent establishment; the allocation of income between related persons; the characterization of particular items of income; the application of source rules with respect to particular items of income; the meaning of a term; increases in amounts specified in the treaty to reflect monetary or economic developments; and the application of domestic law relating to penalties, fines and interest. Much of the work of the competent authorities is to allocate business profits and deductions between a permanent establishment in one state and a home office in the other state or to allocate income and deduction between related taxpayers in different states. For example, if a U.S. corporation sells goods to a wholly-owned Swiss subsidiary which resells to wholesalers throughout Europe, the competent authorities may be called upon to allocate gain between the U.S. and Swiss corporations for tax purposes.

The guidelines for requesting U.S. competent authority assistance are set forth in Rev. Proc. 2015–40, I.R.B. 2015–35. In March 2019 the Government

Accountability Office published a highly critical report on the IRS competent authority/MAP process. GAO–19–81.

The 2016 U.S. Model includes for the first time a provision requiring that the countries resolve MAP disputes through mandatory binding arbitration if they have not been able to settle such disputes otherwise, with detailed procedures for how to conduct such arbitration. The number of U.S. tax treaties in effect that include such a provision has been growing slowly, recently increased to 7 as a result of Senate ratification of protocols to tax treaties with Spain, Japan, and Switzerland. The treaty MAP process—which aside from mandatory arbitration has no fixed deadlines and no penalties in the event the contracting states can't reach an agreement—is generally agreed to be widely flawed in its implementation. The OECD in the course of the BEPS Project introduced a number of measures to try and improve the process, including the conduct of peer reviews of countries' MAP processes. *See* discussion *infra* at § 11.08(C).

(I)   EXCHANGE OF INFORMATION AND ADMINISTRATIVE ASSISTANCE

U.S. bilateral income tax treaties also contain provisions obligating a treaty partner to provide information to the other treaty partner for the purpose of enabling that other treaty partner to enforce its tax law. The information received by the competent authorities might be available for other purposes if allowed by a mutual legal assistance treaty in force between the contracting states. *See* 2016 U.S. Model, Art. 26. The partner that is asked for the information is authorized to use its administrative information gathering powers, including compulsory legal process, to obtain any necessary information. There are several types of exchanges that take place, including: routine or automatic exchanges of information concerning names of payees and amounts of interest, dividends and royalties paid to residents of a treaty partner; exchanges made upon request by a treaty partner; simultaneous examinations of related taxpayers; spontaneous exchanges of information; and exchanges of industry-wide information. If the IRS issues a summons to a third-party record keeper seeking records of business transactions with the taxpayer pursuant to a treaty partner's request for information, the taxpayer must be provided with notice allowing an opportunity to quash the third-party summons. I.R.C. § 7609. There is no requirement that the IRS provide a taxpayer notice if it provides information in its own possession to a treaty partner, although the Treasury may allow an opportunity for administrative review of the decision to exchange information. It was precisely due to concerns over the exchange of information provisions in new protocols/treaties that has resulted in the delay in Senate ratification.

The United States also has entered into tax information exchange agreements (TIEAs) with countries that are not treaty partners to facilitate international cooperation in the enforcement of tax laws. In addition, the United States has ratified the multilateral OECD Convention on Assistance in Tax Matters which also provides for information exchanges.

A treaty partner may decline to provide information if doing so would require administrative measures which violate the law or administrative practice of either treaty partner; the information is not obtainable in the normal tax administration of either treaty partner; or the information requested would disclose any trade or business secret.

While the United States is willing to exchange information pursuant to its treaties, normally one country will not assist in collection of another country's taxes. *Holman v. Johnson*, 1775 WL 22 (Eng. 1775) (Lord Mansfield). It is difficult to defend this common law principle in the tax area when a foreign government can already seek to enforce a foreign judgment based on a breach of contract in a U.S. court. Why shouldn't a U.S. court enforce a foreign tax judgment (and vice versa) as long as the taxpayer has notice, the right to be heard, and the right to raise any constitutional due process defenses. Providing tax administrations with more tools to obtain information about their tax residents' activities in other jurisdictions is another hot—and developing—area of international tax law. Some of the steps the United States has taken in this regard are discussed in the next chapter.

§ 5.06   TREATY ABUSE, THE U.S. MODEL TREATY AND THE GLOBAL TAX TREATY LANDSCAPE

As noted throughout this chapter, the past few years have seen significant changes in the way tax treaties are viewed worldwide in terms of the extent to which they facilitate cross-border income shifting and tax avoidance. As a result, the OECD BEPS Project included recommendations ("minimum standards") for countries to make amendments to existing treaties. Many of the changes incorporated into the U.S. Model by the 2016 U.S. Model reflect similar concerns by the U.S. Treasury related to base erosion and profit shifting.

But despite—or maybe because of—all these changes, the treaty landscape remains in flux. The U.S. Model has no legal significance—it does not impact any existing treaties and is simply a statement of the U.S. starting position for negotiating future treaties. No U.S. treaties have yet been signed that incorporate these changes, and no U.S. treaty has been ratified by the U.S. Senate since 2010 (although 4 protocols/amendments to existing treaties were approved in July 2019).

Although many of the treaty recommendations proposed by the OECD have been incorporated by other countries through their signatures to the OECD's multilateral instrument, considerable uncertainty exists with regard to these changes as well. That's because the changes include new terminology that will have to be interpreted by judges not used to these concepts.

More broadly, although tax treaties have played an important role in the allocation of taxing rights among countries for over a century, recent trends suggest that they are being viewed with increasing skepticism. International organizations such as the International Monetary Fund have questioned whether developing countries benefit from entering into treaties, and their value has also been called into question by the TCJA which enacted several provisions some have characterized as violating U.S. treaty obligations. Tax treaties, and the role they play in determining the taxation of U.S. residents' cross-border income, represent one facet of the rapidly evolving global tax landscape.

CHAPTER 6

FILING, WITHHOLDING, AND REPORTING REQUIREMENTS

This chapter provides a brief overview of the filing and reporting obligations applicable to both U.S. and foreign persons. The requirements are complex and failure to comply may subject the taxpayer to penalties. Reviewing the primary sources in this area is essential.

§ 6.01   FILING REQUIREMENTS

If a nonresident is engaged in a trade or business in the United States, the taxpayer must file a tax return for that year even if the taxpayer has no effectively connected income for the year or is exempt from taxation by statute or treaty. I.R.C. § 6012. Historically, the IRS in regulations has taken the position that if no return is filed or if the return filed is not "true and accurate," a nonresident may not claim any deductions from gross income. I.R.C. §§ 874(a), 882(c)(2) and Reg. § 1.882–4. In *Swallows Holding, Ltd. v. Comm'r*, 515 F.3d 162 (3rd Cir. 2008), the court upheld these regulations.

If a nonresident is not engaged in a trade or business in the United States, the taxpayer often may not be required to file a return if the tax liability is fully satisfied by withholding at the source. Reg. §§ 1.6012–1(b)(2)(i) and 1.6012–2(g)(2)(i).

In many cases, a nonresident taking a position that a treaty of the United States overrules (or otherwise modifies) a U.S. domestic tax law must file a return and disclose this position on a statement (Form 8833) attached to the taxpayer's return. I.R.C. § 6114. For example, a nonresident who contends that the U.S. ECI that it generates is not attributable to a U.S. permanent establishment or a foreign corporation that claims a treaty exemption from the U.S. branch profits tax is required to disclose that position under I.R.C. § 6114. Moreover, a foreign person entitled to a treaty reduction of the 30 percent statutory withholding rate on interest, dividends, etc. (*i.e.*, FDAP income) must provide the withholding agent with the necessary documentation (*e.g.*, a W-8BEN— BEN is short for "beneficial owner"; entities file a W-8BEN-E) prior to the time of payment in order to receive the treaty benefits. Reg. § 1.1441–6(b)(1). Even then, in some cases where the payments are from related parties and exceed more than $500,000, a taxpayer may still be required to file a Form 1120-F (along with a Form 8833). A foreign corporation failing to disclose a treaty-based reporting position can be subject to a penalty of $10,000 ($1,000 for other nonresidents). I.R.C. § 6712.

While an extensive discussion of all the filing requirements and Forms in both an inbound and outbound context is beyond the scope of this book, what follows is a brief summary of some of the more important filing requirements for both inbound and outbound taxpayers.

For a U.S. corporation, Schedule N, which is attached to the U.S. corporation's income tax return, is used to identify whether a U.S. corporation has any foreign operations. Certain U.S. citizens, residents, and corporations who own or acquire the stock of a foreign corporation (including stock treated as owned under constructive ownership rules) may be required to file Form 5471. Additionally, certain officers and directors of the foreign corporation may be required to file Form 5471. The category of the filer determines what information must be disclosed on the form. The information generally consists of an income statement, balance sheet, earnings and profits calculations, details of intercompany transactions, and disclosures concerning acquisitions, dispositions and mergers involving the foreign corporation. As a result of the enactment of TCJA, the IRS has made significant revisions to Form 5471 requiring that taxpayers provide much more information than previously required.

Other important forms for a U.S. corporate taxpayer include the Form 1118 which is used to compute a corporation's foreign tax credit for income taxes paid or accrued to a foreign country or a U.S. possession and is filed as part of the taxpayer's corporate income tax return. Any corporation that claims a foreign tax credit must attach this form to its income tax return. This form has also become more complex as a result of TCJA changes.

Generally, Form 926 must be filed by a U.S. citizen or resident, domestic corporation, or an estate or trust (other than a foreign estate or trust) that transfers tangible or intangible property (even if unappreciated) to a foreign corporation. Form 926 is not used to report transfers relating to foreign estates and trusts and foreign partnerships (Forms 3520 and 8865, respectively, address these transfers).

The U.S. Treasury has promulgated regulations conforming U.S. multinationals' reporting obligations to OECD country-by-country (CBC) reporting requirements (T.D. 9773). Groups with annual gross revenue in excess of $850 million in the preceding reporting period must file Form 8975, which requires the filer to list the group's entities, including information on each entity's tax jurisdiction (if any), country of organization and main business activity. Information regarding financial and employee information for each tax jurisdiction in which the group does business is also required. Under competent authority agreements signed by the U.S. Treasury, this information is exchangeable with tax administrations in other jurisdictions. *See* § 11.06(B) for more discussion on CBC reporting.

A U.S. taxpayer that owns a foreign corporation (treated as a disregarded entity under the U.S. check-the-box regulations) is required to file a Form 8858 that provides information that may help the IRS enforce the branch currency provisions of I.R.C. § 987 when income is remitted from the branch back to the United States. *See* Chapter 12.

For an inbound taxpayer, generally, a foreign corporation must file Form 1120-F if, during the taxable year, the corporation:

- Overpaid income tax that it wants refunded;

- Engaged in a trade or business in the United States, whether or not it had income from that trade or business;

- Had income, gains, losses treated as if they were effectively connected with a U.S. trade or business; or

- With some exceptions, had income from any U.S. source (even if its income is tax exempt under an income tax treaty or code section).

The return is due by the 15th day of the 6th month after the corporation's taxable year if the corporation does not have an office in the United States. Otherwise, the return is due by the 15th day of the 3rd month after the end of the corporation's taxable year. A six-month extension of time for filing the return, but not for paying tax, may be requested on Form 7004.

Form 5472 reports intercompany transactions involving U.S. corporations (or foreign corporations that are engaged in a U.S. trade or business) and certain foreign and domestic related parties. Under 2016 regulations, a disregarded entity may be treated as a corporation for these filing purposes. New for 2019 are reporting obligations for amounts paid that are subject to anti-hybrid rules of I.R.C. § 267A. *See* Prop. Reg. § 1.6038A–2(b)(5)(iii).

In addition to a nonresident filing a U.S. corporate tax return where appropriate, every partnership (domestic or foreign) that engages in a U.S. trade or business or has U.S. source income is required to file a Form 1065. It is due on the 15th day of the 4th month after the end of the partnership taxable year (*i.e.*, April 15th for a calendar year-end partnership). Foreign partnerships that are controlled by U.S. persons must file a Form 8865 even if not engaged in a U.S. business.

§ 6.02   SAILING PERMITS

Aside from any filing requirements, neither a resident alien nor a nonresident alien may depart from the United States without procuring a certificate of compliance with the federal income tax laws. I.R.C. § 6851(d)(1). This provision does not apply to temporary visitors or in the case where a resident alien is planning to return to the United States.

§ 6.03   THE NEED FOR WITHHOLDING

If a foreign taxpayer is not engaged in a trade or business in the United States but receives investment income from U.S. sources, any fixed or determinable annual or periodical income is subject to a 30 percent tax rate (or lower treaty rate). I.R.C. §§ 871(a) or 881. However, because the foreign taxpayer may not have business assets in the United States, it might be impossible to enforce the 30 percent tax against a foreign taxpayer that does not voluntarily pay. Accordingly, the Code contains a variety of withholding provisions which apply to the investment income of foreign taxpayers. A withholding agent who fails to withhold will be personally liable for the requisite tax, penalties, and interest. I.R.C. § 1461.

In general, withholding is required if the following six criteria are met: (a) the recipient is a foreign person; (b) the amount paid is U.S. source income; (c) the amount paid is fixed or determinable annual or periodical income (*i.e.*, generally passive investment income from interest, dividends, royalties, and some rents); (d) the amount paid is not income effectively connected to a USTB; (e) the payor or some agent of the payor is a withholding agent; and (f) no exception applies.

§ 6.04   WITHHOLDING ON DIVIDENDS, INTEREST, AND OTHER PERIODIC PAYMENTS

When a U.S. or foreign payor makes a U.S. source dividend or interest payment (or other U.S. source payment to a foreign investor that is taxable under either I.R.C. §§ 871(a)(1) or 881), the payor may be obligated under I.R.C. §§ 1441 or 1442 to withhold 30 percent of the amount paid from U.S. sources that is not effectively connected with the foreign investor's conduct of a USTB. No additional tax liability is imposed by I.R.C. § 1441; instead, the provision establishes a method of collecting taxes that are imposed and due under I.R.C. §§ 871 and 881 by transferring the initial tax payment responsibility to the payor.

The general withholding obligation arises when there are specified types of payments to a foreign person. Reg. § 1.1441–1(b). Payments to U.S. persons are not subject to the 30 percent withholding requirement of I.R.C. § 1441, but a backup withholding requirement of 31 percent may be imposed by I.R.C. § 3406 if a U.S. recipient fails to provide the required proof of U.S. residence or citizenship to the withholding agent (*e.g.*, a Form W-9). Conversely, payments to foreign persons are subject to 30 percent withholding under I.R.C. § 1441 but are not additionally subject to the backup withholding rules.

Determining the status of a payee as U.S. or foreign is not always easy. The regulations contain a complicated series of presumptions which a withholding agent may use to ascertain the payee's residency in the absence of documentation as to the payee's status. Reg. § 1.1441–1(b)(3). A withholding agent relying on these presumptions will not be liable for any tax or penalties that may result because the payee's actual residency was not as presumed. The presumptions are to be used only for determining a payee's status in reaching a decision to withhold; the presumptions are not to be used for granting a reduced rate of withholding under any income tax treaty. Moreover, withholding agents should be aware that the regulations under I.R.C. § 1441 also contain rules for determining the status of entities that are disregarded under the check-the-box regulations. *See infra* Chapter 14. Payments to a U.S. disregarded entity which is wholly owned by a foreign person are treated as made to a foreign person. Reg. § 1.1441–1(b)(2)(iii).

Normally, the amount withheld on a distribution to a foreign payee is 30 percent of the gross amount of the payment. I.R.C. §§ 871 and 881. A withholding agent may grant a reduced rate of withholding to a beneficial owner that is a foreign person entitled to a reduced rate of withholding in accordance with a tax treaty if appropriate documentation is provided. Reg. § 1.1441–1(b). Moreover, a withholding agent may be absolved of the withholding obligation when making a payment to a foreign person who assumes responsibility for withholding on that payment. Foreign persons eligible to assume this withholding responsibility fall into four categories: qualified intermediaries, U.S. branches of foreign entities, withholding foreign partnerships, or authorized foreign agents. *See infra* § 6.04(E).

(A) INCOME SUBJECT TO WITHHOLDING

The broad withholding requirement of I.R.C. § 1441 does not apply to all items of income. Items that are effectively connected with the conduct of a trade or business within the United States are exempt from withholding if appropriate documentation is presented to the withholding agent (*e.g.*, W-8ECI). Compensation paid to employees is subject to wage withholding rather than withholding under I.R.C. §§ 1441 or 1442. *See* Form 8233. An amount paid as a scholarship or fellowship for study, training or research in the United States (*i.e.*, amounts that do not represent compensation for services) to a nonresident alien individual temporarily present in the U.S. may constitute income to the nonresident if the scholarship is not excluded under I.R.C. § 117. That payment will be subject to a 14 percent withholding requirement, consistent with I.R.C. § 871(c).

In general, income from sources within the United States that is fixed or determinable, annual or periodical income (FDAP income) is subject to withholding. I.R.C. § 1441(b). There are exceptions from the withholding requirement for certain classes of income such as portfolio interest, bank deposit interest, and short-term original issue discount. Reg. § 1.1441–2(a). To be considered a short-term obligation, and thereby exempt from withholding, an obligation must be payable within 183 days of the original issue. I.R.C. § 871(g).

On all other original issue discount (OID) obligations, withholding is required where the payor is able to calculate the amount of OID paid to a foreign beneficial owner. Reg. § 1.1441–2(b)(3). A withholding agent must withhold on OID to the extent that it has actual knowledge of the portion of the payment constituting taxable OID to the beneficial owner or if that knowledge is reasonably available to the withholding agent. The withholding agent will be considered to have actual knowledge of the portion of the payment which constitutes taxable OID if it knows the beneficial owner's holding period, purchase price and the terms of the obligation.

When a foreign beneficial owner of an instrument carrying OID has the instrument redeemed by the corporation, the withholding agent must compute and withhold the requisite tax on the amount of OID that accrued while the foreign person held the obligation up to the time when the instrument is redeemed. Generally, no withholding is required if an OID instrument is sold unless the sale is part of a plan to avoid tax and the withholding agent has reason to know of the plan. Reg. § 1.1441–2(a). However, even in the absence of withholding tax the seller may have to file and pay tax on the accrued interest. Reg. § 1.1441–2(b)(3).

Often it will be necessary for a withholding agent to determine whether a payee is the beneficial owner of a payment or the agent of the beneficial owner. The term "beneficial owner" is defined as "the person who is the owner of the income for tax purposes and who beneficially owns that income." Reg. § 1.1441–1(c)(6). A person "owns" income to the extent that it is required under general U.S. tax principles to include the payment in gross income per I.R.C. § 61. A person who receives income in the capacity of a nominee, agent, or custodian for another person is not the beneficial owner of the income.

In general, the beneficial owners of a payment to a flow-through entity (*e.g.*, a partnership) are the persons who under U.S. tax principles are the owners of the income in their separate and individual capacities. For example, suppose that a payment is made to a partnership. Under generally applicable U.S. tax principles, the beneficial owners of partnership income are the partners in the partnership. Therefore, when a payment is made to that partnership, the beneficial owners of that payment are the partners in their separate and individual capacities. In determining the beneficial owners of payments to a partnership, the withholding agent may be required to look through multiple tiers of pass-through entities in order to find a beneficial owner that is not a conduit. Reg. § 1.1441–1(c)(6)(ii).

Typically, the amount subject to withholding is the gross (*i.e.*, full) amount of the payment. Reg. § 1.1441–3(a). However, a corporation may reduce the amount of a distribution which is treated as a dividend subject to withholding based on a reasonable estimate of available earnings and profits (either current or accumulated). No withholding is required on a distribution that is not paid out of available earnings and profits. Reg. § 1.1441–3(c)(2). If the corporation making the distribution later determines that it under-withheld on the distribution, it will be liable for the amount under-withheld and any related interest. The corporation will not incur a penalty so long as the estimate of available earnings and profits was reasonable. If the FDAP payment subject to withholding is a payment-in-kind (*e.g.*, property used to satisfy an interest obligation), the withholding agent is not obligated to convert the property to cash if the withholding agent is able to obtain payment from another source (*i.e.*, withhold an extra amount on the cash portion of an interest payment to the same recipient). The obligation to withhold is not discharged even when there is no alternative source from which to withhold, and as a result, a withholding agent is authorized to liquidate any property of the beneficial owner into cash if necessary to satisfy the withholding requirements. Reg. § 1.1441–3(e).

Withholding is required at the time when there is a payment of FDAP income to a foreign payee.

Income subject to withholding is considered paid when it is includible in income under U.S. tax principles governing the cash basis method of accounting. Reg. § 1.1441–2(e). A payment may be deemed made even where there is no actual transfer of cash or other property. Accordingly, FDAP income reallocated from a related U.S. person to a foreign recipient under I.R.C. § 482 would be considered a payment for withholding purposes. Reg. § 1.1441–2(e)(2) and *Central de Gas de Chihuahua, S.A. v. Comm'r,* 102 T.C. 515 (1994). Moreover, where a foreign person realizes income from the cancellation of a debt, withholding is required if the withholding agent has control over money or property owned by the recipient. Reg. §§ 1.1441–2(d) and 2(e)(1).

(B) REDUCED RATES OF WITHHOLDING

Nonresidents receiving FDAP income may claim a reduced rate of withholding under a favorable treaty provision. Reg. § 1.1441–6. Withholding will be reduced to the level specified in a particular treaty if the beneficial owner of the payment is a resident of that treaty country and all of the other requirements to obtain benefits of the treaty are satisfied. Reg. § 1.1441–6(b). To prove that a treaty applies, the foreign beneficial owner of the income must provide the withholding agent with a beneficial owner withholding certificate (W-8BEN for individuals or W-8BEN-E for entities). This certificate should establish that the person who is considered to be the beneficial owner of the income under U.S. tax principles is a resident of the signatory treaty country or is somehow otherwise entitled to reduced withholding under that treaty. Reg. § 1.1441–6(b)(1). A beneficial owner withholding certificate is valid only if it is provided on a Form W-8BEN (or W-8BEN-E) or in some cases a substitute form. Reg. § 1.1441–1(e)(2). Generally, a withholding agent may rely upon the beneficial owner's Form W-8BEN(-E) and withhold at a reduced rate if the certificate is received before any payment is made. Reg. § 1.1441–1(e)(1).

(C)   WHO IS A WITHHOLDING AGENT?

A withholding agent is any person that has the control, receipt, custody, disposal, or payment of an item of a foreign person subject to withholding, including a lessee, mortgagee, employer or the payor of dividends. Reg. § 1.1441–7(a). In general, the withholding agent is the last person in the United States who handles an item of income before it is paid over to a foreign person. Under I.R.C. § 1441(a), it is possible to have more than one withholding agent for a single income item. Even where several persons qualify as withholding agents with respect to a single payment, only one tax is required to be withheld and generally only one return must be filed.

The withholding agent is required to deposit any withheld tax in a Federal Reserve or other authorized bank. I.R.C. § 6302. The withholding agent must file an annual return on Form 1042 and a Form 1042S with respect to each foreign recipient. A copy of the Form 1042S goes to the foreign recipient. The withholding agent is personally liable to the IRS for any amount required to be withheld and is indemnified against any claims of the taxpayer. I.R.C. § 1461. Moreover, a withholding agent is obligated to withhold only to the extent that the agent has control over, or custody of, money or property of the payee from which to withhold the required amount. When a withholding agent does not have control over or custody of any money or property owned by the recipient or beneficial owner during the course of the year in which a payment occurs, the withholding agent will be absolved of the withholding obligation unless the payment is a distribution on stock or the lack of control or custody of money or property is a result of a pre-arranged plan to avoid withholding. Reg. § 1.1441–2(d).

If a withholding agent fails to withhold or under withholds, there is no defense that either another withholding agent failed to withhold or that legal counsel advised that withholding was unnecessary. However, a withholding agent may rely on documentation provided by the payee indicating that no withholding is required (*e.g.*, the income is effectively connected or the payee is a U.S. citizen or resident) if appropriate procedures are followed. Where the failure to file or withhold is a willful attempt to evade tax, the withholding agent will be liable for penalties imposed under I.R.C. § 6672, in addition to the withholding agent's liability for the underlying tax.

(D) PAYMENTS INVOLVING PARTNERSHIPS, TRUSTS AND ESTATES

If a FDAP payment is made to a pass-through entity, such as a partnership, the withholding obligation depends on whether the partnership is domestic or foreign. Reg. § 1.1441–5(a)(1). Generally, a withholding agent will be able to rely on documentation from the payee in determining the residence of the payee. A partnership is deemed to be foreign if it is created or organized outside the United States. I.R.C. § 7701(a)(5). A partnership will be presumed foreign under the following circumstances: actual knowledge of the employer identification number (EIN) indicates foreign status; correspondence with the payee is mailed to a foreign address; or the payment is made outside of the United States. Reg. § 1.1441–5(d)(2).

Payments to domestic partnerships are not subject to withholding under I.R.C. § 1441, even if some of the partners are foreign persons. Reg. § 1.1441–5(b)(1). Instead, a domestic partnership is the withholding agent for items of income included in the distributive share of a partner who is a foreign person. Assuming that the domestic partnership withholds on a foreign partner's distributive share of FDAP income received, there will be no withholding obligation when the income is actually distributed to the foreign partner. However, a U.S. partnership must withhold on any distributions of an amount subject to withholding (*i.e.*, an interest payment to a lender) or on making a guaranteed payment to a foreign partner. Reg. § 1.1441–5(b)(2). Similar rules apply to payments to U.S. trusts and estates on behalf of foreign beneficiaries.

A more substantial withholding obligation exists when payments are made to foreign partnerships. Generally, a payment to a foreign partnership is treated as if the payment were made directly to its partners. Reg. § 1.1441–5(c)(1). The partners individually—rather than the partnership—will be considered the payees for purposes of determining whether a payment was made to a U.S. or foreign person. If a partner is itself a partnership or another pass-through entity, the partners of the highest tier foreign partnership will be considered the payees. Reg. § 1.1441–5(c)(1)(i). Essentially, the lower tier partnerships will be looked through for tax purposes, until a partner is reached that is not a pass-through entity. As a result of the look-through, a foreign partner may claim treaty benefits to which the partner is entitled in its own right. To the extent that the payor is unable to determine the amount allocable to each foreign partner or in the event that some partners are not accounted for, the payor may be required to withhold at the highest applicable rate. Reg. § 1.1441–5(d)(3).

Suppose USCo makes a dividend payment of $120 to XYZ, a foreign partnership in Country X. XYZ is comprised of three equal partners, X, Y, and Z. In determining the correct rate of withholding, the withholding agent will look through XYZ and consider the residence of the individual partners, if appropriate documentation is provided. If X is a resident of country X which does not have a tax treaty with the United States, the withholding agent must withhold from the dividend payment 30 percent of the share of the dividend attributable to X. Because X, Y, and Z are equal partners, we can assume that X will be allocated $40 of the dividend. Therefore, on the payment to XYZ, the withholding agent must collect $12 of tax (30% of $40) and remit the $12 to the IRS on behalf of X. If Y is a U.S. resident, no withholding is required by I.R.C. § 1441 on Y's share of the dividend payment. Suppose that Z is a resident of the Netherlands which has a tax treaty with the U.S. Under that treaty, the rate of withholding on dividends is reduced to 15 percent. So the withholding agent must withhold $6 from the dividend payment to XYZ as tax on the $40 share of the payment allocable to Z. In sum, on the $120 dividend from USCo, the withholding agent collects a total of $18 to remit to the IRS, and the payee XYZ actually receives a payment of only $102.

Nonetheless, a withholding agent may treat a payment as made to a foreign partnership—and not to its partners—if certain documentation is provided to the withholding agent which would indicate the payee is a withholding foreign partnership. Reg. § 1.1441–5(c)(1)(ii). In the case of a withholding foreign partnership, the withholding agent will not withhold on the payment to the entity, but rather the partnership itself will become liable for collecting the tax on the distributive shares of its foreign partners. Withholding foreign partnerships are discussed *infra* in § 6.04(E).

Consider also the scenario when a foreign partnership is engaged in a trade or business in the United States. Its ECI is subject to U.S. taxation, but there is no withholding under I.R.C. § 1441 on this income. If the partnership then distributes its effectively connected income to its foreign partners, unless there is a withholding obligation, U.S. source income may escape U.S. taxation entirely (although the partners are obligated under I.R.C. § 875 to pay the tax due as a result of the partners' conduct of a U.S. trade or business).

Section 1446 requires foreign and domestic partnerships to withhold with respect to a foreign partner's distributive share of income effectively connected with the conduct of a U.S. trade or business. This withholding obligation is, in effect, a prepayment of taxes due with respect to the foreign partners' shares of ECI under I.R.C. § 875(1). If the amount withheld exceeds the substantive tax liability, the excess is refunded. The withholding rate is the highest applicable graduated rate for each partner (*e.g.*, 21 percent for a corporate partner). Withholding under I.R.C. § 1446 is required regardless of whether there is an actual distribution.

In tiered partnership situations, the withholding obligation can be pushed down to the bottom tier with proper documentation from the upper tier partnership. For example, suppose that USP1 and USP2, U.S. partnerships with foreign partners, own 100 percent of USP3, a U.S. partnership that generates U.S. ECI. USP1 and USP2 would have

I.R.C. § 1446 withholding obligations, but can shift the obligations to USP3 with proper documentation.

Section 1446(f), enacted as part of the TCJA, imposes new withholding requirements in the case of a disposition of an interest in a partnership where a portion of the gain is treated as ECI under newly enacted I.R.C. § 864(c)(8). If I.R.C. § 1446(f) applies, the transferee must withhold tax equal to 10 percent of the amount realized on the disposition. A number of exceptions are provided, including one that applies if the transferor provides an affidavit affirming that the transferor is not a foreign person.

Proposed regulations issued in May 2019 provide guidance for taxpayers for withholding, reporting and paying tax under I.R.C. § 1446(f) upon the sale, exchange or other disposition of an interest in a partnership earning ECI, including rules for withholding by brokers on transfers of interests in publicly traded partnerships REG–105476–18, 2019–27 I.R.B. 63. These regulations are generally applicable when finalized. Until then, taxpayers may rely on a series of Notices issued by the IRS in 2018 (Notice 2018–08, 2018–7 I.R.B. 352; Notice 2018–29, 2018–16 I.R.B. 495).

(E) PAYMENTS TO FOREIGN INTERMEDIARIES

In the case of investment income, payments often will be made to a foreign intermediary (*i.e.*, a person other than the beneficial owner). Examples of such intermediaries are a nominee recipient, a bank, a brokerage house or a foreign partnership. The

Regulations promulgated under I.R.C. § 1441 identify five different types of intermediaries. They are: (1) nonqualified intermediaries, (2) qualified intermediaries, (3) withholding foreign partnerships, (4) authorized foreign agents, and (5) U.S. branches of foreign financial institutions. Each of these intermediaries serves a slightly different function, and the filing and withholding obligations associated with each are also slightly different. Typically, a foreign intermediary will provide a W-8IMY (IMY for Intermediary) to a withholding agent, in some cases along with the appropriate W-8BEN(-E) for any beneficial owner. Withholding agents must identify situations where an intermediary is involved and take into account the effect of the intermediary on the withholding obligation. Where a qualified intermediary (QI) or withholding foreign partnership (WFP) exists, the withholding agent may be relieved of the withholding obligation if certain documentation is provided to the IRS by the intermediary. If the withholding agent is relieved of the withholding obligation, the QI or the WFP becomes responsible for withholding.

A nonqualified foreign intermediary (NQI) is a foreign person (*e.g.*, a foreign bank) receiving payments for which it is not the beneficial owner and which has not entered into a withholding agreement with the IRS. A withholding agent must obtain certain documentation from a nonqualified intermediary indicating the portion of the payment allocable to each person for whom the intermediary is collecting the payment. This information is necessary so that the withholding agent is able to withhold the appropriate amount. Reg. § 1.1441–1(e)(3)(iii). When a nonqualified intermediary fails to provide the necessary documentation, the withholding agent simply withholds at the statutory rate. Therefore, where a nonqualified intermediary is involved in a transaction, the withholding agent is not released from the responsibility of obtaining the required documentation.

In contrast, a foreign intermediary will be considered to be "qualified" if it has entered into an agreement with the IRS accepting certain information gathering responsibilities with respect to withholding. Reg. § 1.1441–1(e)(5). A qualified intermediary may be a foreign financial institution or clearing organization; a foreign branch or office of a U.S. financial institution or clearing organization; a foreign corporation claiming treaty benefits for its shareholders; a bank holding company (and subsidiaries of a bank holding company); or any other person with whom the IRS may choose to enter into a withholding agreement. Reg. § 1.1441–1(e)(5)(ii). Under a withholding agreement, a qualified intermediary generally will be subject to the same reporting and withholding provisions applicable to withholding agents. The terms of such an agreement may vary depending on the situation and on the circumstances of each qualified intermediary. A qualified intermediary may assume primary withholding responsibility, thereby agreeing to withhold and pay over the required amounts as if the intermediary were a withholding agent. The qualified intermediary must provide specified documentation to the withholding agent indicating that the intermediary has assumed the withholding obligation.

Obviously some intermediaries will not want to assume the legal liabilities inherent in the withholding obligation or to deal with the hassle and additional paperwork created by the withholding responsibility. A QI without primary withholding responsibility (non-PWR), unlike a QI with primary withholding responsibility (PWR), must collect beneficial owner documentation. But unlike a nonqualified intermediary, a non-PWR QI does not need to turn over the information to a withholding agent. Instead, the non-PWR QI provides the withholding agent with withholding rate pool information (*e.g.*, a U.S. beneficial owner pool, a 30 percent pool for nonresident beneficial owners not entitled to a treaty-reduced withholding rate, a 15 percent pool for beneficial owners entitled to a treaty-reduced withholding rate). This pool information allows the withholding agent to withhold in the aggregate the correct amount of tax.

An intermediary may, however, choose to enter into a withholding agreement with the IRS in order to use its status as a qualified intermediary with primary withholding responsibility (*i.e.*, as a withholding agent) to attract customers. For instance, a foreign investor who might be hesitant to invest in U.S. stocks or debt instruments due to various reporting requirements may be persuaded to invest through a qualified intermediary which has a less extensive reporting requirement than a comparable nonqualified intermediary.

Furthermore, the burden created by entering into a withholding agreement with the IRS may be minimal for a large foreign bank or brokerage house which maintains adequate customer records.

Shifting primary withholding responsibility will generally be favorable to withholding agents. For example, suppose the qualified intermediary is a foreign financial institution investing in stock and securities of U.S. corporations on behalf of a group of customers. If the qualified intermediary assumes the primary withholding obligation, then the withholding agent will not face the burden of collecting and reporting on payments to multiple foreign beneficial owners. Instead, the qualified intermediary will be liable for reporting and paying over the requisite tax.

Suppose that USCo is a publicly traded, domestic corporation. FrenchBank is a French financial institution that offers brokerage services to its customers. FrenchBank reaches an agreement with the IRS to act as a qualified intermediary with primary withholding responsibility for payments made to its customers on stocks and other instruments held through FrenchBank accounts. In accordance with this agreement, FrenchBank notifies USCo of its status as a qualified intermediary. A, B, and C are customers of FrenchBank and through their FrenchBank accounts they each purchase 100 shares of USCo stock. USCo declares a dividend of $1/share and pays FrenchBank $300 to credit to the accounts of A, B, and C. USCo does not withhold on the payment to FrenchBank;

rather FrenchBank is obligated to withhold as a result of its agreement with the IRS. If A is a U.S. resident, FrenchBank is not required to withhold and can credit A's account the full $100 dividend. If B is a resident of France which has a tax treaty with the United States reducing withholding on dividend payments to 15 percent, FrenchBank must collect $15 of tax on the dividend payment to B and can credit B's account $85. If C is a resident of Argentina which does not have a tax treaty with the United States, FrenchBank must collect $30 of tax on the USCo dividend for C and can credit C's account $70. Therefore, FrenchBank withholds a total of $45 and remits it to the IRS. FrenchBank disburses the remainder to its clients: $100 to A, $85 to B, and $70 to C.

Moreover, foreign partnerships may enter into agreements with the IRS to assume primary withholding and reporting responsibility. Reg. § 1.1441–5(c)(2). A foreign partnership that has entered into such a withholding agreement is known as a withholding foreign partnership and serves the same purposes and functions as a qualified intermediary. Payments to a withholding foreign partnership are treated as if they are made to the partnership as an entity, rather than flowing through to the partners who are the beneficial owners of the payments. Provided certain documentation, the withholding agent merely reports that it made payments to the partnership; there is no withholding at the time of the payment to the withholding foreign partnership. In this manner, a foreign partnership is accorded the same treatment as a domestic partnership. To achieve this result, a withholding foreign partnership will be required to withhold at the same time and use the same procedures as U.S. partnerships with foreign partners. Reg. § 1.1441–5(c)(2)(iii). When a foreign partner is required by U.S. tax principles to recognize its distributive share of the partnership's taxable income, the withholding foreign partnership will be required to withhold the requisite tax and remit it to the IRS at that time.

Consider again, the XYZ partnership example discussed *supra* in § 6.04(D). XYZ, a foreign partnership in Country X, decides to enter into a withholding agreement with the IRS. XYZ informs USCo of XYZ's status as a withholding foreign partnership and provides USCo with the necessary documentation. Subsequently, USCo makes another $120 dividend payment to XYZ. Because of XYZ's new status as a withholding foreign partnership, the withholding obligation shifts to XYZ, and USCo is absolved of its I.R.C. § 1441 responsibility. USCo pays the full $120 dividend to XYZ and does not remit any tax to the IRS. Instead, XYZ is liable for the requisite withholding tax at the time prescribed by U.S. tax principles applicable to a domestic partnership (*e.g.*, withholding on a foreign partner's distributive share of FDAP income).

A U.S. branch of a foreign bank or insurance company may receive payments on behalf of a foreign person which does not have income effectively connected with the conduct of a U.S. trade or business. Reg. § 1.1441–1(e)(3)(v). Normally, a withholding agent would be required to withhold on a payment to a foreign payee (*e.g.*, the foreign bank) because the U.S. branch is not considered to be a legal entity. Instead, the U.S. branch may enter into an agreement with a withholding agent to be treated as U.S. person with respect to any payments received. Once the withholding agent receives the appropriate documentation, the withholding obligation will be removed from it. Rather, the U.S. branch will be treated as the withholding agent in a manner similar to that of a qualified intermediary.

A withholding agent may shift some of its responsibilities to an authorized foreign agent by mutual agreement. Reg. § 1.1441–7(c). This type of arrangement is advantageous to a withholding agent, because it allows the withholding agent to shift some or all of the burden of collecting documentation and reporting to the IRS. The acts of an authorized foreign agent will be considered the acts of the withholding agent for the purposes of satisfying the withholding obligation. The withholding agent is fully liable for the acts of the authorized foreign agent and continues to be liable if the authorized foreign agent fails to carry out its obligation.

As noted, a beneficial owner of income otherwise subject to FDAP withholding typically files a W-8BEN(-E). An intermediary who collects a payment for the beneficial owners (*e.g.*, a foreign bank or foreign partnership) files a W-8IMY and in cases where it is not a qualified intermediary it should attach each appropriate W-8BEN(-E) so the withholding agent knows how much to withhold. In some cases, a FDAP payment (*e.g.*, payment for services performed in the United States) is made to a nonresident that is engaged in a USTB to which the income is effectively connected. In these cases, the nonresident should provide a W-8ECI which informs the potential withholding agent not to withhold because the nonresident is required to file a U.S. tax return (*e.g.*, a Form 1120-F for a corporation or a Form 1040-NR for an individual). Finally, foreign governments (or their controlled entities) are exempt from withholding under I.R.C. § 892 on certain types of FDAP income. In these situations, a W-8EXP (EXP for Exempt) should be provided to the withholding agent.

§ 6.05   FIRPTA WITHHOLDING

When a foreign taxpayer is engaged in a trade or business in the United States, normally there is no required withholding on the trade or business income. However, when a foreign taxpayer disposes of U.S. real property, withholding is required on the deemed ECI. I.R.C. § 897.

In general, the purchaser of any U.S. real property must withhold 15 percent of the amount realized on a disposition. I.R.C. § 1445(a). Withholding under I.R.C. § 1445(a) is an estimation of the tax due as opposed to withholding under I.R.C. §§ 1441 and 1442 which generally collects without estimation the 30 percent tax imposed by I.R.C. §§ 871(a) or 881. Withholding is required of a purchaser of a partnership interest if 50 percent or more of the value of the partnership's gross assets consist of U.S. real property interests and 90 percent or more of the value of the gross assets consist of U.S. real property interests plus cash (or cash equivalents). Reg. § 1.1445–11T(d).

There are a number of important exceptions to the general rule. If the seller provides an affidavit that it is a U.S. person, no withholding is required. I.R.C. § 1445(b)(2). This is true even if a U.S. partnership with foreign partners sells a United States Real Property Interest to a purchaser. That is because the U.S. partnership itself is responsible for handling the withholding for its partners. If the asset sold is stock of a domestic corporation and the corporation provides an affidavit that it is not a U.S. real property holding corporation (and has not been one during the 5-year testing period), the purchaser is relieved of a withholding obligation. I.R.C. § 1445(b)(3). No withholding is required if the IRS provides a statement that the seller is exempt from tax or has made other satisfactory arrangements. Finally, no withholding is required if the purchaser acquires the property as a personal residence and the purchase price does not exceed $300,000—an increasingly difficult test to meet in today's housing market.

Under I.R.C. § 1445(f)(3), a foreign person does not include (and so an exemption from withholding will apply to) a qualified foreign pension fund as defined in I.R.C. § 897(*l*).

Proposed regulations provide guidance on how foreign pensions funds that are exempt from FIRPTA can certify their exempt status. REG–109826–17, 2019–26 I.R.B. 1349. Until Form W-8EXP is revised, foreign pension funds can provide a certificate of non-foreign status.

Section 897 treats gain and loss from the disposition of a U.S. real property interest (a "USRPI") recognized by a foreign person "as if the taxpayer were engaged in a trade or business within the United States during the taxable year and as if such gain or loss were effectively connected with such trade or business" for purposes of imposing net income-based taxation under I.R.C. §§ 871 and 882. When a foreign person disposes of a USRPI, I.R.C. § 1445 requires the transferee to withhold 15 percent of the total amount paid. A special rule, provided in I.R.C. § 1445(e)(1), applies when a domestic partnership with foreign partners disposes of a USRPI. Under that section, the partnership is required to withhold tax equal to 21 percent of the gain realized and allocable to the foreign partners. Similarly, there is a 21 percent withholding obligation on certain distributions of U.S. real property interests by a domestic or foreign corporation. I.R.C. § 1441(e)(2) and (3). Because the gain is ECI in the hands of the U.S. partnership, there is an overlap of two withholding regimes because the partnership will also be required to withhold on under I.R.C. § 1446. However, there is no double-withholding. In the case of an overlap, only I.R.C. § 1446 shall apply, thereby effectively overriding I.R.C. § 1445. Reg. § 1.1446–3(c)(2)(i). In the case of a foreign partnership that has tax withheld by the transferee under section 1445(a), the Regulations permit the partnership a credit against its I.R.C. § 1446 liability. Reg. § 1.1446–3(c)(2)(ii).

§ 6.06   INFORMATION REPORTING

In addition to the return and withholding requirements, taxpayers may also be subject to information reporting requirements that are imposed to provide the IRS with information needed to verify a taxpayer's tax liability. For example, suppose that a U.S. subsidiary of a foreign corporation purchases inventory from its foreign parent and resells the inventory in the United States. If the purchase price paid by the U.S. subsidiary to the foreign parent is more than an arm's-length price, then the gain taxable in the United States from the subsidiary's sales to customers will be understated (and the foreign parent's income which is not typically taxable in the United States will be overstated). To determine whether, the subsidiary has paid an arm's-length price it may be helpful to know the foreign parent's costs of production or the price which the foreign corporation sells to unrelated purchasers, if any.

Congress has enacted I.R.C. §§ 6038A and 6038C which require certain U.S. taxpayers or foreign taxpayers doing business in the United States to provide a variety of information to enable the IRS to police arm's-length pricing between related taxpayers. Form 8975, discussed *supra*, will provide the IRS and foreign tax administrations with a lot of additional detail on companies' tax profiles by jurisdiction. The details of these disclosure provisions and the intercompany pricing problem in general are discussed *infra* at § 11.06(B).

§ 6.07   FATCA REPORTING
AND WITHHOLDING

(A) BACKGROUND

Estimates that the United States was losing hundreds of billions in tax revenues each year as a result of offshore tax abuse primarily from the use of concealed and undeclared accounts held by U.S. taxpayers or their controlled foreign entities led Congress in 2009 to enact the "Foreign Account Tax Compliance Act of 2009" ("FATCA"). *See* I.R.C. §§ 1471–1474 and accompanying Regulations. The FATCA withholding rules are coordinated with existing withholding rules to prevent duplicate withholding.

These rules are designed to combat offshore tax evasion by requiring non-U.S. financial institutions (foreign financial institutions or FFIs) and other offshore vehicles to report certain information pertaining to U.S. taxpayers holding financial assets abroad. The intent behind the law is to require FFIs to identify and report U.S. persons holding assets abroad and for certain non-financial foreign entities (NFFEs) to identify substantial U.S. owners. In order to comply with these rules, FFIs are required to enter into an FFI Agreement with the U.S. Treasury or comply with intergovernmental agreements (IGAs) entered into by their local government. U.S. withholding agents (USWAs) must document all of their relationships with foreign entities in order to assist with the enforcement of the rules. Failure to enter into an agreement or provide required documentation will result in the imposition of a 30 percent withholding tax on certain payments made to such customers and counterparties. The intent of FATCA is not impose a withholding tax but rather to use the threat of the tax as a stick to compel disclosure.

For example, a payment of interest from a U.S. payor to an FFI will be subject to 30 percent FATCA withholding tax if the FFI is not a "participating FFI" (*i.e.*, one that has entered into an FFI Agreement with the IRS) or has not agreed to comply with any applicable intergovernmental agreement (IGA) with its local government. The tax imposed under I.R.C. § 1471 applies notwithstanding what would be required under I.R.C. § 1441. Even a participating FFI will be required to withhold on a payment to a non-participating FFI based on the applicable pass-thru percentage discussed below.

After the United States enacted FATCA, many other countries followed suit with adoption of a parallel system of reporting and exchange of information known as the Common Reporting Standard, the rules of which are generally established by the OECD and agreed to by countries that have signed a multilateral Convention on Mutual Administrative Assistance in Tax Matters. The United States generally obtains more information from countries under the FATCA regime than it has agreed to provide under bilateral agreements, and has not committed to the Common Reporting Standard.

(B)   WITHHOLDABLE PAYMENTS

FATCA regulations define withholdable payments as "[a]ny payment of U.S. source FDAP income; and [f]or any sales or other dispositions occurring after December 31, 2016, any gross proceeds from the sale or other disposition of any property of a type that can produce interest or dividends that are U.S. source FDAP income." Reg. § 1.1473–1(a)(1)(i). In addition, FATCA does not align directly with many of the withholding exceptions regarding U.S. source FDAP payments expressly granted in other Code sections. For example, a payment of U.S. source portfolio interest or bank deposit interest, both exempt from withholding under I.R.C. § 1441, are treated as withholdable payments for FATCA purposes. While FATCA implements a 30 percent withholding tax on some payments if certain requirements are not met, certain payments are exempt from withholding. Grandfathered obligations, certain short term obligations, effectively connected income (ECI), excluded non-financial payments (*i.e.*, payments made in the ordinary course of business such as wages, rental income, software license payments), gross proceeds from the sale of excluded property, fractional shares and offshore payments of U.S. FDAP income prior to 2017 are all types of exempt payments.

(C)   FOREIGN FINANCIAL INSTITUTION (FFI)

An FFI is generally any non-U.S. entity that functions as a financial institution (*e.g.*, a bank), custodial institution that hold financial assets for third parties, investment entity (*e.g.*, investment or portfolio management company) or insurance company. In addition certain holding companies or treasury centers may be treated as FFIs. A treasury center is defined as an entity primarily involved in financing transactions (*e.g.*, making loans, taking deposits, entering into hedges) for members of its affiliated group. Not all corporate holding companies or treasury centers are subject to FATCA. The holding companies and treasury centers that are primarily affected or those which are part of an affiliated group that has a foreign financial institution (*e.g.*, a bank) as a member or a holding company or treasury center in a private equity type structure.

Even though an entity falls under the definition of an FFI, it may still be excluded where the regulations deem the chances of U.S. persons hiding assets to be low. For example, if the entity is an excepted nonfinancial group entity or a non-profit organization, it is excluded. Many nonfinancial groups that are engaged in active business but have a treasury center entity that enters into hedging activities or other financing activities for the group would be excluded from the definition of an FFI. Similarly, holding companies in nonfinancial group can be excluded as they are generally used for organizational, regulatory or tax purposes.

If an entity falls under the definition of an FFI and is not excluded from the definition, it can nevertheless fall under a deemed-compliant FFI category. Generally deemed-compliant FFIs have less impact in terms of what they are required to do to comply with FATCA, but the impact varies depending on the category of deemed-compliant status. There are three categories of FFIs with varying responsibilities including registered deemed-compliant FFIs, certified deemed-compliant FFIs and owner-documented FFIs. While registered deemed-compliant FFIs will have to manage most of the administrative burdens common to participating FFIs, certified deemed-compliant FFIs will have far fewer administrative requirements because they do not need to register with the IRS. Certified deemed-compliant FFIs include, but are not limited to, nonregistering foreign local banks (*i.e.*, those not likely to have U.S. customers), and low value account FFIs (*e.g.*, no accounts exciting $50,000 and no more than $50 million in assets). The final deemed-compliant status category, an owner-documented FFI, is meant for smaller passive investment vehicles. Treating them as an owner-documented FFI whereby U.S. owner information is provided to the withholding agent and subsequently reported to the IRS serves the same purpose behind FATCA.

(D) NON-FINANCIAL FOREIGN ENTITY (NFFE)

If an entity does not fall under the definition of an FFI or is otherwise excluded from the definition, the entity would be considered a NFFE. Generally if the NFFE is not an excepted NFFE (including an active NFFE described below), the NFFE (*i.e.*, passive NFFE) will have to provide its withholding agent with information on any substantial U.S. owners, or if none exist, a certification to that effect.

Excepted entities include publicly traded corporations and affiliates and active NFFEs. These types of entities generally will likely not be vehicles for U.S. persons to hide their assets because of the nature of their activities. Most U.S. persons tend to use passive vehicles to shield their income rather than conducting an actual business activity, which is why entities that do not qualify for an excepted NFFE status are required to provide substantial U.S. owner certifications.

Active NFFEs are entities that conduct an actual business activity other than holding assets that produce investment income such as interest, dividends, rents, etc. Any entity may be classified as an Active NFFE if: less than 50 percent of its gross income for the preceding calendar year is passive income; and less than 50 percent of the weighted average percentage of assets (tested quarterly) held are assets that produce or are held for the production of passive income.

Any NFFE that is not otherwise excepted will be a passive NFFE and must provide withholding agents with a certification regarding its substantial U.S. owners (if any). Substantial U.S. owners include any specified U.S. person directly or indirectly owning more than 10 percent of the passive NFFE. In IGA countries the term "controlling person" is used instead of substantial U.S. owner, and refers to persons who are considered as having control over an entity. The definition of "control" is interpreted in accordance with the Financial Action Tax Force Recommendations and may vary depending on the

IGA country. For example, it is possible that under a particular IGA country, a controlling person may be defined as having ownership of 25 percent or more or an entity.

(E) FATCA OBLIGATIONS

When a U.S. withholding agent makes a withholdable payment, FATCA's enforcement mechanism is a 30 percent withholding tax on payments made to persons that do not qualify for a FATCA withholding exemption. USWAs must annually report aggregate FATCA withholding on Form 1042 and file Forms 1042-S with respect to each payee for any withholdable payments. The FATCA status of a payee is determined most clearly by a valid Form W-8 or W-9 that can be associated with the payee at the time of payment. For purposes of identifying a payee where the payment is made to a flow-through entity or intermediary, if the flow-through entity or intermediary is not the payee (as defined above) the USWA may associate a payment with a withholding certificate using an intermediary withholding certificate (*e.g.*, a Form W-8IMY) from the flow-through entity that includes documentation of the actual payee or payees of the payment.

Participating FFIs must follow certain procedures to identify and document the FATCA status of each of their account holders to determine whether the account is a U.S. account, non-U.S. account or an account held by a recalcitrant account holder (essentially a holder not providing documentation) or nonparticipating FFI. Participating FFIs can generally document account holders with a Form W-8 or Form W-9.

Under the FFI agreement, a participating FFI agrees to withhold 30 percent on any withholdable payment made to a recalcitrant account holder or nonparticipating FFI. The withholding must take place at the time of payment. A participating FFI acting as a nonqualified intermediary (NQI), non-withholding foreign partnership or non-withholding foreign trust may delegate its withholding responsibility to its withholding agent by providing the information necessary for that withholding agent to withhold and report on any payments *e.g.*, providing a Form W-8IMY, withholding statement, etc. Participating FFIs are however required to withhold to the extent the withholding agent fails to withhold the correct amount.

Under the FFI agreement, a participating FFI agrees to report on specified U.S. individuals, specified U.S. owners of accounts held by owner-documented FFIs, and substantial U.S. owners of accounts held by passive NFFEs. The information is reported on Form 8966. Generally, the information reported consists of identifying information as well as the value of the account and payments with respect to the account.

§ 6.08   PENALTY PROVISIONS

Congress has enacted a welter of penalty and interest provisions to ensure that taxpayers comply with the Code's requirements. For example, there are penalties for failure to file a tax return or to pay tax

(I.R.C. § 6651), failure to pay estimated income tax (I.R.C. § 6655) and failure to deposit withheld taxes (I.R.C. § 6656).

Two of the more important penalty provisions are I.R.C. § 6662 which provides accuracy-related penalties and I.R.C. § 6694 which penalizes a tax preparer when a position on a return lacks a realistic possibility of being sustained on its merits and that position is not disclosed.

Section 6662 penalizes a taxpayer for any underpayment of tax required to be shown on a return which is attributable to specified factors including negligence (or worse), any substantial understatement of income tax or any substantial valuation misstatement. Generally, the penalty is equal to 20 percent of any underpayment but can be 40 percent for substantial valuation misstatements or 75 percent in the event of fraud.

Negligence is defined to include any failure to make a reasonable attempt to comply with the tax laws. If a position lacks a "reasonable basis," negligence penalties may result. Reg. § 1.6662–3(b). Disregarding existing rules or regulations (*e.g.*, regulations, revenue rulings) also can trigger the penalty, although if a taxpayer discloses the existence of the adverse rule and has a "reasonable basis" for the position taken, the penalty can be avoided. Many practitioners think they can take have a reasonable basis for a position if they have a 20 percent likelihood of success in the event of litigation.

Of particular importance is the substantial understatement factor. A substantial understatement occurs if the amount stated on the return exceeds 10 percent of the correct tax liability or $5,000 ($10,000 for a corporation). I.R.C. § 6662(d)(1)(A). No penalty is imposed on an understatement if "substantial authority" exists (some practitioners use a 40 percent likelihood of success benchmark) for the taxpayer's position, or if there is disclosure of the taxpayer's position and there is a "reasonable basis." While substantial authority might include cases, rulings, legislative history, private letter rulings, etc., conclusions reached in articles treatises, legal periodicals, or opinion letters do not constitute substantial authority. Reg. § 1.6662–4(d)(3).

Notably, penalties can apply even when there is no underlying tax owed, if a taxpayer has failed to comply with reporting obligations. Section 6662 provides for penalties for failure to file information returns. Failure to file Form 5471 or Form 8865, for example, is subject to a $10,000 penalty for each failure for each applicable annual accounting period per entity.

For a discussion of the tax shelter listing and reporting requirements, *see infra* § 14.05(A).

PART 3

FOREIGN ACTIVITIES
OF U.S. TAXPAYERS

CHAPTER 7

INTRODUCTION TO U.S. BUSINESS ACTIVITY IN FOREIGN COUNTRIES

§ 7.01 INTRODUCTION

The next several chapters focus on the U.S. tax treatment of U.S. taxpayers doing business or investing abroad. As noted in Chapter 2, the United States differs from most other countries in that it taxes its residents and citizens on a "worldwide" basis. Under a worldwide system, the residence country asserts taxing jurisdiction over all the income earned by its residents, regardless of where earned. Under a territorial system, in contrast, the resident country only asserts taxing rights over income earned in that jurisdiction.

In reality, the U.S. worldwide system historically has operated as such in name only; some scholars have referred to it as a "quasi-worldwide" system. That's because in practice, U.S. taxpayers have been able to defer taxation of foreign earnings because generally speaking, income earned by foreign corporations was not taxed in the United States until repatriated as a dividend. And as any good student of the subject of tax knows, deferring tax for long enough is essential equal to zero tax from a present value perspective.

The TCJA ostensibly moved the United States to a territorial system by providing for a dividends received deduction (DRD) for some dividends paid to U.S. shareholders by foreign corporations, but the reality is much more complex. The participation exemption is extremely limited, while the TCJA also vastly expanded current tax on income earned by companies controlled by U.S. shareholders ("controlled foreign corporation" and "U.S. shareholder" are technical terms defined in the Code and discussed in greater detail in Chapter 9). In effect, the TCJA moved the U.S. international tax system from one that allowed almost unlimited deferral of tax on foreign earnings to one that imposes a type of minimum tax on those earnings. In an unusual display of Congressional humor, the regime pursuant to which this minimum tax is imposed is referred to as GILTI (which stands for "global intangible low-taxed income"). The GILTI regime along with its antecedent and close cousin, the Subpart F regime, are discussed in Chapter 9.

An important feature of the U.S. international tax system is the foreign tax credit, which has been part of the Code since 1913. The foreign tax credit serves to prevent double taxation that could otherwise result from the U.S. and another country both asserting tax on the same income earned by a U.S. resident (the U.S. because of its worldwide tax system and the foreign country because it taxes income earned in its jurisdiction (many other countries relieve double taxation by exempting business income earned in other jurisdictions while using a credit mechanism for investment income earned and taxed in other jurisdictions)). Chapter 8 contains an introduction to the foreign tax credit, which essentially allows a U.S. taxpayer to decrease its U.S. tax liability on foreign source income by the amount of any foreign income taxes paid on the foreign source income. The foreign tax credit can be a "direct" credit (*i.e.*, where the foreign tax is paid directly by the U.S. taxpayer) or "indirect." An indirect foreign tax credit can be claimed in some circumstances for taxes paid by a person (*i.e.*, a foreign controlled company) other than the U.S. taxpayer. After TCJA, an indirect credit generally can only be claimed on foreign earnings taxed to a U.S. shareholder as GILTI or Subpart F, and Chapter 10 goes into more detail as to when the indirect tax credit can be claimed and how its calculated.

In limited circumstances, the United States applies an exemption-type system for foreign earned income. As indicated in § 7.02, for certain foreign earned income there is an exclusion from gross income and therefore no U.S. taxation.

Since the early days of the U.S. income tax, taxpayers have attempted to avoid the tax by shifting income overseas beyond U.S. tax jurisdiction. This is especially desirable from a taxpayer's standpoint if the foreign source income would be subject to little or no tax in the foreign jurisdiction. One of Congress' earlier attempts to prevent such income shifting was through enactment of the subpart F rules, which subject to full U.S. tax income earned from transactions that are viewed as particularly susceptible to income shifting (discussed in Chapter 9).

A U.S. taxpayer also may be able to structure its affairs so that a foreign corporation rather than the U.S. taxpayer earns income. Congress has tried to use to address such types of related-party income shifting by requiring that all transactions between related parties be conducted at arm's length pricing. The arm's length standard, as it's known, and the transfer pricing rules that apply to this standard, are discussed in Chapter 11.

A third major tax issue involving U.S. taxpayers earning income abroad is the treatment of transactions denominated in a foreign currency. Chapter 12 describes how foreign currency gains and losses are computed and treated for U.S. tax purposes.

§ 7.02   CITIZENS AND RESIDENTS OF THE UNITED STATES LIVING ABROAD

(A) INTRODUCTION

Although normally U.S. citizens and residents are taxable on their worldwide income, U.S. citizens and residents who work abroad have historically been able to exclude for tax purposes foreign source earned income and certain excessive housing cost amounts. The congressional purpose behind this exclusion is to make U.S. businesses more competitive abroad by making the use of U.S. employees abroad less expensive (*i.e.*, lower employer reimbursements for extra tax expenses incurred because of overseas transfers).

The exclusion under I.R.C. § 911 for certain income earned abroad is basically a substitute for the foreign tax credit on that income. In the absence of I.R.C. § 911, a U.S. taxpayer with earned income abroad would pay U.S. taxes on that income but could reduce the U.S. taxes by the amount of foreign taxes paid on such income. But notice that I.R.C. § 911 permits an exclusion from gross income even if the income earned abroad is not taxed (or is taxed at a lower rate than it would be taxed in the United States) by the foreign country.

(B) FOREIGN INCOME EXCLUSION

Under I.R.C. § 911 for 2019, a qualified individual can exclude as much as $105,900 of foreign earned income from taxable gross income. This amount is indexed for inflation. A "qualified individual" is one who is a bona fide resident of a foreign country for at least a taxable year or is present in a foreign country for at least 330 days during any consecutive twelve months. I.R.C. § 911(d)(1). In addition, the exclusion under I.R.C. § 911 is generally only available if the taxpayer's tax home (*i.e.*, regular place of business) is in the foreign country. For purposes of I.R.C. § 911, "residence" is defined under U.S. tax principles by looking at factors including: the taxpayer's intention; establishment of a home in the foreign country for an indefinite period of time; and participation in the activities of the community. *See* Reg. § 1.911–2(c); *Sochurek v. Comm'r*, 300 F.2d 34 (7th Cir. 1962). In a liberal interpretation of I.R.C. § 911, an airline pilot for a Japanese airline was deemed to be a "resident" of Japan for purposes of I.R.C. § 911 even though the pilot's wife remained in the couple's historic home in Alaska, the pilot did not speak Japanese, and was not integrated into the Japanese community. *Jones v. Commissioner*, 927 F.2d 849 (5th Cir. 1991). The court found a strong congressional intent to encourage foreign trade by placing U.S. employees seeking foreign employment in an equal position with noncitizens working abroad whose income is exempt in their home countries. But in recent cases, the Tax Court has held the other way. In *Hudson v. Commissioner*, T.C. Memo. 2017–221, it determined that a pilot who worked for Korea Airlines had failed to establish that he ever intended to be anything more than a transient. *See also Leuenberger v. Commissioner*, T.C. Summ. Op. 2018–52 (holding that defense contractor had failed to establish a tax home overseas).

An individual does not have to be taxed as a resident by the foreign country in order to qualify under I.R.C. § 911. Also, a national of a foreign country resident in the United States under I.R.C. § 7701(b) is entitled to the exclusion under I.R.C. § 911(d) for foreign income under most treaty nondiscrimination articles. Rev. Rul. 91–58, 1991–2 C.B. 340.

The exclusion is limited to compensation (pensions and annuities are not covered) not exceeding $105,900 for personal services actually rendered while overseas; it does not cover personal services rendered in anticipation of, or after the conclusion of, an overseas assignment or over international waters. I.R.C. § 911(b)(1)(A) and (d)(2) and *Rogers v. Comm'r*, 783 F.3d 320 (D.C. Cir. 2015). Suppose that a U.S. taxpayer residing in Mexico is engaged in the publishing business in Mexico. Can the taxpayer exclude $105,900 of income from taxation? Under

I.R.C. § 911(d)(2)(B), where both personal services and capital (*e.g.*, printing presses) are material income-producing factors, not more than 30 percent of the net profits are treated as earned income subject to exclusion. Capital is a material income-producing factor if the operation of the business requires substantial inventories or substantial investments in plant, machinery, or other equipment, but not if the capital is incidental to the production of income (*e.g.*, computers for general office use). *Rousku v. Commissioner*, 56 T.C. 548 (1971). If services performed abroad culminate in a product that is either sold or licensed, it is often difficult to determine whether the proceeds are foreign earned income. The IRS has acknowledged that royalties paid to a writer of literary works is earned income for purposes of I.R.C. § 911. Rev. Rul. 80–254, 1980–2 C.B. 222.

The Bipartisan Budget Act of 2018 for the first time allowed certain contractors or employees of contractors supporting the U.S. Armed Forces in designated combat zones to qualify for the foreign earned income exclusion even if their abode is in the United States. I.R.C. § 911(d)(3). *See* IR–2018–173.

(C) HOUSING COST AMOUNT

In addition to the exclusion for foreign earned income, a qualified U.S. taxpayer can "exclude" from gross income a housing cost amount. I.R.C. § 911(a)(2). The base housing amount used in calculating the foreign housing cost exclusion in a taxable year is 16 percent of the amount (computed on a daily basis) of the foreign earned income exclusion limitation (*i.e.*, $105,900 for 2019), multiplied by the number of days of foreign residence or presence in that year.

Reasonable foreign housing expenses in excess of the base housing amount remain excluded from gross income (or, if paid by the taxpayer, are deductible), but the amount of the exclusion is limited to 30 percent of the maximum amount of a taxpayer's foreign earned income exclusion. I.R.C. § 911(c)(2)(A). The IRS is given authority to issue regulations or other guidance providing for the adjustment of this 30 percent housing cost limitation based on geographic differences in housing costs relative to housing costs in the United States. Under the 30 percent rule, the maximum amount of the foreign housing cost exclusion in 2019 is (assuming foreign residence or presence on all days in the year) $14,826 (($105,900 × 30 percent) − ($105,900 × 16 percent)). Certain expenses are ineligible for the exclusion including the costs of purchasing a house or apartment, capital improvements, furniture, mortgage interest, property taxes, wages of housekeepers, gardeners or other laborers, and any costs that are lavish and extravagant. I.R.C. § 911(c)(3). While I.R.C. § 911 uses the term "exclusion," a taxpayer incurring qualifying housing expenses excludes from gross income the amount used by the taxpayer to pay the housing costs.

Where a U.S. taxpayer's employer provides a housing allowance, the housing cost amount can be excluded from gross income. A payment by an employer that is not denominated as a housing cost allowance can still be excluded from gross income under I.R.C. § 911(c). Where the employer does not provide a housing allowance, a qualified U.S. taxpayer can exclude (*i.e.*, deduct) the housing cost amount from gross income, but the exclusion is limited to the taxpayer's foreign earned income not already excluded. I.R.C. § 911(c)(4). Any excess housing cost may be carried forward one year only and deducted then subject to the same limitation.

§ 7.03   PARTICIPATION EXEMPTION

The limited exemption from the principle of worldwide taxation available to individuals in the form of the foreign earned income exclusion has a corporate counterpart enacted as part of TCJA in 2017. Under I.R.C. § 245A, U.S. corporate shareholders that own at least 10 percent of the stock of a foreign company can claim a 100 percent dividends received deduction for the foreign source portion of any dividend received from such company after December 31, 2017. No foreign tax credit is allowed for any dividend for which a deduction under I.R.C. § 245A may be claimed. To be able to claim the dividends received deduction, the shareholder generally must hold its stake in the foreign company for more than 365 days in the two-year period surrounding the dividend date.

The enactment by the United States of the participation exemption was touted as a significant move towards adoption of a territorial system. The reality is that this law change is likely to provide only limited benefits to U.S. residents with foreign business earnings.

Unlike some other participation exemption systems, the U.S. provision only applies to earnings generated by foreign corporations—there is no exemption for foreign branch earnings. There is also only a limited deduction available in the case of sale of foreign stock. And, the participation exemption only is available for corporate shareholders; the deduction is not available to individual owners of foreign companies. Because most of the earnings of controlled foreign companies will be subject to immediate tax in the hands of their U.S. shareholders (as discussed in Chapter 9), only a relatively small amount of the earnings of such companies is likely to be eligible for the deduction.

The dividends received deduction is not available for dividends from controlled foreign corporations that are "hybrid dividends," defined as any dividend for which the foreign company received a deduction or other tax benefit. I.R.C. § 245A(e). The legislative history explains that this rule is a response to international concerns regarding hybrid arrangements used to achieve double nontaxation. A taxpayer that receives a hybrid dividend is in a sense doubly penalized—not only is the dividend ineligible for the I.R.C. § 245A dividends received deduction, but this amount also can't be offset by a foreign tax credit for any taxes paid on the foreign earnings that generated the dividend.

The IRS issued proposed regulations on hybrid dividends in December 2018 (REG–104352–18,

2019–3 I.R.B. 35). Under these rules, a dividend is considered a hybrid dividend if it meets two criteria: the DRD would otherwise be allowed if not for the anti-hybrid rule, and the dividend is one for which the controlled foreign corporation (or a related person) is or was allowed a deduction or other tax benefit under a relevant foreign tax law. Under the proposed rules, notional deductions (such as deemed deductions on equity that some countries allow to equalize the treatment of debt and equity) are also considered hybrid deductions. The proposed regulations also contain rules requiring that U.S. shareholders maintain "hybrid deduction accounts" for each share of stock of a controlled foreign corporation held by a person that could claim the I.R.C. § 245A DRD upon a dividend paid by the controlled foreign corporation on the share.

In June 2019, the IRS issued temporary and final regulations under I.R.C. § 245A to address what it considered abusive transactions that resulted in tax-exempt dividends, namely transactions that could generate earnings that would not otherwise be subject to U.S. tax under one of the anti-deferral regimes but that could generate a tax-free dividend under I.R.C. § 245A. T.D. 9865. As of the date of publication, more general guidance interpreting I.R.C. § 245A has not yet been released.

§ 7.04   OVERSEAS SALES

(A) BACKGROUND

In 1962, Congress enacted the foreign base company rules in an effort to curtail the movement of U.S. export profits into foreign subsidiaries in tax haven jurisdictions (these "Subpart F" rules are discussed in greater detail in Chapter 9). From a tax perspective, enactment of this regime immediately made exporting more costly. In 1971, Congress enacted the domestic international sales corporation (DISC) legislation, the practical effect of which was to exempt a portion of U.S. exporters' profits by funneling export sales through a domestic subsidiary of the U.S. exporter.

The DISC framework angered U.S. trading partners and, following a decision by a panel established under the General Agreement on Tariffs and Trade that the DISC legislation constituted an illegal subsidy, was largely withdrawn in favor of the foreign sales corporation (FSC) legislation (but this process took years). Congress hoped that the FSC legislation would comply with international trade laws because of the statutorily required foreign character of the FSC.

From 1984 until late 2000, the United States offered its exporters a federal income tax subsidy for operating through foreign sales corporations. In 1999, a panel formed by the World Trade Organization held the FSC regime to be an unlawful subsidy. In 2000, the Appeals Body of the WTO confirmed the illegality of FSCs and required the United States to eliminate the subsidy.

Congress quickly fashioned a new law, embodied in the FSC Repeal and Extraterritorial Income Exclusion Act of 2000. It significantly changed how export sales were taxed by the creation of so-called "extraterritorial income." The practical outcome was a continuation of the FSC's benefits, now available under a new regime, intended to meet the WTO objections to the FSC.

This second replacement for the DISC—known as the extraterritorial income exclusion (ETI)—also underwent WTO review and was also deemed to constitute an illegal subsidy. In 2004, Congress replaced the ETI regime with another production incentive, not targeted to export sales. Instead, the incentive was available for domestic production irrespective of the final destination of the produced merchandise. I.R.C. § 199 allowed a deduction generally equal to a percentage of the qualified production activities income (QPAI) of the taxpayer for the taxable year, limited to 50 percent of the W-2 wages paid by the taxpayer.

The qualified domestic manufacturing deduction appeared immune to WTO challenge. But it was repealed for tax years beginning after December 31, 2017 as part of the TCJA. At the same time, Congress included in the TCJA a separate new provision intended to equalize the tax rate on profits earned by U.S. taxpayers selling overseas, regardless of whether the activities generating those profits were undertaken in the United States or overseas.

(B)   FOREIGN DERIVED INTANGIBLE INCOME

U.S. tax law and high U.S. corporate rates prior to enactment of TCJA encouraged U.S. taxpayers to offshore profitable intangibles to related foreign entities to try and achieve lower tax rates on the income generated by those intangibles. In enacting TCJA, Congress also wanted to reduce incentives for U.S. companies to move manufacturing overseas in order to take advantage of lower tax rates. To fulfill the goals of encouraging U.S. ownership of valuable intangible assets, new I.R.C. § 250 provides a special deduction for income defined as foreign derived intangible income. The deduction is currently equal to 37.5 percent of the foreign-derived intangible income of domestic companies, resulting in a corporate tax rate of 13.125 percent (the deduction is reduced, and so the tax rate goes up, after 2025).

Foreign derived intangible income (FDII) is intended as a proxy for income earned by domestic companies in excess of a fixed return on tangible assets located in the United States, derived from the sale of property (broadly defined as indicated in the definition of FDDEI below) sold to foreign persons for foreign use; income earned from services provided to non-U.S. persons or in connection with property located outside of the United States may also qualify.

The formula for determining FDII is as follows:

$$\text{FDII} = \begin{array}{c} \text{Deemed} \\ \text{Intangible} \\ \text{Income (DII)} \end{array} \times \frac{\begin{array}{c}\text{Foreign Derived} \\ \text{Deduction Eligible} \\ \text{Income (FDDEI)}\end{array}}{\begin{array}{c}\text{Deduction Eligible} \\ \text{Income (DEI)}\end{array}}$$

Taking apart all these acronyms, DEI is essentially a U.S. corporation's gross income, minus specific items of income such as subpart F and GILTI inclusions (discussed *infra* in Chapter 9), income from a foreign branch of a U.S. corporation, dividends from controlled foreign corporations, and a few other items.

FDDEI is a subset of DEI that is DEI income generally derived in connection with sales of property intended for foreign use, and services provided to any person, or with respect to property, not located within the United States. For this purpose, a 'sale' includes any lease, license, exchange, or other disposition. Special rules apply to sales or services provided to related parties.

Finally, DII is the excess of DEI over deemed tangible income return (DTIR) which is 10% × Qualified Business Asset Investment (QBAI)— essentially tangible business assets that generate deduction eligible income.

This alphabet soup may be slightly more palatable with an example. Suppose USCo has the following tax profile:

- Sales income to U.S. unrelated customers of $200

- Sales income to foreign unrelated customers for foreign use of $300

- Income generated in a branch of $50

- Income generated by a controlled foreign corporation (discussed *infra* in Chapter 8) of $100 that is immediately taxable in the hands of USCo even if not distributed

- No properly allocable expenses

- QBAI of $400

Based on this profile, the deduction under I.R.C. § 250 is computed as follows:

- DEI = Gross Income − Exclusions − Properly Allocable Deductions

  $650 Total Gross Income

  – $100 income from controlled foreign corporation

  – $50 Foreign Branch Income

  – $0 Properly Allocable Deductions

  – $500 DEI

- DII = $500 DEI − (10% × $400 QBAI) = $460

- FDDEI = $300

Therefore, FDII = $460 DII × $300 FDDEI / $500 DEI = $276 – the income that is deemed to be from intangibles that generate foreign income.

The U.S. tax on the FDII component of USCo's income is computed as follows:

- FDII = $276

- FDII Deduction: 37.5% × FDII = 37.5% × $276 = $103.5

- FDII less FDII Deduction: $276 – $103.50 = $172.50

- U.S. tax on FDII: 21% × $172.50 = $36.225

- U.S. Effective Tax Rate on FDII = 13.125% (36.225/276)

The I.R.C. § 250 deduction is only available for companies with positive taxable income. Proposed regulations issued in March 2019 (REG–104464–18, 84 F.R. 8188–8234) provide ordering rules for coordinating the I.R.C. § 250 taxable income limitation with the taxable income limitations of other Code provisions. The proposed regulations also provide rules as to the type of documentation required to substantiate whether sales of property are to foreign persons for a foreign use and that provisions of services are to persons, or are regarding property, located outside the United States. Many taxpayers have objected to these requirements as overly burdensome, and it is possible that they will be relaxed once the regulations are finalized.

As the latest chapter in a saga that many thought had ended in 2004, questions as to whether the FDII deduction would meet the United States' obligations under its trade agreements and tax treaty commitments began to be raised even before TCJA was passed. Is the deduction available under I.R.C. § 250 prompting taxpayers to repatriate intellectual property to the United States? The evidence has not yet borne that out.

CHAPTER 8

INTRODUCTION TO THE FOREIGN TAX CREDIT

§ 8.01 OVERVIEW

(A) RELIEVING DOUBLE TAXATION

Suppose that a U.S. taxpayer (individual or corporation) earns $100,000 of income in Germany. Assuming a flat 30 percent rate of taxation in the United States for illustration purposes (actual U.S. tax rates depend on who the taxpayer is and in the case of individuals how much the taxpayer earns), the U.S. taxpayer, taxable on worldwide income, potentially faces $30,000 in U.S. taxes. If Germany also taxes the income at a 30 percent rate, the taxpayer may pay an additional $30,000 in taxes. In effect, the U.S. taxpayer might pay taxes at a 60 percent rate before even considering any German or U.S. local taxes. If the taxpayer earns $100,000 in the United States, there is only a $30,000 tax liability (aside from state and local income taxes).

While it is apparent that there is international double taxation, it is not apparent what should be done to ameliorate the situation. There are many possibilities. First, perhaps nothing should be done—neither Germany nor the United States should make any adjustments. But this solution treats the U.S. taxpayer earning foreign source income inequitably when compared to a U.S. taxpayer earning U.S. source income. In addition to the issue of equity or fairness, the failure to relieve such double taxation may cause some taxpayers to structure their affairs to avoid producing income in Germany even though, in the absence of tax considerations, the German investment is more productive than a competing U.S. investment.

A second possibility is that Germany should do something—either exclude the income from its tax jurisdiction or give a credit for U.S. taxes paid thereby reducing German taxation to $0. This solution runs counter to a basic international tax principle—the country of source (*i.e.*, the place where income is earned) has taxing priority over the country of residence (*i.e.*, the place where the taxpayer resides). This international taxation principle recognizes that the source country's economic environment is likely to have played a larger role in the production of income than the economic environment of the residence state. If the income is earned in Germany, Germany has first crack at taxation, and if any adjustment is to be made, the United States as a residence country must make it.

A third possibility is for the United States as the country of residence to relieve the double taxation. The United States could meet this requirement in one of several ways. For example, the United States could allow the taxpayer a deduction for the income taxes paid to Germany just as a deduction would be allowed for any other reasonable cost of earning income in Germany. If a deduction were permitted, the U.S. taxpayer would still pay $30,000 in taxes to Germany, but for U.S. tax purposes the taxable income would be $100,000 minus $30,000, or $70,000 on which U.S. federal taxes would be $21,000. In total, national income taxes (*i.e.*, those of Germany and the United States) would be $51,000 which is less than a $60,000 tax liability if no deduction is permitted. Still, this would leave the taxpayer earning income in Germany paying an extra layer of taxes that a taxpayer earning income in the United States would not have to pay, undoubtedly deterring some taxpayers from making otherwise profitable investments in Germany.

Alternatively, the United States simply could exempt the German income from U.S. taxation. Under this approach, which is the prevailing approach among many countries, Germany would collect $30,000 in taxes and the United States $0 on the German income. The taxpayer would be equitably treated when compared with a U.S. taxpayer earning $100,000 in the United States, and a taxpayer debating an investment in the United States or the same one in Germany would not be influenced by the national income tax consequences. This is the approach taken by I.R.C. § 911 discussed in § 7.02 *supra* which permits a qualified individual to exclude a specified amount of foreign earned income. But suppose that Germany does not tax the income or taxes it at a rate less than 30 percent. In such a case, the U.S. taxpayer earning income in Germany is better off than a U.S. taxpayer earning the same income at home. In such a case, a pre-tax decision to invest in the United States rather than Germany might be reversed in light of the lower German taxes.

Concerned with this problem, the United States— which historically has been a relatively high-tax country—has adopted a tax credit rather than an exemption method for relieving double taxation. Under the tax credit method, the United States essentially taxes the $100,000 earned in Germany but allows a credit against the $30,000 U.S. tax liability for the income taxes paid to Germany on that income. If Germany taxes the income at a flat 30 percent rate, the taxpayer owes no U.S. taxes because the taxpayer credits the $30,000 in taxes paid to Germany against the $30,000 U.S. tax liability.

Note that to the extent foreign taxes are creditable against U.S. tax liability, a U.S. taxpayer may on one level be largely indifferent about the German taxes. The imposition of German taxes does not cost the taxpayer any additional money because the taxpayer would have paid the United States $30,000 in taxes if there were no German taxes. (All things being equal, U.S. taxpayers might prefer the tax money to go to the United States as between the United States and a foreign country.)

The tax credit method at this point may seem no different than if the U.S. taxpayer were allowed to exempt the German income, but there is an important difference. Suppose that the rate Germany imposes on the German income is only 10 percent so that the U.S. taxpayer pays $10,000 in taxes to Germany. Under an exclusion method, the United States would not tax the German income. But the tax credit method allows the United States to impose a $30,000 tax on the $100,000 of German income and then to allow a $10,000 foreign tax credit for the taxes paid to Germany. So the United States still collects $20,000 of tax revenue from the German income, and the overall tax burden on the U.S. taxpayer earning income abroad is not more favorable (as it would be under the exclusion method) than a U.S. taxpayer earning income in the United States.

Now suppose that the German tax rate is 50 percent and further assume that the U.S. taxpayer in addition to the $100,000 of German income has $100,000 of income earned in the United States. The German tax on the $100,000 of German income is $50,000. Assuming a 30 percent tax rate, the U.S. tax on the $200,000 of worldwide income is $60,000. If the United States grants a full foreign tax credit for the $50,000 German tax liability, the total U.S. tax actually paid by the taxpayer will be $10,000. It is true that the taxpayer's total income tax liability (*i.e.*, in Germany and the United States) is $60,000 ($50,000 paid to Germany and $10,000 paid to the United States) on $200,000 of total income just as it would be for a U.S. taxpayer earning $200,000 in the United States. However, if the $50,000 in German taxes is fully creditable, the U.S. taxpayer ends up paying $10,000 of U.S. taxes (instead of $30,000) on $100,000 of U.S. source income. In effect, taxes paid to Germany would reduce U.S. taxes on U.S. source income from 30 percent to 10 percent.

The U.S. tax system does not allow a foreign country's income taxes to reduce U.S. income taxes on U.S. source income. As explained in more detail *infra* in § 10.03, limitations are placed on the creditability of foreign income taxes. The U.S. taxpayer is allowed to credit only $30,000 of German taxes (*i.e.*, the German taxes can only offset the U.S. taxes on the $100,000 of German income). The taxpayer's total tax bill is $50,000 of German taxes and $30,000 of U.S. taxes (on the $100,000 of U.S. source income). To the extent that a U.S. taxpayer cannot credit foreign income taxes against U.S. income taxes on the same income, the foreign tax credit limitation takes away the neutrality a U.S. taxpayer may face in the decision of whether to invest in Germany or the United States. But the United States is unwilling to relieve double taxation that in its view is caused by unwarranted taxation by another country (or by the taxpayer's decision to generate income in a high-tax jurisdiction). Historically, foreign tax credits that were limited in this manner were available as credits in other years under a tax credit carryforward/carryback mechanism; the TCJA has introduced limitations on the carryforward and carryback for some types of credits (*See* § 10.02(B)).

In the situation where the taxpayer has excess foreign tax credits, international tax planning has historically focused on ways to turn the U.S. income into foreign source income. Suppose that the U.S. taxpayer was able to turn all of the U.S. source income into foreign source income in a manner that would not trigger any additional foreign tax. Now the taxpayer would have $200,000 of foreign source income. The potential U.S. tax is $60,000, but the taxpayer may qualify for a tax credit for the $50,000 tax paid in Germany. Notice that in this situation the

German tax would not be offsetting U.S. tax on U.S. source income. With the tax credit, the U.S. tax bill would be $10,000. The result is an overall tax bill of $60,000 rather than the $80,000 tax bill that existed before turning the U.S. source income into foreign source income. Changing the source of income from U.S. source to foreign source income in this case results in a tax savings.

How might a taxpayer and a tax advisor turn U.S. source income into foreign source income in a manner that does not trigger any additional foreign taxes? There are many ways this could occur. For example, suppose that the taxpayer was generating U.S. source income by selling purchased inventory to foreign customers with title passing in the United States. If the taxpayer transfers title abroad, the sales income will be foreign source income. I.R.C. § 861(a)(6). Changing where title passes normally will not affect how a foreign country taxes the sale. Another way to affect source of income would be to decrease expenses currently allocated and apportioned against foreign source income and have them allocated and apportioned against U.S. source income instead. In the example above, if $100,000 of expenses that were allocated and apportioned against the German source income were instead allocated and apportioned against the U.S. income, foreign source income would increase by $100,000 and U.S. source income would decrease by $100,000. Again, the U.S. rules would not impact how a foreign country taxes under its own set of rules.

While there are possible tax planning opportunities to maximize the use of excess foreign tax credits, source cannot be changed by merely waving a wand. Changing the source of income often will involve changes in the way business is conducted. Furthermore, tax planning is best done when business decisions are implemented in a tax-efficient manner rather than making business decisions merely to facilitate tax planning. Also as discussed below and in Chapter 10, the TCJA has significantly restricted the types of foreign tax credit planning opportunities previously available to taxpayers.

(B) THE STATUTORY FRAMEWORK

Section 901(a) authorizes the foreign tax credit subject to the limitations of I.R.C. § 904. The foreign tax credit is elective, and if the taxpayer elects to take the credit, no deduction for foreign taxes paid is available. I.R.C. § 275(a)(4)(A). In most circumstances, a taxpayer will elect to take a credit which offsets U.S. taxes dollar-for-dollar rather than a deduction which may only offset U.S. taxes by 30 cents for every dollar deducted if the tax rate is 30 percent. Of course if foreign taxes are not creditable, then the deduction under I.R.C. § 164(a)(3) becomes attractive. Also, a deduction may be preferable if a U.S. taxpayer has excess credits. For example, if T has $100 of U.S. source income, $100 of business income from country A (subject to a $30 country A income tax), and a $100 business loss from country B, no foreign tax credit can be taken because T has $0 foreign source income overall. However, if T deducts the $30 income tax paid to country A, then T's taxable income is reduced from $100 to $70. It should be noted that even in this situation, a credit may be preferable because of the ability to carry unused credits to other taxable years in many cases. I.R.C. § 904(c).

The credit is available for U.S. citizens and residents including U.S. corporations. I.R.C. § 901(b). Under some circumstances the credit is also available for nonresident aliens and foreign corporations engaged in a trade or business in the United States. I.R.C. § 906. The credit is available for foreign income taxes and for any other tax paid in lieu of an income tax. I.R.C. §§ 901(b) and 903.

Generally the taxpayer accounts for the foreign tax credit in a manner consistent with the taxpayer's method of accounting. However, I.R.C. § 905 permits a taxpayer to claim a foreign tax credit in the year the foreign taxes accrue even if the taxpayer is a cash basis taxpayer. The foreign tax credit provisions contain special rules for the treatment of taxes paid on certain types of income, notably oil and gas income. I.R.C. § 907.

Since 1918, the Code also permitted some shareholders to claim the benefit of an indirect credit upon the receipt of a dividend—a proportionate share of the foreign taxes accumulated (or "pooled) by the paying corporation relative to the percentage of the dividend to its earnings and profits, was considered paid at the time of the distribution. Section 902, the provision that allowed the indirect credit, was repealed by the TCJA. The principles of I.R.C. § 902 survive, however, in I.R.C. § 960, which grants shareholders an indirect credit upon an inclusion under either I.R.C. § 951 or I.R.C. § 951A. Chapter 10 discusses the indirect credit in greater detail.

§ 8.02   ELIGIBILITY

Under I.R.C. § 901(b), U.S. citizens and domestic corporations may credit income taxes paid to foreign countries, except that no credit is available for income taxes paid to any foreign country which the United States does not recognize, or maintain diplomatic relations with, or which provides support for acts of international terrorism. I.R.C. § 901(j). Resident aliens also are eligible for the foreign tax credit. However, I.R.C. § 901(c) authorizes the President to disallow the foreign tax credit to resident aliens who are citizens of a foreign country that does not allow U.S. citizens resident there a similar credit for taxes paid to the United States or other countries.

A foreign corporation or nonresident alien engaged in a trade or business in the United States is taxed on effectively connected income. I.R.C. §§ 871(b) or 882. *See* Chapter 4. It is possible that foreign source income may be effectively connected income. I.R.C. § 864(c)(4). For example, suppose that a Peruvian corporation engaged in a software licensing business in the United States licenses the use of computer software to a licensee in France. The Peruvian corporation may have foreign source royalty income that is subject to U.S. taxation as effectively connected income. I.R.C. § 864(c)(4)(B)(i). If France also taxes such income, the Peruvian corporation may be able to credit the French income taxes against U.S. taxes on the U.S. royalty income. I.R.C. § 906.

Any eligible taxpayer that is a member of a partnership or trust may claim as a credit a proportionate share of the qualifying foreign taxes paid by the entity. I.R.C. § 901(b)(5).

§ 8.03   CREDITABLE TAXES

In order for a taxpayer to receive a U.S. foreign tax credit for an amount paid to a foreign government, there are several requirements that must be met. Not all payments to a foreign government are creditable taxes. First, the foreign levy must be a tax, not a voluntary payment and not a payment for a specific right or service (*e.g.*, a royalty payment). Second, it may be necessary to determine whether the payment is a separate tax or part of a unified tax in order to evaluate creditability. Third, it is necessary to determine if the tax is an income tax when viewed through the lens of U.S. tax principles. Fourth, if the tax is not an income tax, it may still be creditable as an "in-lieu-of" tax under I.R.C. § 903. If a foreign levy is a creditable income tax, then it is necessary to determine who can claim the credit and what is the amount of the creditable tax that is paid.

(A)   IS THE FOREIGN LEVY A TAX?

Essentially, a tax is a forced payment collected by a governmental authority in exchange for a variety of governmental services (*e.g.*, roads, schools, national defense). If the payment is voluntary, it is not creditable. Reg. § 1.901–2(e)(5). A taxpayer must exhaust all effective and practical means of lowering foreign tax payments but need not tilt at windmills. For example, if the IRS makes a transfer pricing adjustment under I.R.C. § 482 that allocates income from a foreign subsidiary to a U.S. parent, the foreign subsidiary must try to reduce the foreign tax paid. Reg. § 1.901–2(e)(5)(ii) Exs. 2 and 3. *See Procter & Gamble Co. v. United States*, 2010–2 U.S. Tax Cas. (CCH) ¶ 50,593 (S.D. Ohio 2010), where the taxpayer failed to pursue whether under the U.S.-Japan treaty, Japan would be willing to reduce taxes it imposed on what Korea taxed as Korean source income. However, a taxpayer need not litigate a foreign tax liability if the taxpayer has obtained in good faith from a foreign tax advisor an opinion that litigation would be unsuccessful. Reg. § 1.901–2(e)(5)(i). *Compare Coca-Cola v. Commissioner*, 149 T.C. 446 (2017), which agreed with the taxpayer that its pursuit of a refund claim in Mexico would have been futile.

Even if a foreign levy is not voluntary, it will not be creditable unless it is a payment to a foreign government as a taxing authority. Reg. § 1.901–2(a)(2)(i). A thorny issue concerning creditability is whether a purported tax payment is in fact a payment for a "specific economic benefit" in which case it is not creditable. A tax payment theoretically is a payment in return for a variety of nonspecific government services (*e.g.*, national defense, use of the highways, national health care). The creditability regulations attempt to distinguish between this variety of broad government services and a payment for a specific economic benefit (*e.g.*, the right to extract oil from the ground). Reg. § 1.901–2(a)(2). The term "specific economic benefit" means an economic benefit that is not made substantially available on substantially the same terms to substantially all persons who are subject to the generally imposed income tax. Reg. § 1.901–2(a)(2)(ii).

In *Exxon Corp. v. Commissioner*, 113 T.C. 338 (1999), the Tax Court held that the U.K. Petroleum Revenue Tax (PRT) was a creditable foreign income tax—a conclusion that was affirmed in a related case by the Supreme Court in *PPL Corp. v. Commissioner*, 569 U.S. 329 (2013). The Tax Court determined that the PRT taken in its entirety did not constitute a royalty payment because the taxpayer did not receive any special benefit for paying the tax. Even though there was some evidence that the tax was imposed because the U.K. had earlier sold the right to explore in the North Sea for what in hindsight was a bargain price, the court did not regard the PRT as a delayed royalty payment.

In some cases, a U.S. taxpayer pays a foreign tax that includes a payment for a specific economic benefit as well as payment for general governmental services. For purposes of determining the amount creditable, the payment is bifurcated into two components: a noncreditable payment for a specific economic benefit and a creditable payment for the excess paid if the payment otherwise satisfies the creditability requirements. Reg. § 1.901–2(a)(2)(i). The taxpayer is referred to as a "dual capacity taxpayer." Reg. § 1.901–2A. A dual capacity taxpayer must establish the creditable portion of the payment under either the "facts and circumstances" method or the safe harbor method. The facts and circumstances method is exactly what it sounds like: if the taxpayer can establish that an otherwise creditable levy is not paid in exchange for a specific economic benefit, the payment is creditable. Reg. § 1.901–2A(c)(2).

The safe harbor method employs the following formula to determine the creditable portion of a levy paid by a dual capacity taxpayer:

$$(A - B - C) \times \frac{D}{1 - D}$$

where:

A = gross receipts

B = expenses computed under the general foreign income tax rules

C = the total "tax" paid by the dual capacity taxpayer

D = the general tax rate

To understand the formula, consider the following example. Country X imposes a levy on every corporation doing business in Country X on 40 percent of its Country X net business income. Net income is computed under U.S. tax principles except that a corporation engaged in mineral exploitation in Country X is not permitted to recover its exploration expenditures. Mineral deposits in Country X are owned by the government which exacts a royalty in exchange for the mining privilege. Assuming that the nonrecovery of exploration expenses does not render the entire income tax noncreditable, a taxpayer engaged in mining is a dual capacity taxpayer paying a general income tax and a levy for the right to extract minerals. For the taxable year in question, USCo, a U.S. corporation engaged in a trade or business in Country X, has gross receipts of $120,000, deductible general business expenses of $20,000 and a tax liability of $40,000. In addition, USCo incurs exploration expenses that would be deductible under normal U.S. income tax principles of $30,000.

Under the safe harbor method, USCo's creditable income tax would be $20,000 (($120,000 − $50,000 − $40,000) × .40 divided by (1 − .40)) and the other $20,000 would be treated as a payment for a specific economic benefit. Stated differently, if Country X had allowed normal deductions, USCo would have only paid $20,000 of income tax at a 40 percent rate on net income of $120,000 minus $20,000 of general business expenses minus $30,000 of exploration expenses minus $20,000 paid for a specific economic benefit.

(B) IS THE TAX A SEPARATE TAX OR PART OF A BROADER TAX?

If the levy in question is determined to be a tax, it is necessary to ascertain whether the tax stands alone or is part of a broader tax. For example, suppose that a U.S. taxpayer is subject to a foreign tax on the gross revenues resulting from sales in that foreign country. Viewed as a tax in and of itself, the tax on gross sales revenue may not qualify as a creditable income tax if no allowance is made for the cost of goods sold. However, if the levy is deemed to be part of an overall tax system that viewed in its entirety is a creditable income tax for U.S. tax purposes, then the levy may be creditable. Conversely, suppose that a U.S. taxpayer pays a foreign tax, based on the net sales income generated in the foreign country. Viewed as a separate tax, the levy may be a creditable income tax. However, if the levy is deemed to be part of an overall tax that has other features that render the tax not creditable against U.S. tax liability, the levy on net sale income will not be a creditable tax.

The creditability of a tax is determined by looking at all taxpayers subject to the tax rather than on a taxpayer-by-taxpayer basis. Reg. § 1.901–2(a)(1). In determining whether a levy is a separate tax or part of a broader tax, the regulations offer several general principles. Reg. § 1.901–2(d)(1). The determination of whether a levy is a separate levy or part of a broader levy is made by looking at U.S. rather than foreign tax principles. Foreign labeling is not relevant. A levy imposed by one taxing authority (*e.g.*, national government) is always separate from a levy imposed by another taxing authority (*e.g.*, local government). A levy is a separate levy if the tax base differs in kind for different classes of taxpayers. For example, a gross base withholding tax on nonresidents is a separate tax from a net income tax on residents. Similarly a gross base withholding tax imposed on nonresidents is a separate tax from a net business tax imposed on nonresidents. Reg. § 1.901–2(d)(3) Ex. 2.

(C)   IS THE TAX AN INCOME TAX?

Because the foreign tax credit is aimed at preventing international double taxation of income, the only payment allowed as a tax credit against U.S. income tax liability is a foreign *income* tax under I.R.C. § 901. Foreign taxes that are income taxes in the U.S. sense can qualify for a tax credit even if imposed by a political subdivision or local authority of a foreign country. By contrast, U.S. state and local taxes are not creditable, but can only be deducted (and not in all circumstances).

Foreign taxes that are not income taxes in a U.S. sense may be deductible for U.S. tax purposes under I.R.C. § 164(a)(3). The issue of what constitutes a creditable foreign income tax is a difficult one. Countries implement all manner of user fees, royalty payments, and profit-splitting arrangements which are sometimes difficult to distinguish from an income tax. Even an exaction that looks like an income tax may not really be an income tax because the tax revenue is rebated to the taxpayer, or the taxpayer receives a direct or indirect subsidy from the government.

The Code provides little guidance as to what constitutes a creditable income tax. The regulations issued by the IRS labor mightily to distinguish an income tax from other payments. Essentially, the regulations provide that a foreign tax is creditable only if its "predominant character . . . is that of an income tax in the U.S. sense." Stated differently, in order to be creditable, a foreign tax must be "likely to reach net gain." Reg. §§ 1.901–2(a)(1)(ii) and (3)(i).

A foreign tax is considered "likely to reach net gain" if it satisfies three requirements: realization, gross receipts, and net income. The "realization" requirement is met, if on the basis of its predominant character, a foreign tax is imposed only upon, or subsequent to, the occurrence of an event that would result in realization under the Code. Reg. § 1.901–2(b)(2). For example, a foreign tax that is generally imposed on mere asset appreciation prior to a sale or other disposition probably would not be creditable. It is possible for a foreign tax imposed prior to a realization event to be creditable if the foreign country does not tax the same income again upon realization, and either the imposition of the tax is based on the difference in property values during the taxable year or the pre-realization event is the physical transfer of inventory. In addition, pre-realization taxation may be creditable if the income taxed is recapture income from deductions (or credits) previously taken by the taxpayer. For example, suppose that a taxpayer purchases an asset for $10,000 and is permitted a depreciation deduction of $3,000 thereby reducing the basis to $7,000 while the fair market value of the property remains at $10,000. A foreign tax on $3,000 of recapture income imposed prior to a sale or disposition does not disqualify a foreign tax from being creditable.

The "gross receipts" requirement is satisfied if the foreign tax uses a tax base of gross receipts from the disposition of property, or if there is no disposition, or the disposition is between related parties, the tax base is computed under a method that is likely not to exceed the fair market value of the property involved. Reg. § 1.901–2(b)(3). For example, a foreign tax based on the assumption that gross receipts from extraction income equal 105 percent of the fair market value of petroleum extracted would not be creditable if the tax is designed to produce an amount that is greater than actual gross receipts. However, if a tax not based on gross receipts is intended to reach the same tax base, it may be creditable. For example, suppose that country A imposes a "headquarters tax" on the country A branch of a U.S. corporation equal to 110 percent of expenses where the branch manages the business activities of the U.S. corporation and its related corporations. If the tax is imposed because of the difficulties of measuring the actual gross receipts of the branch from its management activities, and the headquarters tax base is not likely to be greater than actual gross receipts, the tax may be creditable.

The "net income" requirement is satisfied if a foreign tax is computed by reducing gross receipts by the costs of producing the income (including capital expenditures) determined under "reasonable principles." Reg. § 1.901–2(b)(4). A foreign tax law is deemed to permit the recovery of significant costs even if there are timing differences when compared with U.S. law unless the timing differences effectively deny the deduction. For example, expenses that are deducted under U.S. tax principles may be capitalized under foreign tax principles and recovered on a recurring basis over time or upon the occurrence of a future event (*e.g.*, a sale). Such treatment would not endanger the creditability of a foreign income tax unless the delayed recovery was tantamount to a denial (*e.g.*, capitalization of a U.S.-deductible expense over 100 years). Even if a foreign tax law does not permit the recovery of a significant cost, the tax may be creditable if there is an allowance that effectively compensates for the denial.

While the net income requirement is aimed at producing a tax base similar to that under U.S. tax principles, in some rare circumstances a foreign tax whose base is gross receipts may still be creditable if the tax is almost certain to reach some net gain because the expenses of producing income will almost never be so high as to offset gross receipts. Reg. § 1.901–2(b)(4). For example, suppose a foreign tax is imposed at a 30 percent rate on gross wages earned by an employee with no employee deductions permitted. Because the expenses of employees attributable to wage income are almost always insignificant compared to the gross wages realized, employees subject to the tax are almost certain to have net gain. Accordingly, the tax would satisfy the net income requirement. Reg. § 1.901–2(b)(4) Ex. 3. Gross base withholding taxes similar in nature to the U.S. withholding tax with respect to dividends, interest, rents, royalties and other fixed and determinable annual periodical income can be creditable income taxes. *Bank of America National Trust & Savings Ass'n v. United States*, 459 F.2d 513 (Cl. Ct. 1972).

In some cases, a tax that does not appear to reach net income on its face nevertheless may be a creditable income tax. In *PPL Corp. v. Commissioner*, 569 U.S. 329 (2013), the Supreme Court after reviewing and discussing the I.R.C. § 901 requirements held that a U.K. windfall tax on excess profits was a creditable foreign income tax. The Court determined that the tax taken in its entirety was an income tax even though it was nominally based on the difference between the company's valuation based on purchase price and subsequent performance and on its face did not appear to tax net profits or to meet other income tax criteria. The court found that the difference between the two different valuations was based on net income.

In determining whether a foreign tax satisfies the net income requirement, one of the factors taken into account is whether a loss in one activity (*e.g.*, a contract involving oil and gas exploration) in a trade or business is allowed to offset profits in another activity (*e.g.*, a separate contract) in the same trade or business. If an offset is allowed, it need not be in the same taxable period in order to insure creditability. Furthermore, the fact that no offset is allowed against a different activity in a trade or business does not defeat creditability if an offset is allowed against profitable activity of the same contract in another taxable period. It is not necessary that a foreign tax permit an offset against profits from a different trade or business or profits from investment activity or that losses be allowed to offset profits from related entities in order for a foreign tax to be creditable. Reg. § 1.901–2(b)(4)(ii).

A foreign tax that otherwise might satisfy the creditability requirements is nevertheless not creditable if the tax is designed to tax U.S. residents or citizens only to the extent each $1 of foreign tax reduces U.S. tax liability by $1 (*i.e.*, a "soak-up" tax). For example, a foreign tax that is only imposed if, or to the extent that, it is creditable against U.S. taxes would not be a creditable tax. Reg. § 1.901–2(c). This type of selective tax whose application is dependent on U.S. creditability, like those foreign taxes permitting rebates or which directly subsidize the taxpayer, is not creditable because it is not an income tax in the U.S. sense.

The question of whether another country's tax should be considered an income tax in the U.S. sense is an ever-recurring topic. Consider some recent examples. Beginning in 2011, U.S. companies doing business in Puerto Rico are subject to a 4 percent excise tax on purchases from their Puerto Rican affiliates (over a certain size). An excise tax wouldn't appear to meet the criteria for a tax on net income, but the IRS has said that pending resolution of the issue, it will not challenge any taxpayer's position that this tax paid is a tax in lieu of an income tax described in I.R.C. § 903, and that if it ever determines that the Puerto Rican excise tax is not a creditable tax, the decision will not be retroactive. Notice 2011–29, 2011–16 I.R.B. 663. Puerto Rico's troubled economy may have had something to do with the IRS' leniency here.

In 2015, the United Kingdom enacted a new tax known as a "diverted profits tax" targeted at companies that had "diverted" their profits from the U.K. to lower taxed jurisdictions. Such tax was described in a N.Y. State Bar Association report (that did not explicitly call out the DPT by name) as a tax that would enable the U.K. to tax persons that lack connections to it traditionally recognized as a basis for asserting taxing jurisdiction. The N.Y. State Bar requested that the IRS issue guidance as to whether such types of taxes may be creditable, but to date the IRS has not done so.

In July 2019, France enacted a "digital services tax," which is a tax imposed on the gross revenues of certain types of revenue streams generated by multinational companies of sufficient size. Such a tax on gross revenues wouldn't appear not to meet the definition of a tax on net income as described in the regulations under I.R.C. § 901. *But see* Reg. § 1.901–2(b)(4)(i)(B).

(D) TAXES IN LIEU OF AN INCOME TAX

In some cases, a tax that does not qualify as a creditable foreign income tax may nevertheless be creditable as an "in-lieu-of" tax under I.R.C. § 903 if the tax is imposed in lieu of a tax on income that is generally imposed. In order for a tax to qualify as an in-lieu-of tax, the foreign country must have a general income tax law that would apply to the taxpayer but for the in-lieu-of tax, and the general income tax is not imposed on the taxpayer because of the in-lieu-of tax. Reg. § 1.903–1(a)(2) and (b). However, to qualify for a foreign tax credit, the taxpayer cannot be subject to the general income tax and subject to the in-lieu-of tax.

It is not a requirement that the in-lieu-of tax be imposed because of administrative difficulty in applying the generally imposed income tax. Reg. § 1.903–1(a). Nor is the base of the in-lieu-of tax required to be net income in order for the imposition to be creditable. There is also no requirement that the burden of the in-lieu-of tax be the same as or less than the tax burden that would have resulted under the generally imposed income tax. Reg. § 1.903–1(b). However, a "soak-up" in-lieu-of tax, like a soak-up income tax, will not be creditable. Reg. § 1.903–1(b)(2).

As an example of an in-lieu-of tax, suppose that Country X has a tax that is generally imposed on realized net income of nonresident corporations attributable to a trade or business carried on in Country X. The tax applies to all nonresident corporations, except that corporations engaged in the insurance business are subject to a charge on gross receipts. The tax applicable to nonresident corporations engaged in insurance activities would satisfy the in-lieu-of requirement. Reg. § 1.903–1(b)(1).

A gross base income tax imposed on nonresidents as a substitute for a general comprehensive net base income tax applicable to residents qualifies as an in-lieu-of tax that is creditable. Reg. § 1.903–1(b)(3) Ex. 1. Accordingly, a withholding tax on dividends, interest, and royalties imposed by a foreign country similar to the tax imposed by I.R.C. §§ 871(a) and 881 would qualify as an in-lieu-of tax and is creditable in the United States.

(E)　WHO CAN CLAIM THE FOREIGN TAX CREDIT?

Under I.R.C. § 901(b), U.S. citizens, residents and domestic corporations are entitled to a foreign tax credit. A U.S. partner in a partnership (or a beneficiary in an estate or trust) can claim a credit for a proportionate share of foreign tax paid by the entity. I.R.C. §§ 901(b)(5) (individual partners) and 702(a)(6) (corporations). Also, nonresidents that are subject to U.S. tax on income effectively connected with the conduct of a U.S. trade or business may be able to credit foreign taxes paid with respect to that income. I.R.C. § 906.

Sometimes it is not clear who the taxpayer is with respect to a foreign tax payment. Suppose that U.S. resident R owns a foreign entity E located in country E that is treated for U.S. tax purposes as a corporation but is treated as a transparent, pass-through entity by country E. If country E imposes a tax on R resulting from the activities of E, who is deemed to pay the tax—E, the person that the United States considers as the income earner or R, the person country E considers to be the income earner? The regulations consider the taxpayer of a foreign tax to be the person on whom foreign law imposes legal liability for tax. Reg. § 1.901–2(f)(1). This is known as the "technical taxpayer" rule. Yet, the longstanding case of *Biddle v. Commissioner*, 302 U.S. 573 (1938) is often cited for the proposition that U.S. rather than foreign standards apply in determining U.S. tax consequences.

A taxpayer who is legally liable for a foreign tax that is paid is deemed to pay the tax even if the payment is made by someone else. Reg. § 1.901–2(f)(2). Moreover, even if the foreign government itself assumes the responsibility for a U.S. taxpayer's foreign tax, a credit may be available if the government's assumption of the tax liability is compensation for services rendered or goods sold or leased to the government by the U.S. taxpayer. This Regulation permits a U.S. taxpayer to enter into a "net contract" with a foreign government that assures a taxpayer a fixed after-tax contract price for services rendered or goods sold or leased to the foreign government. *Amoco Corp. v. Commissioner*, 138 F.3d 1139 (7th Cir. 1998). Any tax liability that is assumed by another party (*e.g.*, a foreign government) is considered income for U.S. tax purposes. Reg. § 1.901–2(f)(2)(ii).

Suppose USCo owns all of the "stock" in ForCo1 which is a disregarded entity for U.S. tax purposes but a corporation for Country X purposes. ForCo1 owns all of stock of ForCo2, a regarded Country X corporation. ForCo1 and ForCo2 form a Country X consolidated group. Under Country X law, the parent of the consolidated group is responsible for any taxes on group income. Suppose that ForCo2 earns $100 and Country X imposes an income tax of $30 on ForCo1. Does that mean that USCo can take a tax credit for the taxes imposed on disregarded ForCo1 (and potentially utilize that credit to offset U.S. tax on some other foreign source income that USCo has generated)? Reg. § 1.901–2(f)(3) essentially aligns the tax with the underlying income within a consolidated group regardless of who the technical taxpayer is under local law. So in this example the taxes would be deemed to reside at ForCo2 and would be available, and creditable under I.R.C. § 960, only to the extent they are attributable to income USCo is required to include under the rules of I.R.C. §§ 951 and 951A.

(F) WHEN CAN THE FOREIGN TAX CREDIT BE CLAIMED?

Before the enactment of the TCJA, the government wrestled mightily with how to curtail planning involving structures that permitted U.S. shareholders to claim a foreign tax credit before taking the associated income into account. Congress enacted I.R.C. § 909 in order to address such situations where the foreign tax credits had been made available to a U.S. taxpayer, but the underlying income was not yet subject to U.S. tax. Under I.R.C. § 909, if there is a foreign tax credit splitting event with respect to a foreign income tax paid or accrued by a taxpayer, such tax is not taken into account for federal tax purposes before the taxable year in which the related income is taken into account by the taxpayer—that is, the split tax is suspended. The rule was aimed at limiting taxpayers' ability to use foreign tax credits on income not yet taxable in the United States to offset U.S. tax on other foreign source income of the U.S. taxpayer.

Section 909 does not suspend foreign income taxes if the same person pays the tax but takes into account the related income in a different taxable period (or periods) due to, for example, timing differences between the U.S. and foreign tax accounting rules.

As with a number of other anti-abuse provisions that have been enacted over the past several decades, I.R.C. § 909 remains in the Code but has less continued relevance given that the TCJA eliminated many of the planning opportunities previously available to taxpayers that allowed them to defer income but accelerate credits. *See* § 9.04.

(G) WHAT IS THE AMOUNT OF THE CREDITABLE FOREIGN INCOME TAX?

Even if a foreign income tax satisfies the realization, gross proceeds, and net income requirements, an amount paid to a foreign government is not creditable to the extent that it is reasonably certain that the amount will be refunded, credited, rebated or forgiven. Reg. § 1.901–2(e)(2). For example, a U.S. taxpayer subject to a 30 percent withholding tax by country X on a dividend payment may not claim a credit for the withholding if pursuant to the U.S.-X income tax treaty the taxpayer can file a refund claim. Reg. § 1.901–2(e)(2)(ii) Ex. 1.

If a foreign government either directly or indirectly returns a portion of a tax payment as a subsidy, the tax payment to the extent of the subsidy is not creditable. I.R.C. § 901(i). For example, suppose Brazil imposes a 30 percent tax on interest paid from a Brazilian borrower to a foreign lender. A Brazilian borrower pays $100,000 in interest to a U.S. lender of which $30,000 is withheld for payment to the government. If the government either rebates the $30,000 to the lender or to the Brazilian borrower, the tax is not creditable. The U.S. lender who receives $70,000 of net income would be willing to include an extra $30,000 of income in order to receive a $30,000 tax credit. The "extra" $30,000 inclusion would result in an additional $6300 of U.S. tax if the lender pays taxes at a 21 percent rate. However, a $30,000 tax credit, if available, would provide a dollar-for-dollar offset against U.S. tax liability that would not only offset any additional tax but may effectively decrease U.S. tax on the taxpayer's other foreign source income. Similarly, if a tax payment is directly linked to a government subsidy (*e.g.*, the government provides office space to the lender), the tax is not creditable.

Suppose foreign government F imposes both a noncreditable tax based on asset value (assets tax) and a creditable income tax. Suppose further that the assets tax is allowed as a credit against the income tax. If a U.S. taxpayer has a $4,000 assets tax liability and a $10,000 income tax liability, the taxpayer can take a credit for $6,000. Reg. § 1.901–2(e)(4) and Reg. § 1.903–1(b)(3) Ex. 5. If the rule in country F is that a taxpayer pays whichever is greater, the assets tax or the income tax, then the taxpayer could take a $10,000 foreign tax credit. If the rule in country F is that a taxpayer pay whichever is less, then the taxpayer could take no credit.

Under some circumstances, a tax that qualifies as a creditable foreign tax may not be fully creditable and may be permanently disallowed when there is a base difference with respect to the amount of taxable income in a foreign country resulting from inconsistent views of asset basis. To illustrate, suppose that USCo buys the "stock" of a German disregarded entity for $150 million. From a U.S. perspective, USCo has bought the underlying assets for $150 million, but for German purposes, USCo has bought stock and the basis of the underlying assets carries over. This may lead to a situation where for U.S. purposes, the basis of the assets is $150 million but for German purposes the basis of the assets is, for example, $120 million. Assume that the property purchased is amortizable both in Germany and U.S. over 15 years (*e.g.*, goodwill or other intangibles). For U.S. tax purposes the annual amortization would be $10 million but for German purposes, the amortization would be $8 million. Holding all else constant, the German taxable income each year will be $2 million less under U.S. law than under German law. The "policy" behind I.R.C. § 901(m) is that if there is $2 million of German phantom income from a U.S. perspective, then the German tax on that "phantom income" (*e.g.*, $600,000 assuming a 30 percent German tax rate) should not be creditable in the United States. From a U.S. perspective, there is no income to the extent offset by the excess amortization deduction allowed under U.S. law, and therefore no German tax credit for German taxes imposed on that "phantom income."

Under I.R.C. § 901(m), certain foreign income taxes paid or accrued on "covered asset acquisition" (CAA) transactions may be permanently disallowed. These transactions are targeted by I.R.C. § 901(m) because they result in stepped-up bases in assets that are eligible for cost recovery for U.S. tax purposes, without a corresponding increase to tax basis for foreign tax purposes. For example, when a taxpayer makes an election under I.R.C. § 338(g) as part of a qualified stock purchase of a foreign target, the target is treated as having sold its assets to a new foreign target for fair market value. The deemed asset acquisition treatment also results in the new foreign target taking a cost-basis in the assets deemed purchased from the target. However, because the election is only relevant for U.S. purposes, there is no corresponding increase to the target's asset-basis for foreign tax purposes. The difference may result in a permanent difference in the amounts available for cost-recovery deduction for U.S. and foreign tax purposes.

Two of the most common events that trigger I.R.C. § 901(m) are the purchase of stock in a disregarded foreign entity and an I.R.C. § 338(g) election. But any transaction that gives rise to an asset basis difference may be problematic. Where I.R.C. § 901(m) applies, the disqualified portion of any foreign taxes paid are deductible for U.S. tax purposes.

Proposed Regulations issued by the IRS in 2016 expand the description of CAAs provided in the statute to include any transaction treated as an acquisition of assets for both U.S. and foreign income tax purposes, provided the transaction results in an increase in the U.S. basis of the assets without a corresponding increase in the foreign tax basis. The proposed regulations also include a *de minimis* rule, generally providing that so long as the basis difference is less than $10 million or 10 percent of the total U.S. tax basis in a transaction, the rules of I.R.C. § 901(m) won't apply. REG–129128–14, 2016–8 I.R.B. 356. The *de minimis* exception saves taxpayers from having to maintain extensive and elaborate records for purposes of complying with I.R.C. § 901(m).

§ 8.04   COMPUTING THE DIRECT CREDIT

The computation of the direct foreign tax credit under I.R.C. § 901 is not complicated. If a taxpayer pays a creditable foreign income tax of $15,000 and the taxpayer's U.S. income tax liability before the foreign tax credit is $60,000, the taxpayer only pays $45,000 to the U.S. government. The credit reduces U.S. tax liability dollar-for-dollar. However, it is important to note that the tax credit permitted under I.R.C. § 901 is subject to the limitations under I.R.C. § 904, discussed *supra* and in greater detail in § 10.03. Without additional information concerning the nature and source of the income that generated the foreign tax, the amount of the foreign tax credit permitted for a particular taxable year cannot be determined.

§ 8.05   TAX REDETERMINATIONS

It is not uncommon that in a year after a U.S. taxpayer takes a foreign tax credit, the foreign taxing authority may redetermine the foreign taxes. For example, an audit may require additional taxes due or perhaps the taxpayer receives a tax refund. In some cases, the amount of foreign taxes paid for U.S. tax purposes changes because of currency fluctuations between the time of accrual and that of payment. Section 905(c) addresses tax redeterminations. It will come as no surprise that the rules are quite intricate, but essentially they operate as follows. Any redetermination that affected a direct tax (*e.g.*, a withholding tax or taxes imposed on a foreign branch of a U.S. corporation) requires a U.S. taxpayer to file an amended return to reflect the redetermination. Under prior law, any redetermination that affected an indirect tax under I.R.C. § 902 (*e.g.*, a foreign subsidiary assessed a higher income tax; a subsidiary received a refund; currency fluctuations resulted in a difference between the dollar value of accrued and paid taxes), generally was taken into account prospectively by making the appropriate change to the tax pools of the foreign company. In conjunction with the repeal of I.R.C. § 902 by the TCJA, I.R.C. § 905(c) was also amended. It now provides that any taxes not paid within 2 years after the close of the taxable year to which those taxes relate shall be taken into account in the year in which those taxes relate. These changes raise new questions, such as: What happens with respect to taxes that are only redetermined after the U.S. statute of limitations has expired (unfortunately not an uncommon situation in many foreign countries).

Treasury has yet to issue regulatory guidance on amended I.R.C. § 905(c) addressing the many questions that taxpayers have regarding how to make adjustments or claim credits in the case of foreign tax adjustments in a post-TCJA world.

§ 8.06   EFFECT OF TREATIES ON THE FOREIGN TAX CREDIT

To have trudged through the rules governing the foreign tax credit only to learn that the rules do not apply to income from and taxes paid to U.S. treaty partners would be cruel indeed. But not surprisingly, U.S. bilateral income tax treaties do address the crediting of foreign income taxes. For example, in the U.S. Model Treaty, Article 23 provides relief from double taxation generally in accordance with U.S. domestic law rules governing relief from double taxation. However, treaty relief from double taxation under some treaties may be more favorable for a taxpayer than under U.S. domestic law rules providing relief from double taxation (*e.g.*, the source rules used in limiting the foreign tax credit may provide the taxpayer a larger foreign tax credit under the treaty than under U.S. domestic law). Where treaty resourcing rules permit a foreign tax credit that would not be available under U.S. domestic law, the item of income is put in a separate treaty basket to prohibit any cross-crediting of taxes. I.R.C. § 904(d)(6).

CHAPTER 9

TAXATION OF U.S. PERSONS' FOREIGN INCOME EARNED IN CORPORATE FORM

§ 9.01   OVERVIEW

For the past 100 years, the U.S. has had a worldwide system of taxation, meaning that if a U.S. taxpayer conducted business abroad, the earnings of the foreign business were taxable in the U.S.—either immediately, in the case of a foreign business conducted directly or through a branch, or when those earnings were repatriated to the U.S. via a dividend, in the case of a foreign business conducted through a corporation. (The U.S. tax imposed on that foreign-earned income might be reduced by any applicable foreign tax credit.) The TCJA upended this system in two important ways: First, as discussed in Chapter 7, *supra*, dividends paid to 10 percent U.S. shareholders that are corporations from specified foreign companies now may be entitled to a 100 percent dividends received deduction. I.R.C. § 245A. Second, most of the earnings of controlled foreign companies (a term described in § 9.02) are now subject to tax under I.R.C. § 951A, as global intangible low-taxed income (GILTI) in the hands of their U.S. shareholders, albeit at a reduced rate of taxation. This means that there is much less benefit for U.S. taxpayers from deferring the repatriation of their foreign earnings. At the same time, the tax imposed by I.R.C. § 951A diminishes the relevance of the dividends received deduction.

The statutory requirement to include GILTI of controlled foreign corporations in income is located in a part of the Code known as subpart F. The subpart F regime as enacted in 1962 was intended to prevent U.S. taxpayers from shifting mobile income to low-taxed jurisdictions that could allow for what Congress viewed as inappropriate deferral of U.S. taxation on this income. Until enactment of TCJA in 2017, the subpart F rules generally did not try to impose current U.S. tax at the U.S. shareholder level on the profits of active business operations conducted by a controlled foreign corporation earned from dealing with unrelated parties.

The GILTI provision (I.R.C. § 951A), which sits within subpart F of the Code, significantly broadens the old subpart F regime. In effect, it imposes current U.S. tax on U.S. shareholders on most of the earnings of controlled foreign corporations, by requiring an inclusion at the U.S. shareholder level of all of the earnings of controlled foreign companies in excess of a fixed return on tangible assets, subject to specific exclusions. The rules of subpart F that international tax experts were required to master for the past 50 years were already complex; GILTI—regulations interpreting which are still in the process of being written by the Treasury—increases that complexity many multiples over. There are also discrepancies between the GILTI rules and the historical subpart F rules that raise significant and challenging questions about how to interpret the new provisions.

Much time and energy of international tax practitioners prior to enactment of the TCJA was spent on ensuring that a U.S. taxpayer's controlled foreign subsidiaries would not generate subpart F income, which would subject that income to immediate U.S. tax. The TCJA upended this calculation as well, with an inclusion of subpart F income in some cases now being more preferable to U.S. shareholders than an inclusion of GILTI. This analysis has to do with how foreign tax credit applies to GILTI as compared to subpart F income, a topic that is discussed in detail in Chapter 10.

§ 9.02 DEFINITIONS

In order for an inclusion under subpart F to be triggered, there must be a CFC (controlled foreign corporation). A foreign corporation is a CFC if "U.S. shareholders" own more than 50 percent of the total combined voting power of its stock or more than 50 percent of the stock's total value. I.R.C. § 957(a). A "U.S. shareholder" is defined as a U.S. person (a term defined in I.R.C. § 957(c)) owning at least 10 percent or more of the total combined vote or value of the corporate stock. I.R.C. § 951(b) (note that prior to enactment of the TCJA, the definition of a U.S. shareholder was limited to persons owning 10 percent voting stock; ownership of non-voting stock was irrelevant for this purpose). If 11 unrelated U.S. individuals own equal interests in a foreign corporation, the corporation is not a CFC because each shareholder owns less than a 10 percent interest. Such a corporation would have no U.S. shareholders. If the same 11 individuals are partners in a U.S. partnership that owns 100 percent of the corporation, the corporation would be a CFC because a U.S. partnership is a U.S. shareholder that owns more that 50 percent of the stock of the corporation.

A foreign corporation with ten equal unrelated U.S. individual shareholders is a CFC. On the other hand, if one shareholder owns 50 percent and the other nine own the remaining 50 percent equally, the corporation is not a CFC because U.S. shareholders (*i.e.*, 10 percent shareholders) do not own *more* than 50 percent of the corporation's stock. Notice that if a U.S. shareholder and a foreign shareholder enter into a foreign joint venture conducted through a foreign corporate entity with each participant owning precisely 50 percent of the vote and value of the entity, the entity will not be a CFC.

In testing whether a foreign corporation is a CFC, the Code looks to direct and indirect ownership and to constructive ownership. I.R.C. §§ 957(a) and 958. Suppose that the voting stock of a foreign corporation is owned equally by six U.S. individuals and six foreign corporations (each corporation's stock being owned by one of the six individuals). Each of the twelve shareholders holds directly an 8 $\frac{1}{3}$ percent interest in the foreign corporation and so it appears that there are no U.S. shareholders. However, because the six individuals are deemed to own indirectly the stock owned by their wholly-owned corporations, each individual is deemed to be a 16 $\frac{2}{3}$ percent shareholder and therefore a U.S. shareholder. I.R.C. §§ 957 and 958(a)(2). Because the U.S. shareholders own more than 50 percent of the stock of the foreign corporation (*i.e.*, they own 100 percent), the foreign corporation is a CFC. Similarly, when foreign partnerships or trusts own shares in foreign corporations, it is necessary to attribute the entity's ownership of the shares to the partners or beneficiaries.

Apart from indirect ownership, a U.S. person is deemed constructively to own stock owned by certain related persons. I.R.C. § 958(b). For example, if Parent owns 9 percent of the voting stock of a foreign corporation and Child owns 4 percent, Parent is a U.S. shareholder for purposes of deciding whether the foreign corporation is a CFC. Child is also a U.S. shareholder, but stock cannot be counted twice in determining whether the foreign corporation is a CFC. The constructive ownership rules of I.R.C. § 958(b) employ the constructive ownership rules of I.R.C. § 318 with certain modifications specified in I.R.C. § 958(b)(1) through (3). Note that TCJA repealed a provision (I.R.C. § 958(b)(4)) that previously limited the application of the constructive ownership rules for purposes of determining CFC status. Many structures set up before the enactment of TCJA are now subject to the subpart F rules and many more persons are potentially subject to the obligation to file Form 5471 (*see* Chapter 6) as a result of this change in law.

As an illustration of the change brought about by repeal of prior I.R.C. § 958(b)(4), consider the following. FP, a foreign corporation, owns 100 percent of the stock of FSub, a foreign subsidiary, and 100 percent of the stock of USSub. Is FSub a CFC? Under I.R.C. § 318(a)(3) USSub is deemed to own what its shareholder owns. Under prior I.R.C.

§ 958(b)(4), the constructive ownership rules in I.R.C. § 318(a)(3) could not make a U.S. person (USSub) the owner of stock owned by a foreign person (FP). After the law change, USSub is considered to own 100 percent of FSub, which is now treated as a CFC.

Suppose that USCo owns 10 percent of the voting stock of ForCo1 (the other 90 percent is owned by unrelated foreign shareholders). ForCo1 owns 51 percent of the voting stock of ForCo2 (the other 49 percent is held by a single unrelated U.S. shareholder). Is ForCo2 a CFC? (Assume ForCo1 is not.) Starting with the indirect ownership rules in I.R.C. § 958(a)(2), USCo would appear to own 5.1 percent of ForCo2 (10 percent × 51 percent). So USCo would not be a U.S. shareholder (*i.e.*, 10 percent owner) and ForCo2 would not be a CFC (U.S. shareholders own only 49 percent of ForCo2). However, the constructive ownership rules also apply, and if those rules provide more ownership than the indirect ownership rules, the constructive ownership rules prevail. Reg. § 1.958–2(f)(2). Under I.R.C. § 318(a)(2)(C) attribution rules as modified by I.R.C. § 958(b)(3) and (b)(2), USCo is deemed to own 10 percent of ForCo2 (10 percent × 100 percent) as ForCo1, by owning more than 50 percent, is considered to own 100 percent of ForCo2 under I.R.C. § 958(b)(2). Consequently, U.S. shareholders would be deemed to own 59 percent of ForCo2 which is a CFC.

One could play all day in the indirect and constructive ownership sandbox, but it is beyond the scope of this book to do so, and mental health experts may not permit it.

§ 9.03   INCOME TAXABLE TO SHAREHOLDERS—SECTION 951(a)

If a foreign corporation is a CFC under I.R.C. § 957(a), each U.S. shareholder (who owns stock on the last day of the year) must include in income the sum of the shareholder's pro rata share of subpart F income plus, with respect to taxable years of foreign companies beginning after December 31, 2017, the shareholder's GILTI for the shareholder's taxable year. I.R.C. §§ 951(a) and 951A. The statute also requires U.S. shareholders to include in income their share of U.S. property owned by the CFC, but that requirement has been substantially modified (largely turned off, for corporate shareholders) by regulations. *See* § 9.03.

A taxpayer's pro rata share is based on direct and indirect ownership (but not constructive ownership). In effect, I.R.C. §§ 951(a) and 951A treat U.S. shareholders as having received a current distribution out of a CFC's earnings to the extent that they meet any of the above categories. (Special rules may apply in the case of U.S. shareholders that are partnerships, as discussed below.) For most foreign companies, the majority of their earnings will fall into one of these categories. The result is that much of the earnings of CFCs will be includible in their U.S. shareholders' U.S. taxable income in the year earned.

When income is included under either I.R.C. §§ 951(a) or 951A, the CFC maintains an account of previously taxed earnings (PTEP) so that there is no double inclusion. *See* I.R.C. § 959 (discussed in § 9.05 below).

In many cases, a U.S. shareholder may not actually receive a distribution of income that is deemed to be included under I.R.C. §§ 951(a) or 951A. But a U.S. shareholder is treated as if the shareholder has income. Note that subpart F inclusions are not treated as actual dividends for many purposes under the Code (*e.g.*, for purposes of reduced tax on dividends under I.R.C. § 1(h)(11)). Where there is no actual distribution, the U.S. shareholder is treated essentially as if the shareholder contributed the deemed inclusion amount back to the corporation which in turn results in an increase in the shareholder's stock basis. I.R.C. § 961. On a subsequent distribution of PTEP, there is typically no further taxation, although the stock basis of a U.S. shareholder must be reduced upon the distribution. I.R.C. §§ 959 and 961. The income that is deemed distributed to U.S. shareholders may carry with it an indirect foreign tax credit for any creditable income foreign taxes paid. I.R.C. § 960 (discussed *infra* Chapter 10).

(A) SUBPART F INCOME

For most U.S. shareholders of CFCs, the inclusion of GILTI required by I.R.C. § 951A likely will result in a larger inclusion than an inclusion of subpart F income, a term defined in I.R.C. § 952. But as an ordering matter, the subpart F inclusion comes first: income that is subpart F income is excluded from GILTI.

As noted above, subpart F was designed as an anti-abuse regime to prevent U.S. taxpayers from shifting mobile income to low-taxed jurisdictions. Reflecting that perspective, the definition of subpart F income mostly encompasses income that is easily movable. Subpart F income is composed of several categories: income derived from insurance of U.S. risks, foreign base company income, certain income from countries engaged in international boycotts, and certain illegal payments. I.R.C. § 952(a).

The most important category is foreign base company income, a term that itself is composed of three categories. I.R.C. § 954. These categories were directed primarily at a holding structure where a U.S. parent corporation created a foreign subsidiary (*i.e.*, a base company) in an effort to isolate either passive income or some of the income from the parent company's active business in a low-tax jurisdiction. For example, a U.S. manufacturing parent company might sell its products to a foreign subsidiary in a low tax jurisdiction, which then sells to the product's end-users not located in that jurisdiction. By manipulating prices, some of the income from the manufactured products might be isolated in that low-tax jurisdiction even though there may be no business reason to be there. While it is true that I.R.C. § 482 (discussed *infra* Chapter 11) may allow the IRS to reallocate income between parent and subsidiary, the CFC provisions offer a more targeted weapon that can apply even when the dealings between parent and subsidiary are at arm's length.

Until 2018, much of U.S. international tax planning was focused on making sure that the earnings of CFCs didn't fall within the definition of subpart F income. In an odd twist, tax planning post-enactment of TCJA sometimes operates in reverse: taxpayers can benefit from having income categorized as subpart F income rather than having it includible as GILTI under I.R.C. § 951A. The reason for this has to do with the way the foreign tax credit applies for purposes of the GILTI inclusion. (*See* the discussion of the indirect foreign tax credit in Chapter 10).

(1) Foreign Personal Holding Company Income

The first and most important category of foreign base company income is foreign personal holding company income (FPHCI). I.R.C. § 954(a)(1) and (c). This category generally consists of passive income such as interest, dividends, rents, royalties, and net gains from the sale of assets producing these income flows or sales of non-income producing assets or payments that are considered to be dividend or interest substitutes. (Also gains from commodities transactions or foreign currency gains are FPHCI.) If a U.S. parent corporation (or a U.S. individual) employs a CFC to hold investments in order to isolate the investment income in a low-tax jurisdiction, the income will be in turn: foreign personal holding company income, which is foreign base company income, which is subpart F income, which is subject to U.S. federal taxation of the U.S. shareholders in the United States even if not distributed by the CFC. (Note that some states do not tax subpart F income until the income is repatriated.)

FPHCI also includes income that is the equivalent of interest. For example, suppose an accrual basis U.S. parent corporation sells property (with a $0 basis) or performs services for a third party in exchange for an account receivable of $10,000 which it sells (*i.e.*, factors) to a CFC for $7,000. In the absence of a remedial provision, the U.S. parent company would report net income of $7,000 ($10,000 accrued income minus the $3,000 loss on the sale of the receivable). The CFC would report $3,000 of income when the receivable was paid. Under I.R.C. § 864(d), the transaction is treated as a $7,000 loan by the CFC to the obligor under the receivable with the $3,000 income received by the CFC treated as interest. The $3,000 income characterized as interest is FPHCI that will normally be taxable under I.R.C. § 951(a) to the U.S. parent corporation. So the parent corporation reports $7,000 of net income when the receivable is factored and $3,000 of income when the CFC collects on the receivable.

There is a special rule for interest and income derived in the active conduct of a banking or financing business. Qualified banking or financing income of an eligible CFC will not constitute FPHCI. I.R.C. § 954(h). Generally, an eligible CFC is one that is predominately engaged in the active conduct of banking or financing. To avoid FPHCI, an eligible

CFC must earn qualified banking or financing income. I.R.C. § 954(h)(3). For a similar exception for active insurance income, *see* I.R.C. § 954(i).

There is a similar "active business" exception for rents and royalties reflecting that these income flows can be generated from an active business. If rents or royalties are derived from an active trade or business conducted by the CFC's employees and are not received from related taxpayers, the receipts do not constitute FPHCI. I.R.C. § 954(c)(2)(A). For example, rents received by a CFC from a retail car-leasing business involving substantial maintenance, repair and marketing by the CFC's employees would not be FPHCI. The "active business" exception can be satisfied through either extensive production activities or through marketing and servicing activities. *See, e.g.*, Reg. §§ 1.954–2(d)(1) and 1.954–2T.

Although rents or royalties from a related party cannot meet the active rents or royalties exception, they are excluded from FPHCI if the payments are for use of property located in the country where the CFC is organized. I.R.C. § 954(c)(3). For example, if a CFC incorporated in Ireland leases an Irish factory to Subco, an Irish corporation, which manufactures and sells machine tools, the rent received by the CFC is not subpart F income even though the active business exception does not apply. However, the easing of the related party rule does not apply if the rent payment reduces Subco's subpart F income. I.R.C. § 954(c)(3)(B). For example, if Subco earns $50,000 from passively subleasing the rented property to an unrelated party and pays $40,000 in rent to the CFC, the rental payment it makes to the CFC is FPHCI. Otherwise only $10,000 of $50,000 of rental income would be FPHCI.

Two exceptions are potentially applicable in the case of dividends and interest received from related parties. The first is known as the "same country" exception. Dividends and interest which are normally FPHCI may not be foreign personal holding company income if received from a related person organized and engaged in a trade or business in the same country as the CFC. I.R.C. § 954(c)(3)(A). For example, if a CFC has a subsidiary (organized in the same country) which conducts a trade or business and uses most of its assets (more than 50 percent pursuant to Reg. § 1.954–2(b)(4)(iv)) in that country, dividends or interest paid to the CFC are not FPHCI. If the CFC had conducted the trade or business, there would have been no subpart F income. As in the case of rental payments from related parties, interest paid by a related party that decreases the payor's subpart F income is treated as FPHCI to the CFC (*e.g.*, in addition to its active trade or business the subsidiary has passive income to which any interest paid is allocated).

A look-through rule in I.R.C. § 954(c)(6) is much broader in application than the "same country" exception. Dividends, interest, rents, and royalties from a CFC which is a related person are not treated as FPCHI to the extent attributable to income of the payor which is not subpart F income. The "related person" definition looks to more-than-50 percent common control. Note that the related person does not need to reside in the same country. However, the look-through rule does not apply to payments from a U.S. company. To the extent that the passive payment reduces or is allocable against subpart F income of the payor, subpart F treatment will result to the recipient. *See* Notice 2007–9, 2007–1 C.B. 401, for guidance on how to determine if the payment is allocable against subpart F income of the payor. The look-through rule has been set to expire, and in some years has expired, many times, but has been regularly renewed by Congress.

To illustrate how I.R.C. § 954(c)(6) works, suppose that USCo owns all the stock of two subsidiaries— LuxCo and FrenchCo. FrenchCo is engaged in an active trade or business. Assume that LuxCo is subject to a nominal rate of tax and that FrenchCo is taxed at a 30 percent rate. If FrenchCo pays interest or royalties to LuxCo, which functions as the financing and licensing company for the USCo worldwide group, there may be a deduction in France under its tax system and little or no tax in Luxembourg. So if FrenchCo generates active income, then the interest/royalty payment should not be subpart F income.

Now if the payment of interest or royalties from FrenchCo reduced the subpart F income of FrenchCo, the look-through rule would not apply. Suppose that FrenchCo earned $20 of interest from a loan to an unrelated borrower and $80 of non-subpart F active trade or business income. Under the rules governing how expenses are allocated in CFCs, a $30 interest payment to LuxCo would first offset the $20 of interest income earned by FrenchCo and then offset $10 of active business income of French Co. I.R.C. § 954(b)(5) and Reg. § 1.954–1(c)(1)(i)(C). Accordingly, LuxCo is deemed to receive $20 of subpart F income (*i.e.*, FPHCI) and $10 that would qualify as non-subpart F income under the look-through rule.

Suppose that USCo owns all of the stock of Foreign Holdco, the only asset of which is all of the stock of Foreign Opco, a manufacturing corporation. Assume that the stock of Foreign Holdco and the stock of Foreign Opco are highly appreciated. An unrelated Purchaser wants to acquire the foreign operations. If Purchaser buys the stock of Foreign Holdco, USCo will have a gain for U.S. purposes. If Purchaser buys the stock of Foreign Opco from Foreign Holdco, some or all of the gain on the sale of stock might be subpart F income (*i.e.*, FPHCI).

Suppose instead that Purchaser buys the assets directly from Foreign Opco. Under this scenario, typically there may be no FPHCI because Foreign Opco is selling assets used in a trade or business. Reg. § 1.954–2(e)(3).

Suppose that USCo causes Foreign Opco to check-the-box to be treated as a disregarded entity for U.S. tax purposes. A U.S. check-the-box election has no effect on foreign taxation, but in this situation for U.S. tax purposes, the election is treated as if Foreign Opco liquidated into Foreign Holdco. A foreign-to-foreign liquidation typically has no immediate U.S. tax consequences. *See infra* Chapter 14. Now Foreign

Holdco sells the "stock" of Foreign Opco. For U.S. tax purposes Foreign Opco is not a corporation, and there is no stock. Instead, there is a sale of trade or business assets that does not create subpart F income. *See Dover Corp. v. Commissioner*, 122 T.C. 324 (2004).

(2)   Foreign Base Company Sales Income

The second category of foreign base company income is foreign base company sales income (FBCSI). I.R.C. § 954(a)(2) and (d). This category includes income from property purchased from (or sold to) a related party (defined in I.R.C. § 954(d)(3) using a more than 50 percent ownership test based on value or vote) if the property is manufactured and sold for use outside the CFC's country of incorporation. For example, if a U.S. parent corporation manufactures engines which are sold to its CFC (typically in a low tax jurisdiction) for resale abroad, income received by the CFC is FBCSI to the extent that the engines are sold for use outside the CFC's country of incorporation. Similarly, if the CFC purchases engines from an unrelated foreign manufacturer and sells them to the CFC's U.S. parent corporation for resale in the United States, the CFC's income is FBCSI. If the goods sold by the CFC are intended for use or disposition inside the country of its incorporation, the income is not FBCSI ("destination exception").

In addition to the destination exception, there are two manufacturing exceptions relating to FBCSI. There is a statutory manufacturing exception where the goods sold are manufactured in the country where the CFC is incorporated. I.R.C. § 954(d)(1)(A). Suppose USCo owns all of the stock of Foreign Opco1 and Foreign Opco2, both located in Brazil. If Foreign Opco1 manufactures inventory and sells it to Foreign Opco2 for sale outside of Brazil, there is no FBCSI even though there is a purchase from a related person and sale outside the country of incorporation because the inventory is manufactured in Brazil. The outcome would not change if Foreign Opco2 purchased the inventory from an unrelated Brazilian manufacturer and then sold to a related distributor outside of Brazil.

There is a second manufacturing exception that applies wherever manufacturing takes place. If the CFC manufactures or constructs the property sold, the income is not FBCSI—subject to the branch rule discussed below. Reg. § 1.954–3(a)(4)(iii). Often, determining whether manufacturing has occurred is not clear, but income from a CFC that merely assembles goods manufactured by its parent may not escape classification as FBCSI. Another question is whether a CFC that hires another corporation (whether related or unrelated) to manufacture on its behalf under strict supervision (often referred to as "contract manufacturing" if the CFC buys from the manufacturer or "toll manufacturing" if the CFC pays the manufacturer a service fee to manufacture where the CFC owns the raw materials, works-in-progress and finished inventory throughout the production process) is engaged in "manufacturing." *See* Reg. § 1.954–3(a)(4).

Note that in order for a CFC to have FBCSI, the related corporation need not be a U.S. corporation. Suppose that USCo, a U.S. corporation, has two subsidiaries—MfgCo in high-tax country M and SalesCo in low-tax country S. MfgCo manufactures thermostats and then sells them at an arm's-length price to SalesCo which sells them throughout Europe. Under I.R.C. § 954(d)(1) the income earned by SalesCo is FBCSI which is subject to U.S. taxation under subpart F because SalesCo purchases personal property manufactured outside of country S from a related party (*see* I.R.C. § 954(d)(3)) and sells the property for use outside of country S.

Suppose that a U.S. corporation has a wholly-owned manufacturing subsidiary in Germany which establishes an unincorporated branch office in Switzerland through which all sales are made to European customers. Assume that the sales income in Switzerland is not subject to tax in Germany. At first glance, it appears that there is no subpart F income because the German corporation is a manufacturing corporation. However, under I.R.C. § 954(d)(2) the branch may be treated as a subsidiary so that the sales income of the branch to customers outside of Switzerland will be treated as foreign base company sales income taxable to the U.S. parent corporation. This treatment will occur where the sales branch income is taxed at an effective rate that is less than 90 percent of, and at least 5 percentage points less than, the effective rate of tax that would have applied if the sales were made by the German corporation in Germany. Reg. § 1.954–3(b)(1).

The "branch rule" applies to manufacturing branches as well as sales branches. The manufacturing branch rule only applies if the effective tax rate of the sales subsidiary is less than 90 percent of or more than 5 percentage points less than the effective tax rate that would have applied to the sales income had it been earned in the manufacturing country. Reg. § 1.954–3(b)(1). Therefore, in order for the rule to apply in this example, the income earned by Switzerland must be taxed at an effective tax rate that is less than the effective tax rate had the income been earned and taxed in Germany. The regulations do not provide much guidance on how to determine the "effective tax rate." *But see* GLAM 2015–002. Whether there is a sales branch or a manufacturing branch, subpart F may apply only where the sales unit (whether a branch or the rest of the corporation) is taxed at a lower rate than the manufacturing unit (whether the rest of the corporation or the branch).

There is no end to branch rule permutations and combinations. If a CFC has multiple manufacturing branches with respect to the product being sold, the manufacturing branch with the lowest tax rate (*i.e.*, a pro-taxpayer rule) is used for the rate disparity test. If a CFC has multiple sales branches, the rate disparity test must be performed for each sales branch and the manufacturing branch.

In *Ashland Oil, Inc. v. Commissioner*, 95 T.C. 348 (1990), the IRS argued unsuccessfully that sales income of a CFC in a low tax jurisdiction was subject to tax as subpart F income even though the property sold was purchased from an unrelated manufacturer in another country. The manufacturer was a "contract manufacturer" which manufactured goods according to the CFC's specifications and received compensation equal to the sum of its costs plus a fixed fee. *See also Vetco Inc. v. Commissioner*, 95 T.C. 579 (1990), in which the IRS tried again to expand the branch rule to cover any perceived abuse involving a sales or manufacturing subsidiary.

Suppose that a Hong Kong CFC purchases raw materials from a related Chinese corporation and arranges for an Indonesian contract manufacturer to do the manufacturing. (Note that Hong Kong and China are treated as separate countries for U.S. tax purposes.) Sales are then made throughout Asia. Unless the CFC is viewed as manufacturing, the purchase of goods from a related party and the sale to unrelated parties outside the country of the CFC's incorporation leads to FBCSI in the view of the IRS even though the goods purchased from a related party (raw materials) are not the same as the goods sold by the CFC (finished goods).

A CFC can be a manufacturer where another party (related or unrelated) does the physical manufacturing. Reg. § 1.954–3(b) considers whether the CFC makes a "substantial contribution" to the manufacturing.

(3)   Foreign Base Company Services Income

The third category of foreign base company income is foreign base company services income (FBCSvcsI. I.R.C. § 954(a)(3) and (e). This category is composed of income derived from the performance of specified services for, or on behalf of, a related person (defined in I.R.C. § 954(d)(3)) outside the country where the CFC is organized. The services covered are: technical, managerial, engineering, architectural, scientific, skilled, industrial, commercial, or like services. For example, suppose the U.S. parent corporation manufactures engines for sale abroad, and a wholly-owned Swiss subsidiary—a CFC—services the installed engines throughout the rest of Europe on behalf of its parent company. The income realized by the CFC that is not generated from services performed in Switzerland is FBCSvcsI, which is foreign base company income, which is subpart F income, which is directly taxable to the U.S. parent corporation. The purpose of this category is to discourage the parent corporation from isolating services income in a low-tax jurisdiction.

If the services are performed in the country in which the CFC is organized, the income is not FBCSvcsI. I.R.C. § 954(e)(1)(B). For example, services income earned by the Swiss corporation from servicing engines in Switzerland is not FBCSvcsI. However, suppose that the U.S. parent corporation has a wholly-owned Luxembourg subsidiary that wholly-owns all the "stock" of a French disregarded entity. If the French disregarded entity performs services in France on behalf of the U.S. parent corporation, the income generated will be FBCSvcsI because the services are performed outside of Luxembourg—the CFC that is tested.

Note that if services performed on behalf of the parent corporation are directly related to the sale by the CFC of property it manufactured and are performed before the time of sale, the income is not FBCSvcsI. I.R.C. § 954(e)(2). A CFC's services income directly related to property it manufactures is not FBCSvcsI whenever performed because the services are not "for or on behalf" of a related person.

A CFC's services are performed on behalf of a related person if the CFC receives compensation from a related person, if the CFC performs services that the related party was obligated to perform, if the services are a material part of a sale by a related person, or if the related party provides "substantial assistance" contributing to the performance of services by a CFC to an unrelated person. Reg. § 1.954–4(b). "Substantial assistance" may include the related party providing meaningful supervision or loaning employees or providing financial assistance. Reg. § 1.954–4(b).

For example, suppose that USCo has two wholly-owned subsidiaries, HelperCo and LowTaxCo, in two different jurisdictions. LowTaxCo enters into an agreement with unrelated customers for LowTaxCo to perform services. LowTaxCo then hires HelperCo to perform those services on its behalf. Customers pay LowTaxCo which pays an arm's length fee to HelperCo for performing the services. The income earned by HelperCo may be FBCSvcsI if HelperCo is not a U.S. corporation and if the services are performed outside HelperCo's country of incorporation. Even then, HelperCo may avoid subpart F income under the high tax exception in I.R.C. § 954(b)(4). (*See* discussion below.)

Regardless of the treatment of Helper Co., the net income of LowTaxCo (after deducting the fee to HelperCo) from services performed outside its country of incorporation may be FBCSvcsI because LowTaxCo receives substantial assistance from Helper Co. Reg. § 1.954–4(b)(2)(ii). Whether LowTaxCo will or will not have FBCSvcsI depends on whether HelperCo is a U.S. company and the extent to which HelperCo provides assistance. Notice 2007–13, 2007–1 C.B. 410, provides that "substantial assistance" consists of assistance furnished (directly or indirectly) by a related *U.S.* person or persons to the CFC if the assistance satisfies an objective cost test. If HelperCo is a foreign entity providing assistance, LoTaxCo should not have FBCSvcsI under the Notice. If HelperCo is a related U.S. corporation, then LoTaxCo may have subpart F income to the extent that the cost to LoTaxCo of the services furnished by HelperCo equals or exceeds 80 percent of the total cost to LoTaxCo of performing the services.

(4) Oil and Gas Income

The TCJA repealed a long-standing category of foreign base company income, namely income from the manufacture and distribution of oil and gas products outside the United States unless the products were extracted from, or for use in, the country where the CFC was organized. Prior I.R.C. § 954(a)(5) and (g).

(5) Allocation and Apportionment of Deductions

Under the subpart F rules, a U.S. shareholder is taxed on net foreign base company income. I.R.C. § 954(a)(5). Consider a situation where a CFC earns both subpart F and non-subpart F income. The regulations under the source rules and the foreign tax credit rules apply for this purpose. Reg. § 1.954–1(c). *See* Reg. §§ 1.861–8 *et seq.*, discussed *supra* at § 3.02 and Reg. § 1.904–5. Note though, that interest paid to a related person is allocated first to passive foreign personal holding company income with any remainder allocated to other subpart F or non-subpart F income. I.R.C. § 954(b)(5). Any remaining interest expense at the CFC level is allocated and apportioned against subpart F and non-subpart F income either by apportioning interest expense pro rata based on the CFC's gross income subject to some modifications ("modified gross income method") or pro rata based on the assets of the CFC ("asset method"). The method selected must be used for all CFCs.

(6) Relief Provisions

Any CFC—even one actively engaged in manufacturing—is likely to have some foreign base company income. For example, a manufacturing CFC typically may have interest from bank accounts or interest from financing sales. The Code provides a *de minimis* rule so that if the **gross** foreign base company income (plus certain insurance income) is less than the lower of 5 percent of the CFC's gross income or $1 million, none of the CFC's income is treated as subpart F income. I.R.C. § 954(b)(3)(A). Conversely, if a CFC has gross foreign base company income (and certain insurance income) in excess of 70 percent of the CFC's gross income, the entire gross income for the taxable year is treated as subpart F income. I.R.C. § 954(b)(3)(B).

Even if a CFC has foreign base company income in excess of the *de minimis* amount, upon the taxpayer's election, no item of income that would otherwise be foreign base company income or insurance income is included in those categories if the income is subject to an effective rate of foreign income tax greater than 90 percent of the maximum U.S. corporate tax rate. I.R.C. § 954(b)(4). This "high tax exception" allows a U.S. shareholder to avoid subpart F treatment for an item of income earned by a CFC that is essentially taxed at the same rate at which it would have been taxed had it been earned directly by the U.S. shareholder. Before enactment of the TCJA there were few tax jurisdictions that had a corporate tax rate equal to 90 percent of the U.S. rate (35% × .90 = 31.5%). Income earned in jurisdictions subject to an effective foreign rate of at least 18.9 percent may now qualify for the high-tax exception. The reduction in the U.S. corporate tax rate in the TCJA means that the choice of whether an item of income is includible in income as subpart F may often be elective for the U.S. shareholder.

In determining whether the high tax exception is met, the U.S. dollar amount of foreign income taxes paid or accrued with respect to the net item of income is divided by the U.S. dollar amount of the net item of income, increased by the associated foreign taxes.

The amount included as subpart F income cannot exceed the current earnings and profits (E&P) for the CFC's taxable year. I.R.C. § 952(c)(1)(A). To the extent that the potential subpart F inclusion exceeds the current E&P (*i.e.*, there is a deficit in the non-subpart F E&P), non-subpart F income in future years is "recaptured" as subpart F income. I.R.C. § 952(c)(2). For example, suppose in year 1 a CFC has $10 million of subpart F income and a $6 million loss from non-subpart F activities (*e.g.*, from an active manufacturing business). The subpart F inclusion for the year is limited to $4 million—the net amount of E&P for the year. In year 2, if the CFC earns $7 million of non-subpart F income, $6 million of that income ($10 million − $4 million) will be recaptured as subpart F income. I.R.C. § 952(c)(2).

Suppose a CFC has an E&P deficit from subpart F activities for a prior year. A "qualified" deficit can be carried forward and offset any current earnings and profits so that current subpart F income would not be taxable. I.R.C. § 952(c)(1)(B). To be "qualified," an E&P deficit must arise in the same activity as the current subpart F income. For example, FBCSI in a current year cannot be lowered through a deficit arising from passive activities in a prior year. Also, current FPHCI cannot be offset by an E&P deficit in a prior year even if it arose from passive activities.

Not only can a CFC reduce subpart F income by applying a qualified deficit against the current earnings and profits limitation, it can also reduce subpart F income under the "chain deficit rule" which permits an E&P deficit of certain related corporations to offset current E&P in applying the E&P ceiling rule. I.R.C. § 952(c)(1)(C). For example, suppose that CFC has subpart F income of $100 million and E&P of $100 million. Suppose that CFC owns all the stock of Subco which has an E&P deficit of ($100 million). If the chain deficit rule applies, U.S. shareholders of CFC will have no subpart F income for the year. In order for the chain deficit rule to apply, the two corporations must be incorporated in the same foreign country and there must be 100 percent ownership (constructive ownership rules apply). Also, for subpart F income to be offset, the deficit must arise from the same type of activity and must have occurred while in the chain. If the subpart F income is FPHCI, the chain deficit rule usually will not apply even if the deficit arose from passive activities.

(7) Insurance Income

Another category of subpart F income deserves a brief mention. Under I.R.C. § 952(a)(1), certain insurance income—basically the insurance of risks outside the country in which a CFC is organized—is considered subpart F income. U.S. shareholders historically sought to avoid taxation by organizing a captive insurance company (*i.e.*, one that insured its U.S. shareholders) which had more than 10 equal U.S. shareholders. If each shareholder held less than 10 percent of the stock, there would be no U.S. shareholders within the meaning of I.R.C. § 951(b) and therefore no CFC under I.R.C. § 957. However, under I.R.C. § 953(c) which provides a special rule for captive insurance companies, if even 25 percent of a captive insurance company is owned by any U.S. persons (*i.e.*, not necessarily 10 percent shareholders) the company is a CFC, and the income is taxed to the U.S. persons regardless of their percentage ownership.

(8) Ordering Rules

In determining the potential subpart F inclusion for a U.S. shareholder, Reg. § 1.954–1(a) prescribes the following order:

1. Determine gross foreign base company income.

2. Apply the de minimis and full inclusion rules to arrive at adjusted gross foreign base company income.

3. Subtract properly allocable deductions to arrive at net foreign base company income.

4. Adjust net foreign base company income (to arrive at adjusted net foreign base company income) by making two adjustments: first, the E&P limitation under I.R.C. § 952(c); second, the high tax exception under I.R.C. § 954(b).

5. Consider whether the CFC has any insurance income as defined in I.R.C. § 953.

6. Finally, add to the total any non-subpart F income that is recaptured under I.R.C. § 952(c)(2).

To illustrate how these ordering rules might apply, consider a CFC that under the high tax exception does not appear to have subpart F income. However, if that CFC is subject to I.R.C. § 952(c)(2) recapture, because that step is the last step and comes after the high tax exception, there will be a subpart F inclusion. Moreover, the taxpayer cannot again assert the high tax exception to the I.R.C. § 952(c)(2) recapture amount. Reg. § 1.954–1(a)(7) (last sentence).

The rules for calculating an inclusion of GILTI under I.R.C. § 951A intersect with the subpart F rules in sometimes non-intuitive ways. *See* discussion below.

(B) EARNINGS INVESTED IN U.S. PROPERTY

(1) In General

Under I.R.C. § 951(a), a U.S. shareholder is taxable on the shareholder's portion of the CFC's Subpart F income (primarily foreign base company income) and the CFC's investment of any non-subpart F earnings in U.S. property (I.R.C. § 951(a)(1)(B)). To illustrate the perceived abuse that the rule in I.R.C. § 951(a)(1)(B) was intended to curtail, suppose that, prior to enactment of TCJA, a CFC with $5 million of earnings had no subpart F income, but made a loan of $3 million to its U.S. parent company. Unless the parent corporation was taxed on this transaction, it had the current use of $3 million on which U.S. taxes were deferred. I.R.C.

§§ 951(a)(1)(B) and 956 were intended to deter U.S. taxpayers from repatriating non-subpart F earnings of a CFC through loans and other investments in U.S. property in a tax-free manner where the earnings had not been subject to U.S. tax.

Under I.R.C. §§ 951(a)(1)(B) and 956, a U.S. shareholder is taxed on the shareholder's pro rata share of any increase in the earnings of the CFC invested in U.S. property. In the example above, the parent corporation is taxed on the $3 million invested in the U.S. debt instrument in the current year. The increase in earnings invested in U.S. property is measured essentially by comparing the average adjusted basis of such U.S. property (minus allocable liabilities) for the tax year (using the close of each quarter as a measuring date) with the adjusted basis at the end of the previous year.

The term "U.S. property" refers to any property that is tangible property located in the United States, any security issued by a U.S. payor (i.e., stock issued by a domestic corporation or an obligation issued by a U.S. borrower), or the right to use in the United States certain intangible property such as patents, copyrights, secret formulae, designs or other similar property. I.R.C. § 956(c)(1). For example, if a CFC acquires the right to produce a patented computer chip in the United States, the amount paid for that right (whether a lump sum or periodic royalties) is considered an investment in U.S. property. A CFC's investment in the stock of its U.S. parent company or of a related U.S. corporation also is considered an investment in U.S. property. A CFC that is a partner in either a U.S. or foreign partnership is considered to own a pro rata share of U.S. property owned by the partnership. Reg. § 1.956–4(b)(1).

(2) Post-TCJA Guidance

With the enactment of the TCJA, actual dividends from a CFC are generally tax-free as a result of I.R.C. § 245A. Also, most foreign earnings will give rise to immediate inclusions in income in the hands of their U.S. shareholders from either Subpart F income or as GILTI. As a result, the untaxed earnings of CFCs that could result in an I.R.C. § 956 inclusion are substantially reduced. If a U.S. taxpayer can access foreign earnings with no U.S. tax through a distribution, there's really no reason why a loan of those earnings and profits should be taxable. Treasury and the IRS seemed to agree, and in regulations finalized in May 2019, they largely wrote I.R.C. §§ 951(a)(1)(B) and 956 out of the Code, at least for corporate shareholders. Under Reg. § 1.956–1(a)(2), a corporate shareholder's I.R.C. § 956 amount is reduced by the amount of the deduction under I.R.C. § 245A equal to a hypothetical I.R.C. § 956 distribution.

Although the regulations went a long way towards removing discrepancies between an old Code section and a newly adopted international tax regime, I.R.C. § 956 remains on the books and still could impact unwary taxpayers. For one, it doesn't apply to eliminate potential I.R.C. § 956 inclusions for individual U.S. shareholders. Second, as discussed in Chapter 7, some dividends may not qualify for I.R.C.

§ 245A, such as hybrid dividends. This means that taxpayers still need to be aware of the potential for taxable I.R.C. § 956 inclusions. In addition, in proposed regulations (Prop. Reg. § 1.960–2(b)(1)), the IRS said that no foreign income taxes are deemed paid with respect to an inclusion under I.R.C. § 951(a)(1)(B) thus producing a double whammy for taxpayers that fall unsuspectingly into the I.R.C. § 956 trap.

§ 9.04   GLOBAL INTANGIBLE LOW-TAXED INCOME

As noted above, the subpart F rules were enacted in order to make sure that U.S. persons couldn't shift mobile income to low-tax jurisdictions, and the rules defining subpart F income generally aim to fulfil that goal. The TCJA's expansion of the subpart F regime requires that U.S. shareholders of CFCs include in income each year a new category of income known as GILTI. I.R.C. § 951A. In effect, GILTI functions as a kind of minimum tax on U.S. shareholders' foreign earnings, but it's also not exactly a minimum tax. That's just one reason why it's a complicated provision for students to understand, taxpayers to comply with, and the IRS to administer. Regulations finalized in June 2019 (T.D. 9866) provide some answers to taxpayers' basic questions about how to calculate the GILTI inclusion, but both taxpayers and the government are still navigating their way through this provision that has introduced complex, but also fundamental, changes to the U.S. international tax rules.

(A) CALCULATING GILTI

GILTI sets up numerous traps for the unwary for the beginning student. While the statute requiring the GILTI inclusion is found in subpart F of the Code, GILTI does not come within the definition of subpart F income as described in I.R.C. § 952. Another big difference between subpart F income and GILTI is that while CFCs earn subpart F income, CFCs don't earn GILTI: only U.S. shareholders do. CFCs instead earn what the statute refers to as "tested income." I.R.C. § 951A(b). U.S. shareholders with CFCs must net their pro rata share of tested income from CFCs with positive tested income against any pro rata share of tested losses from CFCs that have tested losses to arrive at "net CFC tested income." I.R.C. § 951A(c)(1). Net CFC tested income is not the same as GILTI. To derive GILTI from net CFC tested income, a U.S. shareholder first has to determine its "net deemed tangible income return" (NDTIR) for the tax year. GILTI is equal to the excess of a U.S. shareholder's net tested income for a tax year over its NDTIR for the same year.

Like "net CFC tested income," the determination of NDTIR requires a calculation that's performed at the shareholder level, rather than at the entity (CFC) level. NDTIR is defined to mean the excess of 10 percent of the aggregate of a shareholder's pro rata share of the qualified business asset investment (QBAI) of each of its tested income CFCs (*i.e.*, only those CFCs with positive tested income) for a tax year, over any net interest expense taken into account in determining net CFC tested income. QBAI is essentially tangible property used in a trade or business. Subtracting the NDTIR from net CFC tested income effectively exempts from U.S. tax the portion of the CFCs' profits that represent a fixed return on tangible assets. As a general rule, it's only this amount (which for highly profitable companies, generally represents only a small portion of their foreign profits) that is entitled to the dividends received deduction under I.R.C. § 245A. (But *see* discussion about proposed high-tax election below).

Tested income generally means the gross income of a CFC minus allocable deductions, except for certain items of gross income that are specifically excluded. I.R.C. § 951A(c)(2). The list of exceptions includes effectively connected income as described in I.R.C. § 952(b) (*see* discussion in Chapter 4 on effectively connected income); any gross income taken into account in determining the CFC's subpart F income; gross income excluded due to the high-tax exception to subpart F; dividends received from related persons; and foreign oil and gas extraction income (defined in I.R.C. § 907). How to determine "properly allocable" deductions is a subject that will be tackled in more detail in the next chapter.

As an example, assume CFC is owned 100 percent by a U.S. corporation, and has non-subpart F income of $300; subpart F Income of $200; expenses (other than taxes) of $400 that are proportionally allocable across all categories of income, and QBAI of $100. Assume that CFC is not subject to any foreign tax.

The simplified example for how to calculate CFC's tested income is as follows:

CFC	Total	Sub F Income	Tested Income
Gross Income	$500	$200	$300
Expenses (other than taxes)	($400)	($160)	($240)
Pre-tax Income	$100	$40	$60
Taxes	0	0	0
Taxable Income	**$100**	**$40**	**$60**

The chart above shows net taxable income in each category.

The next step is to subtract from net CFC tested income of $60 (in the example, there are no CFCs with tested losses, so no offset for tested losses), 10 percent of the $100 QBAI. The net deemed tangible income return on $100 of QBAI is $10, and the U.S. shareholder's GILTI is therefore $50.

In the example, out of $100 of total taxable income, Subpart F and GILTI inclusions together total $90, which is the amount taxable to the U.S. shareholder even if the income is not distributed. As the example illustrates, the result of this complex series of interconnected definitions is that nearly all of the net income of CFC has been included in the income of its U.S. shareholder because it is either Subpart F income or GILTI income (with the exclusion of a 10 percent return on tangible assets). In our example, the QBAI was relatively high as a percentage of net income. For many highly profitable companies the value of which stems from intangible rather than tangible assets, this percentage will likely be much lower, and the mandatory inclusion of combined subpart F and GILTI may be in excess of 90 percent of the CFCs net income.

Regulations finalized in June 2019 provide guidance for how to determine tested income when either the *de minimis* rule or the full inclusion rule of subpart F applies. *See* Reg. § 1.954–1(d). In general, these rules provide that gross income taken into account in determining subpart F income does not include any item of gross income excluded from FBCI under the *de minimis* rule but generally does include any item of gross income included in FBCI under the full inclusion rule.

Suppose that FSub has gross income of $290 from product sales to unrelated persons within its country of incorporation, gross interest income of $10 (an amount that is less than $1,000,000) that does not qualify for an exception to FPHCI, and earnings and profits (E&P) of $300. The regulations say that FSub's $10 of gross interest income (which meets the *de minimis* exception to subpart F) is not excluded from gross tested income and FSub has $300 ($290 of gross sales income and $10 of gross interest income) of gross tested income. *See* Reg. § 1.951A–2(c)(4)(iv) Ex. 2.

Once the GILTI inclusion has been calculated at the U.S. shareholder level, it's necessary to reallocate amounts taxed under GILTI back to each CFC with tested income (this is necessary for purposes of determining the PTEP account at each CFC). *See* § 9.05. Suppose USP, a domestic corporation, owns all of the stock of CFC1, CFC2, and CFC3, and that in a single taxable year, CFC1 has tested income of $100, CFC2 has tested income of $300, and CFC3 has tested loss of $50, while USP has no NDTIR. USP is considered to have net CFC tested income $350, computed as follows: ($100 + $300 – $50) and a GILTI inclusion amount of $350 (because it has not NDTIR). USP's aggregate pro rata share of tested income is $400 ($100 from CFC1 + $300 from CFC2). The portion of its GILTI inclusion amount treated as being with respect to CFC1 is $87.50 ($350 × $100/$400), from CFC2 is $262.50 ($350 × $300/$400). The portion of USP's GILTI inclusion amount treated as being with respect to CFC3 is $0 because CFC3 is a tested loss CFC.

The regulations also provide guidance for how to determine tested income in cases where the I.R.C. § 952(c) recapture rule applies. In short, taxpayers with gross subpart F income that had no inclusions because of E&P limitations in a prior year might have a double inclusion if they have positive non-subpart F income in a subsequent year—once by virtue of the I.R.C. § 952(c) recapture rule and again due to GILTI. The preamble to the final regulations contains a (somewhat counter intuitive) explanation of why Treasury felt this was the right answer.

(B) THE HIGH-TAX EXCEPTION

In proposed regulations issued in June 2019 (REG–101828–19, 2019–29 I.R.B. 412), the IRS proposed allowing taxpayers to elect the high-tax exception of I.R.C. § 954(b)(4) even for income that is not subpart F income. If the election is made, income that met the effective tax rate test under I.R.C. § 954(b)(4) would not be treated as gross tested income. The election proposed has the potential to significantly expand the exclusion from GILTI. The proposed regulations say that they would only apply once finalized and it's likely that the mechanics of how the high-tax election is calculated will be revised before they are finalized.

The election is made by a CFC's controlling U.S. shareholders, but is binding on all U.S. shareholders and would apply to all CFCs that are members of a controlling domestic shareholder group. Taxpayers that elect the high-tax exception may exclude from GILTI income that's been taxed at a rate of at least 18.9 percent. Under the proposed regulations, the calculation of the effective rate of tax is done on a QBU (qualified business unit) basis. This means that either all the income of a QBU is included in tested income, or excluded under the election. *See* Chapter 12 for a discussion of the term QBU.

(C) ENTITY V. SHAREHOLDER CALCULATION

Because the determination of subpart F income is performed at an entity level, whereas the calculation of GILTI can only be done at the U.S. shareholder level, the subpart F rules specified by the statute as being applicable to GILTI don't work that well. To take one example, the statute wasn't clear whether the calculation needed to determine a U.S. shareholder's inclusion of GILTI should be done separately for each U.S. shareholder in a consolidated group, or whether the netting of CFC tested income and CFC tested loss should be done at the level of a U.S. consolidated group as a single U.S. shareholder. It can make a big difference. The regulations provide that the calculation of GILTI is done on a consolidated basis. *See* Reg. § 1.951A–1(c)(4), Reg. § 1.1502–51.

The IRS has historically struggled with trying to reconcile the rules of subchapter K of the Code (dealing with partnerships) and the rules of subpart F. This challenge was made even more difficult by enactment of GILTI, because of the fact that tested income is an entity level concept but GILTI is a shareholder level calculation. Recall that if a U.S. shareholder owns over 50 percent of a foreign corporation, the entity is a CFC, and that a domestic partnership is a U.S. person. *See* I.R.C. § 7701(a)(30). So if a U.S. partnership owns 100 percent of the stock of a foreign corporation, the company is a CFC, even if all the partners in the partnership are foreign persons.

In final regulations, the IRS determined that while a domestic partnership that owns a foreign corporation is treated as an entity for purposes of determining whether the partnership and its partners are U.S. shareholders and whether the foreign corporation is a CFC, its treated as an aggregate of its partners for purposes of determining its partners' GILTI inclusions and for purposes of any other provision that applies by reference and I.R.C. § 951A. What this means in practice is that only partners in a partnership that are themselves U.S. shareholders will have a GILTI inclusion. This is a reversal of the stance the IRS has historically taken with respect to subpart F income earned by CFCs with U.S. partnerships as shareholders. *See Eaton Corp. v. Commissioner*, 152 T.C. No. 2 (2019).

As an example of how this rule works, suppose USP, a domestic corporation, and Individual A, a U.S. citizen unrelated to USP, own 95 percent and 5 percent, respectively, of PRS, a domestic partnership. PRS owns 100 percent of the single class of stock of FC, a foreign corporation. The GILTI regulations do not alter the analysis of whether PRS, USP, and Individual A (each a U.S. person) are U.S. shareholders of FC and whether FC is a CFC, and so because PRS, a U.S. person, owns 100 percent of the FC stock within the meaning of I.R.C. 958(a), PRS is considered a U.S. shareholder under I.R.C. 951(b), and FC is a CFC. However, for purposes of determining the GILTI inclusion under I.R.C. § 951A, PRS is not treated as owning (within the meaning of I.R.C. § 958(a)) the FC stock. In determining the GILTI inclusion amount of USP and Individual A, USP is treated as owning 95 percent of the FC stock and Individual A is treated as owning 5 percent of the FC stock under I.R.C. § 958(a). Because USP is a U.S. shareholder of FC under this definition, it will have a GILTI inclusion based on a 95 percent ownership stake. But Individual A is not treated as a U.S. shareholder of FC, and so would not have a GILTI inclusion from FC.

In proposed regulations, the IRS announced that it was considering expanding this approach to subpart F income as well, to ensure consistency between the calculation of inclusions mandated by I.R.C. § 951A and I.R.C. § 951(a) of earnings from CFCs owned by a U.S. partnership.

(D) QBAI

Remember that the formula for calculating GILTI is net tested income minus NDTIR, and that NDTIR is equal to 10 percent of QBAI. Defining QBAI therefore is important.

QBAI means the average of a tested income CFC's aggregate adjusted bases as of the close of each quarter in "specified tangible property" that is used in a trade or business of the tested income CFC and is of a type with respect to which a deduction is allowable under I.R.C. § 167. *See* Reg. § 1.951A–3(b). Specified tangible property is defined by reference to a tested income CFC and a CFC inclusion year, to mean tangible property of the tested income CFC used in the production of gross tested income for the CFC inclusion year. What if property is only partially depreciable? In such case, only the depreciable portion of the property is relevant for purposes of the QBAI calculation. Although taxpayers can exempt a return on QBAI from a GILTI inclusion, this exemption only applies for CFCs that have positive tested income. If a CFC has a tested loss, the value of any tangible property for producing an amount

exempt from GILTI is essentially lost. *See* Reg.
§ 1.951A–3(h)(1).

The regulations include a broad anti-abuse rule to
protect against taxpayers trying to increase their
QBAI (and hence their tax-exempt income). If a CFC
acquires specified tangible property with a principal
purpose of reducing the GILTI inclusion amount of a
U.S. shareholder, and the CFC holds the property
temporarily but over at least the close of one quarter,
the property is disregarded in determining the
acquiring CFC's QBAI for any CFC inclusion year
during which it held the property (the regulations
refer to this rule as the "temporary ownership rule").
See Reg. § 1.951A–3(h)(1).

Property also is presumed to be acquired
temporarily with a principal purpose of increasing a
U.S. shareholder's DTIR if it's held by the CFC for
less than 12 months and the CFC's holding of the
property as of the tested quarter close would have the
effect of increasing the shareholder's DTIR.
Taxpayers can rebut this presumption only if the
facts and circumstances clearly establish that the
subsequent transfer of the property was not
contemplated when the property was acquired and
that a principal purpose of the acquisition of the
property was not to increase the DTIR. To rebut the
presumption, a statement must be attached to the
Form 5471 explaining the facts and circumstances
supporting the rebuttal. Property is presumed not to
be acquired temporarily with a principal purpose of
increasing the shareholder's DTIR if the property is
held by the acquiring CFC for more than 36 months.

There's also a safe harbor that applies if basically the transfer is within a wholly owned group of CFCs that all follow the same tax year.

The following example illustrates the application of these anti-abuse rules. Suppose USP, a domestic corporation, owns all of the stock of CFC1, which owns all of the stock of CFC2 which owns all the stock of CFC3. As of January 1, Year 1, CFC1 owns specified tangible property Asset A and transfers that asset to CFC2 on December 30, Year 1. On April 10, Year 2, CFC2 transfers Asset A to CFC3. CFC3 holds Asset A for the rest of Year 2. The regulations provide that this fact pattern meets the safe-harbor exception because none of the transfers increase the shareholder's DTIR. *See* Reg. § 1.951A–3(h)(1)(vii) Ex. 1.

Another anti-abuse rule generally disallows, for purposes of calculating tested income or tested loss, any deduction or loss attributable to disqualified basis in depreciable or amortizable property resulting from a disqualified transfer of the property. A disqualified transfer is a transfer of property by a CFC during its "disqualified period" in a gain-recognition transaction to a related person. A disqualified period essentially is one in which there is gain recognized by the CFC, but no inclusion of GILTI by its U.S. shareholder because of a mismatch in year-end dates. Reg. § 1.951A–3(h)(2).

A U.S. shareholder's net deemed tangible income return on QBAI is reduced by interest expense that reduces tested income (or increases tested loss) to the extent the interest income attributable to such expense is not taken into account in determining the shareholder's net CFC tested income ("specified interest expense"). I.R.C. § 951A(b)(2)(B). The regulations adopt a netting approach, defining specified interest expense as the excess of the U.S. shareholder's pro rata share of "tested interest expense" of each CFC over its pro rata share of "tested interest income" of each CFC. In effect, this means that generally speaking only net interest income included in gross tested income is taken into account in determining specified interest expense. There is a special rule for how to calculate specified interest expense of tested loss CFCs. Reg. § 1.951A–4(b)(1)(i) and (iv).

Suppose USP, a domestic corporation, owns all of the stock of each of CFC1 and CFC2, tested income CFCs, and that CFC1 pays $100 of interest to CFC2 which is not foreign personal holding company income because of I.R.C. § 954(c)(6). In the same year, CFC2 pays $100 of interest to a bank, an expense that's allocated and apportioned to its gross tested income. *See* Reg. § 1.951A–2(c)(3). (Assume neither CFC1 nor CFC2 holds qualified assets or stock of another CFC). CFC1 is considered to have $100 of tested interest expense and no tested interest income. CFC2, meanwhile, has $100 of interest expense allocated and apportioned to its gross tested income (*see* Reg. § 1.951A–2(c)(3)) and $100 of interest income included in its gross tested income, and so has $100 of tested interest expense and $100 of tested interest income. USP's pro rata share of CFC1's tested interest expense is $100, its pro rata share of CFC2's tested interest expense is $100, and its pro rata share of CFC2's tested interest income is $100. Its aggregate pro rata share of tested interest expense is $200 and its aggregate pro rata share of tested interest income is $100. Its specified interest expense equals $100 ($200 – $100).

(E) THE GILTI DEDUCTION

The determination of a U.S. shareholder's GILTI is not the end of the story. There are still a few additional important steps. For one, the amount of the inclusion is "grossed-up" by any foreign taxes paid by the CFC that are considered attributable to the CFC's tested income. How to determine this amount, as well as the indirect foreign tax credit generally, is addressed in Chapter 10.

Second, U.S. corporate shareholders with GILTI inclusions have one significant benefit that U.S. shareholders with subpart F inclusions don't have. U.S. corporate shareholders are entitled to deduct 50 percent of the sum of the GILTI inclusion plus the foreign tax gross-up, for an effective tax rate on GILTI of 10.5 percent (in cases where there are no foreign taxes paid). I.R.C. § 250. (The deduction decreases, and thus the rate of tax on GILTI increases, after 2025).

If we go back to our example from the table several pages earlier, the GILTI amount after the deduction would be ($50 minus $25) = $25 of net GILTI. That amount would be subject to a 21 percent corporate tax rate, resulting in a U.S. tax of $5.25 on $50 of GILTI inclusion, or a 10.5 percent effective tax rate. The deduction for GILTI in I.R.C. § 250 is supposed to mirror the deduction in the same Code section that is available for FDII (discussed *supra* in § 7.04(B)), with the apparent intention of ensuring that U.S. multinational corporations are neutral in the decision of where to hold profitable intangible property that is used to generate foreign-derived profits.

Third, once the GILTI inclusion has been determined at the U.S. shareholder level, the amount has to be re-allocated back down to each CFC. This allocation is needed both to determine how much of the foreign taxes paid by the CFC should be considered attributable to the income includible as GILTI, and for purposes of keeping track of the previously taxed earnings of the CFC. Those earnings should not be taxed again upon repatriation. I.R.C. § 959. The discussion below dives into the concept of previously taxed earnings and profits (PTEP) in more detail. There are many open questions as to how those rules, written for inclusions required under I.R.C. § 951(a), will apply going forward to GILTI inclusions required under I.R.C. § 951A. The importance of having earnings classified as PTEP also has been minimized to some extent, given that non-previously taxed earnings would anyway be entitled to the 100 percent dividends received deduction under I.R.C. § 245A. *See* discussion *supra* in Chapter 7.

§ 9.05   PREVIOUSLY TAXED EARNINGS AND ADJUSTMENTS TO STOCK BASIS

The Code's mechanism for ensuring that income taxed to a U.S. shareholder under either I.R.C. § 951(a) or 951A is not subject to tax a second time when actually distributed by the foreign corporation. I.R.C. §§ 959 and 961. To illustrate the nature of the problem I.R.C. § 959 attempts to solve, consider the following scenario: suppose a CFC, wholly-owned by USCo, earns $1,000 of GILTI income in year 1 but makes no actual distributions, and in year 2 (when it has no other earnings) makes a $300 distribution to USCo. USCo includes $1,000 in income in year 1 under I.R.C. § 951A but does not include the $300 distribution because the distribution is out of PTEP (note that for the past 50 years previously taxed earnings have been referred to by the acronym PTI (previously taxed income) but in recently issued guidance the IRS has coined a new term to refer to such previously taxed earnings (PTEP). Don't get confused if you sometimes see references to PTI and sometimes to PTEP. They mean the same thing).

The concept of PTEP is somewhat intuitive: after all, most would agree that the same earnings shouldn't be subject to tax twice in the same shareholder's hands. The challenge, as with much else of international tax, is in the details. In guidance released in late 2018 (Notice 2019–1), the IRS announced that taxpayers needed to track the PTEP of their CFCs in 16 different accounts (up from 3 prior to TCJA). But they also asked taxpayers for help in trying to figure out how to simplify this accounting. Stay tuned.

In addition to tracking a CFC's earnings to ensure that they're not subject to double tax, taxpayers also need to adjust the basis in the stock of CFCs whose earnings were previously subject to U.S. tax. Suppose a U.S. parent company incorporates a CFC by exchanging $20 million for the corporation's stock. In the first year of operation, the shareholder has an inclusion of GILTI from the CFC of $2 million that is taxed to the U.S. parent corporation. When the U.S. shareholder is taxed on the inclusion, the basis of the CFC's stock is increased from $20 million to $22 million as if the CFC had made a distribution to the parent company which had then reinvested the proceeds in the CFC. I.R.C. § 961. In the next year, assume the CFC has no further earnings but distributes $2 million to the U.S. parent corporation. Under I.R.C. § 959(a), the parent corporation is not taxed on the distribution of PTEP, but it must reduce its stock basis in the CFC by $2 million to $20 million. I.R.C. § 961(b)(1). If basis has been reduced to $0, any excess distribution is taxed as a capital gain. Reg. § 1.961–2(c).

If a U.S. parent corporation owns a lower-tier CFC through a series of upper-tier CFCs, any inclusion leads to a basis step-up that ripples down the chain. I.R.C. § 961(c). If an upper-tier CFC disposes of stock of a lower-tier CFC, the basis step-up resulting from an inclusion by the lower-tier entity may decrease or eliminate any gain on the sale of the stock for subpart F purposes (*i.e.*, FPHCI), but the basis step-up is only for that purpose. There is no basis step-up for purposes of determining the E&P of the upper-tier foreign entity resulting from the sale.

In Notice 2019–1, the IRS asked for comments on the extent to which basis created under I.R.C. § 961(c) should be treated as basis for purposes of determining tested income in applying I.R.C. § 951A. In the final GILTI regulations, the government said that it was sensitive to taxpayers' concerns but that taking into account I.R.C. § 961(c) basis adjustments for purposes of determining gross tested income could inappropriately reduce the amount of stock gain subject to tax.

§ 9.06   SALE OF CFC STOCK

The U.S. international tax system as designed in the 20th century was intended to ensure that foreign earnings of a CFC would at some point be subject to U.S. tax at ordinary income rates (*i.e.*, not treated as a capital gain).

In order to ensure that the non-previously taxed earnings of CFCs were taxed at ordinary income rates whenever and however a U.S. shareholder cashed in on the earnings via an actual or deemed sale of the CFC stock at a gain, I.R.C. § 1248 (enacted in 1962) requires that gain on a disposition of stock in a CFC that would otherwise be treated as capital gain be taxed as a dividend to the extent of the CFC's E&P other than those previously included in the U.S. taxpayer's income under subpart F. I.R.C. § 1248(d)(1). This mandatory inclusion also picks up E&P in lower-tier CFCs. The provision generally applies to a sale by any U.S. person owning at least a 10 percent interest in the CFC. For I.R.C. § 1248 to apply, the corporation whose stock is sold need not be a CFC at the time of sale, if it was a CFC at any time during the preceding five years.

As a result of the dividends received deduction enacted as part of the TCJA, I.R.C. § 1248, originally enacted as a backstop to protect worldwide taxation, now generally functions as a taxpayer favorable rule. New I.R.C. § 1248(j) generally provides that any amount treated as a dividend under I.R.C. § 1248 is treated as a dividend for purposes of applying I.R.C. § 245A—thereby entitling the U.S. shareholder to a DRD for the portion of the gain treated as a dividend under I.R.C. § 1248. This rule only applies in the case of stock held for at least one year.

Suppose USCo owns stock of CFC1 with a basis of $3 million and FMV of $10 million. CFC1 has E&P of $2 million and holds stock of CFC2 which has E&P of $1 million. USCo has held the CFC1/CFC2 chain since its formation. Assume that none of the earnings of CFC1 or CFC2 are PTEP but rather constitute earnings generated by tangible assets (specified tangible property). If USCo sells all the stock of CFC1, the $7 million gain will consist of a dividend to the extent of the $3 million of E&P, plus $4 million of capital gain. The amount treated as a dividend will be tax exempt under I.R.C. § 245A.

The principle of I.R.C. § 1248 has been extended to sales of lower-tier foreign subsidiaries by upper-tier foreign subsidiaries. If a CFC sells or exchanges stock in a lower-tier foreign corporation, any gain on the sale or exchange is treated as a dividend to the same extent that it would have been so treated under I.R.C. § 1248 if the CFC were a U.S. person. New I.R.C. § 964(e)(4) says that the foreign source portion of the dividend is treated as subpart F income of the selling CFC, but also says that the U.S. shareholder of the selling CFC is entitled to a deduction under I.R.C. § 245A for any subpart F income included in gross income, in the same manner as if such subpart F income were a dividend received by the U.S. shareholder from the selling CFC.

For example, if USCo owns 100 percent of the stock of CFC1 which owns 100 percent of CFC2, gain on any sale or exchange by CFC1 of stock of CFC2 is treated as subpart F income of CFC1 to the extent of the earnings and profits of CFC2. I.R.C. § 964(e). To the extent that USCo includes any amount of that subpart F income into its income, it is entitled to a dividends received deduction under I.R.C. § 245A. I.R.C. § 964(e)(4).

§ 9.07   SPECIAL CONCERNS RELATING TO INDIVIDUALS

U.S. shareholders, both U.S. corporations and individuals who meet the requisite stock ownership thresholds, are required to include into income the amounts proscribed by I.R.C. §§ 951(a) and 951A. But as described in Chapter 7, *supra*, only corporations are entitled to the 100 percent DRD described in I.R.C. § 245A. Individuals are also not entitled to the deduction that reduces the U.S. effective tax rate on GILTI income that is available to corporate shareholders under I.R.C. § 250. Generally speaking, U.S. individual shareholders of foreign companies are penalized relative to corporate shareholders in a number of respects: unlike corporations, their income tax rates were not substantially reduced in the TCJA; they are required to include amounts in GILTI but aren't entitled to the deduction under I.R.C. § 250 that lowers the effective rate on GILTI income; and they are not entitled to the dividends received deduction for dividends paid out of eligible earnings of a CFC. Finally, as will be discussed further in the next chapter, they cannot claim foreign tax credits with respect to deemed dividends from CFCs required to be included in income as subpart F income or GILTI.

While the DRD is available only for domestic corporations, I.R.C. § 962 provides that an individual who is a U.S. shareholder may generally elect to be taxed on amounts included in gross income under I.R.C. § 951(a) in "an amount equal to the tax that would be imposed under section 11 if such amounts were received by a domestic corporation." There were lots of questions raised about whether the I.R.C. § 962 election was broad enough to allow taxpayers to claim the deduction under I.R.C. § 250, by its terms available only to corporations.

In proposed regulations, the IRS said that GILTI is treated as an amount included under I.R.C. § 951(a) for purposes of I.R.C. § 962, essentially providing that taxpayers who make the election under I.R.C. § 962 are able to claim the deduction under I.R.C. § 250 for GILTI only available to corporate shareholders under the statute. Prop. Reg. § 1.962–1(b)(1)(i).

§ 9.08   TRANSITION TAX

In connection with the transition to a mislabeled territorial system of taxation, the TCJA imposed a one-time transition tax on the accumulated earnings of CFCs (and other foreign corporations with at least one 10 percent U.S. shareholder that is a corporation). I.R.C. § 965. The transition tax was supposed to be the cost of getting into a new more beneficial regime of taxation of foreign earnings.

The transition tax in I.R.C. § 965 is effective for the last tax year of a foreign corporation that begins before 2018, and with respect to U.S. shareholders, for the tax years in which or with which such tax years of the foreign corporation ends. Taxpayers can elect to defer payments of tax due under I.R.C. § 965 over an 8 year period (but only upon an election made with a timely filed return), with more beneficial timing rules available for S corporations and REITs.

A portion of the I.R.C. § 965 inclusion is deductible. Earnings that are invested in "real" assets are taxed at a lower rate than earnings that are invested in cash or cash equivalents, resulting in effective corporate rates of 15.5 percent applicable to cash assets and 8 percent for any remaining assets. Individuals are entitled to a deduction based on the highest rate of tax applicable to corporations in the taxable year of inclusion.

Despite the fact that the transition tax was a one-time event, it will have ripple effects on taxpayers' tax attributes and on structuring and planning considerations for years to come. That's because the earnings taxed under I.R.C. § 965 are considered PTEP under I.R.C. § 959, and the inclusions also resulted in adjustments to stock basis under I.R.C. § 961. *See* Notice 2019–1, 2019–3 I.R.B. 275. The IRS has announced that it will be revising PTEP guidance in order to reflect changes made by TCJA but as of the date of this printing such guidance has not yet been released. Final regulations under I.R.C. § 965 provide rules for basis adjustments that need to be tracked going forward. Reg. § 1.965–2(e).

§ 9.09   PASSIVE FOREIGN INVESTMENT COMPANIES (PFICs)

Having mastered the rules of subpart F and GILTI, it's now time for you to be introduced to an entirely different regime that separately may require U.S. shareholders to include in income earnings of foreign corporations. The passive foreign investment company (or PFIC) rules apply to potentially subject to U.S. tax the earnings of foreign companies by shareholders that are not "U.S. shareholders"—*i.e.*, U.S. persons that own less than 10 percent of the vote or value of a CFC. These rules address Congress' concerns that U.S. persons may be able to defer tax on earnings of foreign companies in which they own but a minority interest, specifically targeted at passive income. A PFIC is defined as a foreign corporation which meets either an income or an asset test. Under the income test, at least 75 percent of the corporation's income must be passive income for the PFIC rules to apply. I.R.C. § 1297(a)(1). Passive income includes dividends, interest, passive rents and other income treated as foreign personal holding company income for purposes of subpart F. I.R.C. § 1297(b).

The passive income test is based on gross income. For example, if a foreign corporation earns interest income, the fact that deductions exceed the interest income does not change the fact that the foreign corporation would be a PFIC with respect to a U.S. owner. In applying the passive income test, under I.R.C. § 1297(c) described below, the income of 25 percent owned subsidiaries can be taken into account. There is also another look-through rule under I.R.C. § 1298(b)(7) for certain foreign corporations that own at least 25 percent (by value) of the stock of a U.S. corporation.

Under the asset test, a foreign corporation is a PFIC if at least 50 percent of the corporation's assets (by value) are held for the production of passive income. I.R.C. § 1297(a)(2). Such a corporation would be a PFIC even if it did carry on an active business such as manufacturing. A non-publicly traded foreign corporation can elect to use adjusted basis rather than fair market value as a measuring rod, but once the election is made it cannot be revoked without IRS consent. I.R.C. § 1297(e)(2).

Under I.R.C. § 1297(c), where a foreign corporation owns, directly or indirectly, at least 25 percent by value of the stock of another corporation (a "subsidiary"), the subsidiary look-through rule generally applies. Where the subsidiary look-through rule applies, the foreign corporation being tested for PFIC status is treated as if it held directly its proportionate share of the subsidiary's assets (both passive and active), and directly earned its proportionate share of the subsidiary's income (both passive and active). Second and more remote tiers of foreign corporations are also subject to this treatment if they are 25 percent or more indirectly owned by the foreign corporation being evaluated for PFIC status.

In July 2019, more than 30 years after the PFIC rules were enacted, the IRS issued proposed regulations providing guidance for how to determine a foreign company's proportion of the share of assets and income of a look-through subsidiary. *See* REG– 105474–18, 2019–31 I.R.B. 493; 84 Fed. Reg. 33120– 33161; Prop. Reg. § 1.1297–2(b)(2).

In applying the income test for testing PFIC status, interest, dividends, rents or royalties which are received from a related party (under I.R.C. § 954(d)(3), more than 50 percent voting power applying constructive ownership rules) receive look-through treatment. I.R.C. § 1297(b)(2)(C). For example, if an entity that is being tested for PFIC status receives interest from a related brother/sister corporation (*i.e.*, a common parent owns both the lender and the borrower) that conducts an active business, the interest income, while normally passive income, will be treated as non-PFIC income for purposes of I.R.C. § 1297(a). If the lender was a wholly-owned subsidiary, presumably the interest income would be disregarded for PFIC testing as the borrower would be deemed to own all of the lender's assets and to receive all of the lender's income. I.R.C. § 1297(c).

Three alternative methods may apply with respect to a U.S. owner of a PFIC. For a qualified electing fund (QEF) under I.R.C. § 1295 that provides information necessary to determine the income and identity of its shareholders, electing U.S. owners are taxed currently on their pro rata portions of the company's actual income under I.R.C. § 1293, subject to an election to defer payment of tax (plus an interest charge) until a distribution is made or a disposition of stock occurs. I.R.C. § 1294. The deemed distribution is not eligible for the dividends received deduction in I.R.C. § 245A. I.R.C. § 245A(a)(2).

The QEF election can be made by any U.S. person holding PFIC stock. If a QEF shareholder is a domestic corporation which owns at least 10 percent of the QEF's stock, the shareholder may be permitted an indirect tax credit. I.R.C. § 1293(f). (Even though I.R.C. § 902 was repealed, I.R.C. § 1293(f) treats the deemed distribution as eligible for the foreign tax credit under I.R.C. § 960. *See* discussion of the indirect foreign tax credit in Chapter 10). A U.S. partnership must make the election for its partners. If a QEF election is in place, any qualifying U.S. shareholders can get the beneficial tax capital gains tax rate under I.R.C. § 1(h)(11) for any capital gains at the PFIC level. Because a QEF shareholder is generally taxed as income is earned by the PFIC, there is no additional PFIC taxation upon distribution or if a QEF shareholder disposes of the PFIC stock where the QEF election is made in the first year the U.S. owner becomes an owner. I.R.C. § 1291(d)(1). A U.S. owner that reports income as a result of a QEF election increases its basis in the stock of the PFIC. I.R.C. § 1293(d).

Note that a taxpayer with a QEF election only picks up the income of the foreign corporation in years that the entity is a PFIC under the asset or income tests in I.R.C. § 1297(a). So if a QEF election is made in Year 1, the electing shareholder would include all of the entity's income in Year 1. If the entity is not a PFIC in Year 2, then the electing shareholder does not include the PFIC's income. If the entity again becomes a PFIC in Year 3, the electing shareholder includes the income. *See* Reg. § 1.1295–1(c)(2)(ii).

A second method, the deferred interest charge method, allows a U.S. owner ex post to compute an annual inclusion based on reasonable assumptions and to defer payment of the taxes (plus an interest charge) until an "excess distribution" from the PFIC or a disposition of stock occurs. I.R.C. § 1291. Under this method, gain recognized on the disposition of stock is considered to be earned pro rata over the shareholder's holding period of the investment. The U.S. tax due on disposition equals the yearly taxes due plus interest running from each year's due date. The tax rate applied is the highest statutory rate for the owner during the time the stock was held. Notice that under this method, no gain on a sale will qualify for capital gains treatment. Note also that the definition of a disposition is quite broad. For example, if a U.S. owner pledges PFIC stock, that pledge is a disposition for PFIC purpose. I.R.C. § 1298(b)(6). Even a nonrecognition event may trigger taxation. I.R.C. § 1291(f).

The portion of the total actual distributions for the taxable year of the U.S. investor that constitutes an excess distribution is determined by comparing the total distributions received to the average amount of distributions received during the preceding three years, or, if shorter, during the taxpayer's holding period prior to the current year (the "base period"). The amount of the excess distribution is the amount by which total distributions for a taxable year exceeds 125 percent of the base period.

If a shareholder has made a timely QEF election (a "pedigreed QEF") to be taxed as if the PFIC were a pass-thru entity, the deferred interest charge method will not apply. For example, if a U.S. owner with a timely QEF election in effect has gain on the sale of PFIC stock, the gain may qualify for capital gain treatment. For this reason, taxpayers who own stock of a PFIC generally try to make timely QEF elections. But if the shareholder has made an untimely QEF election after the first year it is a PFIC with respect to that owner, the deferred interest charge method may apply even though the QEF election is in effect. For example, a shareholder selling stock of a PFIC at a gain will be subject to a deferred interest charge with respect to that gain. In some cases, a shareholder who fails to make a timely pedigreed

QEF election can do so retroactively. Reg. § 1.1295–3.

To illustrate how the deferred interest charge method functions, suppose that a PFIC shareholder has shares of stock in a PFIC with a basis of $100 and fair market value of $600. Suppose that the shareholder has held that stock for five years and that the corporation was a PFIC for each of those five years. Upon the sale, the gain will be spread out over the holding period so that $100 is attributable to each of the five years. With respect to the $100 deemed to have been earned in Year 1, the shareholder will owe tax at the highest marginal tax rate for that year, plus an interest charge equal to the tax that would have been paid if the taxpayer did not defer payment multiplied by an applicable interest rate multiplied by the four years between the end of year 1 and the end of year 5 when the sale takes place. The same analysis applies for the $100 deemed to have paid in year 2, except the interest runs for only three years, and so on. I.R.C. § 1291. Essentially, the interest charge is for the "loan" from the IRS for the tax that should have been paid each year but was not paid. However, note that if there is no gain on the sale of the stock, there is no PFIC interest charge.

This method can be quite punitive. For example, capital gain on the sale of stock may not be due to earnings of the PFIC but may be due to asset appreciation. Also gain on a sale may not have accrued in a pro rata manner but may have occurred shortly before the sale. For these and other reasons, QEF elections are often made where possible.

A third method for reporting PFIC income is the mark-to-market election. I.R.C. § 1296. A U.S. shareholder holding marketable stock in a PFIC (*e.g.*, stock listed on a recognized stock exchange) may elect to recognize either gain or loss annually on the difference between the shareholder's basis at the beginning of the year and the fair market value of the stock at the end of the year. PFIC inclusions are not eligible for the lower tax rate on qualified dividends available to individuals. I.R.C. § 1(h)(11)(C)(iii).

As noted above, essentially a U.S. owner can make a QEF election or if no QEF election is made PFIC liability occurs under the deferred interest charge method. Steps can be taken under either method to minimize potential PFIC liability. Consider first a U.S. owner not making a QEF election.

Once a foreign corporation qualifies as a PFIC with respect to a U.S. owner, it remains a PFIC—the "once a PFIC, always a PFIC" rule—which can lead to some surprising results. For example, suppose that a U.S. shareholder of a PFIC is subject to tax under the deferred interest charge method discussed above. Even if the foreign corporation in a subsequent year no longer meets the PFIC requirements (*i.e.*, when the active business produces profits), any excess distribution or sale of the stock will give rise to a deferred interest charge applied to the shareholder's entire holding period, including that portion when the corporation was not a PFIC.

However, a shareholder can purge the PFIC taint by electing to treat the stock as having been sold on the last day of the last year the foreign corporation met the PFIC qualifications. I.R.C. § 1298(b)(1). This deemed sale is subject to the deferred interest charge but any subsequent gain in the value of the stock or distribution from the foreign corporation will not be subject to the deferred interest charge as long as the foreign corporation does not again become a PFIC. If the deemed sale would not result in any gain, then the purge election is essentially costless. There is also a deemed dividend purge election (instead of the deemed sale purge) for U.S. investors owning stock in a PFIC that is also a CFC. For example, a 7 percent U.S. investor could make the deemed dividend purge as long as the U.S. investor simultaneously elects QEF treatment. I.R.C. § 1291(d)(2)(B).

Recall that a U.S. owner making a QEF election after the first year the owner becomes an owner remains subject to the QEF regime and the deferred interest charge regime. However, there is another purge provision that allows a shareholder of an unpedigreed QEF (*i.e.*, where the QEF election is not timely made in the first year of PFIC status) to avoid the deferred interest charge method on any subsequent sale of stock or excess distribution if the shareholder agrees to treat the stock as sold immediately before the QEF election takes effect in a transaction subject to the deferred interest charge. That purge would mean that any subsequent appreciation in the stock or any subsequent distributions would not be subject to the deferred interest charge method. Reg. § 1.1291–10.

To prevent the dual application of the subpart F rules and the PFIC rules, Congress has enacted an "overlap" rule that essentially provides that any shareholder that is a U.S. shareholder with respect to a CFC will not be subject to the PFIC rules. However, the PFIC rules could apply to any U.S. persons who are not shareholders of that entity. For example, suppose that USCo owns 95 percent of the stock of FC, a foreign corporation, and a U.S. individual owns the remaining 5 percent of the stock. The PFIC rules apply to the U.S. individual even though the subpart F rules apply to USCo. As noted above, the IRS has proposed regulations that would treat partnerships as an aggregate for purposes of determining the subpart F inclusions of partners in a U.S. partnership. How such proposed rules might interact with the CFC/PFIC overlap rule is unclear.

Under I.R.C. § 1298(f) and Temp. Reg. § 1.1298–1T, a U.S. person that is a shareholder of a PFIC must file a Form 8621 annually. The Regulations eliminate some duplicative reporting. For example, a partner in a U.S. partnership that owns stock of a PFIC where a QEF election is in place (or where the mark-to-market rules apply) does not have to file a Form 8621 if the U.S. partnership files the form.

CHAPTER 10

LIMITATIONS ON THE FOREIGN TAX CREDIT AND THE INDIRECT CREDIT

§ 10.01 THE INDIRECT CREDIT: OVERVIEW

Chapter 8 covered how a U.S. taxpayer can claim a foreign tax credit for foreign taxes paid directly (the direct credit). I.R.C. § 901. Since 1918, the Code also permitted some shareholders to claim the benefit of an indirect credit upon the receipt of a dividend on a proportionate share of the foreign taxes paid by the distributing corporation. Section 902, which allowed U.S. corporate shareholders that were 10 percent owners of foreign companies to claim what was known as the indirect tax credit, was repealed by the TCJA in conjunction with the enactment of I.R.C. § 245A, which allows U.S. corporate shareholders a 100 percent dividends received deduction for such dividends. *See* Chapter 7, *supra*. The logic was that there is no need to provide a tax credit against income that is exempt from U.S. taxation.

The principles of I.R.C. § 902 survive, however, in I.R.C. § 960, which allows U.S. corporate shareholders to claim a foreign tax credit upon inclusions of income required by I.R.C. §§ 951(a) and 951A (subpart F income and GILTI, as discussed in Chapter 9). (Note that withholding taxes on distributions from foreign companies, which are considered direct taxes, are still creditable under I.R.C. § 901.) Subject to limitations, when earnings of a CFC are includible in the income of a U.S.

shareholder under the subpart F rules, the U.S. parent corporation may be permitted an indirect tax credit for the foreign taxes on the income earned by the CFC attributable to the inclusion. But there is an important distinction between the credit allowable under I.R.C. § 960 with respect to an inclusion under I.R.C. § 951(a) (of subpart F income) versus an inclusion of GILTI required under I.R.C. § 951A. While an inclusion under I.R.C. § 951(a) entitles the U.S. shareholder to a credit for 100 percent of the foreign taxes paid attributable to the inclusion, an inclusion under I.R.C. § 951A only entitles the U.S. shareholder to a credit for 80 percent of the attributable foreign taxes.

Because the edifice of the indirect credit was built on a foundation that assumed a dividend was taxable income, its mechanics don't always fit well into the post-TCJA regime. In this chapter, we will see how the IRS is attempting to update its regulations to adjust to the new regime, and illustrate some of the many questions that remain to be addressed.

As discussed in Chapter 8, the availability of the foreign tax credit is generally limited to the U.S. tax otherwise due on foreign source income. That's a principle that's simple to articulate but hard to implement. Further, as part of a decades-long effort to limit taxpayers' ability to engage in foreign tax credit planning (what some have referred to as the last legal tax shelter), the Code divides different categories of income into separate baskets for foreign tax credit purposes. Foreign taxes paid on income allocated to one basket are not creditable against income earned in another basket. Closely related to the categorization of gross income into different baskets are questions of how to allocate expenses between and among different baskets to arrive at net income against which foreign taxes are creditable. We'll take on these intellectually stimulating topics in the rest of this chapter.

§ 10.02   AVAILABILITY OF THE INDIRECT CREDIT

(A)   WHO CAN CLAIM THE INDIRECT FOREIGN TAX CREDIT?

The credit allowed under I.R.C. § 901 can be claimed by both individuals and corporations. The indirect credit allowed under I.R.C. § 960, however, is only available to domestic corporate shareholders. Because the credit is only available against inclusions of income required under I.R.C. §§ 951(a) and 951A (or, in some circumstances from PFICs), this means that only persons required to include such amount in income—*i.e.*, U.S. shareholders as defined in I.R.C. § 951(b)—can claim the indirect credit under I.R.C. § 960.

Under the statute, the credit is available to offset inclusions of subpart F income and inclusions required as a result of investments in U.S. property pursuant to I.R.C. § 951(a)(1)(B) (as well as inclusions of GILTI). But the regulations turn off the credit available for I.R.C. § 956 U.S. property inclusions, by providing that any inclusion otherwise required under I.R.C. § 956 is reduced to the extent such deemed distribution would be entitled to the I.R.C. § 245A deduction if received as a distribution from the CFC directly. Reg. § 1.956–1(a). Because dividends eligible for the I.R.C. § 245A deduction don't carry foreign tax credits, neither will such a hypothetical distribution now mandated by I.R.C. § 956 regulations. The denial of the credit applies whether or not the deemed distribution is tax-exempt under I.R.C. § 245A or taxable (either because the shareholder is an individual ineligible to claim the I.R.C. § 245A deduction or because the deemed distribution is one to which I.R.C. § 245A(e) would apply).

The indirect credit allowable under I.R.C. § 960 is only available to domestic corporations that own at least 10 percent of the foreign corporation's voting stock. There is no indirect tax credit for inclusions required by an *individual* owning stock of a foreign corporation doing business abroad even though individuals are required to include amounts in income under the rules of subpart F or GILTI. An individual taxpayer who makes an election under I.R.C. § 962 is eligible to claim a credit for foreign taxes paid in connection with an inclusion of subpart F income or GILTI as if they were a domestic corporation. I.R.C. §§ 962(b), 951A(f). But note that any subsequent distribution of PTEP in this case is subject to tax to the extent the distribution exceeds the tax paid on the inclusion. *See* I.R.C. § 962(d).

Suppose that USCo is a 50 percent partner in a partnership that owns 100 percent of the stock of ForCo, a CFC. Under I.R.C. § 960, because USCo would have an inclusion of 50 percent of any GILTI income earned by ForCo, it should be able to claim a proportionate share of foreign taxes attributable to such income as a credit under I.R.C. § 960. Prop. Reg. § 1.960–2(b)(4) provides that where a domestic corporation that has a distributive share of a domestic partnership's subpart F inclusion and is also a U.S. shareholder with respect to the CFC that gives rise to a subpart F inclusion it's treated as a subpart F inclusion of the domestic corporation for purposes of I.R.C. § 960(a). The GILTI inclusion amount of a domestic corporation that is also a U.S. shareholder of a CFC through its interest in a domestic partnership is generally determined at the partner level; the rules in Prop. Reg. § 1.960–2(c) apply in the same manner as if the domestic corporation included the GILTI inclusion amount directly. Prop. Reg. § 1.951A–5(c).

(B) CARRYBACKS AND CARRYFORWARDS

As noted in Chapter 8, a foreign tax paid but not creditable in the year paid is generally available for a one-year carryback and 10 year carryforward under I.R.C. § 904(c). However, there is a limitation on this carryback and carryforward in the case of foreign taxes paid attributable to GILTI inclusions. Such taxes are not eligible for any carryback or carryforward.

What happens to foreign taxes that were paid but not credited before 2018? The proposed regulations provide a rule for how to categorize these taxes. *See* Prop. Reg. § 1.904–2.

(C) DIRECT V. INDIRECT CREDIT

Suppose that a newly-formed, wholly-owned foreign subsidiary of a U.S. corporation earned $1 million of subpart F income in its first year on which it paid $250,000 in foreign income taxes. The foreign corporation therefore has $750,000 of earnings and profits for its only year of existence, all of which qualify as subpart F income—$1 million of earnings minus the $250,000 tax payment. The U.S. corporate shareholder includes in its taxable income $750,000, plus the $250,000 of foreign taxes deemed paid. If the U.S. shareholder included just $750,000 into income and was able to credit $250,000 of foreign taxes against its U.S. tax liability, the effective tax rate on the subpart F income would be 33 $\frac{1}{3}$ percent ($250,000 tax on $750,000 of income) when the foreign tax rate was actually 25 percent ($250,000 tax on $1 million of income). Instead, the indirect foreign tax credit actually treats the domestic parent corporation as if it directly paid the allocable portion of income taxes borne by the included income. The U.S. corporate shareholder thus is required to include not only the $750,000 dividend but also $250,000 additional dollars. Stated differently, the U.S. parent corporation must "gross up" the deemed tax payment and treat the grossed-up amount as part of the subpart F inclusion. I.R.C. § 78. In sum, the domestic parent corporation reports $1,000,000 of income and can take a $250,000 foreign tax credit so that the effective tax rate on the subpart F income is 25 percent ($250,000 tax on $1,000,000 inclusion)— the same rate applied to the CFC.

U.S. shareholders that receive dividend distributions from 10 percent owned corporations can no longer claim an indirect credit in connection with those dividends, given the repeal of I.R.C. § 902. Also, I.R.C. § 245A(d) specifically provides that no credit is allowable under I.R.C. § 901 for any taxes paid or accrued (or treated as paid or accrued) with respect to any dividend for which a deduction is allowed under I.R.C. § 245A. Such distributions may be subject to withholding taxes in other jurisdictions, which may be creditable under I.R.C. § 901. But taxpayers can still claim a foreign tax credit upon distributions from foreign companies, if the distributions are of previously taxed earnings and profits. Section 960(c) provides rules addressing creditability of taxes on distribution of PTEP. *See* Prop. Reg. § 1.960–3. *See* § 10.05 below.

§ 10.03 LIMITATIONS ON THE FOREIGN TAX CREDIT

(A) OVERVIEW

As noted in Chapter 8, the amount of foreign tax credit a U.S. taxpayer can claim is limited by its foreign source income—specifically, to the U.S. tax that would otherwise be due on such income. In this section we dive into the calculations and complexities of the foreign tax credit limitation in more detail. A word of warning: the computations required by these labyrinthine provisions can boggle the mind.

Suppose T, a U.S. taxpayer (corporation), directly earns net income of $100,000 from business activities in Mexico and $200,000 of income from U.S. sources. Assume that the U.S. tax rate is a flat 21 percent while the Mexican rate is 50 percent. The U.S. tax liability on the $300,000 of worldwide income is $63,000. Absent a limitation provision, T could credit the $50,000 of Mexican taxes against the U.S. tax liability, leaving a net U.S. tax liability of $13,000, or an effective U.S. tax rate of only 6.5 rather than 21 percent on the $200,000 of U.S. source income. In order to prevent foreign income taxes from reducing U.S. income taxes on U.S. source income, I.R.C. § 904 has historically limited the foreign tax credit to foreign income taxes imposed on foreign source income to the extent those taxes do not exceed the U.S. income tax on that foreign source income.

Specifically, I.R.C. § 904 provides that the total amount of the foreign tax credit cannot exceed the same proportion of the tax against which the credit is taken which the taxpayer's foreign source taxable income bears to worldwide taxable income. Stated differently:

$$\frac{X}{\text{U.S. income tax}} = \frac{\text{Foreign source income}}{\text{Worldwide taxable income}}$$

where X = the amount of creditable foreign income taxes that can be credited for the taxable year. Solving the equation for X yields the following formulation:

$$X = \text{U.S. income tax} \times \frac{\text{Foreign source income}}{\text{Worldwide taxable income}}$$

Foreign source income is sometimes referred to as the numerator of the I.R.C. § 904(a) limitation formula, and worldwide taxable income is referred to as the denominator.

Applying the formula to the problem above results in a U.S. income tax credit for the current year of $21,000 of the $50,000 Mexican income tax and a U.S. tax collection of $42,000—essentially $200,000 of U.S. source income taxed at a 21 percent tax rate:

$$\frac{X}{\$63,000} = \frac{\$100,000}{\$300,000}$$

As noted above, other than with respect to credits associated with GILTI inclusions, under I.R.C. § 904(c), any excess creditable taxes that can not be immediately credited because of the I.R.C. § 904(a) limitation generally can be carried back one year (necessitating an amended return) and carried forward ten years, subject always to the I.R.C. § 904(a) limitation. Excess credits cannot be deducted. I.R.C. §§ 904(c), 275(a)(4)(A).

Suppose that T arranges for $100,000 of the U.S. source income (*e.g.*, investment income that may be easily moveable) to be earned in the Cayman Islands, a foreign jurisdiction that imposes no income tax. Now T has $200,000 of foreign source income and $100,000 of U.S. source income. If the I.R.C. § 904(a) formula allows T to look at "overall" foreign income, $42,000 of the $50,000 in Mexican taxes is immediately creditable (instead of $21,000 in the prior example):

$$\frac{X}{\$63,000} = \frac{\$200,000}{\$300,000}$$

In effect under this "overall" method, the taxpayer would be permitted to average the highly-taxed Mexican income with the non-taxed Cayman Islands income so that the United States would only collect $21,000 of U.S. tax instead of $42,000 in the example above where there was $200,000 of U.S. source income. For various periods in U.S. tax history, the taxpayer was permitted to use this "overall" method of determining the foreign tax credit limitation.

To prevent this type of averaging, Congress has at various times enacted a "per country" limitation. Under the "per country" limitation, foreign income taxes from each country are subjected to the I.R.C. § 904(a) limitation separately so that the numerator of the I.R.C. § 904(a) ratio (*i.e.*, foreign source income) is applied country-by-country. In the previous example, only $21,000 of the Mexican income taxes would be immediately creditable. Up to $21,000 of Cayman Islands income taxes would also have been creditable but there are no taxes imposed and the taxpayer cannot credit the excess Mexican income taxes under the Cayman Islands limitation. Crediting $21,000 of Mexican tax against the potential $63,000 U.S. tax liability on $300,000 would leave a $42,000 residual U.S. tax.

The "per-country" limitation method may appear to be a perfect solution to the perceived averaging problem. But consider this additional problem that the per-country limitation creates. Suppose that T has the $100,000 of Mexican income on which $50,000 of Mexican income taxes are paid, $100,000 of U.S. income and a $100,000 loss from the start of a new business in China. In total, T has $100,000 of net income on which there is a $21,000 U.S. income tax. If the "per-country" method is used, the taxpayer can credit $21,000 of Mexican taxes against the $21,000 U.S. tax liability:

$$\frac{X}{\$21,000} = \frac{\$100,000}{\$100,000}$$

If T is allowed to credit $21,000 of Mexican income taxes, the U.S. tax liability is eliminated even though T has earned $100,000 of U.S. source income. For this situation, the "per-country" method results in lower U.S. taxes than the "overall" method which would force T to combine the $100,000 of Mexican income with the $100,000 Chinese loss in the I.R.C. § 904(a) numerator, thereby producing no foreign tax credit:

$$\frac{X}{\$21,000} = \frac{\$0}{\$100,000}$$

It is this conundrum of the "overall" method being preferable in some situations and the "per country" limitation method being preferable in some situations in terms of protecting U.S. taxation of U.S. source income that has led to a shifting back-and-forth over the years in the way in which I.R.C. § 904(a) limitation is applied. The current system introduces new sets of complications.

(B) SEPARATE "BASKETS"

The foreign tax credit limitation applies not just to limit a taxpayer's ability to claim a foreign tax credit to the U.S. tax on its foreign source income. Within foreign source income, Congress has created a regime in which income is categorized into separate "baskets": the taxes paid on income in one basket is generally not creditable against taxes paid on income belonging in a different basket.

Under the "basket" approach laid out in I.R.C. § 904(d) (and in mind-numbing detail in regulations), each specially designated type of gross income is placed into a "basket" to which the I.R.C. § 904(a) limitation is applied. The complexity involved in applying I.R.C. § 904 to the separate baskets has turned many a sane tax professional (oxymoron?) into a "basket case." Nevertheless, the basic Congressional intent is not difficult to understand. Congress wanted to prevent U.S. taxpayers from arranging their affairs to maximize the foreign tax credit at the expense of U.S. taxes on U.S. source income.

The I.R.C. § 904(d) limitation for each basket can be stated as follows:

$$X = \text{U.S. income tax} \times \frac{\text{Foreign source income in the basket}}{\text{Worldwide taxable income}}$$

Where X = the amount of creditable foreign income taxes that can be credited for the taxable year. Solving the equation for X yields the following formulation:

$$\frac{X}{\$21,000} = \frac{\$0}{\$100,000}$$

For years beginning after September 31, 2006, and through enactment of the TCJA, there were only two baskets—the passive basket and the general basket. Prior to that time, I.R.C. § 904(d) created as many as nine separate baskets. Perhaps nostalgic for the previous, more complex system, the TCJA created two new baskets which means that in taxable years after 2017 there are four baskets to which taxpayers' income may be assigned. The two new baskets are the GILTI basket and the foreign branch basket. I.R.C. § 904(d)(1)(A) and (B).

To illustrate how the basket mechanism works, consider again the examples discussed. Assume the $100,000 of Mexican income is generated from business activities (but not from a foreign branch) and is therefore placed in the general income basket. I.R.C. § 904(d)(1)(D). Assume the $100,000 of investment income from the Cayman Islands (also not from a foreign branch) would be placed in the passive income basket and so treated separately under I.R.C. § 904(d)(1)(C). Applying the I.R.C. § 904(a) formula to the general income basket produces only $21,000 of creditable Mexican taxes:

$$\frac{X}{\$63,000} = \frac{\$100,000}{\$300,000}$$

This produces the same result as the "per country" limitation. (Note that separate baskets apply even if the passive interest income is earned in the same country as the active income.) But, recall that the "per country" limitation failed to protect U.S. source income in the situation where T earned $100,000 of Mexican income and suffered a $100,000 business loss in China. Applying the baskets to this situation yields a "correct" result, a result that protects the $21,000 U.S. income tax on the $100,000 of U.S. income. Both the Mexican income and the Chinese loss are placed in the general basket (I.R.C. § 904(d)(1)(D)) so that no Mexican taxes are creditable for the taxable year because the numerator in the I.R.C. § 904(a) ratio is $0:

$$\frac{X}{\$21,000} = \frac{\$0}{\$100,000}$$

In sum, the use of the basket method is intended to provide some of the advantages of the "per country" limitation in preventing averaging of high- and low-taxed income and the advantages of the "overall" limitation in offsetting foreign losses against foreign income for purposes of determining the numerator in the I.R.C. § 904(a) formula.

Computing the foreign tax credit limitation is a daunting task requiring a lot of information. As an act of simplification, Congress has waived the limitation for certain *de minimis* foreign taxes paid by individuals. An individual with $300 ($600 for joint filers) or less of creditable foreign taxes is exempt from the foreign tax credit limitation, provided that the taxpayer has no foreign source income other than qualified passive income. I.R.C. § 904(j).

(1) The GILTI Basket

For most U.S. multinational taxpayers with CFCs, the vast majority of the earnings of their foreign subsidiaries will be includible as GILTI and will be allocated to the GILTI basket. A simplified example of how to calculate the foreign tax credit for GILTI inclusions is presented below. But before getting to the example, an overview of some of the foreign tax credit rules as specifically relevant to GILTI is helpful.

First, as explained above, taxes associated with a GILTI inclusion under I.R.C. § 951A may be creditable under I.R.C. § 960. But that section introduces a wrinkle to the calculation of the GILTI foreign tax credit, by limiting the credit to 80 percent of the taxes attributable to the GILTI inclusion. That calculation is further complicated by an issue highlighted in Chapter 9—while income when earned by a CFC has the character of "tested income," income is not characterized as GILTI at the CFC level. This means that the taxes attributable to tested income of a CFC may not match the inclusion required by I.R.C. § 951A at the U.S. shareholder level.

Suppose that USCo owns 100 percent of CFC1, which has non-subpart F income of $300, subpart F income of $200, expenses (other than taxes) of $400 (allocated proportionately between GILTI and subpart F income), a foreign tax rate of 20 percent and QBAI (*see* § 9.04(D)) of $100.

The calculation of USCo's tested income is as follows:

CFC1	Total	Sub F Income	Tested Income
Gross Income	$500	$200	$300
Expenses (other than taxes)	($400)	($160)	($240)
Pre-tax Income	$100	$40	$60
Taxes	($20)	($8)	($12)
Taxable Income	**$80**	**$32**	**$48**

The calculation of the foreign tax credit associated with the GILTI inclusion of $38 ($48 net tested income − [10% × $100 QBAI]) is as follows:

First, determine the "inclusion percentage" associated with the GILTI inclusion. I.R.C. § 960(d)(2). The inclusion percentage is equal to the $38 of GILTI, divided by the $48 of USCo's aggregate tested foreign income = 79.2 percent. The deemed paid taxes is equal to the $12 of foreign taxes attributable to the tested income, multiplied by the 80 percent limitation and by the 79.2 percent inclusion percentage. The credit for foreign taxes attributable to tested income is thus limited to $7.60.

The I.R.C. § 78 gross-up on the inclusion—unlike the deemed paid credit—is not subject to the 80 percent limitation. The I.R.C. § 78 gross-up therefore equals: 79.2 percent multiplied by the $12 of taxes paid attributable to GILTI, or $9.50 (12 × .792).

The calculation of the residual U.S. tax on the GILTI inclusion is as follows:

GILTI inclusion plus I.R.C. § 78 gross-up is equal to $47.50 ($38 + 9.50). The U.S. corporate shareholder is then entitled to a deduction under I.R.C. § 250 of 50 percent of the inclusion amount, or $23.75 ($47.50 × .5). *See* § 9.04(E), *supra*. U.S. tax before any foreign tax credit is equal to $4.99 (21 percent of $23.75). The foreign tax credit is therefore limited to $4.99.

The residual U.S. tax in this example is equal to $0. But note that $2.61 of foreign tax credits (resulting from the 80 percent limitation and the 79.92 percent haircut associated with the inclusion percentage) are permanently lost and cannot be carried forward.

Extensive regulations under I.R.C. § 861 provide guidance for how to allocate U.S. shareholder expenses to foreign source income for purposes of computing the foreign tax credit limitation. As indicated below, the requirement to allocate U.S. shareholder expense to income in the GILTI basket further reduces the availability of the foreign tax credit and increases the effective tax rate on GILTI inclusions. Full creditability against the U.S. tax is only available in the example outlined above because it assumes no U.S. shareholder expenses allocable to the GILTI income. If there were any such expenses, the foreign source income in the GILTI basket would be reduced, further limiting the U.S. shareholder's ability to credit the foreign taxes attributable to that income.

For example, suppose that $10 of interest expense incurred by the U.S. shareholder was apportioned to the tested income under the interest expense allocation and apportionment rules in Reg. § 1.861–9. Now the net GILTI inclusion is reduced proportionately and the 21 percent hypothetical U.S. tax is correspondingly lower (but note that allocation of U.S. shareholder level expenses doesn't change the amount of foreign tax actually paid). That means a lower foreign tax credit limitation as well.

Hopefully the above very simple example (you may not agree with this characterization) suffices to show how (1) the calculation of GILTI shouldn't be done without a spreadsheet; (2) most taxpayers will be limited in their ability to fully utilize foreign taxes to offset U.S. taxes owed on GILTI inclusions.

(2) The Foreign Branch Basket

In addition to the GILTI basket, the TCJA introduced another new basket: the foreign branch basket. I.R.C. § 904(d)(1)(B). The foreign branch basket includes income from foreign branches other than passive income. A branch is described for this purpose by reference to a qualified business unit (QBU) as defined in I.R.C. § 989(a). The term QBU previously had limited relevance as it was only used in connection with foreign currency calculations (discussed *infra* in Chapter 12). The term now has been elevated in importance.

The statutory description of the foreign branch basket is very brief, and says only that the amount of business profits attributable to a QBU shall be determined under rules established by the Secretary. Proposed regulations under section 904 modify the I.R.C. § 989 definition of QBU for this purpose to say that to constitute a foreign branch, a QBU must carry on a trade or business outside the United States. Prop. Reg. § 1.904–4(f). The proposed regulations would also take into account some disregarded transactions in determining the income of a foreign branch.

(3) Passive Basket

Passive income (*e.g.*, interest and dividends) can be quite portable. For example, a U.S. corporation may be able to arrange its affairs so that interest income that was formerly U.S. source income (*e.g.*, interest from U.S. corporate bonds) becomes foreign source income (*e.g.*, the taxpayer purchases foreign bonds) often subject to little or no foreign taxation. The relative ease of changing the source of investment income in the absence of some limitation could allow the taxpayer to average high-taxed business income with low-taxed investment income.

The most important categories of income that fall into the passive income basket include dividends, interest, rents, royalties, annuities, net capital gains, and commodities transactions. I.R.C. §§ 904(d)(2)(A)(i), 954(c)(1). Much of this income when earned by a CFC is likely to be subpart F income; remember that as an ordering matter, subpart F income is characterized as such before consideration of whether an item of income is "tested income" under I.R.C. § 951A. *See* § 9.04.

But there are some important exceptions to these inclusions. Rents and royalties derived in an active trade or business from a related or an unrelated person may not be considered passive. Reg. § 1.904–4(b)(2).

There is also an exception for high-taxed passive income which is referred to in the legislative history as the "high-tax kick-out." I.R.C. § 904(d)(2)(B)(iii)(II). The term "high-taxed passive income" refers to income subject to an effective foreign tax rate exceeding the highest applicable U.S. rate (*i.e.*, corporate or individual, depending on the taxpayer) on the income. I.R.C. § 904(d)(2)(F). Rules for how to allocate high-taxed passive income to the passive income basket have been modified by proposed regulations. Prop. Reg. § 1.904–4.

Financial services income (*e.g.*, interest earned by a bank) is not considered passive income. Proposed regulations also provide guidance on the allocation of financial services income to different baskets, needed because the foreign branch basket and the GILTI basket both take precedence over the passive basket. Prop. Reg. § 1.904–4(e).

(4) General Basket

The general basket in I.R.C. § 904(d)(1)(D) is defined to include any income that does not go in the other three baskets. I.R.C. § 904(d)(2)(A)(ii). Historically, foreign source business profits were general basket income. Under the new regime, foreign source business profits earned by a CFC are most likely to be tested income, includible as GILTI, while foreign source business profits earned by a U.S. person may be considered foreign branch income and allocated to the foreign branch basket. The general limitation basket is most likely limited to income that falls within two categories: subpart F income that is active business income and foreign active business income earned directly by a U.S. person from U.S. operations with foreign customers (not through a foreign branch).

Under I.R.C. § 904(d)(2)(H) prior to TCJA, where there was a tax base difference (i.e., a difference in the tax base as calculated for U.S. and foreign tax purposes) the taxes were placed in the general basket. But it appears that Congress neglected to amend I.R.C. § 904(d)(2)(H) when it created additional baskets. As a result I.R.C. § 904(d)(2)(H) now sends all income on which there is a base difference to the foreign branch basket. This cannot be the result Congress intended but it is not clear when there might be a technical correction to address this situation. The proposed regulations incorporate the faulty cross-reference. Prop. Reg. § 1.904–6(a)(1)(iv).

But the proposed regulations also say that base differences arise only in limited circumstances (for example, for categories of items such as life insurance proceeds or gifts, that are excluded from income for Federal income tax purposes but may be taxed as income under foreign law). All other differences between U.S. and foreign tax bases are essentially referred to as a "timing difference." For example, a difference between U.S. and foreign tax law in the amount of deductions that are allowed to reduce gross income, like a difference in depreciation conventions or in the timing of recognition of gross income, is not considered to give rise to a base difference. In the case of a timing difference, the proposed regulations say that taxes on such income are allocated and apportioned to the appropriate separate category or categories to which the tax would be allocated and apportioned if the income were recognized under Federal income tax principles in the year in which the tax was imposed. Prop. Reg. § 1.904–6(a)(1)(iv).

(C) LOOK-THROUGH RULES

Income may appear to be one type of income, *e.g.*, passive income, but under a look-through rule may end up characterized as general basket income. Where a foreign subsidiary is a CFC, a U.S. taxpayer owning at least 10 percent of the voting stock historically was required to "look through" any distribution of dividends, interest, rents and royalties to the distributing corporation's underlying income. I.R.C. § 904(d)(3). Regulations under that Code section generally allocated such income to the basket to which it is allocable in the hands of the payor.

Proposed regulations alter this approach. Under Prop. Reg. § 1.904–5, look-through applies only to determine whether income is allocated to the passive basket (*i.e.*, royalty income received form a CFC is treated as passive income only to the extent the CFC has allocated the royalty expense to its passive income). Other income is allocated based on general principles. Thus, dividends, interest, rents, or royalties paid from a CFC to its U.S. shareholder are not assigned to a separate category (other than the passive category) under the look-through rules, but are assigned to the foreign branch category, a specified separate category (as described in Prop. Reg. § 1.904–4(m)), or the general category (under the rules of Prop. Reg. § 1.904–4(d)). This means that income received from CFCs can't be allocated to GILTI—under the paradigm of the proposed regulations, that is only a shareholder level I.R.C. § 904(d) category and so income can't be allocated to it at the CFC level. This rule introduces further restrictions on U.S. taxpayers' ability to fully credit taxes paid on tested income.

(D) THE I.R.C. § 78 GROSS-UP

To what basket does the I.R.C. § 78 gross-up belong? The question was a controversial one given that if the government applied the same principle as applies to the look-through rules, the I.R.C. § 78 gross-up could never be allocated to GILTI category income. But that would have severely limited the ability of taxpayers to credit taxes imposed on GILTI category income. The proposed regulations provide taxpayers with some relief in this case by stating that the I.R.C. § 78 gross-up related to GILTI basket taxes is allocated to the GILTI basket. Prop. Reg. § 1.904–4(*o*).

§ 10.04 ALLOCATION AND APPORTIONMENT OF DEDUCTIONS

(A) IN GENERAL

Allocating gross income to and among the different I.R.C. § 904(d) baskets is only one part of the exercise. The next step—perhaps the most complex one—is to allocate expenses among the different categories of income. To understand the importance of allocating expenses in general, consider that to the extent expenses are allocated and apportioned against foreign source income, a U.S. taxpayer may have its foreign tax credit limited. For this reason, U.S. taxpayers generally prefer expenses to be allocated and apportioned against U.S. source income. The same principle applies when allocating expenses among the different baskets, but the analysis is more dependent on the taxpayer's individual circumstances.

To recap the rules for allocation of expenses discussed above in § 3.03, in general a taxpayer is required to: (1) allocate deductions to a class of gross income; and then, if a statutory provision requires, (2) apportion deductions within the class of gross income between the statutory grouping (*e.g.*, effectively connected income for a nonresident taxpayer and foreign source income for a U.S. taxpayer) and the residual grouping (*i.e.*, everything else). Reg. § 1.861–8(a)(2). Often expenses bear a definite relationship to a class of gross income in which case no further allocation is necessary although it may be necessary to apportion the income between U.S. and foreign sources (or for a nonresident, between effectively connected income and all other income). For example, direct business expenses deductible under I.R.C. § 162 can often be allocated to specific income. Proposed regulations (Prop. Reg. § 1.861–8(e)(14)) provide that the I.R.C. § 250 deduction allowed for a GILTI inclusion is generally considered definitely related and allocable to the GILTI category of income.

Proposed regulations (Prop. Reg. §§ 1.861–8 through 1.861–13 and 1.861–17) amend existing regulations to clarify how deductions are allocated and apportioned in general, and provide new rules to account for the specific changes made to I.R.C. §§ 864(e) and 904 by TCJA.

For example, TCJA essentially created a large category of an asset that could be considered a tax-exempt asset (*i.e.*, an asset that doesn't give rise to taxable income). That's because stock of a CFC theoretically gives rise to tax-exempt income to the extent that it produces income that is distributed tax-free under I.R.C. § 245A. Section 864(e)(3) generally provides that, for purposes of allocating and apportioning any deductible expense, any tax-exempt asset (and any income from the asset) is not taken into account. If stock of a CFC was treated as a tax-exempt asset, that could result in fewer deductions being allocated to foreign source income, or to income in the GILTI category.

The proposed regulations grant taxpayers partial relief here. Instead of treating stock that gives rise to a tax-free dividend as tax-exempt, they provide that for purposes of applying the expense allocation and apportionment rules, the gross income offset by the I.R.C. § 250 deduction is treated as exempt income, and the stock or other asset giving rise to that income is treated as a partially exempt asset. Prop. Reg. § 1.861–8(d)(2)(ii)(C)(1). But this also means that the value of a domestic corporation's assets that produce FDII is reduced to reflect the fact that the income from the assets is treated in part as exempt. The proposed regulations also provide that that a distribution of PTEP doesn't result in any portion of the stock in a CFC being treated as an exempt asset.

(B) INTEREST

The allocation and apportionment of interest expense often plays a significant role in determining a taxpayer's tax posture. Some interest is directly allocated to a specific class of income if the loan proceeds are applied to purchase and improve real property or depreciable personal property and the creditor can look only to the identified property for security. Reg. § 1.861–10T(b). But if money is borrowed for general business purposes, the interest accrued or paid (depending on method of accounting) is first allocated against all of the taxpayer's gross income and then is apportioned under I.R.C. § 864(e) between U.S. and foreign sources generally according to the basis of all of the taxpayer's assets (according to either a tax book value or alternative tax book value method). For purposes of this apportionment, the assets of all affiliated corporations (generally members of a U.S. consolidated group but sometimes other corporations are included as well) are taken into account. I.R.C. § 1504. This allocation based on assets is premised on the notion that money is fungible, making it difficult to trace accurately interest expense to a particular item of income.

Suppose that a U.S. parent corporation with $30 of interest expense on a $400 loan owns two assets: stock of a wholly-owned U.S. subsidiary with a basis of $600 and stock of a foreign subsidiary (that has no earnings and profits) with a basis of $200. The U.S. subsidiary owns assets used to produce U.S. source income with a basis of $700 and assets used to produce foreign source income with a basis of $100. Because a foreign subsidiary is generally not part of an affiliated group, there is no "look-through" to the assets of the foreign corporation for purposes of allocating interest (although the basis of the stock in the foreign corporation is adjusted for a foreign corporation's earnings and profits under I.R.C. § 864(e)(4)). However, the parent is deemed to own the U.S. subsidiary's U.S. assets with a basis of $700 and the foreign assets with a basis of $100. In total, the U.S. parent is deemed to own foreign assets with a basis of $300 ($200 basis in the foreign stock and $100 basis in the U.S. subsidiary's foreign assets) and U.S. assets with a basis of $700 (the U.S. subsidiary's basis in its assets used to produce U.S. source income). Accordingly, 30 percent of the $30 interest expense of the U.S. parent corporation, or $9, is apportioned against foreign source income and the other $21 of interest expense is allocated against U.S. source income. The same result would occur if the U.S. subsidiary had borrowed the money and paid the interest. Notice that how the borrowed funds are actually used is irrelevant in determining the allocation and apportionment of interest expense. Notice also that the amount of gross U.S. source or foreign source income the taxpayer generates is irrelevant. The formula is mechanical.

One important modification in calculating the tax book value basis of stock of a foreign corporation is the "basis bump" for E&P of 10 percent owned foreign corporations. In a typical case for a wholly-owned foreign subsidiary, the stock basis would be adjusted upwards for E&P of the foreign subsidiary or downwards if there was an E&P deficit. Reg. § 1.861–12(c)(2).

Because U.S. depreciable assets are generally depreciated using accelerated depreciation methods (or under the TCJA, through immediate expensing) while foreign assets held by a U.S. taxpayer are depreciated using a straight-line method, a U.S. taxpayer's calculation under the tax book method may result in apportioning more interest expense against foreign source income for purposes of calculating the foreign tax credit. The alternative tax book value method allows a taxpayer to elect to calculate the tax book value of all depreciable tangible property under the straight-line method in apportioning certain expenses, including interest for foreign tax credit limitation purposes. This may result in less interest expense apportioned against foreign source income. (Note that existing regulations (§ 1.861–9T(h)) provide that a U.S. taxpayer can elect to use an additional method—the fair market value (FMV) method of allocating and apportioning interest expense but that taxpayers' ability to utilize this method was eliminated by the TCJA.)

(C) RESEARCH AND EXPERIMENTAL EXPENDITURES

As noted in § 3.02(C), the government has requested comments on whether the rules for allocating R&D expenses should be revised in light of the changes to I.R.C. § 904(d), in particular the addition of the GILTI category. Revised rules for allocating R&E expenses will likely be an expanded topic in the next edition of this book.

§ 10.05 DISTRIBUTIONS OF PTEP

As discussed in Chapter 9, *supra*, amounts includible in income under subpart F are not taxable to shareholders when subsequently distributed. I.R.C. § 959. Notice 2019–01 describes 16 categories of PTEP, and says that forthcoming regulations will provide for ordering rules for distributions of PTEP.

For purposes of calculating the foreign tax credit, the proposed regulations provide for 10 groups of PTEP within each of the I.R.C. § 904 categories. Taxes may be attributable to a PTEP group, but only if they are imposed solely by reason of receipt of a distribution of PTEP.

Each CFC is required to establish a separate, annual PTEP account for its E&P for its current taxable year to which subpart F or GILTI inclusions of the CFC are attributable, corresponding to the inclusion year of the PTEP and to the I.R.C. § 904 baskets. The PTEP in each annual account is then assigned to one of the 10 possible groups of PTEP.

The proposed regulations provide complex rules for how a CFC should account for a distribution of PTEP that it receives. *See* Prop. Reg. § 1.960–3(c)(3). Similar rules apply for a CFC that makes a distribution of PTEP.

§ 10.06   AMOUNT OF TAX DEEMED PAID

(A) OVERVIEW

All of the rules considered in the earlier parts of this chapter—how to allocate income among different baskets, and how to allocate deductions among the baskets, are applied for one purpose: determining how much of the foreign taxes paid by a CFC are creditable to its U.S. shareholder.

Assuming that the foreign income taxes paid by a foreign subsidiary are creditable income taxes and that the ownership requirements are satisfied, the amount of foreign taxes deemed paid by a U.S. shareholder is the amount of the foreign corporation's foreign income taxes considered properly attributable to the item of income includible under the subpart F rules of I.R.C. §§ 951(a) or 951A.

(B) ALLOCATING TAXES TO BASKETS

The proposed regulations provide an ordering rule for how to compute foreign taxes deemed paid under I.R.C. § 960 and how to allocate foreign income taxes among the different baskets. To apply this ordering rule, you'll need to pull together all the knowledge you've gained from this and prior chapters.

The ordering rule requires that taxpayers perform a set of calculations for each CFC, beginning with the lowest-tier CFC in a chain. For each CFC, taxpayers are required to allocate income among the different income groups. Note that the income groups at the CFC level do not exactly coincide with the I.R.C. § 904(d) baskets, which are determined at the U.S. taxpayer level. At the CFC level, there are three groups to which income can be assigned: the general category, the passive category, and a special I.R.C. § 901(j) category (discussed in Chapter 15). Note that the categories at the CFC level differ from the I.R.C. § 904(d) baskets because the IRS views the GILTI basket as only existing at the shareholder level—at the CFC level, there is only "tested income" but not GILTI. Taxes are allocated to income groups within each category based on the taxable income (as computed under foreign law) in each group. At the CFC level, taxpayers also have to allocate income among the different PTEP accounts, as discussed above.

The next step—once gross income has been allocated among the different categories at the CFC level—is to allocate and apportion deductions, including taxes, to the different categories. Once this has been done, the current year taxes deemed paid for purposes of I.R.C. § 960 can be determined. This whole process then needs to be repeated for the next CFC up the chain. As a final step, the taxpayer needs to determine the taxes deemed paid for any distributions of PTEP to the shareholder.

Once taxable income and current year taxes for each income group have been determined, the amount of foreign income taxes deemed paid for each of the subpart F inclusion and I.R.C. § 951A inclusion can be determined. The amount of foreign taxes considered properly attributed is based on a ratio equal to the product of the current year taxes in the relevant income group times the ratio of the relevant income group inclusion to the amount of income in that group.

As you are by now well aware, calculating the deemed paid tax limitation is not for the faint of heart.

§ 10.07   TREATMENT OF LOSSES

(A) TREATMENT OF FOREIGN LOSSES

Because U.S. taxpayers are—with limited exceptions—taxed on worldwide income, a foreign loss has the potential of decreasing U.S. taxes on U.S. income. That seems appropriate in light of the fact that foreign gains increase U.S. taxes. But, suppose a U.S. taxpayer has an overall foreign loss (OFL) in one year and foreign income in a subsequent year that is not offset by the earlier foreign loss (*e.g.*, the loss was in one country and the income was in a different country). An OFL arises when foreign deductions exceed foreign source income. The excess loss is then available to offset U.S. source income. Once an OFL (the excess of foreign source deductions over foreign source income) offsets U.S. income, it becomes an "OFL account." In the absence of a corrective provision, the impact over a 2 year period could be to lower U.S. taxation of U.S. source net income.

To illustrate, suppose that USCo earns $1,000 of U.S. source business income and suffers a $1,000 loss from business operations in Germany. The U.S. taxation for the year is $0 on the worldwide income of $0. In the next year, USCo earns $1,000 from U.S. business operations and $1,000 from business operations in Switzerland. Assuming a 21 percent rate, the U.S. tax on the $2,000 of worldwide income is $420. If the Swiss income tax is also a 21 percent rate, USCo is able to credit the $210 of Swiss tax on $1,000 of Swiss income against the U.S. tax liability, resulting in a $210 U.S. tax liability. Over the two year period, the United States collected only $210 on $2,000 of U.S. source income for an effective tax rate of 10 1/2 percent. That result arises because on net foreign income of $0 over a two-year period, the taxpayer paid $210 of foreign taxes that were creditable against U.S. taxes.

To prevent this result, I.R.C. § 904(f)(1) generally requires USCo to treat the foreign source income earned in the second year as domestic source income for purposes of the foreign tax credit. With this resourcing, none of the Swiss income tax is creditable in the second year under the I.R.C. § 904(a) limitation because the numerator (*i.e.*, foreign source income) of the I.R.C. § 904(a) fraction is $0. Notice that over a two-year period, the correct result is reached from a U.S. standpoint: USCo earned $2,000 of U.S. source income and pays $420 in U.S. income taxes. Unfortunately, USCo earned $0 net foreign income but still paid a $210 Swiss income tax. Those Swiss taxes may be available in the prior year or in the next ten years under I.R.C. § 904(c).

The recapture rule for OFL accounts under I.R.C. § 904(f)(1) is actually more lenient than indicated above. In many cases, only 50 percent (or greater if the taxpayer so elects) of a taxpayer's foreign earnings (limited by the amount of the OFL) is resourced as U.S. source income for purposes of the foreign tax credit limitation. Taxes on the other 50 percent of the foreign earnings are still creditable. In the example, $105 of the Swiss income taxes would still be immediately creditable ($420 × ($500 foreign source income/$2,000) worldwide income) reducing U.S. tax liability in the second year to $315.

The principle of recapturing foreign losses by recharacterizing future foreign source income also applies where foreign losses in one basket offset income in another basket. (Remember that foreign losses offset U.S. source income only if there are foreign losses left after offsetting foreign source income.) The following rules apply under I.R.C. § 904(f)(5): (1) for any taxable year, a foreign loss in one basket (separate limitation loss) is allocated to income in the other basket before offsetting U.S. source income; (2) in a subsequent taxable year, foreign income attributable to the loss basket is first treated as U.S. source income to the extent U.S. source income was previously offset (OFL account recapture) and then is treated as foreign source income placed in the other basket the income of which was previously offset (separate limitation loss recapture).

The rules governing separate limitation losses are complex, and historically OFL account recapture was a significant problem for many U.S. multinationals. But as is the case with many of the rules designed to protect the U.S. fisc against taxpayers' planning opportunities with respect to the foreign tax credit, the OFL rules don't really address the post-TCJA foreign tax credit regime. That's because taxes attributable to income of a CFC includible as GILTI are only creditable to the extent of GILTI income, and are not available to be carried forward. Taxpayers with GILTI inclusions subject to the OFL rules may be doubly penalized.

Nevertheless, I.R.C. § 904(f) remains in the Code, imposing further limits on taxpayers' ability to claim foreign tax credits post-enactment of the TCJA.

(B) TREATMENT OF U.S. LOSSES

The flip-side of the OFL is the overall domestic loss, or ODL. If a U.S. taxpayer has income from foreign sources but a loss from U.S. sources, the U.S. loss is allocated among the taxpayer's foreign income baskets. I.R.C. § 904(f)(5)(D). If a U.S. taxpayer has both a loss from U.S. source income and a loss in a foreign income basket, the loss from the foreign basket is allocated against foreign source income in the other basket and then the U.S. loss is allocated to the income remaining in that basket.

If an overall domestic loss (ODL) in one year offset foreign income, there is a counterpart to the OFL rules in a subsequent year that changes U.S. source income to foreign source income. I.R.C. § 904(g). To illustrate, suppose in year 1 USCo has a $1,000 U.S. loss and $1,000 of foreign source income. In year 2, USCo has $1,000 of U.S. source income and $1,000 of foreign source income. Because the U.S. source loss in year 1 offset foreign source income, the U.S. source income in year 2 should be treated as foreign source income. That is, in year 1 USCo reports no net income, and in year 2 USCo should report $2,000 of foreign source income to reflect accurately the source of the net income earned during the 2-year period (*i.e.*, no net U.S. income and $2,000 of net foreign source income). However, under I.R.C. § 904(g)(1), 50 percent of the $1,000 U.S. source income in year 2 is treated as foreign source income. This is consistent with the 50 percent recapture rule for OFLs discussed above. An ODL is a positive attribute for a U.S. taxpayer. ODL recapture may permit a U.S. taxpayer to utilize foreign tax credits more efficiently (because there will be $1,500 of foreign source income in year 2 rather than $1,000 of foreign source income). The flip-side of the OFL double penalty in the case of GILTI inclusions is that the ODL also provides less of a benefit to taxpayers in a regime in which GILTI foreign tax credits cannot be carried forward or back.

Proposed regulations provide for transition rules for OFLs and ODLs. They also provide an ordering rule to coordinate with the limitation in I.R.C. § 904(b)(4). Prop. Reg. § 1.904(b)–3(d).

CHAPTER 11
INTERCOMPANY PRICING

§ 11.01 OVERVIEW

Transfer pricing—addressed by the United States in I.R.C. § 482 and in much of the rest of the world through adoption of OECD transfer pricing guidelines—represents the policies and procedures associated with the way in which a company prices goods, services, and intangibles transferred within an organization. From an international tax standpoint, transfer pricing concerns itself with transactions between affiliates domiciled in different taxing jurisdictions. Transfer pricing is significant for both taxpayers and tax administrations because it affects the allocation of profits from intra-group transactions, which impacts the income and expenses reported and therefore taxable profits of related companies that operate in different taxing jurisdictions. One of the most challenging issues that arises from an international tax perspective is determining income and expenses that reasonably can be considered to arise within a territory.

Suppose ParentCo, a U.S. corporation, has a wholly-owned foreign subsidiary, SubCo, organized and operated in Hungary. ParentCo manufactures tractor parts in the United States and sells them to SubCo which in turn sells the parts to unrelated Hungarian customers. If the tax burden in Hungary is lower than that in the United States, or if Hungary offers special tax incentives for income earned in Hungary, or perhaps if SubCo has large net operating losses, it may be advantageous for ParentCo and its subsidiary to structure transactions so that much or all of the combined profit of ParentCo and SubCo is recognized by SubCo. For example, assume that for a particular transaction the cost of manufacturing is $60,000 and that the final sales price received by SubCo is $150,000 on sales to Hungarian customers, a $90,000 combined profit. In the absence of a remedial provision, if ParentCo sells the tractor parts to SubCo for $60,000, then SubCo would report $90,000 of income on the ultimate sale and ParentCo would report $0. If Hungarian tax rates are low, the overall tax liability of ParentCo and its subsidiary may be minimized.

Historically, ParentCo may not have been liable for U.S. taxes on SubCo's income because SubCo is a foreign corporation earning foreign source business income. Post-TCJA, most of the income earned in Hungary likely would be subject to U.S. tax as GILTI under I.R.C. § 951A. But even if the income is taxable as GILTI to ParentCo, the I.R.C. § 250 deduction for GILTI lowers the effective tax rate on GILTI to 10.5 percent, which means that it still may be preferable to generate profits in Hungary rather than directly by ParentCo, or in Hungary rather than another jurisdiction with a higher tax rate.

Conversely, if ParentCo is a foreign corporation (Hungarian ParentCo) which manufactures the tractor parts and sells them to US SubCo, a U.S. corporation, which resells the tractor parts throughout the United States, US SubCo might pay $150,000 to Hungarian Parentco. Hungarian

ParentCo would report a $90,000 gain which normally would escape U.S. taxation, and US SubCo would report $0. Because Hungarian Parentco and US SubCo are related, and the amount paid by US SubCo to Hungarian Parentco remains within the controlled group, the amount paid is artificial. But in the absence of a remedial provision, the tax savings achieved by manipulating prices can be significant. Note that the BEAT (discussed *supra* in 4.09(B)), which is intended to address inbound base erosion, likely would not catch this transaction because of the exception for cost of goods sold.

On the flip side, transfer pricing adjustments also can lead to international double taxation. Suppose that in Table 1 below, country A (*e.g.*, Japan) under its transfer pricing rules determines that in addition to the $200 reported as income, an additional $400 of income reported by a foreign subsidiary in country B is really taxable in the United States. Assume that country B does not agree and continues to tax the $800 of income reported on the return. The results are as follows:

Table 1—Detrimental Impact of Double Taxation on Effective Tax Rate (ETR)			
	Parent (Country A)	Subsidiary (Country B)	Consolidated
Total profit reported on tax return	200	800	1,000
Tax rate	40%	40%	
Tax liability before Country A transfer pricing adjustment	80	320	400
Global ETR			40%
Double taxation effect on ETR			
Total profit after 400 Country A adjustment	600	800	1,000
Tax rate	40%	40%	
Tax liability after Country A transfer pricing adjustment	240	320	560
Global ETR			56%

The other side of the coin is that careful attention to transfer pricing can be used to lower effective tax rates. In Table 2, failure to consider local country tax rates in setting intercompany prices might result in $600 of additional taxable income in country A where it really should be taxable income in country B. Adjusting the transfer pricing can lead to a significant effective tax rate reduction—from 34 percent to 16 percent.

Table 2—Potential Benefit of Transfer Pricing on Global Effective Tax Rate (ETR)			
	Parent (Country A)	Subsidiary (Country B)	Consolidated
Total profit reported on tax return	800	200	1,000
Tax rate	40%	10%	
Tax liability before change to transfer price	320	20	340
Global ETR			34%
ETR Effect of Transfer Pricing Change			
Total profit after using transfer pricing to shift 600 of income	200	800	1,000
Tax rate	40%	10%	
Tax liability after 600 transfer pricing change	80	80	160
Global ETR			16%

Because of the planning opportunities (as well as the potential pitfalls) it presents, transfer pricing is one of the most controversial and contested issues in international taxation today. It is an area closely scrutinized by the IRS and where most multinational taxpayers perceive the highest risk in connection with their activities in multiple jurisdictions. The technical tax issues involved in determining the correct transfer price under U.S. rules or OECD guidelines have been exacerbated by the growth in global supply chain structures in recent years as well as the increased contribution of the value of intangibles to multinationals' profits. Because of the importance and complexity of transfer pricing, it has become a sub-specialty for international tax practitioners—that is, a significant subset of international tax professionals focus solely on transfer pricing issues. It's a topic that's also become highly political—blamed for the failure of developing countries to generate sufficient revenue to meet growth targets, and commonly associated in the public realm with abusive tax planning. In short, transfer pricing rules, while extremely technical, also implicate a wide range of philosophical, political and economic questions about how income and profits should be allocated across borders, and who gets to write the rules determining how that should be done. These controversies are exacerbated by the lack of an effective means for resolving tax disputes between countries; the great majority of cross-border tax disputes over allocation of tax revenues involve transfer pricing issues. *See* § 11.08. The result of these political tensions has been the launch of a major project for rewriting the international tax rules that may involve a significant revision of current transfer pricing rules. *See* § 14.06.

Although questions involving transfer pricing are most often associated with the cross-border business practices of large multinationals, the topic is not just relevant for large companies. Potentially every company engaging in cross-border transactions with related parties needs to consider the implications of these rules. For example, issues under I.R.C. § 482 can arise whenever related parties are involved in sales, purchases, or use of tangible or intangible property; provision and receipt of services or know-how; joint development of intangible property, or loans and guarantees.

Transfer pricing examinations by tax authorities can lead to tax adjustments and in some cases penalties. In the most extreme cases, they have resulted in the shut-down of taxpayers' foreign operations.

Transfer pricing is generally implemented by means of what is referred to as the "arm's length standard," generally considered the best means of ensuring that fair and consistent prices are charged among related parties in cross-border transactions (but not everyone would agree with this positive characterization of the arm's length standard). Many countries—including the United States—have had trouble enforcing the arm's length standard. The increasing critiques of the standard are rooted in a number of concerns, including governments' unhappiness with what they consider asymmetry of information. To address this situation, extensive documentation requirements and protocols for sharing of information among jurisdictions have been adopted as part of the OECD's BEPS Project. *See* § 11.06.

§ 11.02   THE ARM'S LENGTH STANDARD

(A)   THE GROUNDWORK OF I.R.C. § 482

The arm's-length standard that serves as the basis for pricing intercompany transactions has its roots in Congress' assumption that the transactions between related parties may not take place at arm's length pricing, allowing taxpayers to achieve tax savings to the detriment of the fisc. Section 482 (and its predecessors), which has been part of the Code since 1917, is intended to ensure that transactions between related taxpayers take place on an "arm's length" basis that is consistent with transactions between independent parties. To ensure this result, I.R.C. § 482 empowers the Secretary of Treasury to distribute, apportion, or allocate gross income, deductions, credits, or allowances between or among related parties if its determined that such distribution, apportionment, or allocation is necessary in order to prevent evasion of taxes or clearly to reflect their income.

Section 482 doesn't only apply to reallocate income among different jurisdictions; it also can be used to reallocate income between two U.S. entities. But its use by the IRS has most often been in the cross-border arena because the incentives for taxpayers to shift income in this context are much greater. Section 482 operates by treating a controlled taxpayer (as defined below) as equivalent to an uncontrolled taxpayer in determining true taxable income. Reg. § 1.482–1(a).

The statutory language leaves a lot of room for the government and taxpayers to disagree as to whether the price set by a taxpayer reflects a clear reflection of income, and IRS regulations attempt to fill in the gap. The first set of regulations under I.R.C. § 482 was adopted in 1968 and the rules have been regularly revised since. In 1993 the government issued temporary regulations that emphasized the "best method" approach and described how comparability principles applied in determining the arm's length standard. Since 1993, the IRS has continued to revise, update and expand the guidance under I.R.C. § 482, attempting to bring more conformity into the area and protect the fisc. The IRS has struggled in this regard. Congress' most recent attempt to try and bring some clarity to this area and provide the IRS with greater enforcement tools was in December 2017 pursuant to the TCJA. *See* discussion *infra* at § 11.06.

(B) OECD STANDARDS

The U.S. government exported the principle behind I.R.C. § 482 worldwide via the OECD Model Treaty. (*See* Chapter 5 for more discussion on tax treaties). In the 1930s, a report that served as the basis for the League of Nations model treaty recommended that the business income of enterprises engaged in cross-border transactions be allocated among jurisdictions using the separate accounting method and based on the arm's length principle. That provision of the League of Nations draft model treaty ultimately became current Art. 9(1) of the OECD Model Treaty; the wording of Art. 9(1) has remained little changed since 1963.

Article 9(1) of the OECD Model permits contracting states to adjust profits of affiliated entities in line with the arm's length principle. These adjustments can be made, for example, by imputing income or reducing expenses based on domestic law. A contracting state is entitled to make an adjustment to a taxpayer's taxable income under Art. 9(1), regardless of whether the other contracting state agrees with the adjustment.

To achieve the corresponding adjustment from the other state, taxpayers must look to Art. 9(2). Article 9(2) of the OECD Model Treaty provides for the possibility of re-examining transfer prices and then determining a new transfer price via a corresponding adjustment. A contracting state is only committed to making a (corresponding) adjustment if it feels that the arm's length standard has been met. The challenges this creates for dispute resolution purposes are discussed *infra* at § 11.08.

In 1979, the OECD published its first transfer pricing report with interpretations of Art. 9 of the OECD Model Treaty. This report—like the I.R.C. § 482 regulations—has been supplemented regularly by additional detailed transfer pricing reports. The OECD's "Transfer Pricing Guidelines for Multinational Enterprises and Tax Administrations" were first published in 1995. As with the Commentaries to the OECD Model Treaty, the OECD Transfer Pricing Guidelines are not legally binding under international tax law, but they are considered a valuable means of interpretation. The OECD subscribes to an "ambulatory theory" of international law, under which later-in-time amendments to the commentaries to the OECD Model Treaty could be authoritative in interpreting treaties previously signed.

Although I.R.C. § 482 and the regulations thereunder are largely consistent with the OECD

Transfer Pricing Guidelines, there are important differences. For practical purposes, this means that if the United States makes a reallocation under I.R.C. § 482, the other country won't necessarily agree with that reallocation and so may decline to make the corresponding adjustment. If the other country does not agree with the reallocation of income, the two countries have generally agreed (in Art. 25 in the OECD Model Treaty) to reach a compromise under the mutual agreement procedures contained in the treaty. If the countries fail to reach a compromise, a taxpayer may confront international double taxation. *See infra* § 11.08.

Not all countries follow the OECD transfer pricing guidelines. A significant outlier is Brazil, which has adopted a more formulaic approach. Taxpayers with transactions between Brazil and another country that has adopted the OECD guidelines or between Brazil and the United States are left in a bind—the intercompany price often must conflict with the rules of one of the jurisdictions in question. (But note that Brazil's potential ascension to the OECD may result in revisions to its transfer pricing rules to bring them more in line with international standards.) Some other countries—particularly emerging market countries—ostensibly adhere to the OECD transfer pricing guidelines but enforce them through methodologies that don't necessarily comport with the OECD's view of arm's length pricing.

The OECD's work on the BEPS project was focused on reconciling gaps in domestic and international tax rules that allowed taxpayers to shift profits to low-taxed jurisdictions where there was little or no real activity taking place. *See supra* § 1.06 and Chapter 14 for more discussion of BEPS. Revising and updating the OECD's transfer pricing guidelines formed a significant part of the work on the BEPS project. The transfer pricing work also represented the biggest part of the project that remained unfinished when the project supposedly wrapped up in 2015; additional guidelines and discussion drafts on transfer pricing matters spawned by BEPS continue to be released.

(C) SECTION 482 CONTROL

Section 482 applies to "controlled" taxpayers, and for this purpose, the meaning of control is very broad. Unusually for a tax rule, legal formalities are not the most significant factor in analyzing whether I.R.C. § 482 control exists. The courts have held that such control may be present even in the absence of strict legal relationships, so long as "genuine and real control is actually exercised." (*Grenada Industries v. Comm'r*, 17 T.C. 231 (1951), *aff'd*, 202 F.2d 873 (5th Cir. 1953), *cert. denied*, 346 U.S. 819 (1953), *acq. in part and nonacq. in part*, 1952–2 C.B. 2, 5.)

Section 482 control does not require ownership of more than 50 percent of a company's stock. Instead, the courts tend to look at whether one party exercises actual authority over the business affairs of another party. The IRS has said that for purposes of I.R.C. § 482, it is "the reality of control that is decisive, not its form or the mode of its exercise." (Rev. Rul. 2003–96, 2003–34 I.R.B. 386.)

The OECD definition of control may be even broader than the I.R.C. § 482 meaning. Under Art. 9(1) of the OECD Model Treaty, the arm's-length standard applies when an enterprise of one contracting state participates directly or indirectly in the management, control, or capital of an enterprise of the other contracting state; it also may apply where the same persons participate directly or indirectly in the management, control, or capital of an enterprise of a contracting state and an enterprise of the other contracting state, and if conditions are made or imposed between the two enterprises that differ from those that would be made between independent enterprises.

§ 11.03   ARM'S LENGTH PRINCIPLE

The I.R.C. § 482 regulations develop and expand upon what it means to apply the arm's length standard in practice. A controlled transaction should satisfy the arm's length standard if its results are consistent with those that would have been realized if uncontrolled taxpayers had engaged in the same transaction under the same circumstances (the "arm's length result"). Reg. § 1.482–1(b)(1). The test is focused on the result, rather than the selection of the right method. Deriving a satisfactory arm's length price requires analyzing what uncontrolled parties do (referred to as a "comparability analysis").

Under the arm's length standard as interpreted and applied by the regulations, taxpayers can apply different methods even to related transactions if the most reliable way of evaluating them is to analyze them separately. For example, if one entity provides services to an affiliated party while also transferring property to the same party, the taxpayer is entitled to use different methodologies to determine whether the pricing for the transfer of property and for a services transaction is arm's length. But analyzing the combined effect of separate transactions may be appropriate if they are sufficiently interrelated to make such analysis the most reliable means of determining the arm's length price. Reg. § 1.482–1(b)(2)(ii).

The arm's length principle has received enormous scrutiny from scholars, practitioners, and governments. All of this study can be summarized in two key conclusions. First, there is little reason to expect that observations of actual arm's length prices (for comparability purposes) exist for most goods traded by multinational corporations. Where observations of comparables are unavailable, taxpayers often resort to methodologies that require allocations of profits. But profit-based applications of the arm's length principle produce, at best, a range of prices within which any price could be characterized as an arm's length price. In other words, arguably the primary means that governments have developed for allocating cross-border profits among themselves, in the more complicated cases, is essentially a failure. But most would still argue that it's the best method that has been developed to date.

§ 11.04   TRANSFER PRICING METHODOLOGIES

The regulations under I.R.C. § 482 provide a detailed guide to the implementation of the arm's length principle. For purposes of applying the transfer pricing rules, transactions that take place between related entities that sell or purchase tangible or intangible property or provide services are considered "controlled" transactions, also referred to as "related party" transactions. Uncontrolled transactions involve the sale or purchase of tangible or intangible property or the provision of services between two unrelated entities. These transactions are also referred to as "unrelated" or "third-party" transactions.

There are two main approaches generally used to assess whether cross-border, related party transactions produce arm's length results: transaction-based methodologies and profit-based methodologies. Transaction-based methods require the identification of prices or margins from individual transactions or groups of transactions involving related entities and comparing these results to price or margin information involving independent third parties. Profit-based methods seek to benchmark the profits earned by controlled entities and unrelated parties performing similar functions and incurring similar risks.

The transaction-based methods include the Comparable Uncontrolled Price ("CUP") method, the Comparable Uncontrolled Transaction ("CUT") method (essentially, the CUP method applied to intangibles), the resale price method ("RPM"), and the cost plus method. The profit-based methods include the profit split and the Comparable Profits Method (CPM)/Transactional Net Margin Method (TNMM). The following methods may be used, according to the regulations, to analyze tangible property transactions: CUP, Resale Price, Cost Plus, Profit Split (Comparable and Residual), and Comparable Profits Method. The regulations allow CUT, Profit Split (Comparable and Residual), and CPM to analyze intangible property transactions. The OECD Guidelines describe the following methods: CUP, Resale Price, Cost Plus, Profit Split (Comparable and Residual), and TNMM (TNMM is CPM's counterpart under the OECD Transfer Pricing Guidelines.).

(A) TRANSACTION-BASED METHODOLOGIES

(1) Comparable Uncontrolled Price Method

The CUP method compares the amounts charged in controlled transactions with the amounts charged in comparable third party transactions. Comparable uncontrolled transactions may be between two unrelated parties or between one of the related parties and an unrelated party. The CUP method is generally the most reliable measure of an arm's length result if the transaction is identical, or if only minor readily quantifiable differences exist for which appropriate adjustments are made. It requires a high degree of comparability of products and functions, but taxpayers can improve comparability by making adjustments to the prices being compared.

Suppose a parent company ("CanCo"), located in Canada manufactures "product X". CanCo sells product X to both related ("USCo") and unrelated distributors in the United States and the circumstances surrounding the controlled and uncontrolled transactions are substantially the same. Under the CUP method, if CanCo sells product X to the unrelated distributors for $10/unit, then CanCo should sell product X to USCo at the same price, *i.e.*, $10/unit, to satisfy the arm's length principle. However, assume that CanCo arranges for and pays to ship product X to USCo whereas the unrelated entities pick up product X directly from CanCo's manufacturing facility. Because CanCo performs more activities for USCo than it does for the unrelated parties, it should be compensated accordingly. Assuming the additional compensation CanCo should receive for performing the additional activities equals $1/unit, then CanCo should charge USCo $11/unit.

In practice, there may be more than one comparable transaction, which would result in a range of potentially arm's length results rather than an individual result.

(2) Comparable Uncontrolled Transaction Method

The CUT method compares the amount charged in a controlled transfer of intangible property to the amount charged in a comparable uncontrolled transaction. Essentially, it is the CUP method applied to intangibles.

(3) Resale Price Method

The RPM compares the gross margin earned in the controlled transaction to the gross margins earned in comparable uncontrolled transactions. The RPM is most often used for distributors that resell products without physically changing them or adding substantial value. Under this method, the arm's length price at which a distributor would purchase finished products from a related party is determined by subtracting the appropriate gross profit from the applicable resale price of the property involved in the controlled transaction. The RPM requires detailed comparisons of functions performed, risks borne, and contractual terms of controlled and uncontrolled transactions.

Returning to the previous example of CanCo and USCo, suppose that USCo buys teddy bears from CanCo and also acts as a distributor of toy racing cars purchased from unrelated manufacturers. Although each of the individual products is similar to one another (*i.e.*, both are children's toys), they are not exactly the same. To apply the RPM, compare the gross margins earned by USCo on products purchased from CanCo to the gross margins earned by USCo on products purchased from the unrelated manufacturers. USCo's gross margins on purchases of racing cars from unrelated manufacturers form an arm's length range of gross margins. For example, consider the following gross margins resulting from USCo's purchases of toy racing cars from five manufacturers under terms comparable with those in purchases from CanCo:

Unrelated Manufacturer 1   29%

Unrelated Manufacturer 2   32%

Unrelated Manufacturer 3   33%

Unrelated Manufacturer 4   35%

Unrelated Manufacturer 5   36%

To satisfy the arm' length principle, USCo's purchases of teddy bears from its related parties should be set at a price that will allow USCo to earn a gross margin of between 32 percent and 35 percent on the sale to third party customers.

(4) Cost Plus Method

The cost plus method (Reg. § 1.482–3) compares gross margins of controlled and uncontrolled transactions. Under this method, the arm's length sales price to a related party is determined by adding the appropriate gross profit to the controlled taxpayer's cost of producing the property involved in the controlled transaction. The cost plus method is most often used to assess the mark-up earned by manufacturers selling to related parties. The cost plus method requires detailed comparisons of the goods produced, functions performed, risks borne, manufacturing complexity, cost structures and embedded intangibles between controlled and uncontrolled transactions.

Suppose that USCo manufactures similar but not identical products both for CanCo and for unrelated parties. In both cases, USCo acts as a contract manufacturer (an arrangement in which USCo generally does not undertake sales and marketing activities; does not develop its own products; uses patents and designs owned by the purchaser; and does not assume significant inventory and production planning risks). Application of the cost plus method requires a comparison of the gross profits generated relative to the manufacturing costs (gross costs) incurred based on sales to CanCo and unrelated companies. For example, consider the gross mark-ups realized by USCo when selling products manufactured for five different unrelated parties:

Unrelated Co1	42%
Unrelated Co2	45%
Unrelated Co3	41%
Unrelated Co4	44%
Unrelated Co5	39%

USCo needs to earn a gross mark-up between 41 percent and 44 percent for transactions with CanCo to satisfy the arm's length principle.

(B) PROFIT-BASED METHODOLOGIES

(1) Profit Split Methods

Profit split methods allocate the combined operating profits or losses from controlled transactions in proportion to the relative contributions made by each party in creating the combined profits or losses. Relative contributions must be determined in a manner that reflects the functions performed, risks assumed, and resources employed by each party to the controlled transaction.

(a) Comparable Profit Split Method

Under the comparable profit split method, transfer prices are based on the division of combined operating profit between uncontrolled taxpayers whose transactions and activities are similar to those of the controlled taxpayers in the relevant business activity. Under this method, the uncontrolled parties' shares of the combined operating profit or loss is used to allocate the combined operating profit or loss of the relevant business activity between the related parties. This method is not often used because it is very difficult to find two companies in an uncontrolled circumstance with similar functions, risks, and transactions as well as detailed information on how they allocate the business' profits between them.

(b) Residual Profit Split Method

The residual profit split method involves two steps. First, operating income is allocated to each party in the controlled transaction to provide a market return for its routine contributions to the relevant business activity. Second, any residual profit or loss is divided among the controlled parties based on the relative value of their contributions of any valuable intangible property to the relevant business activity. This method is particularly suited to transactions involving highly profitable intangibles that are contributed by multiple parties.

(2) Comparable Profits Method

The Comparable Profits Method ("CPM") evaluates whether the amount charged in a controlled transaction is at arm's length by comparing the profitability of one of the entities involved in the controlled transaction (the "tested party") to that of companies that are comparable in terms of functions performed, risks borne and assets employed. The tested party should not use intangible property or unique assets that distinguish it from unrelated comparable companies.

The degree of comparability between the tested party and the comparable company affects the reliability of the CPM analysis. Reliability may also be adversely affected by varying cost structures, differences in business experience, or differences in management efficiency. However, less functional comparability is required for reliable results than under the transactional methods (*e.g.,* the CUP method, the RPM, or the cost plus method). In addition, less product similarity is required for reliable results under the CPM than under the transactional methods.

The comparable profits method examines the operating profit margin relative to an appropriate base (*e.g.,* costs, sales, assets), in contrast with the RPM and Cost Plus both of which examine gross profits. In this regard, the CPM is less sensitive to differences in accounting classifications between costs and expense items between the tested party and the comparable companies.

The fact that the reliability of results under the CPM is relatively less dependent on product and functional comparability and less sensitive to inconsistencies in accounting practices means that this is the transfer pricing method most frequently used by tax payers as it commonly allows for a broader sample of arm's length references.

(C) BEST METHOD RULE

The arm's length result of a controlled transaction has to be determined under the method that provides the most reliable measure of the arm's length result. There is no strict priority of methods, and no method is invariably considered to be more reliable than any other. Reg. § 1.482–1(c).

In determining the best method, the factors that are relevant include the degree of comparability between the controlled and uncontrolled transactions and the quality of the data and assumptions used in the analysis.

(D) ARM'S LENGTH RANGE

When applying any of the specified transfer pricing methods, a taxpayer may arrive at a single arm's length reference if it is determined that a single uncontrolled transaction presents a high enough degree of comparability or if a number of comparable uncontrolled transactions arrive at the same arm's length reference. But frequently the application of the methods arrives at a number of results all of which could reasonably be considered as arm's length. In such cases, Reg. § 1.482–1(e)(2)(iii)(C) requires reliability of the analysis to be increased by adjusting the range through the application of a statistical method (the interquartile range). Put simply, the interquartile range represents the middle 50 percent of prices or returns observed in uncontrolled transactions.

(E) COMPARABILITY ANALYSIS

The regulations generally require use of the interquartile range to increase the reliability of the comparison unless there are sufficient data to identify, and to make adjustments to eliminate the effects of, all material differences between the tested party and the comparable companies.

Because a transaction is evaluated by comparing the results of the controlled transaction to the results of the uncontrolled transaction, factors that could affect prices or profits must be included in the analysis and adjustments made where warranted. *See* Reg. § 1.482–1(d)(3).

(F) CONTROLLED SERVICES TRANSACTIONS

When one corporation performs services for, or on behalf of, a related corporation, the corporation purchasing the services is deemed to pay an arm's length price to the corporation performing the services. The IRS has wrestled with whether the arm's length price should not only cover actual costs of performing the services but should also include a profit mark-up.

For example, if in-house accountants at ParentCo perform services for SubCo, the arm's length payment to ParentCo should include deemed payments for both the direct and indirect costs of providing the services. The direct costs might include employee salaries and benefits; indirect expenses might include a portion of depreciation, rent, property taxes and other overhead expenses of ParentCo attributable to its accounting services. But should there also be a deemed payment from SubCo to ParentCo for some level of profit in performing the services?

Historically, intercompany payments for services generally did not require a profit mark-up. However, current regulations require a profit mark-up for certain services performed for related parties. Still, there are some services where the arm's length price is considered to be the cost to the related party performing the service with no additional mark-up (the services cost method or SCM). Reg. § 1.482–9(b).

(1) Services Cost Method

The services cost method evaluates the arm's-length nature of the services transaction by reference to the total cost of providing the service with no additional charge or mark-up. In addition to the services cost method, there are rules for shared service arrangements, which permit cost sharing for services. The services cost method and the rules for shared services arrangements are intended to preserve the beneficial aspects of the safe harbor allowing certain routine back-office and other low-value services to be charged out at cost.

(2) Shared Services Arrangements

Shared services arrangements can present advantages for taxpayers. Under a shared services arrangement, if a taxpayer reasonably allocates cost among affiliates, the IRS will not adjust the allocation, even though another method may be more reasonable. Taxpayers are permitted to aggregate or group service costs even though not all services in the group will similarly benefit all participants, and the arrangements are likely to be consistent with similar arrangements adopted by other OECD countries.

To qualify as a shared services arrangement, the agreement must include two or more participants, include as participants all controlled taxpayers that reasonably anticipate a benefit from one or more covered services specified in the shared services arrangement, and be structured so that each covered service (or each reasonable aggregation of services) confers a benefit on at least one participant in the shared services arrangement. Reg. § 1.482–9(b)(5)(ii)(A).

(3) Additional Transfer Pricing Methods for Controlled Services Transactions

For services that cannot qualify for the SCM method, the regulations provide five additional specified transfer pricing methods and unspecified methods for determining taxable income in connection with a controlled services transaction. The selection and application of these methods is subject to the general transfer pricing principles described in Reg. § 1.482–1, including the best method rule, comparability analysis, and the arm's-length range.

(G) CUSTOMS CONSIDERATIONS

Separate from I.R.C. § 482, there is a special rule to prevent U.S. purchasers from inflating the price paid to a related foreign corporation in order to minimize the gain on eventual resale. I.R.C. § 1059A prevents a U.S. purchaser of inventory from a related party from taking as its basis for determining gain on resale an amount greater than the price used in determining the amount of customs duties. But some taxpayers may prefer to pay higher customs duties in order to inflate basis for income tax purposes.

§ 11.05 SPECIAL PROBLEMS WITH INTANGIBLES

(A) THE COMMENSURATE WITH INCOME STANDARD

No area of transfer pricing has proven more challenging for governments to enforce than the pricing of intangible transactions. The IRS and other countries' tax administrations have often struggled to apply transfer pricing rules in connection with transactions that raise questions about the appropriate compensation to be paid for the transfer and/or use of intangibles. Even after the first set of regulations issued under I.R.C. § 482 was promulgated, taxpayers were able to, and did, transfer high-value intangibles—such as drug patents—to low-tax affiliated companies without incurring U.S. tax. Once owned in a low-tax jurisdiction, the intangibles were able to generate high profits without the original or new owners being subject to much in the way of U.S. tax.

Congress responded to concerns over such weaknesses in I.R.C. § 482 in 1986, and amended the statute to provide that in the case of any transfer (or license) of intangible property, the income with respect to such transfer or license shall be commensurate with the income attributable to the intangible (a rule often referred to as the "commensurate with income" or "CWI" standard). This phrase was not otherwise described in the statute, and as a result has created controversy between the IRS and taxpayers ever since (with taxpayers most often on the winning side). At the same time that it amended I.R.C. § 482 in 1986, Congress also amended I.R.C. § 367 to ensure that the outbound transfer of intangibles was a taxable event for U.S. tax purposes. *See* § 13.02.

In theory, the CWI standard could allow the IRS to adjust royalty arrangements between related parties periodically in order to reflect changing market conditions. In practice, the IRS had a difficult time convincing the courts that the CWI standard is consistent with the arm's length standard. In 1988, the Treasury issued a White Paper that said that the CWI standard was intended to work consistently with the arm's-length standard, an interpretation that has caused trouble for the government in litigation ever since. The courts have held the Treasury to that interpretation and have ruled that regulations that applied a rule with an outcome inconsistent with what unrelated parties would do was inconsistent with the arm's length standard and hence the statute, despite the CWI standard. *See Xilinx Inc. v. Commissioner*, 125 T.C. 37 (2005), *aff'd*, 598 F.3d 1191 (9th Cir. 2010). The issue remains unresolved, although it may be tilting in the government's favor. *See Altera Corp. v. Commissioner*, 145 T.C. 91 (2015), *rev'd*, No. 16–70496, 16–70497 (9th Cir. 2019), petition for rehearing en banc pending.

(B) COST SHARING AGREEMENTS

A cost-sharing agreement is an agreement that governs the development, use, and share of profits from joint ownership of an intangible asset. The owner of existing intangible property rights generally agrees to make the rights available to an affiliate in return for other resources and funds that will be applied in the joint development of a new marketable product or service. Rights may be transferred to other cost-sharing participants either through a sale or a license. In return, the owner generally receives a payment from the other participants for the initial contribution. The prior owner may also receive compensation for a portion of the costs of research and development that it performs on a contractual basis. A cost sharing arrangement will result in the foreign affiliate owning some or all of the rights to the new technology developed under the arrangement for tax purposes. Future profits may accrue to the foreign affiliate, which is generally located in a low-tax jurisdiction.

IRS regulations provide that parties to a cost sharing arrangement are required to share costs in proportion to their shares of reasonably anticipated benefits from exploitation of their interests in the intangible. Reg. § 1.482–7(b)(1). A cost-sharing agreement constitutes a qualified cost sharing arrangement within the meaning of the regulations if it includes two or more participants that expect to use the intangible in the active conduct of a trade or business; the agreement contains specified information, including each participant's interest in the intangible, each participant's share of the development costs for the intangible, and the method by which costs will be determined; and the agreement provides for adjustments to each participant's interest in the intangible to account for changes in the economic relationship. If a qualified cost-sharing agreement exists, all participants are considered owners of the intangible and no royalty payment for its use is imputed under I.R.C. § 482.

A fundamental principle of the cost sharing regulations is that each participant's share of costs is reasonably related to the anticipated benefits. But this amount can be difficult to determine because it often involves projected costs and benefits. During the life of the agreement, the participants make payments to each other to adjust the costs of the project to prearranged formulas.

The treatment of stock-based compensation in the calculation of the cost base to determine cost-sharing payments has been an important issue facing taxpayers and the IRS. *See* Reg. § 1.482–7(d)(3). It remains an open question. In *Altera Corp. v. Commissioner*, 145 T.C. 3 (2015), the Tax Court found invalid part of the transfer pricing cost sharing regulations, which required taxpayers to include stock based compensation in the pool of costs that need to be shared in a qualified cost sharing arrangement. This decision was reversed by the Ninth Circuit in June 2019. In July, the taxpayer has filed a petition requesting a rehearing *en banc*. Stay tuned.

(C) BUY-IN PAYMENTS

If one of the participants to a cost sharing arrangement has existing valuable intangibles, then other participants must make a buy-in payment at the arm's length price as compensation for use of the intangible. Reg. § 1.482–7(c). Similarly, if a participant leaves a cost sharing arrangement, then the other participant(s) must make buy-out payments in proportion to the value of the exiting party's interest in the jointly developed intangible. The pricing of buy-in payments has been one of the most challenging issues for the government in enforcing its rules on cost sharing arrangements. The IRS has lost a number of important cases in this area involving large dollar amounts.

Updates made in 1994 to I.R.C. § 482 regulations provide that the IRS may price transactions based on the realistic alternatives available to the taxpayer or aggregate multiple transactions if that provides the most reliable result. But the IRS has failed to persuade the Tax Court to apply these rules in a way that would allow the government treat business as an aggregate, or to use profit-based methods in cases involving transfer of intangibles, in cases such as *Veritas Software Corp. v. Commissioner*, 133 T.C. 297 (2009); and *Medtronic Inc. v. Commissioner*, T.C. Memo. 2016–112, vacated and remanded, No. 17–1866 (8th Cir. 2018). Most recently, the Tax Court in *Amazon.com Inc. v. Commissioner*, 148 T.C. No. 8 (2017), overturned the IRS' adjustment to the taxpayer's pricing of a cost-sharing buy-in payment.

In *Amazon*, the company transferred its technology and marketing intangibles relating to the European market to a Luxembourg subsidiary through a cost-sharing arrangement. The IRS rejected the $255 million buy-in payment made by the Luxembourg subsidiary in favor of its proposed value of nearly $3.5 billion, based on a discounted cash flow approach. The IRS and the taxpayer argued over the use of profit-based valuation approaches versus transactional methods, aggregation of interrelated transactions, and the useful life of intangibles. The Tax Court came down squarely on the side of the taxpayer. The government has appealed.

(D) TEMPORARY I.R.C. § 482 REGULATIONS

The IRS decision in the *Amazon* case highlights why the IRS felt it necessary to issue temporary and proposed regulations in 2015 (Temp. Reg. § 1.482–1T) that expanded the prior standard for when the IRS could require multiple interrelated transactions to be aggregated for valuation purposes. These temporary regulations were issued in response to a perception that taxpayers were engaging in abusive transactions involving the outbound transfer of intangibles, in particular by assigning artificially low values to transferred intangibles. The temporary regulations say that aggregate analysis of two or more controlled transactions may be necessary to determine whether the compensation is consistent with the value provided (Note that the temporary regulations have expired but the proposed regulations remain outstanding and IRS officials have indicated an intent to finalize the proposed rules.)

The temporary regulations provide that where synergies exist among transferred items, valuing them in the aggregate may be a more reliable method than valuing them separately (Reg. § 1.482–1T(f)(2)(i)(B)). Whether two or more transactions should be evaluated separately or in the aggregate depends on the extent to which they are economically interrelated and on the relative reliability of the measure of an arm's length result provided by an aggregate analysis compared to a separate analysis of each transaction. The valuation of separate transactions may need to be coordinated to ensure that the overall value of the transactions is properly taken into account (Reg. § 1.482–1T(f)(2)(i)(C)). In some cases it may be necessary to allocate one or more portions of the arm's length result under a coordinated best method analysis.

Suppose USCo enters into a license agreement with its wholly owned foreign subsidiary, FSub1, that permits FSub1 to use a proprietary manufacturing process and to sell the output from this process throughout a specified region. FSub1 uses the manufacturing process and sells its output to another wholly-owned foreign subsidiary of USCo, FSub2, which in turn resells the output to uncontrolled parties in the specified region. Under the temporary regulations, the evaluation of whether the royalty paid by FSub1 to USCo is an arm's length amount may require an evaluation of the royalty in combination with the transfer prices charged by FSub1 to FSub2 and the aggregate profits earned by these entities from the use of the manufacturing process and the sale of FSub1's products to uncontrolled parties.

Recognizing that the courts have generally looked askance at the IRS' attempts to prevent taxpayers from transferring valuable intangible assets outbound while incurring a minimal tax bill, Congress tried to strengthen the government's position by adding a new sentence to I.R.C. § 482 in the TCJA that permits aggregation of the properties transferred and the consideration of realistic alternatives if this produces the most reliable means of valuation. The statute says that the Secretary shall require the valuation of transfers of intangible property (including intangible property transferred with other property or services) on an aggregate basis or the valuation of such a transfer on the basis of the realistic alternatives to such a transfer if the Secretary determines that such basis is the most reliable means of valuation of such transfers.

The statutory language basically mimics the temporary regulations, which sunset in 2018; one may question how effective the statutory change may prove to be, given that the courts have repeatedly rejected the government's attempts to require taxpayers to use an aggregate approach. Time will tell; this saga is obviously not yet over.

(E) OECD INTANGIBLES GUIDELINES

Tax administrations worldwide—not just in the United States—have struggled with enforcing transfer pricing rules as applied to intangibles. For this reason, the BEPS Project took on a number of related projects that attempted to clarify transfer pricing guidelines with respect to transactions involving intangibles. The updated 2017 version of the OECD Transfer Pricing Guidelines includes new guidance on transfer pricing rules as relates to intangibles.

The revised chapters on intangibles and cost contribution arrangements apply guidance developed by the OECD that places greater reliance on parties' control of risks. Under these new guidelines, a taxpayer's entitlement to returns from intangibles is based on whether it controls intangible development risk. Specifically, the revisions identify development, enhancement, maintenance, protection, and exploitation (DEMPE) as important functions in assessing control of intangible development risk.

The new OECD transfer pricing standards are a departure from the OECD's previous full-fledged allegiance to the arm's-length principle. Under the new guidelines, legal ownership of intangibles alone does not determine the returns from intangibles and related parties that perform important value-creating functions regarding the development, enhancement, maintenance, protection, and exploitation of the intangibles are required to be appropriately compensated. But it's not sufficient to simply perform those functions; a related party that assumes risks also must exercise control over those risks and have the financial capacity to assume the risks. The United States has not updated its transfer pricing regulations to reflect the new focus reflected in revised OECD guidelines.

As with the IRS attempts to apply the commensurate with income standard, its questionable whether the revised OECD transfer pricing guidelines are really consistent with the arm's length standard. But as noted in § 14.06, an even greater departure from the arm's length standard may be in the works.

§ 11.06   DOCUMENTATION REQUIREMENTS AND PENALTIES

(A)   CONTEMPORANEOUS DOCUMENTATION REQUIREMENTS

In the attempt to enforce its transfer pricing rules, the government has adopted specific documentation requirements and penalties applicable to taxpayers' obligations under the transfer pricing regulations. Regulations under I.R.C. § 6662 have effectively shifted the burden of accumulating transfer pricing documentation from the IRS to the taxpayer.

The purpose of the I.R.C. § 6662 penalty regulations, as stated in the preamble, is to encourage taxpayers to make a serious effort to comply with the "arm's length" standard. The preamble follows by stating its intent for taxpayers to report arm's length results on their tax returns. A taxpayer's last two obligations under I.R.C. § 6662 are to document its transfer pricing analysis in a formal report and to be prepared to provide this documentation to the IRS upon request.

Taxpayers may avoid penalties by meeting the contemporaneous documentation requirements under Reg. § 1.6662–6(d). These regulations require contemporaneous documentation (documentation in existence at the time the taxpayer file its tax return) that shows that the taxpayer reasonably concluded that the transfer pricing methodology chosen and its application provide the most reliable measure of an arm's-length result under the best method rule. Taxpayers must be able to explain how they selected their pricing method and the reasons for their rejection of other possible methods.

The focus on contemporaneous documentation reflects Congress' belief that administration of, and compliance with, I.R.C. § 482 could be improved if taxpayers were required to document the methodology used in establishing intercompany transfer prices prior to filing their tax return. If a taxpayer does not have contemporaneous documentation and the IRS concludes that a transfer pricing adjustment is appropriate, the taxpayer may be subject to the following penalties:

	Transactional	Net Adjustment
Substantial Valuation Misstatement (20% Penalty of the Underpayment of Tax)	Price or value is 200% or more (50% or less) than the correct amount	Net adjustment exceeds the lessor of $5 million or 10% of gross receipts
Gross Valuation Misstatement (40% Penalty of the Underpayment of Tax)	Price or value is 400% or more (25% or less) than the correct amount	Net adjustment exceeds the lessor of $20 million or 20% of gross receipts

(B) COUNTRY BY COUNTRY REPORTING

Like the IRS, other countries have similarly sought to correct what they perceive as information asymmetries in the transfer pricing area. Adopting a coordinated approach to transfer pricing documentation was another significant focus of the OECD's BEPS Project, as well as one of its most successful ones. The OECD recommended in the BEPS Project that tax administrations adopt rules requiring that multinational companies headquartered in their jurisdiction with group revenues in excess of €750 million complete a "country-by-country" (CBC) report, along with a master file and a local country file. As of February 2019, over 75 jurisdictions had introduced, or taken steps to begin an introduction of, CBC reporting requirements for multinational groups, many for fiscal years beginning in January 2016.

Based on the OECD template, the CBC report is supposed to be filed by the parent company of a group with its local tax authority. The report is then shared with other tax authorities under multilateral or bilateral tax agreements, including information exchange agreements. The data required by the template is intended, along with the transfer pricing master file and local files, to provide tax administrations with sufficient information to conduct transfer pricing risk assessments and examinations. Taxpayers that are obligated to file the report must report information, on a country-by-country basis, related to the group's income and taxes paid, together with certain indicators of the location of the group's economic activity. Specifically, companies are required to include the following information with respect to each jurisdiction in which they do business:

- Revenue generated from transactions with other constituent entities;

- Revenue not generated from transactions with other constituent entities; profit or loss before income tax;

- Total income tax paid on a cash basis to all tax jurisdictions, and any taxes withheld on payments received by the constituent entities;

- Total accrued tax expense recorded on taxable profits or losses;

- Stated capital of all constituent entities;

- Total accumulated earnings; and

- Net book value of tangible assets other than cash or cash equivalents.

The IRS regulations implementing CBC reporting can be found at Reg. § 1.6038–4 (T.D. 9773). Under these regulations, the ultimate parent entity of a U.S. multinational group with $850 million or more of revenue in the relevant preceding annual reporting period is required to file Form 8975 and Schedule A (the CBC Report) with its annual income tax return. While most other countries have agreed to exchange CBC reports by signing the Multilateral Competent Authority Agreement, which allows them to exchange the reports under the Multilateral Convention for Mutual Administrative Assistance in Tax Matters, the IRS has opted to do so via bilateral competent authority agreements.

The global landscape for CBC reporting is still evolving. It's not yet clear what tax administrations will do with this new information and how it will impact transfer pricing audits and adjustments.

§ 11.07 ADVANCE PRICING AGREEMENTS

In an effort to ensure compliance with I.R.C. § 482 and at the same time provide taxpayers with some certainty in planning their business transactions the IRS has provided taxpayers with the opportunity to obtain an "advance pricing agreement" (APA). (The IRS procedures for obtaining an APA, last amended in 2015, can be found in Rev. Proc. 2015–41, 2015–35 I.R.B. 263; the IRS issued a draft template to be used in drafting APAs in 2017). Other countries have also adopted procedures for taxpayers to enter into bilateral or multilateral APAs. An APA is a binding agreement between a tax administration and a taxpayer and applies an agreed-upon transfer pricing methodology to specified transactions between the taxpayer and a related party. Because the term of an APA is generally 3 to 5 years, an APA provides a taxpayer with some level of certainty before a transaction is consummated, rather than having to justify pricing after a transaction is consummated. From a business perspective, an APA makes it easier to evaluate whether to undertake a transaction.

Although an APA is supposed to be binding on the government and on the taxpayer, the IRS has tried to cancel an APA with at least one taxpayer. *Eaton Corp. v. Commissioner*, T.C. Memo. 2017–147, involved a case in which the IRS retroactively cancelled APAs it had entered into with Eaton Corp., claiming that Eaton did not comply in good faith with the terms and conditions of the APAs and failed to satisfy the APA annual reporting requirements. The Tax Court ruled in Eaton's favor, agreeing with the company that the IRS abused its discretion by cancelling the APAs.

APAs offer many benefits for taxpayers, including the ability to prospectively achieve certainty for the tax treatment of cross-border transactions, reduce or eliminate financial statement reserves, streamline audits, and avoid expensive tax controversies. Verifying compliance with the terms of an APA is often a key focus in later audits. Another major benefit of securing an APA is avoiding U.S. transfer pricing penalties and those of foreign treaty partners. The APA process generally allows taxpayers to budget more effectively and better predict costs, expenses, and tax liabilities.

A major downside of this process, however, is the extensive time commitment and work involved in negotiating the APA with the IRS, which is done with no guarantee that the parties will reach an agreement in the end. Obtaining an APA can require significant resource expenditures by companies. Additionally, the APA process requires taxpayers to disclose to the IRS lots of detailed information about the way their business is conducted. Although APA negotiations can produce better outcomes than historic audit results, they could also result in application of a transfer pricing method that is less advantageous for the taxpayer. Taxpayers also need to consider the length of the APA's term; there is an ongoing obligation to timely update the material facts and information submitted in connection to the APA request.

APAs have come under public scrutiny, meanwhile, as there is no public disclosure of the terms on which the government grants what have been portrayed as special benefits for individual taxpayers. The European Union has launched (under the auspices of its competition agency, pursuant to a legal doctrine known as "state-aid") investigations into tax rulings granted to multinational taxpayers. In addition, bilateral and multilateral APAs may be subject to exchange under BEPS action 5 and EU requirements.

§ 11.08   RESOLVING TRANSFER PRICING DISPUTES

(A)   CORRELATIVE ADJUSTMENTS

Where the IRS makes an adjustment under I.R.C. § 482 to the income of one related party, a correlative adjustment should also be made to the income of the other related party. Reg. § 1.482–1(g)(2). For example, if USCo sells property to SubCo, a foreign corporation, and the IRS adjusts the purchase price upwards under I.R.C. § 482, an adjustment downwards should be made for the income recognized by the related purchaser on the ultimate sale of the property to unrelated purchasers. Or if USCo makes an interest-free loan to SubCo, the interest imputed to USCo should be treated as interest paid by SubCo for purposes of determining whether SubCo has an interest deduction under I.R.C. § 163.

In a domestic context, such correlative adjustments usually mean an increase in the tax liability of one party and a decrease in the tax liability of the other party. In an international context, the United States may not have tax jurisdiction over a related party resident in a foreign country. However, to the extent that the income of a foreign corporation is relevant for U.S. tax purposes (*e.g.*, for purposes of determining the indirect foreign tax credit), the E&P account of the related foreign corporation reflects the correlative adjustments.

Suppose that USCo only charges SubCo, a foreign corporation, $10,000 for property SubCo purchases from USCo instead of $15,000, the arm's length price. If the IRS on audit allocates $5,000 of additional income to USCo as a transfer pricing adjustment, USCo will not have in fact received the extra $5,000 from SubCo. The IRS has administratively ruled that a taxpayer to whom income is allocated may receive a dividend from the related party in the year of the I.R.C. § 482 allocation that is excludable from U.S. income if the transaction which gave rise to the I.R.C. § 482 adjustment did not have as one its principal purposes the avoidance of U.S. federal income tax. Rev. Proc. 99–32, 1999–2 C.B. 296. (This ruling is less valuable since enactment of I.R.C. § 245A means that such dividends are likely anyway tax-free.) Alternatively, the taxpayer can set up an account receivable on its books which can then be paid by the related party with no further tax consequence.

As children we are often taught that "two wrongs don't make a right." That is not always the case in tax law. A taxpayer can avoid a proposed adjustment under I.R.C. § 482 in some cases by showing that it engaged in other transactions not at arm's length to their detriment. For example, if ParentCo overcharges SubCo for services by $25,000, but also permits SubCo free use of property with a fair rental value of $25,000, no I.R.C. § 482 adjustment is warranted. Reg. § 1.482–1(g)(4) Ex. 1.

(B) I.R.C. § 482 AND U.S. TREATIES

Suppose that UKCo is a U.K. holding company that owns 100 percent of the stock of IrishCo, an Irish manufacturing company. IrishCo manufactures computer storage devices at a cost of $100. IrishCo sells the devices to USCo, a wholly-owned U.S. corporation, which resells them to unrelated distributors for $200. Which country gets to tax the $100 profit? Ireland might claim that the arm's length price for the sale to USCo is $200 so that all of the profit is taxable in Ireland. The United States might claim that the arm's length price should be $100, so that the $100 profit is taxable in the United States. Finally, the United Kingdom might argue that both Ireland and the United States are wrong. The arm's length price ought to be $150. Moreover, in the view of the United Kingdom, IrishCo ought to have paid a $50 royalty to UKCo for various manufacturing intangibles (*e.g.*, patents, knowhow), and USCo ought to have paid a $50 royalty to UKCo for various marketing intangibles (*e.g.*, trademarks, customer lists). Under this U.K. view, the United

Kingdom should be able to tax the $100 profit. Hopefully, the three countries involved will be able to resolve their differences, often through the mutual agreement procedures in the applicable treaties, so that the related taxpayers do not have to confront the possibility of being assessed tax on $300 of income when only $100 of net income was earned. Unfortunately, sometimes agreement cannot be reached and a taxpayer faces multiple taxation of the same income.

Article 9(2) of the U.S. Model Treaty (and a similar provision of the OECD Model Treaty) attempts to resolve these types of issues, by providing that when one country makes an adjustment and taxes profits that have already been taxed in the other contracting state, that second country should make an appropriate adjustment to the amount of the tax charged on those profits. But the provision only applies to the extent that the second country agrees that the first jurisdiction's adjustment reflects the arm's length standard. Furthermore, not all treaties include Art. 9(2). And finally, there is no effective means for enforcing the principle of Art. 9(2) or resolving differences between countries with respect to which jurisdiction should be allocated the arm's length price. As a result, the outcome of the fact pattern outlined above may remain unresolved.

(C) THE MUTUAL AGREEMENT PROCEDURE

To resolve disagreements over the types of issues that may come up in the fact pattern highlighted above, Art. 25 of the U.S. Model Treaty (and similar provisions in the OECD and UN Model Treaties) establishes a "mutual agreement procedure" (MAP). The MAP is supposed to enable the parties to a bilateral treaty to resolve situations of double taxation caused by differences in interpretation and application of a treaty. The MAP is administered by the "competent authorities", the persons (generally, representatives from the finance ministry or the tax authority) designated to administer the treaty. Mostly, MAP is used where a taxpayer resident in one country contends that it is not being taxed in another country in accordance with the rules of the treaty, but it can also be used in cases where the competent authorities on their own initiative resolve questions of interpretation or application of the treaty. Although the MAP process can be used for any treaty dispute, most MAP disputes today involve transfer pricing adjustments.

The MAP process faces many challenges. There is no timeframe that binds countries to achieve resolution, and there are no real penalties if countries can't agree who gets to tax the profits under dispute. Action 14 of the BEPS Project focused on improving the effectiveness and efficiency of the MAP process. It set out a minimum standard intended to make dispute resolution mechanisms more effective, consisting of measures that jurisdictions need to take to ensure that treaty-related disputes are resolved effectively and efficiently. Specifically, the action 14 minimum standard requires countries to ensure that treaty obligations regarding MAP are fully implemented in good faith and that MAP cases are timely resolved; that administrative processes promote the prevention and timely resolution of treaty-related disputes; and that taxpayers have appropriate access to MAP. The action 14 minimum standard is supplemented by 11 best practices that relate to those objectives but are not part of the minimum standard.

In the BEPS Project, the United States pushed hard for the OECD Model Treaty to include a provision that would require mandatory binding arbitration as a means of resolving MAP disputes. It was unsuccessful in this regard. Nonetheless, the final action 14 report includes a commitment by 20 jurisdictions to incorporate a mandatory binding arbitration provision in their treaties. *See* § 5.05(H) for a list of U.S. tax treaties that include a mandatory arbitration clause.

Over 130 jurisdictions have signed on to the BEPS inclusive framework, which includes as a minimum standard the action 14 dispute resolution requirements. These countries have also agreed to have their implementation of MAP examined through a peer review process.

(D) OTHER DISPUTE RESOLUTION MECHANISMS

Recognizing that the MAP process does not always produce successful outcomes, is time consuming and expensive, the OECD is working on two other programs with the hope of streamlining cross-border tax disputes. One of these programs is known as the International Compliance Assurance Program ("ICAP"). ICAP is intended to provide assurance to taxpayers as to whether they may be viewed as "low-risk" by tax administrations, after a multilateral review of the information in a CBC report. While the ICAP pilot has received positive reviews, it is limited to just a few companies and countries and so is unlikely to provide a holistic solution to the overarching challenges facing resolution of cross-border tax disputes.

The OECD has also been working to strengthen the process of joint audits, and has developed a Joint Audit Implementation Package that includes model agreements to facilitate and streamline joint audits.

CHAPTER 12
FOREIGN CURRENCY

§ 12.01 OVERVIEW

Foreign exchange markets work very much like markets in general. When demand is great, the price of a particular currency rises; if supplies of a currency are increased, each unit of currency is worth less when compared to other currencies. For example, suppose that the demand for Dutch tulips in the United States increases. Other things being equal, the demand for the Euro (€) needed to pay for the tulips will increase, and the price of the Euro relative to other currencies will rise. The exchange rate may move from, say, $1.00 = 1€ to $1.00 = .8€.

Notice that this process has a stabilizing element in that once the price of the Euro rises to meet increased demand for tulips, the demand for tulips will decrease because their cost to American customers whose functional currency is the U.S. dollar has increased. In addition, if the Euro becomes more expensive for Americans, the dollar becomes cheaper for the Dutch, thereby making U.S. goods more attractive. As the Dutch buy more U.S. dollars needed to purchase the U.S. goods, the price of the dollar will tend to increase relative to the Euro.

U.S. tax liability is determined in U.S. dollars. With foreign exchange rates constantly fluctuating, the tax issue that arises is how and when a taxpayer's foreign exchange gains and losses are converted to dollars? For example, if a U.S. taxpayer purchases

Japanese yen (with U.S. dollars) as an investment and following a shift in exchange rates sells the yen (for U.S. dollars), how is any gain (or loss) to be treated? Or suppose a French branch of a U.S. business conducts its activities using the Euro, how and when should the gains (or losses) of the branch be converted from Euros to dollars?

Tax issues involving foreign currency usually arise in one of the following contexts: (1) isolated business or investment transactions of a U.S. business involving foreign currency; (2) the translation from foreign currency into dollars of the income or loss from continuous activities of a foreign branch or foreign subsidiary of a U.S. business; (3) isolated transactions not connected with the conduct of business or investment (*e.g.*, currency conversion on a vacation). These topics are considered below after an introduction to some of the basic definitional elements of the foreign currency provisions. Even before looking at the statutory apparatus, consider the following three principles that guide the U.S. tax treatment of currency transactions.

First, foreign currency is generally considered to be property the purchase and sale of which are treated in the same manner as the purchase and sale of any other type of property. This general principle has more application to isolated transactions involving the acquisition and disposition of foreign currency than the translation from foreign currency into U.S. dollars for the operation of a foreign branch or foreign subsidiary of a U.S. business. For example, a foreign branch or foreign subsidiary of a U.S. corporation does not have to compute gain and loss every time the branch or subsidiary acquires and then exchanges foreign currency for office supplies. Instead, the translation into dollars typically occurs at the end of the taxable year using the average exchange rate for the year.

Second, gain (or loss) from currency transactions is generally treated as ordinary income (or loss) rather than capital gain (or loss). This treatment stems from the fact that Congress views currency fluctuation, in effect, as an interest substitute. To illustrate, suppose that a taxpayer purchases 130,000 Japanese yen (¥) for $1,000 at an exchange rate of $1.00 = 130¥. At the same time the taxpayer lends the yen for three months at a nominal interest rate of 2 percent per year. Suppose that the interest rate is low relative to interest rates in the United States because the Japanese yen is a strong currency that is expected to get stronger relative to the U.S. dollar. In fact, the taxpayer upon purchasing the yen also agrees in the forward market to sell the yen in three months at a rate of $1.00 = 128¥. The $15.63 gain ($1,015.63 at a conversion rate of $1.00 = 128¥ minus the $1,000 original cost of the yen) that the taxpayer experiences at the end of three months when the loan is repaid and the yen are sold for dollars is really an interest substitute to supplement the low rate of interest on the yen-denominated loan.

Conversely, suppose that a taxpayer purchases foreign currency of a country experiencing high rates of inflation (so that the currency is weak relative to the dollar), and at the same time enters into a forward contract to sell the currency in three months at a specified rate which is less favorable than the exchange rate on the day of the purchase. If the taxpayer then lends the purchased currency, the nominal interest rate in the loan agreement would be high relative to U.S. interest rates. At the end of three months when the taxpayer sells the foreign currency pursuant to the forward contract, the sales price (in dollars) would be less than the purchase price (in dollars). In effect, the taxpayer would have to "give back" some of the high nominal interest earned on the loan.

Both the gain in the first example and the loss in the second example resulting from the forward contracts are treated, respectively, as ordinary income and loss under the currency exchange rules. While this treatment may be appropriate where the taxpayer locks in the gain or loss by hedging in the forward market, not all currency fluctuations result from changes in interest rates. Issues such as trade and capital flows, the political climate and the credit worthiness of the sovereign all influence currency fluctuation.

Moreover, even where interest rates influence currency fluctuation, treating exchange gains (or loss) as ordinary income (or loss) transactions may be unwarranted. To treat the gain (or loss) from foreign currency transactions as ordinary income (or loss) is inconsistent with the treatment of gain (or loss) from dispositions of other types of property. For example, suppose that the rental value of real property increases because a new road is built nearby. If a taxpayer sits back and collects the rents, the income will be ordinary income. However, if the taxpayer sells the real estate at a profit representing the expected increased rental value, the gain will nevertheless be a capital gain. It is not clear why gain (or loss) from foreign currency dispositions should assume the character of the periodic payments (*i.e.*, interest) generated by the property.

As a third general principle governing currency transactions, currency gains and losses are treated separately from related transactions. For example, suppose that a taxpayer borrows Euros which the taxpayer uses to purchase Italian real property. Any gain or loss on the sale of the real property is determined separately from any gain or loss on the ultimate purchase of Euros to repay the loan. The gain or loss on the sale of the real property may be a capital gain or loss while the currency exchange transaction will produce ordinary income or loss. However, in some cases a taxpayer is permitted to integrate currency gain/loss with gain or loss on the underlying property if ahead of time a taxpayer designates the currency transaction as a qualified hedge. Reg. § 1.988–5(b).

§ 12.02   FUNCTIONAL CURRENCY

Under I.R.C. § 985(b), a U.S. taxpayer's functional currency is typically the U.S. dollar in which case a taxpayer must measure income or loss from dealings in foreign currency in U.S. dollars on a transaction-by-transaction basis. In some circumstances, a taxpayer may use a foreign currency as its functional currency. For example, if a U.S. taxpayer has a self-contained, unincorporated foreign branch in England which conducts all of its business in pounds sterling (£), then the pound sterling may be the functional currency of the branch of the U.S. taxpayer. *See infra* § 12.04. Generally, the use of a foreign currency as a functional currency results in deferral of exchange gain or loss, compared with a transaction-by-transaction approach.

The use of a foreign currency as a taxpayer's functional currency is appropriate for a "qualified business unit" (QBU) if the selection is the currency of the "economic environment" in which the QBU's operations are conducted, and the QBU maintains its books and records in such currency. I.R.C. § 985(b)(1)(B). A QBU is defined as any separate and clearly identified unit of a trade or business of the taxpayer which maintains separate books and records. I.R.C. § 989(a).

A taxpayer can have several QBUs. Every foreign corporation is a QBU, and the activities of a foreign branch may constitute a QBU if they include every operation that forms a part of the process of earning income. The regulations allow taxpayers to treat all directly owned QBUs with the same functional currency as a single QBU for most purposes. Reg. § 1.987–1(b)(2).

Suppose that a U.S. corporation that manufactures and sells product X in the United States has a French sales office with one salesperson whose only function is to solicit orders for product X in France. The French office may not constitute a QBU and would likely use the U.S. dollar as its functional currency because it is not a clearly identified, self-sustaining unit.

Even if the activities a foreign branch or subsidiary constitute a QBU, if the economic environment of the QBU is deemed to be the United States, the dollar will be the functional currency. Determining the economic environment depends on the facts and circumstances surrounding the QBU. The regulations list several factors which may be considered in making this determination, but they all basically turn on what currency the QBU uses in its day-to-day activities. *See* Reg. § 1.985–1(c)(2). For example, suppose that a U.S. taxpayer has a wholly-owned subsidiary in Belgium that sells its parent's exports throughout Europe with transactions denominated for the most part in U.S. dollars while maintaining its Euro-based books. Under these circumstances the U.S. dollar may be the functional currency.

In some cases, a U.S. taxpayer with business activities in a foreign branch or subsidiary that is a QBU might nevertheless like to use the dollar as its functional currency and can elect to do so under I.R.C. § 985(b)(3). For example, suppose that USCo has a foreign branch that conducts activities that constitute a QBU in a foreign country that uses the "h" as its currency. Suppose that the branch purchases goods for 100,000h at a time when the conversion rate is $1.00 = 4h. Because of inflation, the "h" currency becomes worth 1/100 of its previous value so that $1.00 = 400h. If the branch sells the goods for 10,000,000h (*i.e.*, 100 times the purchase price) there is no real gain; the nominal gain of 9,900,000h is due solely to inflation. Nevertheless, the taxpayer faces a $24,750 gain (9,900,000h/400h) for U.S. income tax purposes if $1.00 = 400h is the weighted average exchange rate under I.R.C. § 989(b)(4).

A taxpayer is required to use the U.S. dollar as its functional currency for any QBU whose functional currency would be a "hyperinflationary currency" absent a U.S. dollar election. Reg. § 1.985–2(d). A hyperinflationary currency is defined as the currency of a country in which there is cumulative inflation of at least 100 percent during the 36 calendar months immediately preceding the last day of such taxable year. Under I.R.C. § 985(b)(3), the QBU is required to keep its books and records in U.S. dollars and the taxpayer is required to use a method of accounting that approximates a separate transactions method (*i.e.*, converting the gain or loss from each transaction into dollars when the transaction occurs), referred to as the "U.S. **D**ollar **A**pproximate **S**eparate **T**ransactions" **M**ethod (DASTM, pronounced "dastum").

In the example above, the application of I.R.C. § 985(b)(3) allows the taxpayer to avoid any gain recognition due to the hyperinflation. The goods would have a $25,000 dollar basis (100,000h/4h) at the conversion rate ($1.00 = 4h) existing when the goods were purchased. The amount realized would be $25,000 (10,000,000h/400h) at the $1.00 = 400h conversion rate existing at the time of sale.

When DASTM is required, the taxpayer prepares an income or loss statement in the hyperinflationary currency from the books of the QBU. Then that account is conformed to U.S. financial and tax principles and translated into U.S. dollars (usually on a monthly or shorter basis). Reg. § 1.985–3(b). To that income or loss, the taxpayer adds DASTM gain or loss. The DASTM gain or loss that the taxpayer must recognize is equal to the dollar value of the sum of the QBU's net worth at the end of the year plus any dividends or remittances to the home office, minus the sum of the net worth at the end of the preceding year and the QBU's income or loss for the current year and any capital contributions to the QBU. Reg. § 1.985–3(d)(1). Net worth is translated into dollars on a monthly or shorter basis. Dividends and net remittances are translated into dollars using the spot rate. To study DASTM in action, *see* the example in Reg. § 1.985–3(d)(9).

§ 12.03   FOREIGN CURRENCY TRANSACTIONS

Once the functional currency is established, the Code provides a comprehensive set of rules for nonfunctional currency transactions. A nonfunctional currency is treated as property so that its disposition is a taxable event. For example, if the U.S. dollar is the functional currency, a disposition of Mexican pesos (*e.g.*, the exchange of pesos for Mexican goods or U.S. dollars) can be a taxable event. If the Mexican peso is a taxpayer's functional currency, then the purchase and disposition of Euros (or U.S. dollars) can be a taxable event, but the disposition of pesos (*e.g.*, in exchange for Mexican goods) would not be a taxable event.

Statutorily, I.R.C. § 988(a) provides that any foreign currency gain or loss attributable to a "section 988 transaction" constitutes ordinary income (or loss). A "section 988 transaction" includes: (1) the acquisition of a debt instrument or becoming the obligor under a debt instrument; (2) the accrual of any item of expense or gross income that is to be paid or received after the date of accrual; (3) the entering into of certain forward contracts; or (4) the disposition of any nonfunctional currency. I.R.C. § 988(c). Gain or loss realized is generally sourced by reference to the residence of the taxpayer. I.R.C. § 988(a)(3). However in the case of a QBU, the source of gain or loss is the location of the principal place of business of the QBU.

The best way to understand how I.R.C. § 988 operates is to consider a range of transactions involving foreign currency. In the examples that follow, assume that the taxpayer's functional currency is the U.S. dollar (USD) and that the transactions described are business or investment (*i.e.*, not personal) transactions.

(A) ACQUISITION AND DISPOSITION OF FOREIGN CURRENCY

Because foreign currency is treated as property for U.S. tax purposes, the acquisition and disposition of such property follows normal U.S. domestic tax rules. I.R.C. § 988(c)(1)(C). To illustrate, if a U.S. taxpayer buys 1.2 million Hong Kong dollars (HKD) and the conversion rate is 1 USD = 6 HKD, the taxpayer's basis in the HKD is $200,000. When the HKDs are "sold" (*i.e.*, exchanged for U.S. dollars), there is a gain or loss if the conversion rate has changed. I.R.C. § 988(c)(1)(C). For example, if the conversion rate changes to 1 USD = 5 HKD, a taxpayer has a $40,000 gain (treated as ordinary income) on the sale of the HKDs ($240,000 amount realized on the conversion to USD minus the $200,000 basis in the HKDs). The gain is treated as U.S. source income. I.R.C. § 988(a)(3).

If instead of converting HKDs to USD, the taxpayer disposes of the nonfunctional currency by purchasing Hong Kong goods for 1.2 million HKDs when the conversion rate is 1 USD = 5 HKDs, the result is again recognition of $40,000 of U.S. source, ordinary income. The taxpayer will have an adjusted basis in the purchased Hong Kong goods of $240,000 (the original basis of $200,000 plus the recognized gain of $40,000 or the value of 1.2 million HKDs (at 1 USD = 5 HKD) at the time of the purchase). *See* Reg. § 1.988–2(a)(2)(iii)(A).

If instead of purchasing property, the taxpayer lends the HKDs to a borrower, the exchange of the HKDs for a debt instrument issued by the borrower again constitutes a taxable disposition. However, depositing a foreign currency in a bank or other financial institution does not cause recognition of gain or loss until there is a disposition of the currency. I.R.C. § 988(c)(1)(C)(ii). Note that if a taxpayer acquires HKDs and immediately lends to a borrower, there may be no gain or loss on the disposition of the nonfunctional currency.

(B) LENDING AND BORROWING FOREIGN CURRENCY

Both acquiring a debt instrument (*i.e.*, lending) denominated in a nonfunctional currency or becoming an obligor under such a debt instrument (*i.e.*, borrowing) are section 988 transactions that may have U.S. tax consequences. I.R.C. § 988(c)(1)(B)(i). Suppose that a U.S. taxpayer purchases a Brazilian bond paying 7 percent interest at a cost of 1,800,000 Brazilian Real (BRL) at a time when the conversion rate is 1 USD = 1.8 BRL. Under these circumstances there may be two times when gain or loss is recognized. As discussed above, if the exchange rate fluctuates between the time the taxpayer purchases BRLs for dollars and the time the BRLs are exchanged for the bond, gain or loss must be recognized. There may be additional gain or loss recognized if there is a currency fluctuation between the time the taxpayer purchases the bond and when the taxpayer disposes of the bond.

Suppose the bond is redeemed after more than a year at face value (1,800,000 BRL) at a time when the exchange rate is 1 USD = 1.7 BRL. The taxpayer's gain on the section 988 transaction is equal to an amount realized of $1,058,824 (the bond was redeemed for 1,800,000 BRL when 1 USD = 1.7 BRL) minus an adjusted basis of $1,000,000 (the bond was purchased for 1,800,000 BRL when 1 USD = 1.8 BRL) or $58,824. In addition, the taxpayer typically would accrue any interest payable by the borrower and convert that interest to dollars at the average spot rate of interest for the year in question, or if the taxpayer was a cash basis taxpayer, interest would be translated into dollars at the spot rate of exchange on the day of payment.

Now consider a situation where a cash-basis taxpayer with a USD functional currency borrows foreign currency rather than lends it. Suppose a taxpayer borrows £100 when 1 GBP = 1 USD, promising to repay the lender £100 plus 10 percent due in one year. Suppose that the taxpayer uses the £100 to purchase office equipment. A month before repayment is due, the taxpayer purchases on the open market £110 when 1 GBP = .70 USD, and deposits it in a bank. A month later when 1 GBP = .60 USD, the taxpayer pays off the loan.

This series of events results in the following section 988 transactions:

(a) the initial borrowing and repayment (I.R.C. § 988(c)(1)(B)(i));

(b) the disposition of the borrowed currency in exchange for the office equipment (I.R.C. § 988(c)(1)(C)(i));

(c) the acquisition of currency in the open market and its subsequent disposition (I.R.C. § 988(c)(1)(C)(i)).

The £100 borrowing by the taxpayer constitutes a section 988 transaction so that a $40 gain (*i.e.*, the taxpayer borrowed the equivalent of $100 and repaid the equivalent of $60) is recognized resulting from currency fluctuations between the booking date (*i.e.*, the date of the loan) and the payment date (*i.e.*, the day the loan is paid off). I.R.C. §§ 988(c)(1)(B)(i) and 988(b). If there is no currency fluctuation between the date the currency is borrowed and the date it is used to purchase the machinery, the disposition of the borrowed funds does not produce a currency gain or loss. The purchased machinery has a basis equal to the dollar purchase price on the date of purchase at the spot exchange rate of the dollar and the pound sterling.

When the taxpayer purchases £110 in the open market, the basis in the currency is $77. When that currency is transferred to the lender to repay the loan (with interest) at a time when the £110 has a value of $66, the taxpayer suffers an $11 foreign currency loss. The deposit of pounds sterling in the bank is not a section 988 transaction. I.R.C. § 988(c)(1)(C)(ii). Finally, although not a section 988 transaction, the payment of interest generally generates a deduction. For a cash basis taxpayer, the deduction is the U.S. dollar equivalent of the £10 payment, or $6 at the spot exchange rate on the date of repayment.

Suppose a U.K. controlled foreign corporation wholly-owned by USCo uses the pound sterling as its functional currency. If the CFC generates a currency gain (*e.g.*, a U.S. dollar-denominated loan made by the CFC was settled at a time when the dollar strengthened relative to the pound), is that currency gain subpart F income (*i.e.*, foreign personal holding company income) for U.S. tax purposes? Under I.R.C.

§ 954(c)(1)(D), foreign currency gains generally are considered subpart F income unless the gains are directly related to the business needs of the CFC (*e.g.*, loans to customers to encourage inventory purchases).

(C) ACQUISITION AND DISPOSITION OF ASSETS DENOMINATED IN FOREIGN CURRENCY

Generally, fluctuations in exchange rates producing gains and losses upon the purchase and disposition of non-debt assets are not treated as section 988 gains or losses. Instead, the amount of gain or loss, the character, the timing and the source are determined under general tax principles. For example, suppose a U.S. taxpayer purchases 1,000 shares of Toyota stock on the Tokyo stock exchange at ¥13,000 per share at a time when $1.00 = ¥130. More than one year later, the shares are sold for ¥15,000 per share at a time when the conversion rate is $1.00 = ¥125. The taxpayer's gain is $20 per share ((¥15,000/¥125) minus (¥13,000/¥130)), or an overall gain of $20,000. The gain consists of a market gain of $16 per share (¥15,000/¥125 minus ¥13,000/¥125) and a $4 currency gain per share (¥13,000/¥125 minus ¥13,000/¥130). But because I.R.C. § 988 does not apply to the transaction, the entire gain of $20 per share, or $20,000 overall is treated as long-term capital gain. Similarly if a taxpayer purchased business plant or equipment any gain or loss attributable to currency fluctuation would probably be a capital gain or ordinary loss under I.R.C. § 1231;

gain or loss from the disposition of inventory would produce ordinary income or loss.

(D) ACCOUNTS RECEIVABLE AND PAYABLE

While gain or loss on the sale of goods due to currency fluctuation is not normally subject to tax as a section 988 transaction, currency gain or loss resulting from deferred payments for the sale or purchase of goods or services is taxable as a section 988 transaction. If an accrual basis U.S. taxpayer sells goods (or performs services) in exchange for an account receivable denominated in a nonfunctional currency, any gain or loss due to currency fluctuation while the taxpayer holds the receivable will be U.S. source, ordinary income when the receivable is paid. I.R.C. § 988(c)(1)(B)(ii).

For example, suppose an accrual basis U.S. taxpayer sells inventory in Spain in exchange for an account receivable calling for payment of 1,220 Euro at a time when the conversion rate is 1 USD = 1.22 Euro. At the time of the sale, the accrual basis taxpayer accrues any gain on the sale of the inventory itself. If the conversion rate is 1 USD = 1.00 Euro when the purchaser pays the receivable, the seller must account for any gain or loss resulting from fluctuations in the value of the receivable. Under these circumstances, the taxpayer would report U.S. source, ordinary income of $220 ($1,220 amount realized minus $1,000 adjusted basis in the receivable). If the receivable was received by a QBU in Spain that was using the dollar as a functional currency, the gain would be foreign source income. I.R.C. § 988(a)(3)(B).

The same principles govern accounts payable. A change in exchange rates between the time the taxpayer accrues an account payable and the time of payment will also result in ordinary income or loss for the taxpayer. I.R.C. § 988(c)(1)(B)(ii). For example, suppose an accrual basis U.S. taxpayer for business purposes hires the architectural services of a Spanish architect for 1,220€ at a time when the conversion rate is 1 USD = 1.22 Euro. Between the time the U.S. taxpayer accrues the liability and the time payment is made, the conversion rate changes to 1 USD = 1.00 Euro. Under these circumstances, the taxpayer would report an ordinary loss of $220 ($1,220 cost of acquiring the 1,220 Euros minus the $1,000 deduction previously accrued).

(E)   FORWARD, FUTURES AND OPTION CONTRACTS

A section 988 transaction includes entering into or acquiring any forward, futures or option contract or any similar financial instrument if the contract is not subject to the annual accrual (*i.e.*, marked to market) rules of I.R.C. § 1256. I.R.C. § 988(c)(1)(B)(iii). These contracts generally obligate the taxpayer either to sell or purchase foreign currency at some point in the future for a price designated in the present upon entering the contract. For example, suppose a U.S. taxpayer enters into a forward contract to sell 30,000 Taiwan dollars (TWD) in six months at a conversion rate of 1 USD = 30 TWD. At the end of six months when the conversion rate is 1 USD = 40 TWD, the purchaser pays the taxpayer $250 (*i.e.*, the difference between the $1,000 contract price and the $750 cost of 30,000 TWD on the spot market) to cancel the contract, or the taxpayer sells the contract for $250, producing a foreign currency gain. I.R.C. § 988(c)(1)(B)(iii).

In general, I.R.C. § 988 will not apply (and the mark-to-market rules will apply) to a contract to purchase or sell currency if the contract is of a type traded on the interbank market. I.R.C. § 1256. Under the mark-to-market rules, a forward contract is subject to tax at the end of the year as if it had been sold and then repurchased. If I.R.C. § 1256 applied to the example above, the taxpayer would recognize $250 of foreign currency gain if the conversion rate was 1 USD = 40 TWD on the last day of the year even if the payment date was in the following year. No further gain would be recognized upon payment of the TWD under the contract if there were no subsequent change in the exchange rate.

(F) HEDGING

A section 988 hedging transaction is typically a mechanism to reduce the effect of currency fluctuation on taxable income. Under I.R.C. § 988(d)(1), if a section 988 transaction is part of a section 988 hedging transaction, all transactions should be integrated and treated consistently. There are three requirements of a 988 hedging transaction: (1) a "qualified debt instrument" and (2) a "hedge" that is part of (3) an "integrated economic transaction." Reg. § 1.988–5(a)(1). Any debt instrument will qualify as a "qualified debt instrument" unless it is an account receivable or payable. Reg. § 1.988–5(a)(3). A "hedge" is any instrument or series of instruments that when combined with the qualified debt instrument will allow the calculation of yield to maturity in a currency other than that of the qualified debt instrument. Reg. § 1.988–5(a)(4)(i). A qualified debt instrument and a hedge will constitute an "integrated economic transaction" if the hedge fully covers the payments under the qualified debt instrument, the parties to the hedge are unrelated, and the transaction is identified by the taxpayer as a section 988 hedging transaction no later than the close of business on the day the hedge is acquired. Reg. § 1.988–5(a)(5). If all these requirements are met the qualified debt instrument and the hedge will be treated as a single "synthetic debt instrument" denominated in the currency received under the hedge.

For example, assume a taxpayer borrows 1,000 units of a weak foreign currency ("F") for 2 years at 30 percent interest—the market interest rate. Interest payments are F300 in each of the next 2 years, plus a principal payment of F1,000 in 2 years. The high interest rate reflects the anticipated devaluation of the foreign currency relative to the dollar.

If the spot market for the F currency is 1 USD = F2, the loan would be the equivalent of $500 (F1,000/F2). Suppose the F foreign currency can be purchased one year ahead in the forward market at $1.00 = F2.5 and 2 years ahead at 1 USD = F2.75. Under these facts, the taxpayer can protect against any unexpected exchange rate fluctuation (*e.g.*, a stronger F currency relative to the dollar) by purchasing F300 1 year ahead for $120 (F300/F2.5) and F1300 2 years ahead for $473 (F1300/F2.75). These transactions will lock in the F300 interest payments in Years 1 and 2 plus the repayment of F1,000 principal at the end of Year 2. With this full hedge, the foreign currency borrowing is converted into a dollar borrowing of $500 with a payment of $120 in Year 1 and $473 in Year 2, resulting approximately in a 10 percent yield to maturity, rather than the nominal 30 percent.

Instead of deducting $120 of interest in Year 1 (F300/F2.5) and reporting a $27 gain in Year 2—$136 of currency income ($500 minus F1,000/F2.75) minus a $109 interest deduction (F300/F2.75)—the taxpayer would have a $50 deduction ($500 × 10 percent) under the OID rules of I.R.C. §§ 1271 *et seq.* The remaining $70 paid in Year 1 is considered a repayment of principal, leaving $430 of principal to be repaid at the end of Year 2. In Year 2, the taxpayer would deduct $43 of interest ($430 principal outstanding × 10 percent). Over the 2 year period, the application of the hedging rules does not change the amount of the overall deduction (*i.e.*, $93), but the effect is to prevent an acceleration of the deduction into year 1 (with a recognition of gain in year 2).

Similar rules apply to hedged executory contracts to purchase or sell goods or services or stock. For example, suppose that a U.S. taxpayer makes a contract to purchase engineering services in six months for a price denominated in a foreign currency. To protect against exchange rate fluctuation (taxpayer wants to be in the engineering business not the currency fluctuation business), the taxpayer might immediately enter into a forward contract to purchase the foreign currency needed to pay for the engineering services at a fixed price. Under these circumstances, the purchase of the engineering services and the forward contract hedge are integrated with the cost of the services being the locked-in dollar price of the foreign currency.

Suppose that a U.S. corporation enters into an agreement to sell stock in a German corporation for €80 million. If the seller is worried about fluctuating rates between the date the sales agreement is signed and the day the transaction closes, the U.S. corporation might enter into a forward contract to sell the €80 million. By locking in the exchange rate when the agreement is signed, the seller can eliminate currency risk. If the Euro strengthens relative to the U.S. dollar, then the amount received at closing will buy more dollars, but there will be a corresponding loss on the forward contract. Conversely, if the Euro weakens relative to the U.S. dollar, the amount received at closing would buy fewer dollars, but the forward contract would have increased in value. In either case, the dollar value of the sale is locked in.

In this situation, the taxpayer may not want to risk capital loss on the sale and ordinary income on the forward contract. For the corporate seller, capital loss cannot offset ordinary gain. Fortunately, the seller can integrate the forward with sales contract as a hedged executory contract. Reg. § 1.988–5(b)(2). To create a hedged executory contract, the following requirements must be met:

1. The executory contract and the hedge are identified as a hedged executory contract. The Regulations do not detail exactly how the identification is achieved other than to say: a taxpayer must establish a record before the close of the date the hedge is entered into which contains a clear description of: (a) the executory contract; (b) the hedge; and (c) that the hedge is entered into in accordance with Reg. § 1.988–5(b)(3).

2. The hedge itself is entered into after on or after the date the executory contract is entered into.

3. The hedge continues and ends on or after the accrual date.

4. The hedge is not with a related party.

5. The hedge and the executory contract are entered into by the same person (e.g., parent hedging a subsidiary's contract cannot be a hedged executory contract).

As noted, Reg. § 1.988–5 provides for the integration of a section 988 transaction in two limited circumstances. First, Reg. § 1.988–5(a) provides for the integration of a nonfunctional currency debt instrument and a § 1.988–5(a) hedge. Second, Reg. § 1.988–5(b) provides rules for the integration of a hedged executory contract.

Even if a hedging transaction cannot be integrated with an underlying transaction under Reg. § 1.988–5, it still may be considered in some circumstances a hedging transaction under I.R.C. § 1221(b)(2)(A) and Reg. § 1.1221–2(b). If the definitional requirements were satisfied and the identification requirements are satisfied, then the gain or loss under the forward contracts would be subject to the hedge timing rules under Reg. § 1.446–4 which essentially provides that while the underlying transaction and the hedge are not integrated, the timing of gain or loss with respect to both are taken into account in the same year.

A hedging transaction is defined under I.R.C. § 1221(b)(2)(A) to include any transaction entered into by the taxpayer in the normal course of its trade or business primarily (i) to manage risk of price changes or currency fluctuations with respect to ordinary property which is held or to be held by the taxpayer, and (ii) to manage risk of interest rate, price changes or currency fluctuations with respect to borrowings made or to be made, or ordinary obligations incurred or to be incurred, by the taxpayer. Property is ordinary property of the taxpayer only if a sale or exchange of the property by the taxpayer could not produce capital gain or loss under any circumstances.

Under proposed regulations applicable to hybrid transactions, I.R.C. § 988 gain or loss generally is not taken into account under I.R.C. § 267A, with certain exceptions for I.R.C. § 988 gain or loss recognized by an issuer of a debt instrument with respect to accrued interest or relating to items of expense or gross income or receipts to be paid after the date accrued. If a deduction is disallowed under I.R.C. § 267A, a proportionate amount of foreign currency loss under I.R.C. § 988 is also disallowed, and a proportionate amount of foreign currency gain under I.R.C. § 988 reduces the amount of the disallowance.

§ 12.04 FOREIGN CURRENCY TRANSLATION

If a U.S. taxpayer operates abroad through either an unincorporated branch or a foreign subsidiary and the activities are conducted in a foreign currency (*i.e.*, the branch is a QBU) it is necessary to convert the operating results of the foreign business into U.S. dollars at some point in order to determine U.S. tax. For a branch (including a hybrid entity treated as disregarded for U.S. tax purposes but as a corporation for local country purposes), the converted profit or loss is included currently in the taxable income of the U.S. taxpayer. For a foreign subsidiary, any actual or deemed distributions (*e.g.*, subpart F income) must be translated into U.S. dollars in order to determine the taxable income of the U.S. parent. In addition, foreign taxes paid must be converted to U.S. dollars for purposes of computing the foreign tax credit.

(A) FOREIGN BRANCHES

Under I.R.C. § 987, a taxpayer with a QBU must account for currency gain/loss from both operations and remittances back to the home office. I.R.C. § 989 and Reg. § 1.989(a)–1(b) generally treat a corporation or a partnership as a QBU. Moreover, activities of a corporation, partnership, trust, estate, or individual also rise to the level of a QBU if the activities constitute a trade or business, and a separate set of books and records are maintained. Reg. § 1.989(a)–1(c) defines a trade or business as a "specific unified group of activities that constitutes (or could constitute) an independent economic enterprise carried on for profit . . ." A vertical, functional, or geographic division of the same trade or business can constitute a trade or business for this purpose. But a QBU does not include activities that are merely ancillary to a trade or business (Reg. § 1.989(a)–1(c)).

On December 7, 2016, over 32 years after the enactment of I.R.C. § 987 in 1986, the government finally released final (and temporary) regulations providing taxpayers with guidance for how to apply that provision. Until then, guidance in this area consisted of proposed regulations issued in 1991 (the 1991 proposed regulations), which were withdrawn in 2006 when another set of proposed regulations was released (the 2006 proposed regulations). The final 2016 regulations mostly adopt the approach of the 2006 proposed regulations.

These 2016 final regulations generally had a deferred effective date, which was further extended by Notice 2017–57, and then again by Notice 2018–

57, 2018–26 I.R.B. 1 until 2020. As a result, for calendar year taxpayers, the final regulations apply as of January 1, 2020. In the Notices, the government also indicated that it was considering changes that would allow taxpayers to elect to apply alternative rules for transitioning to the final regulations and for determining I.R.C. § 987 gain or loss.

Executive Order 13789 (2017) instructed the Treasury to review all significant tax regulations issued in 2016 or later and to the extent that they imposed undue financial burdens on U.S. taxpayers and added undue complexity to the tax laws, to take concrete action to alleviate their burdens. Treasury has identified the I.R.C. § 987 2016 final regulations as meeting these criteria. In a report published on October 16, 2017 (82 Fed. Reg. 48013), Treasury indicated that it intended to propose modifications to the 2016 final regulations to reduce burden and compliance challenges associated with those regulations and that it was actively considering other rules in connection with that proposal. Notwithstanding the government's (finally!) issuing final regulations in this area, the uncertainty continues at least for some time.

While in the process of undertaking a review of the final regulations, in May 2019 the government nevertheless finalized certain aspects of the temporary regulations issued in 2016, specifically to address policy concerns relating to taxpayers' selective recognition of losses upon the transfer or deemed transfer of QBU assets. More on that below.

Until the final regulations become effective, taxpayers for all intents and purposes are able to choose—as for practical purposes, they've been able to do for many years—among any reasonable method (taxpayers can also make an election to adopt the 2016 final regulations prior to their effective date, provided the regulations are applied consistently). The "head-in-the-sand" approach, which has been adopted by some taxpayers, is not endorsed by this book.

The regulations under I.R.C. § 987 are very complicated. But the general principle is fairly straightforward. For purposes of the discussion that follows, assume that USCo owns DE, a disregarded entity for U.S. purposes and a corporation for foreign purposes, and that DE conducts a foreign trade or business in a non-U.S. dollar functional currency. The rules that follow could also apply if instead of DE, there is a true foreign branch (*i.e.*, branch for U.S. and foreign purposes) engaged in the same activities. Similarly, if USCo was a partner in a partnership that carried on the same activities, the activities would constitute a QBU. Finally, suppose USCo owned all the stock of CFC, a controlled foreign corporation. If CFC operates a trade or business through a branch, disregarded entity or partnership that uses a functional currency different from the functional currency of the CFC, section 987 gain/loss may occur on a remittance to the CFC. In some cases, section 987 gain could be subpart F income, taxable to a U.S. shareholder.

A key difference between the approach taken in the final regulations and the 2006 proposed regulations, versus the 1991 proposed regulations, is that the newer versions of the regulations are intended to make it harder for taxpayers to trigger the realization and recognition of section 987 gain or loss without a fundamental change in the QBU's business. The government's primary concern was taxpayers' ability to intentionally trigger section 987 losses that could be used as a deduction resulting in less U.S. tax, while deferring section 987 gain that might increase U.S. tax. As with many other of the rules we have examined in prior chapters, the history of the government's various iterations of I.R.C. § 987 rules is the story of its attempts to prevent taxpayers from taking advantage of complex rules to their advantage in the cross-border business environment.

(1)   2016 Final Regulations

As stated above, the 2016 final regulations generally adopt the method of the 2006 proposed regulations (often referred to as the 'foreign exchange exposure pool' method or 'FEEP' method).

Some basic principles apply in these regulations. First, the rules apply to activities, not entities. For example, a foreign disregarded entity (*i.e.*, corporation for foreign purposes but disregarded for U.S. tax purposes) that merely holds stock in a foreign corporation does not carry on an activity that is a QBU. Second, currency gain/loss with respect to day-to-day operations of a QBU (*i.e.*, income and deductions) will flow through to the owner, reflected in the income or loss related to the operations themselves. Third, there may be unrecognized foreign currency gains/losses relating to assets and liabilities held in connection with the QBU. The mechanism for keeping track of the net unrecognized section 987 gain or loss is the FEEP method. These net unrecognized currency gains/losses will be recognized upon a remittance from the QBU to the owner. For example, if a QBU owns foreign currency or a note receivable or a note payable denominated in a foreign currency, as that foreign currency fluctuates there may be unrecognized section 987 gain/loss. Assets and liabilities that give rise to potential unrecognized section 987 gain/loss (primarily financial assets) are referred to as "marked" assets. These assets and liabilities are valued in U.S. dollars at the year-end exchange rate. All other assets/liabilities (*e.g.*, property, plant, equipment, and inventory) are referred to as "historic" assets/liabilities and are valued at the historic exchange rates when acquired by the QBU. Changes in currency rates are not deemed to affect these historical assets/liabilities and therefore no section 987 unrecognized gain/loss arises with respect to them.

Fourth, the unrecognized section 987 gain/loss is computed by comparing the balance sheet (with appropriate adjustments to reverse out any additions to, or subtractions from, the QBU) of the QBU at the beginning of the year and the end of the year. Any change is deemed to be a net unrecognized section 987 gain/loss. Fifth, on any remittance from the QBU, a proportionate amount of the net unrecognized section 987 gain/loss is recognized. To see these rules in operation consider the following example.

USCo forms a Japanese branch on 7/1/Year 1 with the following attributes:

- $1,000 of cash (immediately converted to ¥100,000)

- a building with an adjusted basis of $500 (depreciation ignored)

- Branch borrows ¥10,000 on 7/1/Year 1

- Branch earns ¥10,000

Exchange rates:

- Average Exchange rate for Year 1 from 7/1/Year 1 to 12/31/Year 1 = $1 : ¥110.01 (¥1 : $0.009090)

- Spot rate on 7/1/Year 1 = $1.00 : ¥100

- Spot rate on 12/31/Year 1 = $1.00 : ¥120 (¥1 : $0.00833)

Year 1	Beginning Yen	Beginning Dollars	Ending Yen	Ending Dollar	Comments
Cash	0	0	120,000	1,000.00	Marked item $1.00 : ¥120
Building	0	0	50,000	500.00	Historic item $1.00 : ¥100
Liabilities	0	0	(10,000)	(83.33)	Marked item $1.00 : ¥120
Net Value	0	0	160,000	1,416.67	
Increase				1,416.67	
Adjust-ments:					
Transfers In				(1,500.00)	
Taxable income				(90.90)	Yearly Average Exchange Rate
Net Unrecog-nized section 987 G/(L)				(174.23)	

Section 987 requires a comparison of the balance sheet (in U.S. dollars) at the beginning of the year and the end of the year with certain adjustments. In the first year of this QBU, the beginning balance sheet is $0. At the end of the year, the balance sheet reflects "marked items" (essentially, financial assets and liabilities) at the year-end conversion rate (*i.e.*, the items are marked-to-market) while historic assets (*e.g.*, the building) reflect their historical U.S. dollar conversion rate. Then adjustments are made to the balance sheet. Items contributed during the year (*i.e.*, dollar basis in cash and building) are subtracted and income during the year is also subtracted as the currency gain with respect to that income is already taken into account by USCo. The net unrecognized section 987 loss that results therefore reflects the following.

Components	Yen	Value Before Dollars	Value After Dollars	Change Dollars
Cash Contributed	100,000	1,000 $1.00 : ¥100	833.33 $1.00 : ¥120	(166.67)
Cash Earned	10,000	90.90	83.33 $1.00 : ¥120	(7.56)
Cash Borrowed	10,000	(100.00) $1.00 : ¥100	83.33 $1.00 : ¥120	(16.67)
Liability	−10,000	(100.00) $1.00 : ¥100	(83.33) $1.00 : ¥120	16.67
Total				(174.23)

There is no unrecognized section 987 gain or loss attributable to the historic assets (*e.g.*, the building). The net unrecognized section 987 loss is not taken into account by USCo until there is a remittance.

Now let's follow the same example into Year 2 where the following occurs.

- Branch borrows another ¥10,000 on 5/31/Year 2 and purchases equipment (depreciation ignored)

- Branch earns ¥25,000 during Year 2

- Branch transfers ¥70,000 to owner on 12/31/Year 2

Exchange rates:

- Average Spot rate for Year 2 = $1.00 : ¥131.58

- Spot rate on 5/31/11 = $1.00 : ¥130

- Spot rate on 12/31/11 = $1.00 : ¥140

The balance sheet of the QBU is as follows at the end of Year 2.

Year 2	Beginning Yen	Beginning Dollars	Ending Yen	Ending Dollar	Comments
Cash	120,000	1,000	75,000	537.71	Marked item $1.00 : ¥140
Building	50,000	500.00	50,000	500.00	Historic item $1.00 : ¥100
Equip-ment			10,000	76.92	Historic item $1.00 : ¥130
Liabilities	(10,000)	(83.33)	(20,000)	(142.86)	Marked item $1.00 : ¥140
Net Value	160,000	1,416.67	115,000	969.77	
Decrease				(446.90)	
Adjust-ments:					
Transfers Out				500.00	Spot rate
Taxable income				(190.00)	Average rate
Net Unrecog-nized section 987 G/(L)		(174.23)		(136.90)	Total = (311.13)

Notice that the ending value of the QBU (in dollars) has decreased by $446.90 but adjustments must be made to reflect section 987 inflows and outflows. To get a true picture of how currency fluctuation affected the QBU, any distributions out must be added back (*i.e.*, ¥70,000 distribution = $500). Next, the income of the QBU must be subtracted in computing net unrecognized section 987 gain or loss because any currency gain or loss in connection with the income event is already recognized by USCo when it reports the $190 of income. That leaves an additional net unrecognized section 987 loss of $136.90. The following table illustrates what accounts for the additional unrecognized loss.

Components	Yen	Value Before Dollars	Value After Dollars	Change Dollars
Beginning Cash	120,000	1,000 $1.00 : ¥120	857.14 $1.00 : ¥140	(142.86)
Cash Earned	25,000	190.90	178.57 $1.00 : ¥140	(11.43)
Cash Borrowed	10,000	(100.00) $1.00 : ¥100	83.33 $1.00 : ¥120	(16.67)
Beginning Liability	–10,000	(83.33) $1.00 : ¥120	(71.43) $1.00 : ¥140	11.90
New Liability	–10,000	(76.92) $1.00 : ¥130	(71.43) $1.00 : ¥140	5.49
Total				(136.90)

In Year 2, there was a remittance of ¥70,000. To determine whether a remittance has taken place, all of the contributions to the branch and distributions from the branch for the year are netted. In this example, there is only one transfer—the ¥70,000 distribution. That remittance results in USCo recognizing a portion of the $311.13 total net unrecognized I.R.C. § 987 loss. Notice that while the ¥70,000 remittance is a remittance of a marked asset, even if an historical asset (*e.g.*, the building) were remitted, section 987 gain/loss might occur. The portion of the loss that is recognized is equal to the "remittance proportion" multiplied by the net unrecognized section 987 gain/loss ($311.13 loss). The remittance proportion is the $500 remittance in dollars (¥70,000/¥140 spot rate at year-end) divided by the dollar basis of the gross assets in the QBU at year-end increased by the amount of the remittance (*i.e.*, $969.77 plus $500), or 34.02%. Accordingly, the section 987 loss that is recognized on the otherwise tax-free remittance from the branch is $105.84 ($311.13 × 34.02%) which can be deducted against other income USCo may generate. The gain or loss is ordinary and its character is based on the type of income that the assets in the QBU generate. Going into Year 3, the net unrecognized section 987 loss would be $205.29 ($311.13 − $105.84).

The final regulations do not apply to certain 'specified entities,' including banks, insurance companies, leasing companies, finance coordination centers, RICs and REITs. Treasury has said that it is still considering how to apply the regulations to these excluded entities.

All QBUs are required to transition to the FEEP method described in the 2016 final regulations on the 'transition date'—the first day of the first taxable year to which the regulations apply to the taxpayer. Under the proposed 2006 regulations, taxpayers were able to choose between two transition methods ('deferral' and 'fresh start'). The 2016 final regulations attempt to crack down on taxpayers' planning opportunities by disallowing the deferral method.

Under the fresh start method, a QBU is deemed to terminate (only for purposes of transitioning to the final regulations) on the day prior to the transition date and to reform on the transition date, and no section 987 gain or loss is recognized on this deemed termination. The assets of the deemed "re-formed" QBU are recorded on the QBU's balance sheet with a historic exchange rate.

In Notice 2017–572, Treasury said that it is considering changes to the regulations that would allow taxpayers to elect to apply alternative rules for determining section 987 gain or loss as well as alternative transition rules (reiterated in Notice 2018–57, 2018–26 I.R.B. 1).

(2)   Final Loss Deferral Regulations

When a QBU terminates, generally all section 987 gain or loss of the QBU is recognized by the owner. The 2019 regulations that finalized the 2016 temporary regulations generally make it more difficult to trigger section 987 losses through technical QBU terminations and in related party transactions (*e.g.*, transferring a QBU to a related party).

The 2019 final regulations defer section 987 losses resulting from some termination events, partnership transactions, and other transactions involving outbound transfers. They also generally apply to defer the recognition of section 987 gain as well as losses in certain cases.

(3) 1991 Proposed Regulations

The 2006 proposed regulations represented a significant departure from the 1991 proposed regulations, and were a response to perceived abuses attributable to those earlier regulations. Under the 1991 proposed regulations, section 987 gain/loss is determined by calculating an "equity pool" and a "basis pool." Essentially, the equity pool is the taxpayer's investment in the branch stated in the branch's functional currency. The basis pool is the investment in the branch in the taxpayer's overall currency which for a U.S. taxpayer is probably the U.S. dollar. A remittance from a QBU is taxable to the extent that the U.S. dollar value on the date of remittance exceeds that portion of the basis pool allocable to the remittance. Note that a remittance would also include any payment of principal or interest on a disregarded "loan" from the home office to the branch.

For example, suppose a U.S. corporation with a U.S. dollar functional currency organizes a branch in country X that uses the "u" as its functional currency. During Year 1, the taxpayer transfers 1000u to the branch when 1u = 1 USD and transfers $1,000 to the branch when 1u = 2 USD. At this point, the equity pool is 1,500u and the basis pool is $2,000. In the same year, the branch has profits of 1,000u which is translated into dollars at the weighted average rate for the year of 1u = 2 USD. The equity pool is increased by 1,000u to 2,500u; the basis pool is increased by $2,000 to $4,000. Finally, in Year 1 the branch remits 1,000u to the taxpayer's home office when 1u = 2 USD. The taxable portion of the remittance is equal to the excess of the dollar value of the remittance at the spot rate ($2,000) minus the portion of the basis pool that is attributable to the distribution. That portion is determined by the following formula:

$$\frac{1,000u \text{ remittance}}{2,500u \text{ equity pool}} \times \$4,000 \text{ basis pool} = \$1,600$$

Accordingly, the section 987 gain is $400, and the 1,000u remitted is given a basis of $2,000. The equity pool at the end of year 2 is 1,500u (2,500u minus the 1,000u remittance) and the basis pool is $2,400 ($4,000 minus the $1,600 charge to that pool on the remittance).

(B) FOREIGN CORPORATIONS

A distribution or a deemed distribution from a foreign corporation to its U.S. shareholders may be a taxable event for U.S. tax purposes (but note that 10 percent U.S. shareholders of specified foreign corporations are entitled to a 100 percent dividends received deduction for non-hybrid dividends). *See* § 7.03. When a distribution is made (or deemed made), it is necessary to translate into dollars the amount of the distribution, the amount of the E&P from which the dividend is paid and, for a distribution of previously taxed earnings and profits (PTEP) resulting from a previous subpart F or GILTI inclusion, the amount of the foreign tax associated with the distribution. In general, pools of E&P of the foreign corporation are maintained in the functional currency. I.R.C. §§ 986(a) and 989 require that both actual distributions and the E&P out of which they are paid are translated into dollars at the spot rate on the date of the distribution. Under I.R.C. § 989, a deemed distribution required by § 951(a)(1)(A) is translated at the average exchange rate for the taxable year, but the statute is silent on the calculation with respect to § 951A deemed distributions. Final regulations confirm that the same principle applies for I.R.C. § 951A. Reg. § 1.951A–1(d)(1).

Foreign taxes paid by the subsidiary are generally translated into dollars using the average exchange rate for the year the taxes were accrued. I.R.C. § 986(a)(1). For distributions of PTEP, I.R.C. § 986(c) requires currency gain or loss. The transition tax enacted by TCJA in I.R.C. § 965 resulted in a lot of PTEP in foreign corporations. Final I.R.C. § 965 regulations also amend the I.R.C. § 986 regulations to provide guidance regarding the treatment of currency gain or loss upon subsequent distributions of PTEP created by a I.R.C. § 965 inclusion. These rules provide that the foreign currency gain or loss recognized on the distribution of PTEP resulting from I.R.C. § 965 is generally based on any fluctuations between December 31, 2017 and the distribution date. Reg. § 1.986(c)–1. But adjustments may be made based on the deduction provided under I.R.C. § 965(c) or to the extent of any deficit E&P corporations.

When issuing the I.R.C. § 965 final regulations, the government said that it intended to study the proper amount of gain or loss, including foreign currency gain or loss, to be recognized on distributions of PTEP, including PTEP other than I.R.C. § 965 PTEP. Proposed foreign tax credit regulations issued in December 2018 generally provide that foreign currency gain or loss recognized under I.R.C. § 986(c) with respect to a distribution of PTEP is assigned to the category of PTEP from which the distribution is made. *See* § 10.03(B) regarding allocation of income and credits to separate baskets under I.R.C. § 904.

The following examples illustrate the application of the rules for translating and recognizing currency gain or loss on distributions under I.R.C. §§ 986 and 989.

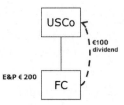

- FC has a euro (€) functional currency
- FC has never incurred any foreign taxes
- FC pays €100 dividend on 3/31/Year 1

On..........€ is worth...	
01/01/Yr. 1	$1.3
03/31/Yr. 1	$1.3
12/31/Yr. 1	$1.5
Average Year 1	$1.4

USCo would include a $130 dividend, translated at the spot rate on date of distribution under I.R.C. § 989(b)(1). Note that USCo likely would be able to claim a 100 percent dividends received deduction on the distribution.

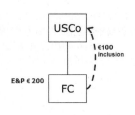

- FC has a euro (€) functional currency
- FC has never incurred any foreign taxes
- FC has a subpart F inclusion of €100 for Year 1 under §951(a)(1)(A)

On..........€ is worth...	
01/01/Yr. 1	$1.3
03/31/Yr. 1	$1.3
12/31/Yr. 1	$1.5
Average Year 1	$1.4

USCo would have a $140 inclusion, translated at the average exchange rate for Year 1 under I.R.C. § 989(b)(3).

- USCo owns stock in an unrelated foreign corporation
- USCo is an accrual basis taxpayer
- USCo receives a €100 dividend on 3/31/Yr. 1
- The dividend is subject to a 10% withholding tax (i.e., €10)

On..........€ is worth...	
01/01/Yr. 1	$1.3
03/31/Yr. 1	$1.3
12/31/Yr. 1	$1.5
Average Year 1	$1.4

USCo would have a dividend of $130 under I.R.C. § 989(b)(1) and would be deemed to pay a foreign withholding tax of $14 under I.R.C. § 986(a)(1), assuming no election was made under I.R.C. § 986(a)(1)(D).

Now consider the implications under I.R.C. § 986(c) of a distribution of PTEP that arose from an inclusion of subpart F income. In this situation, any currency gain/loss between the time of inclusion and the date of distribution must be taken into account.

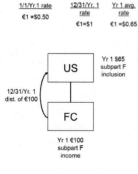

- FC earns €100 of subpart F income in Yr 1
- FC distributes €100 on 12/31/Yr 1

The subpart F income is translated into $65, the average exchange rate for Yr 1, under I.R.C. § 989(b)(3). US has a $65 subpart F inclusion for Yr 1. The distribution is translated at the spot exchange rate on 12/31/Yr. 1 of 1 Euro = 1 USD, under I.R.C. § 989(b)(1). US has a $65 basis in its PTEP for Yr 1, and U.S. receives the equivalent of $100 on 12/31/Yr. 1. Accordingly, US has $35 of foreign currency gain under § 986(c). The source of I.R.C. § 986(c) gain (or loss) is the same as the underlying subpart F— typically foreign source. Under Notice 88–71, 1988–2 C.B. 374, the basket of the gain/loss is also the same as the underlying inclusion. Proposed regulations apply the same principles for purposes of inclusions required under I.R.C. § 951A. *See* Prop. Reg. § 1.904–4(p).

§ 12.05   TREATMENT OF INDIVIDUALS

Section 988 does not apply to "personal transactions" entered into by an individual. Personal transactions are any transactions except to the extent that expenses attributable to such transactions would be deductible under I.R.C. § 162 as a trade or business expense or I.R.C. § 212 as an expense of producing income. I.R.C. § 988(e)(3). For personal transactions entered into by individuals, general tax principles apply. Suppose that a U.S. taxpayer goes to Europe on vacation, purchasing 2,000 Euros when the conversion rate was 1 USD = 1 Euro. There are no tax consequences as the taxpayer spends the Euros on vacation even if there is currency fluctuation. At the end of the vacation suppose the taxpayer converts 600 Euros into $900 at a time when the conversion rate is 1 USD = .67 Euro. Under general tax principles, the taxpayer recognizes a $300 capital gain for tax purposes. Had the gain been less than $200 the *de minimis* rule of I.R.C. § 988(e)(2) would have applied and the taxpayer would have recognized no gain. If the taxpayer received $450 dollars on reconversion because the exchange rate was 1 USD = 1.33 Euro, the taxpayer would have a $150 capital loss for tax purposes. *See* Rev. Rul. 74–7, 1974–1 C.B. 198. However, a loss resulting from a foreign currency transaction by an individual in a non-profit-seeking context normally is not deductible.

Suppose a U.S. citizen purchases a personal residence in country U for 95,000u, paying 10,000u in cash and borrowing 85,000u. At the time of the purchase the conversion rate is 1 USD = 1u. Later, at a time when the conversion rate is 1 USD = .95u, the taxpayer sells the residence for 142,500u, of which 85,000u is used to repay the mortgage. The taxpayer must recognize gain of $150,000 (142,500u/.95u) minus $95,000 (95,000u/1u) on the sale of the residence. The taxpayer also has a loss on the repayment of the mortgage equal to the $89,474 value of the amount paid in satisfaction of the mortgage (85,000u/.95u) minus the $85,000 value of the amount borrowed (85,000u/1u). However, the loss is nondeductible because it is not incurred in a trade or business or a transaction entered into for profit. *See* Rev. Rul. 90–79, 1990–2 C.B. 187.

§ 12.06 A NOTE ON CRYPTOCURRENCY

Is cryptocurrency foreign currency or something else? The IRS is still trying to figure out how transactions in cryptocurrency should be taxed. In Notice 2014–21, 2014–16 I.R.B. 938, the IRS said that virtual currency is not treated as currency that could generate foreign currency gain or loss. Instead, its treated as property for federal tax purposes. Under that Notice, a taxpayer who receives virtual currency must include the fair market value of the virtual currency, measured in U.S. dollars, as of the date the virtual currency was received.

Taxpayers are asking for more guidance in this area. Keep an eye on this evolving area of law.

CHAPTER 13

INTERNATIONAL TAX-FREE TRANSACTIONS

§ 13.01 OVERVIEW

Transfers of property across international boundaries—particularly transfers from taxpayers within the United States to taxpayers outside the United States—create the possibility of tax avoidance in circumstances where nonrecognition provisions would normally render the transaction tax-free. They also potentially allow taxpayers to transfer valuable intangible property developing in a high-tax jurisdiction to a low tax jurisdiction. For example, suppose a U.S. corporation holds an appreciated asset with a basis of $8 million and a fair market value of $30 million that it intends to sell. If it sells the asset, it must recognize the $22 million gain for U.S. tax purposes. Suppose instead that the corporation transfers the asset in a nonrecognition transaction governed by I.R.C. § 351 to a foreign subsidiary which (without negating I.R.C. § 351 treatment) then sells the asset. Under prior law, if the foreign subsidiary wasn't engaged in a U.S. trade or business, the gain from the sale of the asset likely wasn't subject to U.S. tax (unless the subpart F rules applied) even though the appreciation occurred while the asset was held by the U.S. entity. Under current law, such gain would likely be taxed under GILTI, but likely at a rate lower than the U.S. statutory rate. *See* Chapter 9. Taxpayers also developed elaborate structures that utilized the non-recognition rules as a way of repatriating earnings in a tax-efficient manner at a time when straight dividends were taxed at the full 35 percent corporate rate. As the most extreme way to escape U.S. tax on worldwide earnings, taxpayers engaged in "inversion" transactions to reincorporate with headquarters overseas.

This problem was particularly acute under the pre-TCJA international tax regime, but still exists today. A complex statutory and regulatory regime has evolved to prevent what Congress and the IRS viewed as different types of cross-border tax avoidance that mostly reflects the prior tax regime. It's unclear how these rules might evolve to reflect the new "territorial" system but in the meantime these somewhat outdated rules need to be taken into account by taxpayers engaging in taxable and otherwise non-recognition cross-border transactions.

Generally speaking, I.R.C. § 367 operates to impose a "toll charge" on the transfer of assets across international boundaries in transactions which might otherwise be tax-free. While I.R.C. § 367 addresses a variety of nonrecognition transactions, it essentially governs three categories of transactions: (a) "outbound" transactions where U.S. assets are transferred to a foreign taxpayer; (b) "inbound" transactions where assets used by a foreign taxpayer are transferred to a U.S. taxpayer; (c) foreign-to-foreign transactions in which assets used by a foreign taxpayer are transferred to another foreign taxpayer. Generally, I.R.C. § 367(a) and (d) (focusing on intangibles) address outbound transactions; I.R.C.

§ 367(b) addresses the other two categories. I.R.C. § 367(e) contains a rule that specifically addresses outbound liquidations and outbound divisive reorganizations. The statute is short; the regulations expand upon the statute exponentially.

In order to effectively apply the toll charge, I.R.C. § 367 denies U.S. taxpayers the benefits of several corporate nonrecognition rules. Within the three categories of nonrecognition transactions outlined above, the most important kinds of transactions are: (1) transactions that implicate I.R.C. § 351 or otherwise constitute contributions to the capital of foreign corporations; (2) transactions where a U.S. subsidiary of a foreign parent or a foreign subsidiary of a U.S. parent is liquidated in accordance with I.R.C. §§ 337 and 332; and (3) transactions involving corporate reorganizations governed by I.R.C. § 368 and related provisions. Without attempting to plumb the inner recesses of these provisions, a basic understanding is helpful in explaining the operation of I.R.C. § 367.

First, under I.R.C. § 351, a transferor of property does not recognize gain or loss when property is transferred in exchange for stock of a corporation if the transferors receive stock of the transferee corporation, and if immediately after the exchange, the transferors of property own at least 80 percent of each class of stock of the transferee corporation. I.R.C. § 368(c). Nonrecognition under I.R.C. § 351 can apply both to the formation of a new corporation and to transfers to an existing corporation. Under I.R.C. § 367(c)(2), a contribution to capital (*e.g.*, where the transferor contributes property but does not receive stock in return) is essentially treated as a transaction under I.R.C. § 351.

Second, amounts distributed in complete liquidation of a corporation are generally treated as received by the shareholders in exchange for their stock, thereby triggering gain or loss equal to the difference between a shareholder's stock basis and the fair market value of the distributed assets. I.R.C. § 331. Moreover, the liquidating corporation also recognizes gain to the extent that it distributes appreciated assets. I.R.C. § 336. But under I.R.C. §§ 337 and 332, when a parent corporation satisfying an 80 percent ownership test liquidates a subsidiary corporation, the parent corporation does not normally recognize gain on the difference between the parent's basis in the subsidiary's stock and the fair market value of the property distributed. Instead, the parent corporation takes a basis in the distributed assets equal to the basis of those assets in the hands of the subsidiary. In a parent/subsidiary liquidation, the subsidiary can avoid the recognition of gain inherent in any appreciated assets that are distributed. I.R.C. § 337.

Third, there are a variety of forms that a corporate reorganization can take. Consider this common form: suppose X Corp. merges into, or transfers its assets to, Y Corp. before ending its corporate existence with the shareholders of X Corp. becoming shareholders of Y Corp. (In the cross-border context, this commonly occurs when the shareholders of X transfer their X Corp. stock to Y Corp. and then "check-the box" on X

Corp. to make it disregarded—stepped together this "drop and check" is simply an asset transfer from X Corp. to Y. Corp.) Sometimes the former shareholders of X Corp. will end up with stock of Y Corp.'s parent corporation. These transactions are generally "asset reorganizations."

Alternatively, the X Corp. shareholders may transfer their X Corp. stock to Y Corp. in exchange for Y Corp. stock (or stock of Y Corp.'s parent). These reorganizations are sometimes referred to as "stock reorganizations."

Where two corporations reorganize as a single corporate entity (or an acquired corporation becomes a subsidiary of an acquiring corporation) and no cash is involved, normally there are no tax consequences to the transferor-corporation, the transferee-corporation or the shareholders. *See* I.R.C. §§ 368, 361, 354. The surviving corporation in such an acquisitive reorganization (*e.g.*, a merger) takes a carryover basis in the assets that it receives, while the shareholders of the transferring corporation substitute their stock bases in the transferring corporation's stock as the bases of their new stock in the surviving corporation.

These types of acquisitive reorganization can be contrasted with a divisive reorganization where a single corporation divides into multiple corporate entities. Suppose X Corp. is owned by A and B who want to go their separate ways. It is possible for X Corp. to transfer one of its businesses to newly-formed Y Corp., distributing the Y Corp. stock to B in exchange for B's X Corp. stock in a tax-free reorganization where X Corp. is not taxed on its transfer and B is not taxed on the exchange of stock. Similarly, A and B may want to remain as investors together but separate two businesses. It may be possible for X Corp. to contribute one of the businesses to Y Corp. and then distribute the Y Corp. stock pro rata to A and B. Of course, these simplified reorganization patterns do not capture the complexity of the reorganization provisions but perhaps give enough of a flavor to make I.R.C. § 367 somewhat intelligible.

When it applies, I.R.C. § 367 overrides the nonrecognition patterns outlined above by denying corporate status to the foreign corporation involved in the transaction. For example, if a U.S. taxpayer transfers appreciated property to a foreign corporation in a transaction that would otherwise qualify as tax-free under I.R.C. § 351, the application of I.R.C. § 367 will deny the transferee-corporation corporate status for purposes of calculating gain (although I.R.C. § 351 applies to other aspects of the transaction), thereby resulting in taxation of the built-in gain to the transferor under I.R.C. § 1001. As indicated below, the denial of corporate status would also override nonrecognition in the context of subsidiary liquidations and reorganizations. Similarly if the assets of a U.S. corporation are merged into, or otherwise acquired by, a foreign corporation in an asset reorganization, nonrecognition under I.R.C. § 361 may not be available.

§ 13.02 OUTBOUND TRANSACTIONS

(A) GENERAL RULE

The general rule of I.R.C. § 367(a) is that, in certain transactions, gain (but not loss) must be recognized when a U.S. person transfers property to a foreign entity. In order to effectuate this outcome, I.R.C. § 367(a) denies a transferee-corporation its corporate status for purposes of determining the recognition of gain on the transfer. In the case of a transaction apparently governed by I.R.C. § 351, the transferor must recognize gain on the exchange of appreciated property for stock, because the transferee is not considered to be a corporation. I.R.C. § 367(a). As a result, I.R.C. §§ 351 and 1001(c) do not provide nonrecognition, but rather I.R.C. § 1001(a) requires recognition of any gain. Similarly, on a contribution to the capital of a foreign corporation, the transfer will be treated as a sale or exchange of the contributed property for an amount equal to its fair market value, thereby forcing the transferor to recognize gain on the transfer. I.R.C. § 367(f). Where I.R.C. § 367(a) requires recognition of a built-in gain, the character and source of the gain is determined as if the property had been disposed of in a taxable exchange with the transferee foreign corporation. Reg. § 1.367(a)–1T(b)(4).

Suppose that a U.S. person transfers loss property to a corporation in a transaction meeting the requirements of I.R.C. § 351. If the transferee is a U.S. corporation, then the transferor would be denied recognition of the loss by I.R.C. § 351. On the other hand, where loss property is transferred to a foreign corporation which is denied corporate status by I.R.C. § 367, the logical inference would be that I.R.C. § 351 does not apply to the transfer and the transferor might be able to recognize the loss (subject to the loss disallowance rules in I.R.C. § 267). Congress recognized the potential for selective transfers (*e.g.*, only loss property) in this type of transaction. Therefore, I.R.C. § 367(a) only applies to gain—loss recognition is not permitted. Reg. § 1.367(a)–1T(b)(3)(ii). Furthermore, when multiple items of property are transferred simultaneously, the provision is applied to each item separately, so that it denies nonrecognition treatment to the transfer of appreciated property and forces nonrecognition where loss property is transferred, thereby maximizing the taxable income of the U.S. transferor. *See* Reg. §§ 1.367(a)–1T(b)(1) and (b)(3)(ii).

If a U.S. subsidiary liquidates into its foreign corporate parent, I.R.C. § 367(e) will preclude the liquidating U.S. corporation from relying on I.R.C. § 337 to avoid taxation. Normally, I.R.C. § 337 provides nonrecognition of gain for a subsidiary on a distribution of appreciated property to its parent corporation, but the application of I.R.C. § 367(e)(2) causes the U.S. subsidiary to be taxed on the distribution of appreciated property to its foreign parent. There are exceptions if the foreign parent continues to operate a U.S. business distributed by the U.S. subsidiary for ten years (but any appreciated intangibles that are liquidated out of the United States cannot qualify for this exception even if used in a U.S. trade or business) or if the distributed property is a United States Real Property Interest or if the U.S. subsidiary distributes stock of its own U.S. subsidiary in which there is at least 80 percent ownership of the voting power.

If a U.S. corporation transfers its assets to, or merges into, a foreign corporation in exchange for stock of the foreign corporation and that stock is distributed to the former shareholders of the U.S. corporation, normally the U.S. corporation would not be required to recognize gain on the transfer. I.R.C. § 361. However, if I.R.C. § 367 denies the foreign entity corporate status in determining the recognition of gain, the U.S. corporation-transferor will be forced to recognize gain on the transfer of its appreciated assets to the foreign corporation.

In some cases, as discussed below, if a U.S. shareholder transfers stock of a U.S. corporation in exchange for stock of a foreign corporation in what would otherwise be a tax-free reorganization, the U.S. shareholder will have to recognize gain in accordance with I.R.C. § 367. Reg. § 1.367(a)–3(c). In some cases a U.S. transferor will be deemed to transfer stock of a U.S. corporation to a foreign corporation even though no actual transfer has taken place.

(B) THE (REPEALED) ACTIVE TRADE OR BUSINESS EXCEPTION

Until recently, I.R.C. § 367(a)(3) provided an important exception to the automatic toll charge rule of I.R.C. § 367(a) when the property transferred to the foreign corporation by a U.S. person was intended for use in the active conduct of a trade or business outside the United States. TCJA repealed this exception. Now I.R.C. § 351 is turned off on all transfers of appreciated property from a U.S. taxpayer to a foreign corporation. Extensive implementing regulations for prior I.R.C.§ 351(a)(3) remain on the books (Reg. § 1.367(a)–2), until IRS and Treasury get around to withdrawing them. In the meantime, don't get confused.

The transfer of certain intangible assets is addressed below in § 13.02(D).

(C) BRANCH LOSS RECAPTURE RULE

The transfer of an active trade or business to a foreign person could still be subject to tax even under prior law pursuant to a "branch loss recapture rule." Under prior I.R.C. § 367(a)(3), the active trade or business exception would not apply to the transfer of the assets of a foreign branch of a U.S. person to a foreign subsidiary to the extent that the branch sustained net losses before the transfer. The TCJA codified this branch loss recapture rule in I.R.C. § 91, which applies to subject the transfer of a loss business outbound to U.S. tax; the provision seems somewhat redundant given that the active trade or business exception has been repealed. Under I.R.C. § 91, a domestic corporation that transfers substantially all of the assets of a foreign branch to a 10 percent owned specified foreign corporation with respect to which it is a U.S. shareholder has to include the transferred loss amount in taxable income. I.R.C. § 91 (note that unlike I.R.C. § 367(a)(3)(C), the branch loss recapture rule in I.R.C. § 91 only applies in the case of transfers by corporations). A specified 10 percent owned foreign corporation is defined in I.R.C. § 245A (*see* § 7.03), to mean any foreign corporation with respect to which a domestic corporation is a U.S. shareholder (10 percent owner).

The transferred loss amount is generally equal to losses incurred by the branch before the transfer for which the taxpayer was able to claim a deduction, minus any taxable income recognized in the year of transfer or a prior year and any gain recognized in the transfer. The income recognized is U.S. source. While I.R.C. § 91 forces a recapture of prior losses claimed in a manner similar to I.R.C. § 367(a)(3)(C), loss recapture under I.R.C. § 91 is not limited to the built-in gain associated with the transferred assets.

The loss recapture rule is prompted by the fact that often there may be losses during the start-up period of a branch of a U.S. corporation which are deducted by the taxpayer against non-branch income (*e.g.*, foreign source income generated by the home office). If the assets of the branch are then transferred to a foreign corporation at the point when the branch starts to show a profit, the United States in effect has permitted deductions without taking into account the income generated by expenses deducted. The solution is to require the recognition of gain on the incorporation transfer to the extent of the losses of the branch that were previously deducted.

If a branch has suffered losses, those losses may have offset other foreign source income of the U.S. corporation that operates the branch. Alternatively, those losses may have offset U.S. source income of the U.S. corporation that operates the branch in which case there will be overall foreign loss (OFL) account recapture. *See supra* § 10.07. In both cases the recapture is triggered by the incorporation of a branch in an I.R.C. § 351 transaction or a reorganization. If there is potential OFL and branch loss recapture, OFL recapture occurs first (*i.e.*, if there is not enough built-in gain in the transferred assets to permit both OFL and branch loss recapture). I.R.C. § 91(b)(2)(B).

For example, suppose USCo, a U.S. corporation, has operated a foreign branch, B1, that produced a loss of $300,000 three years ago and no income or loss for the last two years. The loss offset income USCo had from other foreign sources. In the current year, USCo transfers the assets of B1—which have a basis of $500,000 and a fair market value of $700,000—to FSub, a newly formed foreign subsidiary of USCo. USCo must recognize a gain of $200,000 for the year under I.R.C. § 367(a). Under I.R.C. § 91, it must also include an additional $100,000 in taxable income in the current year ($300,000 of losses, minus $200,000 of gain recognized), treated as U.S. source income. I.R.C. § 91(c). If the branch losses had been used to offset U.S. income (rather than other foreign source income), the loss would be treated first as OFL recapture. *See* I.R.C. § 91(b)(2)(B). If USCo had both $50,000 of potential OFL recapture and $300,000 of potential branch loss recapture, USCo would recognize $300,000 of income on the I.R.C. § 351 transaction, consisting of $50,000 of OFL recapture, $200,000 of gain, and $50,000 of branch loss recapture.

On the incorporation of a foreign branch, there may also be recapture of dual consolidated losses (*see infra* § 14.03(B)).

(D) INTANGIBLE ASSETS

Concerned that U.S. taxpayers would offset U.S. taxable income with the costs of producing certain intangible assets and then transfer the intangibles beyond the U.S. taxing jurisdiction when they became income producing assets, Congress enacted I.R.C. § 367(d) specifically to address the transfer of intangibles to a foreign corporation. When intangibles are transferred to a foreign corporation in a transaction that falls under I.R.C. §§ 351 or 361, the transferor is treated as having sold the intangibles in exchange for royalty payments (*i.e.*, ordinary income) over the life of the property. I.R.C. § 367(d). The transferor must continue to recognize the deemed royalties for the property's entire "useful life". Deemed royalty payments under I.R.C. § 367(d) are treated as foreign source income to the same extent that an actual royalty payment would be considered foreign source income.

For example, suppose USCo, a U.S. corporation, incurs various research expenses deductible under I.R.C. §§ 162 or 174 (thereby reducing USCo's taxable income) in developing a patented pharmaceutical product. When the product is commercially feasible, USCo transfers the foreign rights to the patent to FSub, a wholly-owned foreign subsidiary in a transaction normally accorded nonrecognition under I.R.C. § 351 or as a contribution to capital. FSub uses the patent to manufacture and sell the product. Under I.R.C. § 367(d), USCo has to report foreign source ordinary income each year equal to an arm's-length royalty for the deemed contingent sale of the patent.

Deciding whether a foreign corporation ought to pay an actual royalty on the acquisition of an intangible from a shareholder or be deemed to pay a royalty under I.R.C. § 367(d) may be affected by foreign tax rules as the U.S. tax treatment will be the same in either case. A deemed royalty payment may not attract a foreign withholding tax although an actual royalty might. On the other hand, an actual royalty payment may be deductible for foreign tax purposes whereas a deemed royalty payment may not.

"Intangible property" (a term previously defined in I.R.C. § 936(h)(3)(B) but now included in I.R.C. § 367(d)) includes manufacturing intangibles such as patents, formulas, processes, designs, patterns, and know-how; marketing intangibles such as franchises, trademarks, trade names and brand names; and operating intangibles such as long-term purchase and supply contracts, surveys, studies, customer lists, and similar property not ordinarily licensed to unrelated parties. Reg. § 1.367(d)–1T(d). Copyrights or literary, musical or artistic compositions may fall under I.R.C. § 367(d) if the transferor created the property by its own personal efforts or has a basis in the property determined with reference to the creator's basis.

Under I.R.C. § 367(d)(4) as amended by the TCJA, gain with respect to foreign goodwill or going concern value of a business conducted outside of the United States is now also included in the definition of intangible property for this purpose. Prior to enactment of the TCJA, Treasury attempted to address this issue through controversial regulations that remain outstanding. T.D. 9803. In a report mandated by Executive Order 13789 which required the Treasury Secretary to identify significant tax regulations issued on or after January 1, 2016, that (i) impose an undue financial burden on U.S. taxpayers, (ii) add undue complexity to the Federal tax laws, or (iii) exceed the statutory authority of the IRS, Treasury recommended that these regulations be substantially revised because statutory reform had substantially addressed the concerns underlying the regulations. But no action has yet been taken.

The amount of gain that a transferor must recognize on the transfer of intangibles to a foreign transferee is accelerated if the transferor severs its relationship to the intangibles either by the transferee disposing of the intangibles or the transferor disposing of the stock of the transferee. I.R.C. § 367(d)(2)(A)(ii)(II) and Reg. § 1.367(d)–1T. Essentially, the re-transfer rules subject a U.S. transferor to a one-time recognition in lieu of future royalties equal to the difference between the amount realized on the sale and the adjusted basis of the intangibles on the original transfer date. If the re-transfer is a sale of stock by the transferor, gain recognized on the sale of stock is decreased by gain recognized under I.R.C. § 367(d). If the re-transfer of intangibles is to a related party, the original U.S. transferor continues to report annual royalty payments. If the stock of the original transferor is transferred to a related foreign person, the transferor continues to report the annual royalty payments. If the transferor goes out of existence (*e.g.*, on an outbound reorganization), then unless the shareholder of the transferor is essentially a U.S. corporation, the transferor must recognize gain on the I.R.C. § 367(d) intangibles. Notice 2012–39, 2012 C.B. 95. If the transferor of the foreign acquiring corporation's stock transfers it to a U.S. related corporation, the U.S. corporation must continue to report the annual payments. Reg. § 1.367(d)–1T(e).

In some situations, a U.S. person transferring intangibles in an outbound transaction would prefer to have the transaction treated as an immediate sale (assuming that nonrecognition treatment is unavailable) rather than as a licensing agreement producing annual deemed royalties that for tax purposes may increase under the "super royalty" provision (*see supra* Chapter 11). I.R.C. § 367(d)(2)(A). The regulations permit a deemed sale election in three limited circumstances: (1) if operating intangibles (*e.g.*, a customer list) are transferred outbound (because operating intangibles are not likely to be sold or licensed by the transferee); (2) where there is a compulsory transfer of any intangible required by the government of the transferee-corporation; or (3) if intangibles are transferred to a foreign corporation pursuant to a joint venture as specified in the Regulations. Reg. § 1.367(d)–1(g)(2); Reg. § 1.367–1T(g). For purposes of the deemed sale election, an operating intangible is an intangible of a type not ordinarily licensed for consideration contingent upon the licensee's use. For example, customer lists and supply contracts might be considered operating intangibles.

Finally, suppose that I.R.C. § 367(d) does create a deemed royalty, but in fact no payment is made from the foreign transferee to the U.S. transferor. Because the deemed royalty is already taxed in the U.S. each year, Reg. § 1.367(d)–1T(g) creates an account receivable each year. If a royalty is actually paid, it will not be taxable again but will instead be a return of basis. If no royalty is paid (perhaps more likely as there was no actual license), then after three years, the receivable is deemed to be contributed to capital so that the transferor at least gets additional stock basis for the deemed inclusion.

One way taxpayers have tried to avoid I.R.C. § 367(d)'s application while still moving valuable intellectual property (IP) offshore is through the use of partnerships. Under what is referred to as a "partnership freeze structure," the U.S. owner of IP might set up a partnership with a related foreign corporation. The U.S. partner would transfer appreciated IP to the partnership in exchange for a preferred partnership interest that paid a fixed return but essentially shifted any future appreciation in the value of the IP to the related foreign corporation. By its terms, I.R.C. § 367(d) does not apply to a transfer to a partnership.

However, Temporary and Proposed Regulations (T.D. 9814 (2017)) limit U.S. taxpayers' ability to shift income from the IP to related foreign entities that may not be subject to U.S. taxation. In some cases, the very transfer of IP itself to a partnership might be taxable event. (Note that, as is the case with many of the other transactions described in this chapter, this type of planning has become less beneficial to U.S. headquartered companies because I.R.C. § 951A likely renders the profits of the foreign entity/partner from intangibles subject to current U.S. tax, albeit at a reduced rate.)

The TCJA made two other changes intended to limit taxpayers' benefits from such outbound transfers of intangibles. It amended I.R.C. § 367(d) to authorize Treasury to write regulations to require that upon the transfer of IP, the IP would be valued on an aggregate basis, or on the basis of the realistic alternatives to such a transfer, if this represents the most reliable means of valuation. I.R.C. § 367(d)(2)(D). It made a similar amendment to I.R.C. § 482.

As discussed *supra* in § 11.05(C), the IRS has not been very successful in its attempts to argue for higher valuations in cases of outbound transfers of IP. It remains to be seen whether the amendments to TCJA will make a material difference in its track record in this area.

(E) THE STOCK OR SECURITIES
EXCEPTION—FOREIGN CORPORATION

In general, if a U.S. person transfers appreciated stock of a foreign corporation to a foreign corporation in what would otherwise be a tax-free transaction (*e.g.*, a § 351 transaction or a reorganization), nonrecognition is nevertheless permitted if the U.S. transferor owns less than five percent—measured by voting power or value—of the stock of the transferee foreign corporation, or if a U.S. transferor which owns five percent or more of the stock of the transferee enters into a five-year gain recognition agreement (GRA). I.R.C. § 367(a)(2).

For example, suppose that USCo owns all of the stock of FSub1 and FSub2, both foreign corporations. If USCo transfers the appreciated stock of FSub2 to FSub1 in exchange for additional FSub1 voting stock, the transaction qualifies as a B reorganization. I.R.C. § 368(a)(1)(B) and as an I.R.C. § 351 transaction. After the transaction USCo owns all of the stock of FSub1 which now owns all of the stock of FSub2. Under the reorganization provisions (or I.R.C. § 351), USCo is not taxed on the exchange of appreciated stock in FSub2 for stock in FSub1. I.R.C. § 354. Section 367(a) does not overrule this nonrecognition if USCo meets the conditions outlined above, including entering into a GRA.

Suppose that instead of transferring the FSub2 stock in exchange for FSub1 stock, USCo sells the stock of FSub2 to FSub1 for cash or a note. This would be a transaction described in I.R.C. § 304. Basically, I.R.C. § 304 treats the transfer as if USCo first received stock of FSub1 which is then redeemed for cash or a note in a transaction that is treated as an I.R.C. § 301 distribution under I.R.C. § 302(d). Note that the deemed stock for stock exchange also requires a GRA (on which gain is triggered on the deemed redemption unless USCo enters into a new GRA). *See* Notice 2012–15, 2012–1 C.B. 424.

A GRA obligates the transferor to recognize any gain that was not recognized on the transfer to the foreign transferee if the transferee disposes of the transferred stock or securities (or the underlying assets are disposed of) during the gain recognition period. Reg. § 1.367(a)–8. The purpose of the GRA is to prevent U.S. taxpayers from transferring stock or securities to a foreign transferee corporation in a manner that does not require recognition under I.R.C. § 367(a), where the foreign transferee subsequently disposes of the transferred property often beyond U.S. tax jurisdiction.

If a transferee disposes of the transferred property during the period that the GRA is in effect, the transferor must not only recognize any previously unrecognized gain but also an appropriate interest charge for the deferral of that recognition. In the example above, such an agreement would require USCo to amend its earlier tax return and report the unrecognized gain on its original transfer of the FSub2 stock to FSub1 (plus an appropriate interest charge for the tax deferral) if FSub1 disposes of the FSub2 stock or if FSub2 disposes of substantially all of its assets. Reg. § 1.367(a)–8(c) and –8(j). Alternatively, USCo with proper identification can elect to have the gain, plus interest, reported on its current return.

The need for a GRA can also apply is situations where there is deemed to be an indirect stock transfer. Reg. § 1.367(a)–3(d). For example, suppose that USCo owns all of the stock of FSub1 and all the stock of FSub2. In a transaction described in I.R.C. § 368(a)(1)(D), all of the assets of FSub1 are transferred to FSub2 and FSub1 liquidates. This is not considered a stock transfer even though pursuant to I.R.C. § 354, stock of FSub1 is exchanged for stock of FSub2. Reg. § 1.367(a)–3(d), Ex. 16. However, if FSub2 were to drop the newly-acquired assets of FSub1 into FSub3 pursuant to I.R.C. § 368(a)(2)(C), the transaction is an indirect stock transfer and a GRA is necessary for USCo to avoid recognition on the deemed transfer of FSub1 stock.

(F) THE STOCK OR SECURITIES EXCEPTION—U.S. CORPORATION

Instead of transferring foreign stock, suppose a U.S. person transfers the appreciated stock or securities of a domestic corporation (a U.S. target company) to a foreign corporation. In this situation, the transferor may be forced to recognize the built-in gain under I.R.C. § 367(a) without the opportunity to enter into a GRA. Reg. § 1.367(a)–3(a). However, there is a narrow exception that allows this transfer to be exempt from recognition under I.R.C. § 367(a) if the U.S. target company complies with certain reporting requirements and the following four conditions are met. Reg. § 1.367(a)–3(c). First, the transferors must not receive more than 50 percent of both the total voting power and the total value of the foreign transferee corporation's outstanding stock after the transaction. Reg. § 1.367(a)–3(c)(1)(i). Second, immediately after the transfer, U.S. persons who are officers or directors of the U.S. target or who own by vote or by value at least 5 percent of the U.S. target company must not own more than 50 percent—both by vote and by value—of the transferee's outstanding stock. Reg. § 1.367(a)–3(c)(1)(ii). Third, the transferor either must not own 5 percent or more of the stock of the foreign transferee corporation by vote or value immediately after the transfer or must enter into a gain recognition agreement with the IRS. Reg. § 1.367(a)–3(c)(1)(iii). Finally, the foreign transferee corporation or a qualified subsidiary must have been engaged in an active trade or business outside the United States for at least 36 months before the transfer transaction and the fair market value of the foreign transferee is at least equal to the fair market value of the U.S. target company. Reg. § 1.367(a)–3(c)(1)(iv).

Both the "more than 50 percent" and the "active trade or business" requirement are intended to prevent manipulation by the U.S. person who may seek to move the appreciated assets of the U.S. target company beyond U.S. tax jurisdiction. This type of manipulation is sometimes referred to as a corporate "inversion" or corporate "expatriation" (*i.e.*, a U.S. corporation (often with foreign subsidiaries) owned by a U.S. shareholder becomes a U.S. subsidiary of a foreign corporation). The concern here is that by interposing a foreign corporation between the U.S.

shareholders and the U.S. target company, the opportunity to avoid U.S. taxation may be enhanced.

For example, suppose that individual shareholders of USCo (*e.g.*, 100 shareholders each owning 1 percent) transfer their stock in USCo in exchange for 100 percent of the stock of ForCo. This is both a transaction under I.R.C. § 351 and a B reorganization. The government's concern is that this inversion may allow tax to escape the U.S. tax net. If USCo were able to transfer stock of a CFC that it owned to ForCo in a tax free manner (or to "freeze" current foreign operations in the CFC and put new operations in a new foreign corporation owned by ForCo), then there may be no U.S. shareholders (*i.e.*, 10 percent owners) required to include amounts in income under I.R.C. § 951 or § 951A (*see* Chapter 9). Furthermore, inverting a U.S. corporation may facilitate "earnings stripping" where a USCo erodes the U.S. tax base by paying interest to its foreign parent. For discussion of measures the United States has taken to combat earnings stripping, *see supra* at § 4.09, as well as below. To prevent these perceived abuses, if the shareholders receive back more than 50 percent of the stock of ForCo, they will be taxed on the exchange of stock in USCo for the stock in ForCo, and no GRA is available to avoid this gain.

(G) INVERSION—U.S. CORPORATION

Given that much publicly traded stock is now held by tax-exempt entities, shareholder-level gain is not a concern for many public companies (alternatively, if the market price of a company's stock is depressed, for many of its shareholders there may be no gain in the stock). In this situation I.R.C. § 367(a), which treats an otherwise tax-free transaction as a taxable transaction to the shareholders, is not likely to prevent the transaction from taking place (alternatively, company management may decide that shareholder gain is a small price to pay for long-term corporate benefits). To address situations where I.R.C. § 367(a) was not achieving the intended results of preventing expatriation transactions, Congress in 2004 enacted a special anti-inversion rule. I.R.C. § 7874. An "expatriated entity" under I.R.C. § 7874 is essentially one that has acquired substantially all the assets of a domestic entity, without a sufficient change in ownership. By definition, an expatriated entity is a domestic corporation or partnership with respect to which a foreign corporation is a surrogate foreign corporation.

A foreign corporation is treated as a "surrogate foreign corporation" if, pursuant to a plan or a series of related transactions: (i) the foreign corporation directly or indirectly acquires "substantially all" of the properties held directly or indirectly by a domestic corporation, or substantially all the properties constituting a trade or business of a domestic partnership; (ii) after the acquisition at least 60 percent of the ownership interest of the foreign entity is held by former owners of the domestic entity; and (iii) the expanded affiliated group (EAG—essentially, 50 percent related corporations) that includes the foreign corporation does not have business activities in the foreign country in which the foreign corporation was created or organized that are substantial when compared to the total business activities of the EAG.

The tax treatment of expatriated entities and surrogate foreign corporations varies depending on the level of owner continuity. If the percentage of stock (by vote or value) in the surrogate foreign corporation held by former owners of the domestic entity, by reason of holding an interest in the domestic entity, is 80 percent or more, the surrogate foreign corporation is treated as a domestic corporation for all purposes of the Code. That is, the inversion is not respected for U.S. tax purposes. If the ownership percentage is 60 percent or more (but less than 80 percent), the surrogate foreign corporation is treated as a foreign corporation but some income or gain required to be recognized by the expatriated entity on the inversion itself or for a 10-year period cannot be offset by net operating losses or credits (other than credits allowed under I.R.C. § 901). Section 4985 also imposes a 20 percent "excise tax" on the value of the specified stock compensation of certain officers and directors of the inverted company.

In determining the level of stock ownership for purposes of testing for a change in ownership, stock owned by the EAG is disregarded. To illustrate, assume a domestic corporation (DC) is wholly owned by a U.S. parent corporation (USP), and that USP transfers all the DC stock to a newly formed foreign corporation (FA) in exchange for all of the stock of FA. Absent the EAG rule, the ownership fraction would be 100 percent and the foreign acquiring corporation would be treated as a surrogate foreign corporation and therefore as a domestic corporation (assuming the EAG does not have substantial business activities in the relevant foreign country). However, under the EAG rule, the stock of FA held by USP is excluded from the numerator and the denominator of the ownership fraction, so that the numerator and the denominator of the ownership fraction are zero and FA is not treated as a surrogate foreign corporation but is respected as a foreign corporation.

Application of the EAG rule does not always lead to the appropriate result, for example, when a domestic entity has minority shareholders. To illustrate, assume that DC is owned 90 percent by USP and 10 percent by individual A, and that USP and individual A transfer all of their DC stock to newly formed FA in exchange for 90 percent and 10 percent, respectively, of the stock of FA. Absent an exception to the EAG rule, the stock of FA held by USP would be excluded from the numerator and the denominator of the ownership fraction, so that the ownership fraction would be 100 percent (10/10) and FA would be treated as a domestic corporation.

To address this and other inappropriate results, Reg. § 1.7874–1 provides two exceptions to the statutory EAG rule: the internal group restructuring exception and the loss of control exception. When either of these exceptions applies, stock of the foreign acquiring corporation held by members of the EAG is excluded from the numerator but not the denominator of the ownership fraction. Thus, both exceptions have the potential to decrease the ownership fraction. In general, the internal group restructuring exception applies when the domestic entity and the foreign acquiring corporation are members of an affiliated group (membership generally being based on an 80 percent vote and value requirement) with the same common parent both before and after the acquisition. The loss of control exception applies when the former owners of the domestic entity do not hold more than 50 percent of the stock of any member of the EAG after the acquisition. In the example, the internal group restructuring rule would apply and the fraction would be 10/100 so that FA would not be treated as a domestic corporation.

In determining ownership under the 60 or 80 percent tests, certain stock—"disqualified stock"—is not taken into account. Reg. § 1.7874–4. The type of transaction giving rise to the "disqualified stock" rules can be illustrated as follows. Suppose shareholders of a domestic corporation (DC) transfer all their DC stock to a newly-formed foreign corporation (New ForCo) in exchange for 79 percent of the stock of New ForCo and, in a related transaction, an investor (perhaps a private equity fund) transfers cash to New ForCo in exchange for the remaining 21 percent of the New ForCo stock. The shareholders of DC have inverted—DC is now owned by ForCo—but because ownership by shareholders of DC in ForCo is less than 80 percent, absent a special rule I.R.C. § 7874 would not apply to deem ForCo to be a domestic corporation.

Treasury thought that this fact pattern did not present a legitimate case for allowing inversion transactions to be exempted from the penalties imposed by I.R.C. § 7874. To prevent this result, stock issued for "nonqualified property"—cash or cash equivalents, marketable securities, certain notes, etc., is considered disqualified and not taken into account in calculating whether the ownership continuity tests have been met. In the example above, the former owners of DC would be deemed to own 100 percent of ForCo and I.R.C. § 7874 would apply to treat ForCo as a domestic corporation. There is a *de minimis* rule that turns off the disqualified stock rule where a shareholder ends up with less than 5 percent of the foreign acquirer (*e.g.*, if the investor had transferred enough cash to constitute 96 percent of the value of ForCo and shareholders of DC ended up with 4 percent of the stock of ForCo). Reg. § 1.7874–4(d).

I.R.C. § 7874 will not apply (and the foreign parent will not be treated as a U.S. corporation) where the "substantial business activities" test is met (*i.e.*, Congress assumed that in such case that the new foreign parent and/or related entities have a business reason to invert). Unfortunately for taxpayers, Reg. § 1.7874–3 takes a hard line approach based on a very hard-to-meet objective test in interpreting the substantial business activities test. An expanded affiliated group will have substantial business activities in the relevant foreign country only when the number of group employees, the employee compensation and the group assets is at least 25 percent of those in the EAG as a whole throughout the world. Note that each of these three metrics must be satisfied. It is not sufficient if the average of the three metrics is at least 25 percent if any one metric is less than 25 percent. There are no exceptions to this objective test.

There is little doubt that both Congress and Treasury regard inversions as pernicious, and a wave of inversion transactions beginning in the late 2000s, combined with Congressional inaction, prompted Treasury to take extraordinary measures—which many observers felt exceeded its regulatory authority—to combat these transactions. In the last year of the Obama administration, Treasury and the IRS issued a number of proposed and temporary regulations that implemented a series of notices previously issued in an attempt to curtail inversion activity. Among other things, these regulations operate to prevent attempts by domestic companies to "skinny down" their assets prior to an inversion through non-ordinary distributions in an effort to bring ownership of a foreign acquiror below 80 percent (or in some cases 60 percent) and to strip out the tax base of the inverted company through leverage. Other rules group together multiple different transactions to treat them as a single inversion, and discourage nontaxable ways of converting CFCs to non-CFCs after an inversion. These rules were largely finalized as proposed in 2018 (T.D. 9834).

As another instrument in the anti-inversion toolbox, the IRS and Treasury issued regulations under I.R.C. § 385 in 2016. These rules were intended to address inversions by making it hard to load up an inverted U.S. company with internal debt after an inversion transaction. Section 385 authorizes the Secretary to issue "such regulations as may be necessary or appropriate" to determine when an interest in a corporation should be treated as stock or debt. The provision was added to the Code in 1969; the only final regulations under this section previously issued in 1980 were withdrawn in 1983 (T.D. 7920 (48 FR 50711) 1983).

The 2016 I.R.C. § 385 regulations, which recharacterize debt issued in certain intercompany transactions as equity (with the result that the interest expense is denied) also mandate that taxpayers comply with extensive documentation requirements in order for interest on the instrument to be allowed as a deduction. The regulations recharacterize debt instruments as stock if they are issued in one of a number of specified tainted transactions or fund a tainted transaction. As an example of the type of transaction the rules target, consider ForCo (a foreign parent corporation) that owns two subsidiaries, USSub and FSub. Under the regulations, a debt instrument distributed by USSub to ForCo may be recast as equity provided certain conditions are met. Similarly, a distribution of cash or property by USSub that was funded by issuance of a debt instrument to FSub may be recast as equity. Reg. § 1.385–3.

In Notice 2017–36, 2017–33 I.R.B. 208, the IRS announced that it would delay the effective date of the documentation rules until 2019. And pursuant to a mandate from the Trump administration to review tax regulations with the goal of reducing tax regulatory burdens, Treasury has said that it is considering a proposal to revoke the documentation regulations as issued altogether, and considering the development of revised documentation rules that "would be substantially simplified and streamlined." Treasury Report 2018–03004 (Oct. 2, 2017). The documentation rules have not yet been withdrawn, but the Notice also says that pending the issuance of such regulations, taxpayers may rely on the delay in application of the documentation regulations as set forth in the Notice.

In the same Report, Treasury also said that U.S. tax reform might obviate the need for the substantive recharacterization rules of the regulations and make it possible for these regulations to be revoked. Nonetheless, the current administration doesn't seem inclined to backtrack on the need for strong anti-inversion rules and so it seems likely that some version of the I.R.C. § 385 regulations will remain in effect.

(H) INTERPLAY OF I.R.C. §§ 367(a) AND 7874

If the transferors end up with 50 percent or less of the transferee corporation and file a GRA, then neither I.R.C. § 7874 nor § 367(a) should apply (but note that under regulations multiple transactions could be "stepped together" to result in an "inversion" for this purpose. Reg. § 1.7874–8). Suppose that USCo owns USSub, a U.S. corporation. Suppose that ForCo, a foreign corporation not owned by USCo, acquires all of the stock of USSub from USCo in exchange for ForCo stock in a transaction that qualifies as a B reorganization. If after the transaction USCo owns 50 percent or less of ForCo stock, I.R.C. § 367(a) would not force USCo to recognize any gain inherent in the USSub stock if USCo enters into a 5-year gain recognition agreement and the "active trade or business" requirements are satisfied. I.R.C. § 7874 should not apply in this situation where ownership in ForCo by U.S. shareholders is less than 60 percent.

Other reorganizations that indirectly resemble a stock transfer also can trigger I.R.C. §§ 367(a) and 7874. For example, suppose USCo owns all of the stock of USSub, and unrelated ForCo owns all of the stock of Newco, a newly-formed U.S. corporation. Suppose that in a reorganization described in I.R.C. § 368(a)(1)(C), USSub transfers all of its assets to Newco in exchange for stock of Newco's parent, ForCo. USSub then liquidates with USCo receiving the ForCo stock. In this situation for purposes of I.R.C. § 367(a), USCo is treated as if it had transferred the stock of USSub to ForCo in exchange for ForCo stock even though USCo did not exchange the stock directly with ForCo. If USCo receives 50 percent or less of the ForCo stock, meets the active trade or business test of Reg. § 1.367(a)–3(c) and enters into a 5-year gain recognition agreement, there will be no immediate tax resulting from I.R.C. § 367(a). If USCo receives more than 50 percent of the ForCo stock, USCo must recognize any gain on the transfer of the USSub stock. The same analysis would apply if USSub merges into Newco or if Newco merges into USSub in a transaction in which USCo receives ForCo stock. *See* I.R.C. § 368(a)(2)(D) and (E). Furthermore, I.R.C. § 7874 may apply to an indirect transfer if the U.S. shareholders acquire 60 percent or more of the ForCo stock. In such a case, ForCo may be treated as a U.S. corporation for U.S. tax purposes (if ownership is 80 percent or more) or certain tax attributes may be unavailable if U.S. ownership is between 60 and less than 80 percent.

(I)   OUTBOUND SPIN-OFFS

Suppose that USCo distributes all of the stock of ForSub to its shareholder ForCo, a foreign shareholder. Generally speaking, such a transaction might be tax-free under the rules of I.R.C. § 355. But because ForCo generally would not be subject to U.S. tax on any gain in the ForSub stock, USCo must recognize gain on the distribution of the appreciated stock of ForSub. I.R.C. § 367(e). Note that there would be no tax imposed on USCo if stock of a U.S. rather than a foreign subsidiary were distributed regardless of whether the recipient is a U.S. or foreign distributee. Reg. § 1.367(e)–1(c).

Section 1248 generally provides for a recharacterization of the gain on sale of 10 percent owned CFC stock as a dividend to the extent of the company's E&P accumulated during the period the selling U.S. shareholder owned the stock. *See supra* § 9.06. Section 1248(f) applies the general I.R.C. § 1248 result to transactions that would otherwise qualify as tax free under specified non-recognition provisions, including I.R.C. § 355. The policy behind enactment of this rule was to ensure that a U.S. shareholders' gain on the sale of foreign company stock would be taxed as ordinary income, rather than capital gain, to the extent it hadn't otherwise been subject to U.S. tax. Because of the participation exemption enacted as part of TCJA, this provision now applies to treat the I.R.C. § 1248 amount as eligible for the dividends received deduction available under I.R.C. § 245A. I.R.C. § 1248(j).

(J) OUTBOUND LIQUIDATIONS

The focus of I.R.C. § 367(e)(2) is to force gain recognition when appreciated assets are removed from U.S. tax jurisdiction through a liquidating distribution. When a U.S. subsidiary liquidates into its foreign parent in what would be a tax-free liquidation under I.R.C. §§ 332 and 337 had the transaction occurred in a domestic context, I.R.C. § 367(e)(2) provides for taxation of the U.S. subsidiary on the distribution of appreciated property in the liquidation. However, no recognition under I.R.C. § 367(e)(2) is required if the foreign parent uses the distributed property in the conduct of a trade or business in the United States for at least 10 years after the liquidation. Reg. § 1.367(e)–2(b)(2). The logic for this exception from immediate recognition by a liquidating subsidiary on the distribution of appreciated assets to a foreign parent is that the foreign parent would be taxed on the effectively connected income of its U.S. branch under I.R.C. § 882, on any repatriation of those earnings under the branch profits tax of I.R.C. § 884, and on any sale of the branch's assets under I.R.C. § 882.

The exception will not apply to the extent that an intangible is distributed by the U.S. subsidiary as part of the liquidating distribution even if the intangible remains in the United States as part of a U.S. trade or business.

Similar logic excepts a liquidating U.S. subsidiary from recognizing gain on an outbound liquidation to the extent that the liquidating corporation (if it is not a U.S. Real Property Holding Company distributing stock of a U.S. corporation that is not a U.S. Real Property Holding Company) distributes stock of a U.S. subsidiary (at least 80 percent ownership) to its foreign parent, Reg. § 1.367(e)–2(b)(2). Also, nonrecognition is permitted on a liquidating distribution of a U.S. real property interest (*e.g.*, U.S. real property or stock in a U.S. real property holding company) because the foreign shareholder of the liquidating U.S. subsidiary would be subject to U.S. tax on any sale of the U.S. real property interest.

(K) TRANSFERS TO ESTATES, TRUSTS AND PARTNERSHIPS

In the waning days of the Obama administration, the IRS and Treasury issued temporary regulations denying the nonrecognition treatment provided by I.R.C. § 721, a provision in the partnership context that is parallel to I.R.C. § 351 in the corporate context, in the case of certain transfers to partnerships with a foreign partner. Reg. §§ 1.721(c)–1T *et seq.* The regulations address transfers by a U.S. partner to a partnership where any gain inherent in the contributed property ultimately will be recognized by a foreign person. In effect, the regulations look through the partnership to determine if the gain will be recognized by a foreign person. The regulations fulfil the commitment made by the government in Notice 2015–54, 2015–34 I.R.B. 210, to issue guidance to prevent what it viewed as abusive transactions in the partnership context. These regulations expire if not finalized by January 2020.

When a U.S. person transfers appreciated property to a foreign trust or estate, the transferor must recognize gain. Therefore, a transfer of property by a U.S. person to a foreign trust or estate is treated as a sale or exchange of the property for its fair market value. If a U.S. trust becomes a foreign trust, all trust assets are treated as having been sold to the foreign trust.

§ 13.03   NON-OUTBOUND TRANSACTIONS

Without a full explanation of the tax law of corporate reorganizations, it is difficult at best to understand the operation of I.R.C. § 367 to non-outbound transactions. What follows is a skeletal summary of I.R.C. § 367(b), the provision that governs the treatment of such transfers.

While I.R.C. § 367(a) is concerned with U.S. taxpayers transferring appreciated assets beyond U.S. tax jurisdiction without recognizing the gain inherent in the appreciation, I.R.C. § 367(b) historically has been focused on a different set of concerns. Until enactment of the TCJA, if a U.S. corporation operated a business through a foreign subsidiary, the income was not normally taxable in the United States unless it qualified as subpart F income. *See supra* § 9.01. However, those foreign earnings were subject to a U.S. corporate-level tax at ordinary income rates when a dividend was paid from the foreign subsidiary to its U.S. parent. Of course if the income was subpart F income, it was subject to a U.S. tax at ordinary income rates when earned by the foreign corporation. In sum, the U.S. tax system was designed to ensure that foreign earnings were subject to a U.S. corporate-level tax at ordinary income rates at some point in time.

The purpose of I.R.C. § 367(b) was to ensure that foreign E&P was subject to a U.S. corporate-level tax at ordinary income tax rates when certain otherwise tax-free transactions resulted in the repatriation or deemed repatriation of those earnings to the United States, or when the United States might otherwise lose the ability to tax those earnings in the future. Section 367(b) is itself quite general, providing essentially that in most reorganizations (or subsidiary liquidations) to which the outbound rules of I.R.C. § 367(a) do not apply, a foreign corporation is accorded treatment as a corporation, thereby paving the way for appropriate nonrecognition under I.R.C. §§ 332, 351, 354, 355, 356 or 361, except to the extent that the regulations provide otherwise. *See* Reg. § 1.367(b)–1(b).

The following types of transactions are governed by I.R.C. § 367(b): (1) the repatriation of foreign assets in an inbound liquidation or inbound reorganization; (2) certain foreign-to-foreign reorganizations; and (3) certain divisive reorganizations involving a foreign corporation. In these transactions, the primary tax policies reflected in the regulations are: (a) to provide immediate taxation when untaxed (by the United States) earnings of a foreign corporation are repatriated to U.S. corporate shareholders; and (b) to prevent a U.S. transferor from avoiding taxation as ordinary income under I.R.C. § 1248.

Applying these policies to the transactions outlined above yields the following results under I.R.C. § 367(b) and the regulations. In a complete liquidation of a foreign subsidiary into its U.S. parent corporation that would otherwise be tax-free under I.R.C. §§ 332 and 337, the parent is treated as receiving a distribution of the "all E&P amount"— essentially the E&P of the liquidating corporation attributable to the U.S. shareholder's ownership. Reg. § 1.367(b)–3. This rule was intended to ensure that any foreign E&P that would otherwise escape tax in the United States would be taxable at the U.S. corporate level.

Similarly, if a foreign subsidiary of a U.S. parent corporation reorganizes into a U.S. subsidiary, the U.S. parent must include in income the E&P of the foreign subsidiary attributable to the parent's stock in the foreign subsidiary. For example, suppose that USCo owns all of the stock of FSub, a foreign subsidiary with earnings and profits. FSub transfers all of its assets to USSub, a U.S. subsidiary, in exchange for the stock of USSub. FSub then liquidates, distributing the USSub stock to USCo.

This asset reorganization (probably a D reorganization under I.R.C. § 368(a)(1)(D)) would normally be tax-free to all parties in the purely domestic context. However, note that the foreign earnings and profits have been repatriated to the United States. In the absence of I.R.C. § 367(b) those earnings would not be taxed in the United States at the corporate level. Section 367(b) will force USCo to include those foreign earnings in income at the time of the reorganization.

In these transactions, the amount that is treated as ordinary income recognized by the U.S. parent corporation is "the all earnings and profits amount." Reg. § 1.367(b)–2(d). Essentially, the "all E&P amount" consists of the foreign E&P (not previously subject to U.S. tax) of the subsidiary involved in the inbound liquidation or reorganization that accrued while the U.S. taxpayer held the stock. Accordingly, any foreign earnings that were subject to inclusions as subpart F income or GILTI would not be part of the all E&P amount. Because post-TCJA most foreign earnings will either constitute subpart F or GILTI, the importance of I.R.C. § 367(b) as a backstop to U.S. taxation of foreign earnings has waned. Moreover, in light of the 100 percent dividends-received deduction available under I.R.C. § 245A, the all E&P amount should be exempt from U.S. taxation upon the inbound event, rendering the historical policy behind I.R.C. § 367(b) moot. But the statute and accompanying (very complex) regulations remain "on the books" until repealed and/or withdrawn.

In an inbound transaction, the E&P of any lower tier subsidiaries is not counted, as that E&P remains potentially subject to tax to the ultimate U.S. shareholder. The all E&P amount includes earnings of a foreign corporation attributable to a U.S. shareholder's stock, even if that corporation was not a CFC at the time the earnings accrued.

Historically, a U.S. taxpayer that had to include the all E&P amount under I.R.C. § 367(b) as a deemed dividend was entitled to credit foreign income tax paid attributable to the E&P in accordance with I.R.C. § 902. But I.R.C. § 902 has been repealed, and instead the dividend distribution from a CFC to the U.S. shareholder should qualify for a 100 percent dividends received deduction under I.R.C. § 245A.

A similar disconnect exists with respect to extensive regulations under I.R.C. § 367(b) applicable to foreign-to-foreign reorganizations, an area in which the IRS and Treasury have been especially active in issuing anti-abuse rules over the past few decades. As an example of the type of transaction that concerned the government, suppose USCo is a shareholder in FC1, a foreign corporation, the assets of which are acquired by FC2, another foreign corporation, in a reorganization with USCo receiving FC2 stock; the shareholder generally should not recognize any gain or loss on the transaction under I.R.C. § 354. Reg. § 1.367(b)–1(b). However, if FC1 is a CFC and FC2 is not (or the shareholder is not a 10 percent shareholder of FC2), then the potential I.R.C. § 1248 recognition on a sale or exchange of FC2 stock (which should reflect the potential I.R.C. § 1248 amount in the FC1 stock) is eliminated, because I.R.C. § 1248 does not apply to the stock of FC2 if it is not a CFC. Similarly, even if FC2 is a CFC, I.R.C. § 1248 does not apply if the U.S. shareholder does not own at least a 10 percent stock interest. In these and similar situations, I.R.C. § 367(b) generally requires the U.S. shareholder to recognize the E&P of FC1 that is allocable to the stock held by the U.S. shareholder. Reg. § 1.367(b)–4.

Note that in this foreign-to-foreign context the amount that is recognized by USCo is "the section 1248 amount" rather than "the all E&P amount." The section 1248 amount consists of foreign E&P and, unlike the all E&P amount, may include the E&P of subsidiaries. To understand why the all E&P amount was limited to the E&P of the top tier company while the section 1248 amount includes E&P of lower tier entities, consider the following. USCo owns all the stock of FSub1 which in turn owns all the stock of FSub2. If FSub1 liquidates, there is no need for the E&P of FSub2 to be taxable to USCo because later distributions or a later liquidation would have resulted in U.S. corporate level taxation. But suppose USCo transfers the stock of FSub1 to FSub3 in a reorganization under I.R.C. § 368(a)(1)(B) where USCo receives only 20 percent of the stock of FSub3 and assume that unrelated foreign shareholders hold the remainder of the stock. Now FSub1 and FSub2 are no longer CFCs. If USCo was not taxed on all of the E&P in both FSub1 and FSub2 on the transaction, that E&P may never have been subject to U.S. corporate level taxation.

Foreign-to-foreign reorganizations were an important planning tool for taxpayers prior to enactment of the TCJA as they provided a means of repatriating foreign cash tax-free or with "hyped" foreign tax credits. The government in response issued a series of notices and regulations. *See,* for example, Notice 2006–85, 2006–2 C.B. 677; Notice 2007–48, 2007–1 C.B. 1428; Notice 2014–32, 2014–20 I.R.B. 1006; 1.367(b)–10; Notice 2016–73, 2016–52 I.R.B. 908.

Like the inbound transactions that require inclusion of the all E&P amount, the requirement to include the section 1248 amount in foreign-to-foreign reorganization transactions appears no longer fit for purpose given that an inclusion of the section 1248 amount in income should be tax-exempt to the recipient U.S. corporate shareholder. I.R.C. § 1248(j).

The third general type of transaction governed by I.R.C. § 367(b) (the first two being liquidations/ reorganizations into the United States and certain foreign-to-foreign reorganizations) is the non-outbound divisive reorganization. In a divisive reorganization, essentially a corporation makes a distribution to one or more of its shareholders, consisting of stock of a controlled corporation (assuming both the distributing and distributed corporations conduct active trades or businesses). I.R.C. §§ 368(a)(1)(D) and 355. If all of the statutory requirements are met, the parties are not taxed in a divisive reorganization. Section 367(b) alters this nonrecognition treatment where either the distributing or controlled corporation is foreign.

If a domestic corporation distributes stock of a CFC to a U.S. corporation, the CFC is deemed to be a corporation and the reorganization is generally tax-free as long as basis adjustments in the stock of the CFC preserve the section 1248 amount. *See* Reg. § 1.1248(f)–2(b)(2) and (3). If the distributee is a U.S. individual, the distributing corporation recognizes gain on the distribution. Reg. § 1.367(b)–5(b).

If the distributing corporation is a CFC, the level of complexity escalates. But essentially if the divisive reorganization distribution is pro rata to the shareholders, the bases in the stock of both the distributing corporation and the corporation whose stock was distributed (the controlled corporation) are adjusted downwards to ensure that any pre-reorganization potential section 1248 amount is preserved in the hands of the shareholders if they dispose of the stock of either the distributing or the controlled corporation. That is, there is no immediate income to the shareholders, but they face the potential for an inclusion of the same section 1248 amount that they faced before the divisive reorganization. If the distribution is not pro rata, but instead a shareholder gives up the stock in the distributing corporation in exchange for the stock in the distributed corporation, then the shareholder has a deemed distribution equal to the shareholder's pro rata share of the earnings and profits of the stock surrendered in the reorganization. Reg. § 1.367(b)–5(d)(2). For those readers with problems getting to sleep, there is a numerical illustration of the rules in this paragraph. *See* Reg. § 1.367(b)–5(g) Ex. 1.

As with the other two sets of regulations described above, there are questions that remain to be answered as to the continued applicability of Reg. § 1.367(b)–5 in a post-TCJA world.

§ 13.04   CARRYOVER OF TAX ATTRIBUTES

Suppose that USCo owns all of the stock of CFC1 and CFC2 (for ease of computation, assume all entities use the USD as functional currency). CFC2 owns all of the stock of CFC3. In year 2 CFC1 merges into CFC2 in a transaction described in I.R.C. § 368(a)(1)(A). What happens to the E&P and PTEP accounts of CFC1? In accordance with I.R.C. § 381 and Reg. § 1.367(b)–7, in an asset reorganization essentially the E&P and taxes of CFC1 combine with those of CFC2. Similar treatment would result if CFC3 were to liquidate into CFC2 in year 4 in a tax-free liquidation under I.R.C. §§ 332 and 337.

As with the rules mandating inclusions of taxable income in the case of otherwise tax-free reorganization and liquidation transactions, it's unclear how the rules governing carryover of attributes in the cross-border reorganization context should apply post-TCJA. Note in this regard that the government has never been able to figure out how to write rules governing the carryover of previously taxed income accounts, and that issue remains reserved in the regulations in Reg. § 1.367(b)–7. As with other areas under I.R.C. § 367(b), the rules governing carryover of attributes in non-recognition transactions will likely be subject to revision by the government in the upcoming days (or should that be years or decades or centuries . . .?).

CHAPTER 14

TAX ARBITRAGE AND AN EVOLVING GLOBAL TAX LANDSCAPE

§ 14.01 INTRODUCTION

Double taxation can occur when two competing jurisdictions claim to have the primary authority to tax the same income with neither providing any relief for taxes imposed by the other jurisdiction. For example, suppose that USCo renders services training Indian computer programmers in the United States. The Indian programmers use their newly-acquired skills in India. Under U.S. law, the training services are considered rendered in the United States and USCo's compensation for those services is U.S. source income. If India treats the services as having been performed in India (*i.e.*, where the services are used), India may impose a tax on the compensation paid. Because the United States will not generally give a tax credit for foreign taxes imposed on what the United States regards as U.S. source income, the result may be double taxation (although in some cases the credits may be available to offset U.S. tax on other foreign source income in the same income basket, or Indian taxes may be creditable under the U.S.-India tax treaty).

One job of the international tax advisor in serving clients is to avoid double taxation. The intersection of different tax systems can produce double taxation, as outlined above, but it can also provide opportunities to minimize and, at times, eliminate tax liability (sometimes referred to as double non-taxation). When two countries classify the same transaction differently or even within a country when tax treatment is inconsistent, the opportunity for tax arbitrage arises. Tax arbitrage is simply the process of exploiting the differences between two different countries' tax treatment of the same transaction. Through tax arbitrage, taxpayers may receive a tax benefit in more than one jurisdiction.

Suppose A, a U.S. resident who has worked in Country X for many years and is now retired, receives a distribution from a Country X payor which the United States considers to be similar to a social security payment but which Country X considers to be a pension distribution. If a treaty based on the 2016 U.S. Model Treaty is applicable, the United States would refrain from taxing the distribution because Art. 17(3) cedes exclusive taxing authority to Country X over payments similar to social security, while Country X would refrain from taxing the distribution because Art. 17(1) grants exclusive taxing authority to the United States over pensions. The result would be double nontaxation. This result arises because of differing views of the transaction by the United States and Country X. The differing views which can sometimes lead to double taxation can also sometimes lead to double nontaxation.

Suppose XCo is incorporated in country X but is managed and controlled in country Y (*e.g.*, important corporate decisions are made in country Y). XCo earns business income in country X but does not have a permanent establishment there. If Country X uses a "place of effective management" test to determine residence while country Y uses a "place of incorporation" test, the result may be that the income of XCo escapes taxation. Country X may not exercise source state taxing authority because XCo's presence there does not rise to the level of a permanent establishment. Country X may not exercise residence-based taxing authority because it considers XCo to be a country Y resident, while country Y may not exercise residence-based or source-based taxation because it considers XCo to be a Country X resident that earns income in Country X.

The ability to arbitrage differences between tax systems can arise in a variety of circumstances where two countries characterize transactions inconsistently. Differing rules with respect to source, residence, transfer pricing, etc. have historically offered openings for taxpayers to avoid or minimize overall taxation from cross-border transactions. The history of the evolution of international tax rules is essentially the story of taxpayers' efforts to engage in tax arbitrage and governments' efforts to prevent them.

International efforts in this regard took on additional force beginning in 2013, when the OECD initiated a project (at the behest of the G7) to crack down on cross-border tax arbitrage engaged in by multinational companies, with the Base Erosion and Profit Shifting project ("BEPS"). *See supra* Chapter 1. This project was focused on taxpayers' ability to shift income and profits from one jurisdiction to another by exploiting the types of differences in rules mentioned above. Although the project formally was concluded in 2015 with the release of reports on 15 separate BEPS action items, work on a number of the areas identified as particularly susceptible to base erosion and profit shifting continues. In the meantime, the BEPS project has morphed into another project that is an attempt to write tax rules to address the digitalized economy. That project in turn has evolved into an effort to rewrite large parts of international tax rules that have been settled since the early 20th century (termed BEPS 2.0). More on that in § 14.06 below.

The discussion below includes a sampling of how tax arbitrage opportunities can shape cross-border transactions, and how the United States and other countries have responded to these transactions. As is usually the case, a crackdown against one type of transaction often leads innovative taxpayers and their advisors to develop other types of tax-efficient structures. There is no end to taxpayers' willingness to save money on their tax burdens and their apparent willingness to pay advisors to help them achieve lower rates spurs advisors to develop creative and ingenious solutions. Although taxpayers inevitably will continue to look for ways to exploit different countries' tax rules to minimize their overall tax rate on cross-border investments, the rest of this chapter will illustrate how the landscape of tax arbitrage has fundamentally shifted as a result of both the BEPS project and the enactment of TCJA.

§ 14.02   THE CHECK-THE-BOX REGULATIONS

Regulations issued by the U.S. Treasury in 1996 have been blamed (or credited, depending on one's perspective) for spawning what has been referred to as "the golden age of cross-border tax planning" in part through the use of hybrid entities. The check-the-box regulations (Reg. §§ 301.7701–1 through –4) allowed many taxpayers to simply choose (*i.e.*, by checking the box) how an entity should be treated— as a corporation or transparent entity—for U.S. tax purposes. Prior to issuance of these regulations, the classification of an entity as a corporation or a partnership absorbed a lot of advisors' time (and lots of taxpayer fees). The regulations were touted as bringing simplification to an unnecessarily complex area of the law. Conceived with the domestic context in mind, the drafters arguably missed their implications in the cross-border arena, where their ancillary effects have been significantly broader.

The regulations permit "eligible entities" to choose among various business classifications. Both domestic and foreign businesses may be "eligible entities" if they meet the requirements of the regulations. Generally, once a change in classification is made, a subsequent change in classification cannot be made for five years. However, an election by a newly formed eligible entity is not considered a change. Reg. § 301.7701–3(c)(1)(iv). An "eligible entity" may be classified as a corporation, partnership or a single member entity. A single member entity (sometimes informally referred to as a "tax nothing" or "disregarded entity") provides flow-through taxation and resembles a partnership but with only one member. This creates an "entity" that is ignored for tax purposes in the United States. When an entity is transparent for U.S. tax purposes but is recognized as a corporation in the country of operation, it is a "hybrid entity." When an entity is recognized as a corporation in the United States but is treated as a transparent entity in a foreign country, it is sometimes referred to as a "reverse hybrid entity."

The check-the-box regulations have a number of requirements. The first requirement is that a separate entity must exist for federal tax purposes. Reg. § 301.7701–1(a). A mere contractual relationship (*e.g.*, joint tenancy) does not qualify as an entity. Once an organization is deemed to be an entity separate from its owners, the next step is to determine if it is a business entity. A business entity is any entity that is not classified as a trust or subject to special treatment under the Code. Reg. § 301.7701–4. A business entity with two or more members is classified as either a corporation or a partnership for federal tax purposes. A business entity with only one owner is classified as either a corporation or a single member entity. Once a business entity exists, a determination of eligibility must be made.

A business entity is ineligible to choose its classification as a transparent or corporate entity if the business form appears on a "per se" list. There is one list for domestic business entities and another for foreign business entities. For example, an entity incorporated in any U.S. state cannot elect to be treated as a transparent entity. Similarly, a U.K. Public Limited Company (PLC) or a Brazilian Sociedade Anonima (SA) cannot choose to be treated as a transparent entity. Reg. § 301.7701–2.

Eligible entities failing to make an election are classified under default rules in the regulations. Reg. § 301.7701–3(b). The regulations attempt to classify entities as they would most likely classify themselves if an election had been made. If two or more members create an unincorporated domestic entity (*e.g.,* a U.S. partnership or a U.S. limited liability company (LLC)), the entity is treated as transparent treatment and classified as a partnership. If only one member creates an unincorporated domestic entity (*e.g.,* a U.S. LLC), it is treated as a single member entity and disregarded.

Foreign eligible entities are classified depending on whether there is unlimited liability or not. A foreign eligible entity consisting of more than one member, when all members have limited liability (*e.g.,* a limited liability company), is deemed a corporation under the default rules. A single member foreign entity with limited liability is also a corporation. On the other hand, a foreign eligible entity with more than one member is a partnership if any member has unlimited liability (*e.g.,* a limited partnership where the general partner has unlimited liability). A single member foreign eligible entity with unlimited liability is disregarded (*i.e.,* treated as transparent).

A check-the-box election can be made retroactively effective up to 75 days before the election is made. In some cases, in the initial year it is possible to make the election retroactive more than 75 days.

Recognizing the flexibility the check-the-box rules provided to taxpayers, Treasury has at various points tried to limit their reach. (*See* Notice 98–11, 1998–1 C.B. 433 (withdrawn); 66 T.D. 8767, 1998–1 C.B. 875; REG–104537–97, 1998–16 I.R.B. 21 (withdrawn)). Taxpayers successfully lobbied Congress on this point, arguing that while the rules facilitated foreign tax planning, they were not being used to reduce taxpayers' U.S. tax burdens. (*See* Notice 98–35, 1998–2 C.B. 34). But while the check-the-box regulations remain in effect, other law changes limit their use as a tax planning tool, including the enactment of anti-hybrid rules by TCJA and anti-hybrid recommendations released as part of the BEPS project.

Under I.R.C. § 267A, deductions for royalty or interest payments are disallowed if a payment (or accrual) is a "disqualified related party amount" and is pursuant to a hybrid transaction or by or to a hybrid entity. A payment is considered a disqualified related party amount if it is paid or accrued to a related party and not included in the income of the related party under its country's tax laws or the related party is allowed a deduction for such amount under its tax laws. Proposed regulations issued in 2018 (REG–104352–18, 2019–3 I.R.B. 357) significantly expand the scope of the statutory provision, closely mimicking the 450-page BEPS report on this topic (BEPS action 2).

For an illustration of how the anti-hybrid proposed regulations apply to hybrid entities and reduce their usefulness as a planning tool, consider the following example: FX, a foreign corporation, holds all the interests of US1, which is treated as a disregarded entity of FX for Country X tax purposes. US1 pays $100x to FX pursuant to a debt instrument, an amount that is treated as interest for U.S. tax purposes but is disregarded for Country X tax purposes. Assume US1 has no other income or expenses. Prior to the enactment of I.R.C. § 267A, US1 could deduct the interest payment but there would be no offsetting inclusion in the income of FX.

Post-TCJA, I.R.C. § 267A (as interpreted by the proposed regulations) would deny the deduction to US1 based on the following analysis: US1 meets the definition of hybrid entity for this purpose (a "specified party" as defined in the regulations) and so its deduction for the $100x payment is subject to disallowance. The $100x payment is not regarded under the tax law of country X because under its laws the payment is a disregarded transaction involving a single taxpayer. In addition, were the tax law of country X to regard the payment (and treat it as interest), FX would include it in income. The payment is a disregarded payment to which Reg. § 1.267A–2(b) applies. *See* Prop. Reg. § 1.267A–6(c)(3) Ex. 3.

§ 14.03   ARBITRAGE AND ITS RESPONSES

Tax arbitrage can occur when different countries provide different tax treatments with respect to: (a) entities; (b) character of income; (c) source of income; (d) tax base. The examples below illustrate some of the structures taxpayers have used in their attempts to exploit these differences, and government responses thereto.

(A)   WHO IS THE TAXPAYER

Tax arbitrage advantages can arise because of conflicting characterizations of the taxpayer. Suppose USCo is a domestic corporation and the sole shareholder of ForCo, a foreign corporation doing business in country X. Prior to enactment of the TCJA, if ForCo's income was non-subpart F income, neither it nor USCo would be subject to current U.S. tax on its income. Assume ForCo had net profits of $1 million that were subject to a foreign tax of 45 percent, or $450,000. Now suppose that USCo set up another entity, Reverse Hybrid, in Country X, treated as a corporation for U.S. purposes but as a partnership for Country X purposes (assume the second owner of Reverse Hybrid is another member of the USCo consolidated group). Assume Reverse Hybrid made a loan to ForCo and received interest from ForCo in the amount of $250,000. The United States likely did not tax the interest received by Reverse Hybrid as subpart F income (*see* I.R.C. § 954(c)(6) and I.R.C. § 954(c)(3), discussed *supra* at 9.03(A)). But Country X thought the interest payment was made to a partnership with U.S.

partners. ForCo might have been able to deduct the $250,000 in interest income it paid out to Reverse Hybrid, which left it with taxable income of $750,000 that would be subject to a 45 percent rate, or $330,750 with no further Country X tax imposed. The total foreign tax liability of $330,750 represented a reduction of $119,250 from the tax liability ForCo would have incurred in the absence of the loan by Reverse Hybrid.

The tax arbitrage allowed ForCo to reduce its overall foreign tax liability through an "interest" payment that under U.S. law was treated as received by a foreign corporation, Reverse Hybrid, as non-subpart F income, but was treated for U.S. tax purposes as received by Country X. This transaction capitalized on the inconsistent classifications countries have for business entities.

TCJA and BEPS address many of the benefits taxpayers previously could achieve from this structure. First, the GILTI provisions of I.R.C. § 951A likely would subject much of the income of Reverse Hybrid to tax. So the benefits of reducing ForCo's income while simultaneously not increasing U.S. taxable income is reduced. But note that there the structure still may be tax-efficient, because the 10.5 percent effective corporate tax rate on a GILTI inclusion may still make the transaction beneficial for the taxpayer if the foreign country imposes tax at a high rate and allows an interest deduction. Changes implemented by countries in response to the BEPS recommendations (including anti-hybrid rules) mean that there may be limitations on ForCo's ability to deduct interest expense. Consideration of the value of the transaction requires a much more complex balancing of the overall picture: taxpayers need to take into account that the ability to claim a full foreign tax credit on the taxes imposed on ForCo may be limited due to new foreign tax credit basketing and expense allocation rules.

(B) ENTITIES

(1) Hybrid Entities

The reverse hybrid structure—in which an entity is considered to be a corporation for U.S. tax purposes but transparent for foreign tax purposes—has over the years provided taxpayers with a number of arbitrage opportunities. Suppose that a Country X partnership with Country X partners is engaged in a U.S. trade or business. All of the partners are required to file U.S. tax returns because the U.S. trade or business is attributable to them. I.R.C. § 875(1). This prospect is burdensome and the partners may regard it as intrusive as well. If the partnership checked the box to be treated as a corporation for U.S. tax purposes, only the corporation and not the "shareholders" would be required to file a U.S. tax return (there would be U.S. corporate-level tax instead of tax of effectively connected income earned by foreign investors). But for Country X tax purposes, the income earned would be taxable directly to the "partners." There would not be any Country X corporate tax imposed.

Reverse hybrids were commonly used as financing mechanisms to create "nowhere income"—income not currently subject to tax in any jurisdiction. Suppose that USCo owned all the stock of Foreign Opco, a Country X corporation with a high rate of tax. USCo could form (by exchanging cash for stock) Foreign Reverse Hybrid (FRH), a Country X corporation for U.S. tax purposes but a flow-through entity for Country X tax purposes. If FRH then made a loan to Foreign Opco, interest accrued or paid by Foreign Opco could then be deductible from the Country X perspective against the income of Foreign Opco. The interest payment would then flow through FRH to the United States from a country X perspective. If Country X concluded that the applicable treaty provided for 0 percent withholding on interest paid by a Country X resident to a U.S. recipient, then Country X would not tax the interest received. At the same time, the U.S. might not tax the interest received as subpart F income. From the U.S. perspective, the interest is received by FRH which is a foreign corporation. To sum up, there was a deduction in Country X and, prior to enactment of the TCJA, no tax on the inclusion for either U.S. or Country X tax purposes.

Section 951A, combined with I.R.C. § 267A, reduces the benefits of this structure. Most of the income of FRH would likely qualify as tested income and be subject to immediate tax in the United States under I.R.C. § 951A. Depending on the extent to which Country X has adopted the BEPS recommendations on hybrids (action 2), the interest payment may not be deductible to Foreign Opco. But note that this structure could still be beneficial if the overall foreign tax rate is reduced and the higher foreign taxes would not have been creditable in the United States because of limitations on the foreign tax credit for GILTI basket income. *See* § 10.03.

Prior to wholesale reform of the international tax rules in the TCJA, the U.S. taxing authorities tried to address the tax benefits available through check-the-box structures with targeted changes. These targeted anti-abuse rules remain on the books as traps for the unwary even with the enactment of TCJA. Under the anti-abuse rule of I.R.C. § 909, the tax imposed is not creditable until the underlying income is taxable in the United States. *See* § 8.03(F). When I.R.C. § 909 was drafted, this rule meant that the foreign tax ordinarily would not be creditable until a distribution was made. But post-TCJA, foreign earnings of CFCs will mostly either be includible in income of the U.S. shareholder immediately (under either I.R.C. § 951 or § 951A) or eligible to be repatriated as a tax-exempt dividend (with no credit for any attributable foreign taxes). As with some other Code sections, the role of I.R.C. § 909 post-TCJA is unclear.

Suppose that a U.S. corporation pays interest to a U.K. reverse hybrid entity owned by Singapore shareholders. In determining whether the U.S.-U.K. tax treaty applies to reduce the withholding tax from 30 percent under U.S. domestic law to 0 percent under the treaty, the U.S. will extend benefits only if the United Kingdom sees the interest payment as taxable in the hands of a U.K. resident (and the resident meets the limitation on benefits requirements). Because that is not the case where the entity is a flow-through for U.K. purposes, no treaty benefits would be available under I.R.C. § 894 and under Art. 1(8) of the treaty itself. *See* I.R.C. § 894(c) (denying treaty benefits for certain payments through hybrid entities) and Reg. § 1.894–1(d). Section 267A also would now apply to deny the deduction to the U.S. payor in such a structure.

(2) Dual Resident Corporations

A dual resident corporation is an entity that is considered to be a resident in two jurisdictions. For example, suppose that XCo, a Country X corporation, owns all of the stock of DRC. DRC is managed and controlled in Country X and is therefore a Country X resident under the Country X residence rules. However, DRC is incorporated in the United States and is a U.S. resident for U.S. tax purposes. DRC owns all of the stock of USCo, a U.S. corporation. During the taxable year, suppose that XCo earns $100 and that USCo earns $100. DRC's only activity is the payment of $100 of interest on a bank loan. In the absence of special rules and assuming consolidated tax treatment both in Country X and the United States, in Country X DRC and XCo would file a consolidated return showing $0 net income. In the United States, DRC and USCo would file a return showing $0 net income. Yet, in the aggregate, these affiliated entities earn $100 of net income. The disconnect arises because the DRC deduction for interest paid to the bank is deducted twice—once in Country X and once in the United States. (Note that

I.R.C. § 267A would not appear to disallow the deduction in the United States to DRC in this case, because the payment is made to an unrelated party. But a special anti-abuse rule in the proposed regulations could deny the deduction if the transaction is considered a "structured arrangement." *See* Prop. Reg. § 1.267A–5(a)(20)).

The use of dual resident corporations is not limited to true corporations. For example, suppose that USCo owns 100 percent of XDE, a Country X entity that is disregarded for U.S. tax purposes but is treated as a corporation for Country X tax purposes. Suppose further that XDE owns all the stock of XCo. Assume that XCo and USCo each earns $100 and that XDE's only activity is $100 interest expense on a bank loan. Again, notwithstanding $100 of overall income, there may be no income for tax purposes in the United States and Country X. In the United States in the absence of remedial legislation, XDE's interest expense flows through and can be used by USCo to offset its income. In Country X, if XDE and XCo can consolidate, the interest expense will offset XCo's interest income. Even though XDE is not a corporation for U.S. tax purposes, it can generate a dual consolidated loss.

A dual consolidated loss transaction capitalizes on inconsistent characterization by multiple tax jurisdictions to permit a double deduction for losses. The transaction usually involves a corporation (or hybrid entity) that has connections to both a foreign country and the United States and, because of inconsistent tax residence requirements, is a resident of both countries—a DRC. The DRC may, in the absence of remedial legislation or regulations, be able to make use of the same deduction in two jurisdictions because the dual resident corporation (or hybrid entity) is treated inconsistently by the two jurisdictions involved.

The benefits of these structures might be caught by I.R.C. § 267A and proposed regulations, and by the BEPS recommendations. But even before that, Congress had acted to try and address such "double dip" structures in a more targeted fashion through I.R.C. § 1503(d)—the dual consolidated loss provision. Section 1503(d) generally prohibits domestic corporations or disregarded entities or branches from using "dual consolidated losses" to offset the income of other members of the corporation's affiliated group. A "dual consolidated loss" (DCL) is a net operating loss of a U.S. corporation that is also subject to residence-based taxation in a foreign country because the corporation is considered to be a resident there. Such a corporation is a "dual resident corporation."

The detailed operation of the DCL rules is explained in the regulations and is beyond the scope of this book. But some of the key concepts are discussed in general terms below.

First, what is a "dual resident corporation"? In general, a dual resident corporation (DRC) is an entity that is subject to residence based tax both in the United States and in a foreign country. A DRC can include a hybrid entity. For example, if USCo owns Foreign Hybrid which owns Foreign Opco,

Foreign Hybrid can be a DRC because its income is included in the U.S. group and it is a corporation taxed as a resident in a foreign country.

Second, what constitutes a DCL? In general, the U.S. rules govern this determination. If there is a loss determined under U.S. tax principles incurred by a DRC, then there is a DCL regardless of whether the items that give rise to that loss are deductible under the tax laws of the foreign country. Conversely, even if a payment is deductible for foreign tax purposes, it will not give rise to a DCL if there is no deduction for U.S. tax purposes. Suppose that USCo owns 100 percent of a foreign disregarded entity (FDE) that owns 100 percent of the stock of Foreign Opco. Suppose USCo borrows from a bank and in turn FDE "borrows" from USCo. If FDE accrues an interest deduction on the loan, the loan and the interest deduction are ignored for U.S. tax purposes. If FDE's only activity is to generate a deduction, that deduction is not a DCL because there is no loss from a U.S. perspective (*i.e.*, the "interest payment" on a "loan" from USCo to FDE is disregarded for U.S. tax purposes).

While the DCL rules eliminate some types of double deductions, they do not eliminate all of them (for the same reason, the transaction is not caught by the anti-hybrid proposed regulations). In this case, USCo receives a deduction for interest paid to the bank and FDE has a deduction which may be usable to offset income of Foreign Opco but which is not includible in income by USCo. However, there is a "booking rule" that allows the IRS to treat the bank loan as borrowed by FDE, thereby creating a DCL where a principal purpose of the arrangement is to avoid booking the bank loan directly to the FDE. In addition, in proposed regulations issued in 2018 Treasury says it is studying this structure because it raises policy concerns similar to ones that are addressed elsewhere in the DCL rules and anti-hybrid rules.

Third, if there is DCL, what are tax consequences? Generally, a U.S. taxpayer with a DCL cannot use the loss generated by the DRC to offset income of another member of the U.S. group. That is, if USCo owns DRC which owns Foreign Opco, a loss incurred by DRC (*e.g.*, the only activity is an interest expense on a bank loan) cannot be used to offset income of USCo. Note that the DCL rules do not prohibit DRC from using its own deductions to offset its own income. For example, if the $100 interest expense on a bank loan were used to offset $100 of DRC's own income, there would be no DCL. In this case, the $100 could be deducted in the United States and in the foreign jurisdiction. That is because the $100 of income is also taken into account twice—once in the United States and once in the foreign jurisdiction. But if DRC generates no income, DRC cannot use the $100 deduction on a consolidated return to offset income of USCo where the deduction also is used to offset income in a foreign jurisdiction.

Fourth, under specified circumstances, DRC can make an election not to use the loss to offset income of another foreign taxpayer (a "domestic use election" under Reg. § 1.1503(d)–6(d)). If a domestic use election is made, the loss of the dual resident corporation then can be used to offset income of another member of the U.S. group. That election can only be made if the taxpayer can certify that under no circumstances that loss can be used to offset income of another foreign entity over a five-year period. In sum, a DCL can either be taken to offset income of another U.S. taxpayer or to offset income of another foreign taxpayer—but not both.

Fifth, if a domestic use election is made to use a DCL to offset income of another member of the U.S. group (upon the promise not to use the loss to offset income of another foreign taxpayer), then when the DRC is sold or moves outside the control of the taxpayer that made the election, the potential for that loss to be used by another foreign taxpayer arises. In this situation, one of two things happens, depending on the nature of the disposition. If the IRS can be sure that that acquiring entity will not or cannot under applicable foreign law use the DCL to offset income of another person, then from a DCL perspective the transaction is insignificant. But if there is no way to ensure that the DCL won't ever be used to offset income of another person, then the U.S. group must give up the benefits it enjoyed (*i.e.*, the use of a deduction to offset income of another member of the U.S. group) by recapturing the losses deducted plus interest upon the disposition (basically interest on the taxes that would have been paid if the domestic loss had not been taken). There is an opportunity to mitigate the DCL recapture to the extent that the DRC itself earned income subsequent to the use of the DCL losses to offset income of another member of the U.S. group, or if the domestic use election resulted in the foreign losses merely becoming part of a U.S. net operating loss rather than actually offsetting income.

(3) Tax-Exempt Entities

Suppose an entity that is not taxable under U.S. law (*e.g.*, a tax-exempt pension fund or a foreign entity not subject to U.S. tax) has a tax attribute that has no value to the entity (because it is tax-exempt) but has value to other tax-paying entities. In this scenario, one can expect a market to exist that would allow the taxpaying entity to "purchase" the tax attribute in a way that benefits both the buyer and the seller at the expense of the U.S. government because the tax attribute has gone to the highest and best use.

For example, suppose that a tax-exempt entity owns $100 million worth of foreign stock on which a $20 million dividend is about to be paid. The dividend is subject to a $3 million foreign withholding tax which is not creditable by the tax-exempt organization. So the tax-exempt entity sells the stock to USCo for $100 million. Assume that USCo has a large capital gain from some other transaction. USCo receives the dividend and then sells the stock back to the tax-exempt entity for $82 million.

The tax-exempt entity ends up with an $18 million profit (more than the $17 million net dividend it would have received). USCo reports a $20 million dividend and takes a $3 million foreign tax credit. With the credit, USCo has a $1.2 million net U.S. tax liability on the $20 million dividend (assuming a 21 percent U.S. tax rate). On the sale back to the tax-exempt entity, USCo takes an $18 million loss deduction which saves $3.78 million in U.S. taxes (assuming a 21 percent rate). In total, USCo receives a $17 million net dividend and suffers an $18 million real loss on the stock sale. But the $3.78 million tax saving on the loss deduction not only covers the $1.2 million net U.S. tax on the dividend (after the foreign tax credit) but also covers the $1 million economic loss and produces a $1.58 million profit for USCo. This transaction appears to be a win-win situation for the tax-exempt entity and USCo.

Congress enacted I.R.C. § 901(k) to prevent the benefits otherwise available from transactions like these. That provision denies a foreign tax credit to USCo if it has not held the stock for a specified number of days. Stated differently, I.R.C. § 901(k) seeks to prevent taxpayers from buying tax benefits without undertaking the risk that comes with true ownership of property. A similar provision applies to payments other than dividends (*e.g.*, royalties). I.R.C. § 901(*l*). Treasury has also acted on a variety of fronts to deter taxpayers from entering into transactions that are perceived to take undue advantage of arbitrage possibilities or are motivated by tax considerations.

For example, suppose that USCo purchases for $75 all rights to a copyright that is about to expire. The expected income from the copyright is a $100 royalty subject to a 30 percent Country X withholding tax. Economically, USCo has paid $75 to receive $70 (*i.e.*,

$100 royalty minus the $30 Country X withholding tax). USCo might engage in this transaction because the $30 tax credit not only will offset any U.S. tax on the royalty income but will also save more than $5 of U.S. tax on other foreign source income USCo might have. For example, USCo might have $100 of gross income from the royalty and $40 of expenses associated with the royalty. On the $60 of net income, the United States would impose a tax of $12.6 (assuming a 21 percent rate) which will be fully offset by the $30 withholding tax on the royalty. In some cases, USCo will be able to use the $17.4 of withholding tax that did not offset U.S. tax on the royalty to offset potential U.S. tax on other foreign source income. Taking taxes into account, the $75 investment will produce more than $75 of cash flow (*i.e.*, the $70 net royalty and potential additional U.S. tax savings). But unless USCo meets the holding period requirement of I.R.C. § 901(*l*) (more than 15 days), no foreign tax credit is available.

(C)   CHARACTER OF INCOME

While a hybrid entity is an organization that is characterized as a corporation by one jurisdiction and a transparent entity by another jurisdiction, a hybrid instrument is an obligation that is classified as equity by one jurisdiction and as debt by another jurisdiction. Suppose that USCo transfers cash to ForCo in exchange for a financial instrument. Under the terms of the instrument, ForCo is obligated to make an annual payment equal to 6 percent of the amount it received. USCo is obligated upon repayment of the instrument to use the proceeds to purchase additional ForCo stock (*i.e.*, USCo has entered into a forward contract). For foreign tax purposes, the instrument might be classified as debt and each periodic payment as interest which may be deductible when accrued by an accrual basis taxpayer in Country X and could therefore reduce the tax on ForCo's income from operations. Moreover, under an applicable treaty Country X may not impose a withholding tax on interest payments actually paid to a U.S. resident.

For U.S. tax purposes, the "loan" coupled with a forward contract to buy stock may be treated as an equity investment so that periodic payments would be dividends rather than interest and would only be taxable when paid and not on accrual. AM 2006–001. In many cases, Country X may allow ForCo to accrue an interest deduction thereby generating a deduction while for U.S. tax purposes a dividend was not taxable unless and until it is actually paid. Reg. § 1.301–1(b).

The recommendations in BEPS action 2 apply with respect to hybrid instruments as well as hybrid entities, and would suggest that Country X deny the deduction to ForCo. In addition, if ForCo is a CFC of USCo, the 100 percent dividends received deduction that might otherwise be available to USCo upon receipt of a dividend from ForCo on the hybrid instrument would be disallowed. I.R.C. § 245A(e).

Suppose that ForCo, a Country X taxpayer, owns all the stock of USCo which owns stock of USSub. Suppose that USCo "sells" the stock of USSub to ForCo for cash with an obligation to repurchase in three years. When USSub pays a dividend, the cash ends up in the hands of ForCo. What is the tax treatment?

From a Country X tax perspective, ForCo has purchased the stock of USSub and if dividends are exempt from Country X taxation or if there is a tax credit for underlying taxes that USSub might have paid on its earnings, there may be no Country X liability. For U.S. tax purposes, this sale with an obligation to repurchase—commonly referred to as a "repo" (as in—**repo**ssession of the underlying stock)—may be treated as a loan. That is, ForCo loaned cash to USCo (*i.e.*, the so-called purchase price is treated as a loan) which is secured by the stock of USSub; when it comes time for repayment, USCo will repay the loan (*i.e.*, payment to "repurchase" the stock) and receive back the stock of USSub.

The result—prior to enactment of the TCJA— would be a nontaxable dividend between members of a U.S. consolidated group followed by a deduction in the United States for a deemed interest payment to ForCo. Proposed regulations under I.R.C. § 267A would deny this deduction. *See* Prop. Reg. § 1.267A– 2(a)(3).

Some character mismatches have been addressed by U.S. taxing authorities in other ways. For example, if a nonresident sells U.S. real estate at a gain, the gain may be taxable in the United States under I.R.C. § 897. *See* § 4.07. But rather than buy the real estate directly and be subject to tax on an eventual sale, suppose instead that the nonresident enters into a notional principal contract ("NPC") with a U.S. counterparty which agrees to buy the property. Under the NPC the nonresident profits if the real estate appreciates (that is, to the extent the underlying U.S. real property appreciates in value) over certain levels. Conversely, the nonresident suffers a loss if the real estate depreciates (or fails to appreciate more than at a specified rate). Has the nonresident successfully converted the character of real estate gain into gain under the NPC that would not be subject to U.S. tax under I.R.C. § 897? Presumably, the IRS would treat the nonresident as the beneficial owner of the property and apply I.R.C. § 897. *See* Revenue Ruling 2008–31, 2008–1 C.B. 1180 (which reaches the opposite result where the benefit to the nonresident is based on an index of real estate, rather than one particular parcel of real estate).

(D) SOURCE OF INCOME

Suppose that USCo manufactures product in the United States and sells to both U.S. and Canadian purchasers. Suppose further that USCo has a $21 excess foreign tax credit (*i.e.*, foreign taxes that have not yet been used to offset potential U.S. tax on foreign source income). If USCo can shift $100 of U.S. source income to foreign source income, then the excess foreign tax credit could be used to save $21 of U.S. tax, assuming that all income generated in these transactions is in the same basket. The problem is that if USCo manages to shift $100 of U.S. source income to foreign source income, the foreign jurisdiction (*e.g.*, Canada) may tax the income. This would result in additional cash tax and would not increase the ability to use excess foreign tax credits.

But suppose that income could be treated as Canadian source income for U.S. tax purposes but Canada would not see the income as Canadian source income subject to tax in Canada? In that case, there may be no additional Canadian tax but $100 of additional foreign source income the U.S. tax on which could be offset by the excess foreign tax credit. To illustrate, suppose that USCo sells $200 of product to a Canadian purchaser with title passing in the United States. The income would all be U.S. source income. But if USCo passes title (and all the benefits and burdens of ownership) in Canada, then under I.R.C. § 863(b) (prior to its amendment by the TCJA), 50 percent of the income would have been sourced in the United States where the manufacturing took place and the other 50 percent of the income would have been sourced for U.S. purposes by where title passes. So $100 of income would have been foreign source income but there may be no additional Canadian tax because Canada does not use mere title passage to determine whether income is taxable in Canada.

It was precisely because of planning like this that Congress amended I.R.C. § 863(b) in 2017 to provide that income from the sale of inventory manufactured in the United States and sold overseas would be sourced solely on the basis of production activities. I.R.C. § 863(b). In the example above, 100 percent of the income is now U.S. source regardless of where title passes. The planning opportunities associated with sourcing arbitrage also have been reduced by changes to I.R.C. § 904(d), specifically through the addition of new foreign tax credit baskets and limitations on the carryover of foreign tax credits associated with GILTI inclusions. But ensuring that the category of income matches the basket in which taxes are allocated remains an important part of planning.

As is the case with income character, the source of income has the potential to be changed through the use of a derivative instrument. For example, a nonresident seeking returns from the U.S. equity markets could purchase stock in U.S. companies. Dividends paid on this stock generally would be considered U.S. source and therefore would be subject to withholding tax at a 30 percent (or reduced treaty) rate. Instead of actually owning the stock, however, the non-U.S. investor could create synthetic ownership by entering into a "total return swap." Under a typical "total return swap," the investor would enter into an agreement with a counterparty under which returns to each party would be based on the returns generated by a notional investment in a specified dollar amount of stock. The investor would agree for a specified period to pay to the counterparty interest on the notional amount of stock and any depreciation in the value of the stock, and the counterparty would agree for the specified period to pay the investor any dividends paid on the stock and any appreciation in the value of the stock. Typically, amounts owed by each party under a total return swap are netted so that only one party makes an actual payment.

Although the equity swap resembles a leveraged purchase of stock, the tax treatment of the foreign investor would be different. Because the source of income from an equity swap (in tax terms, a notional principal contract) is determined by reference to the residence of the recipient of the income, amounts representing dividends in this example would be foreign source and therefore would not be subject to U.S. withholding tax. Reg. § 1.863–7(b). In response to this perceived type of source rule manipulation, I.R.C. § 871(m) treats certain dividend equivalent payments that might otherwise be foreign source as U.S. source payments.

(E) TAX BASE

(1) Timing Differences

Different countries may have different rules to determine for tax purposes when a deduction can be taken or when income must be reported. Suppose USCo wholly owns a foreign reverse hybrid (FRH) treated as a corporation for U.S. tax purposes but a flow-through for foreign purposes. When FRH earns income, the local country imposes the tax on USCo, but for U.S. tax purposes the E&P is "split" from the taxes and resides at FRH. Historically, the resulting foreign tax credit was available to offset U.S. taxes on other foreign source income. This result was essentially a timing issue as the taxes would have been available in the U.S. before the E&P was distributed to USCo by FRH. Congress addressed the benefits available in this structure with enactment of I.R.C. § 909 in 2010, but TCJA does so more broadly by subjecting most of the income of FRH to current U.S. tax. I.R.C. § 951A.

On some occasions, the timing arbitrage is not based on different U.S. and foreign treatment but rather on inconsistent treatment within the U.S. tax system. For example, suppose that ForCo wholly-owns stock of USCo. When USCo earns gross income, some of the tax base may be eroded by accrued interest or other deductions resulting from payments to ForCo. However, any U.S. withholding tax that might be imposed on the U.S. source FDAP income is normally only imposed upon payment rather than accrual. In the absence of a remedial provision, the result is tax base erosion in the U.S. without an offsetting collection of a withholding tax which may arise later upon actual payment of the interest or other payment.

I.R.C. § 267(a)(3) essentially puts USCo on the cash basis method for purposes of the interest expense deduction to match up with the cash basis orientation of Reg. §§ 1.1441–1(a) (requiring "payment") and 1.1441–2(e) (defining "payment"). I.R.C. § 59A (the BEAT alternative minimum tax) also targets this benefit in the case of large taxpayers. *See supra* § 4.09.

(2) Permanent Differences

Differences in the measurement of income by the United States and another country can also lead to tax arbitrage opportunities. For example, suppose USCo purchases all of the stock of ForCo and makes an election under I.R.C. § 338(g). The effect of the election for U.S. tax purposes is to treat ForCo as if immediately prior to USCo's purchase it had sold its assets to a new ForCo—unrelated to old ForCo. Often that deemed sale does not give rise to any U.S. tax, but if the assets of ForCo are appreciated, the effect of the election is to step up the basis of the assets for U.S. tax purposes. This generally results in foreign goodwill with a stepped-up basis. The stepped-up basis in the goodwill or other assets can be amortized or depreciated for U.S. tax purposes (*e.g.*, goodwill can be amortized over a 15-year period under I.R.C. § 197). This I.R.C. § 338(g) election has no impact for local country tax purposes. The result can be an amortization or depreciation deduction for U.S. tax purposes that results in lower E&P for U.S. purposes than for foreign tax purposes—a permanent difference in the amount of income.

Transactions that have the impact of producing amortization or depreciation for U.S. federal tax purposes but not for local country purposes gave rise to the enactment of I.R.C. § 901(m)—the "covered acquisition transaction" provision. *See* the discussion of I.R.C. § 901(m) *supra* in § 8.03(G). Essentially, I.R.C. § 901(m) disallows credits for any foreign taxes paid that are associated with the slice of income that exists for foreign purposes but not for U.S. tax purposes because of the extra deductions resulting from the basis step-up of a I.R.C. § 338(g) election or the purchase of "stock" of a hybrid entity.

The ability to "hype" foreign tax credits may have been severely reduced, but an I.R.C. § 338(g) election can still be beneficial for a U.S. taxpayer. For example, by increasing the basis of tangible assets for purposes of the GILTI calculation (*see* discussion of QBAI, *supra* at § 9.04(D), the step-up can reduce a CFC's tested income and ultimately, the U.S. shareholder's GILTI inclusion. But note that regulations under I.R.C. § 951A prohibit certain "disqualified transfers" that inappropriately result in basis step-ups in tangible property. Even without increasing QBAI, reducing U.S. taxable income relative to foreign income can still be beneficial for the calculation of the foreign tax credit limitation for the GILTI basket.

(F)   WHAT'S NEXT FOR TAX ARBITRAGE?

As the above discussion highlights, many of the structures that taxpayers previously utilized with great effect for tax planning that relied on differences between U.S. and foreign treatment of entities, instruments, and tax base computations have seen their benefits reduced or eliminated as a result of both U.S. and foreign tax law changes. But while cross-border planning has become harder, it's far from over. Instead, arbitrage post-TCJA is more likely to involve a component of substance, with taxpayers looking to invest in assets and operations in jurisdictions where the tax rules are most beneficial. Because the U.S. foreign tax credit continues to apply on a blended basis to foreign income, planning to achieve an optimal overall foreign tax credit mix is essential, as is the balance of the mix of types of the alphabet soup of income, all at different rates and with different associated foreign tax credit baskets: GILTI, FDII, foreign branch income and subpart F income. Character of income and differences in tax base always will remain important. Because the differences in characterization of income continue to matter for the anti-hybrid rules, one can expect taxpayers to continue to seek out transactions that allow them to play off one jurisdiction off another.

For example, consider a taxpayer that is considering whether to own its intellectual property (either newly developed or pre-existing) in the United States v. overseas. The decision of where to locate the ownership of the IP will need to take into account whether income from the IP, if held in the United States, might be subject to a lower tax rate under I.R.C. § 250; whether, if held overseas, continued spend on research and development might qualify for special incentives offered by a foreign jurisdiction, whether there is enough substance overseas to satisfy tax administrators that the income belongs in the jurisdiction where the IP is located; and the total mix of the foreign taxes paid and foreign income. Complex modeling would be needed to determine the optimal solution from a tax perspective of the answers to all of these questions, which would also depend on the taxpayer's profit margin on tangible v. intangible assets.

Similarly, consider a multinational taxpayer that needs to finance an acquisition via a bank loan. In what jurisdiction should it take out the financing? How can the taxpayer ensure that it will be able to fully deduct all of the interest being paid by the group? Here again, the answers will depend on the taxpayer's ability to navigate different countries' limitations on deduction of interest expense, together with the mix of income and expenses in each of the jurisdictions in which it operates.

Taxpayers also will want to consider whether to bring their foreign operations back into the United States, such as by "checking-the-box" on their foreign subsidiaries. What might be the advantages of doing so? Remember the discussion about the limitations on the GILTI foreign tax credit (80 percent of taxes paid) and the restrictions of carryforwards and carrybacks of GILTI-related foreign tax credits. Foreign taxes paid by foreign branches are not subject to those restrictions. But they still reside in a separate basket, and the income earned by a foreign branch cannot qualify for the I.R.C. § 250 deduction for FDII income. Once again, a complex model taking into account multiple factors likely will be needed to reach the optimal result.

For individual taxpayers and small businesses, the questions are different but the balancing act is the same. Should an I.R.C. § 962 election be made, which could allow individual taxpayers the ability to claim foreign tax credits and the I.R.C. § 250 deduction for income earned by a CFC? Should CFCs previously owned in individual or partnership structures be restructured so that they are now owned by corporations (which can claim the I.R.C. § 245A deduction)? Should investment into the United States made by foreign persons be held in partnership or corporate form?

The tax arbitrage landscape remains unsettled after TCJA, but taxpayers' desire to generate profits in the lowest tax jurisdiction possible and willingness to structure their affairs accordingly continue.

§ 14.04 ECONOMIC SUBSTANCE AND OTHER DOCTRINES

Other countries, led by the OECD, made significant efforts to crack down on cross-border tax avoidance beginning in 2013. But the United States had gone through its own moment of recognizing the consequences of unfettered tax avoidance years earlier, in part sparked by the tax shelter activity of the 1990s. This focus eventually resulted in Congress' enactment in 2010 of I.R.C. § 7701(*o*), representing the codification of the long-standing economic substance doctrine. At the same time, Congress also enacted I.R.C. § 6662(b)(6), a strict liability penalty set at 40 percent (reduced to 20 percent in the case of disclosure on the return) of any underpayment attributable to any disallowance of claimed tax benefits by reason of a transaction lacking economic substance.

Under I.R.C. § 7701(*o*), in the case of any transaction to which the economic substance doctrine is relevant, a transaction is treated as having economic substance only if:

- It changes in a meaningful way (apart from federal income tax effects) the taxpayer's economic position, and

- The taxpayer has a substantial purpose (apart from federal income tax effects) for entering into the transaction.

Notice 2014–58, 2014–2 C.B. 746 provides additional guidance regarding the codification of the economic substance doctrine and the related penalty amendments.

The legislative history to I.R.C. § 7701(*o*) makes it clear that the provision was not intended to alter the tax treatment of certain basic business transactions that, under longstanding judicial and administrative practice are respected, merely because the choice between meaningful economic alternatives is largely or entirely based on comparative tax advantages. It provides four non-exclusive examples of such basic business transactions:

- The choice between capitalizing a business enterprise with debt or equity;

- A U.S. person's choice between utilizing a foreign corporation or a domestic corporation to make a foreign investment;

- The choice to enter into a transaction or series of transactions that constitute a corporate organization or reorganization under subchapter C; and

- The choice to utilize a related-party entity in a transaction, provided that the arm's length standard of I.R.C. § 482 and other applicable concepts are satisfied.

The enactment of I.R.C. § 7701(*o*) represented a codification of principles developed in the courts over decades. Unlike the IRS' track record with respect to I.R.C. § 482, discussed *supra* in Chapter 11, the IRS has been somewhat more successful in convincing judges to deny benefits to taxpayers in light of taxpayers' failure to comply with principles of the economic substance doctrine. *See e.g.*, *Santander Holdings v. United States*, 844 F.3d 15 (1st Cir. 2016), *cert. denied*, 137 S.Ct. 2295 (2017); *Bank of NY Mellon Corp. v. Commissioner*, 801 F.3d 104 (2d Cir. 2015), *cert. denied sub nom.*, *Am. Int'l Grp., Inc. v. United States*, 136 S. Ct. 1375 (2016), *and cert. denied*, 136 S. Ct. 1377 (2016); *Salem Fin. Inc. v. United States*, 786 F.3d 932 (3d Cir. 2015)*; Klamath Strategic Inv. Fund v. United States*, 568 F.3d 537 (5th Cir. 2009); *H.J. Heinz Co. v. United States*, 76 Fed. Cl. 570 (2007); *Coltec Industries, Inc. v. United States*, 454 F.3d 1340 (Fed. Cir. 2006); *Compaq Computer Corp. v. Commissioner*, 277 F.3d 778 (5th Cir. 2001).

Note that each of these cases typically features the following: large-dollar transactions where either no or little economic analysis took place, non-existent or poor documentation of the economic benefit to be derived from the transaction, and witnesses and/or documents that were harmful to the taxpayer's position. Terms such as "sham transaction," "economic substance," "business purpose," "step transaction," and "form over substance" pepper these opinions, the thrust of which are that the taxpayer was unable to justify the reported tax results by showing objectively that there were economic factors, aside from tax ones, that made the transaction worthwhile or that in the absence of objective economic substance, there was at least a subjective business purpose, even if misplaced.

Under the economic substance doctrine, the IRS requires the taxpayer to prove that the transaction has a pre-tax profit potential. In applying this test, the IRS has put taxpayers on notice that foreign tax should be treated as an expense rather than a creditable item. *See* Notice 2010–62, 2010–2 C.B. 411.

Every case that focuses on economic substance also examines whether the taxpayer has a "business purpose" in engaging in the transaction in question. The business purpose doctrine arises out of a domestic tax case *Helvering v. Gregory*, 69 F.2d 809 (2d Cir. 1934), *affirmed* 293 U.S. 465 (1935), where the taxpayer carefully followed the divisive reorganization statute, but the transaction had no business purpose. The Court ruled for the government in disallowing the favorable tax treatment taxpayer had sought. The factors that establish a positive business purpose include the following: the transaction originated in a nontax function of the taxpayer; even though the transaction originated in the tax function of the taxpayer, the structure was adopted and supported by nontax function and management; the transaction addressed business concerns raised by a nontax function; the ultimate decision whether to undertake the transaction was based primarily on nontax factors; the transaction involved restructuring the exiting business or the formation of a genuine business; the transaction was expected to generate returns in excess of capital cost but also has a corresponding risk of loss. Negative business purpose factors include: the transaction was planned and executed without regard to pre-tax economic consequences; internal memoranda prior to the execution of the transaction focused on tax benefits; the transaction was structured in a manner to preclude generating pre-tax profit; the plan was marketed to the taxpayer by a promoter as a tax-driven instrument; the business purpose was the effect of tax savings on financial statements; the taxpayer's investigation and due diligence with respect to the transaction was not business-like.

The "business purpose" test appears to have a low threshold. As the court in *Compaq* stated: "To treat a transaction as a sham, the court must find that the taxpayer was motivated by no business purposes other than obtaining tax benefits . . . and that the transaction has no economic substance." *See generally Wells Fargo & Co. v. United States*, 2015–2 U.S. Tax Cas. (CCH) P50,558 (D. Minn. 2015).

In general, the federal courts have incorporated the business purpose requirement into a broader "sham transaction" or "economic substance" doctrine. Under this doctrine, a transaction will be respected if: (1) the transaction has objective economic substance; and/or (2) the taxpayer has a subjective non-tax business purpose. Some courts apply a disjunctive test (*i.e.*, taxpayer must satisfy either economic substance or business purpose). *See e.g.*,

IES Industries v. United States, 253 F.3d 350 (8th Cir. 2001); *Rice's Toyota World v. Commissioner*, 752 F.2d 89 (4th Cir. 1985). Other courts apply a conjunctive test (*i.e.*, the taxpayer must show both economic substance and business purpose). *See e.g.*, *United Parcel Service, Inc. v. Commissioner*, 254 F.3d 1014 (11th Cir. 2001). Still other courts seem to combine the two tests rather than applying a rigid two-part test. *See e.g.*, *ACM Partnership v. Commissioner*, 157 F.3d 231 (3d Cir. 1998).

In *Coltec Industries Inc. v. United States*, 454 F.3d 1340 (Fed. Cir. 2006), Coltec had recognized a 1996 capital gain of $240.9 million but through one of its subsidiaries faced substantial asbestos-related litigation claims. As part of same plan, the Coltec consolidated group made transfers to a formerly dormant Coltec subsidiary in exchange for stock, assumption of the asbestos liabilities and managerial responsibility of litigation claims. Coltec then sold its newly-acquired stock and under the applicable basis rules of I.R.C. § 358 Coltec properly reported a capital loss which was used to offset its capital gain.

The court determined that the assumption of liabilities did not effect any real change in the flow of economic benefits, provide any real opportunity to make a profit, or appreciably affect Coltec's interest aside from creating a tax advantage; it served no purpose other than to artificially inflate stock basis. The decision identified five principles of economic substance:

- The law does not permit the taxpayer to reap tax benefits from a transaction that lacks economic reality;

- The taxpayer has the burden of proving economic substance;

- The economic substance of a transaction must be viewed objectively rather than subjectively;

- The transaction to be analyzed is not the overall transaction but rather the step that gave rise to the alleged tax benefit; and

- Arrangements with subsidiaries that do not affect the economic interest of independent third parties deserve particular close scrutiny.

The focus on the particular step that gave rise to the tax benefit marked a shift in the longstanding approach to viewing a transaction in its entirety.

In an effort to get to the substance of a transaction, courts will often "step" together purportedly independent transactions in order to view the steps as a whole. The courts have generally developed three methods of testing whether to invoke the step transaction doctrine: (1) the end result test; (2) the interdependence test; and (3) the binding commitment test. The end result test is the broadest of the three articulations. The end result test examines whether it is apparent that each of a series of steps are undertaken for the purpose of achieving the ultimate result. The interdependence test attempts to prove that each of the steps were so interdependent that the completion of an individual step would have been meaningless without the completion of the remaining steps. The binding commitment test is the narrowest of the three articulations and looks to whether, at the time the first step is entered into, there is a legally binding commitment to complete the remaining steps.

As an example of the step-transaction doctrine in the international tax context, consider *Del Commercial Properties, Inc. v. Commissioner*, 251 F.3d 210 (D.C. Cir. 2001). In *Del Commercial*, the court ruled that an interest payment from a U.S. borrower to a purported Dutch lender which then paid interest to a Canadian lender was really a loan directly from the Canadian lender to the U.S. borrower which was subject to a 15 percent withholding rate under the U.S.-Canada treaty rather than 0 percent rate under the U.S.-Netherlands treaty. Under modern treaties (including the current treaty with the Netherlands), limitation-on-benefits provisions (*see supra* § 5.05(F)) might prevent unintended treaty benefits. The conduit financing regulations under Reg. § 1.881–3 have the same effect under U.S. domestic law (*see supra* § 4.04(A)(2)). In *Illinois Tool Works v. Commissioner*, T.C. Memo. 2018–121 a debt/equity case involving the IRS' attempt to recharacterize a repatriation transaction in part on economic substance grounds, the court found that the transaction was undertaken for a bona-fide business purpose and respected what it said was the substance as well as the form of the transaction as a loan.

There has yet to be a court case interpreting the codified economic substance doctrine. *Pilot Series of Fortress Insurance LLC v. Commissioner*, Dkt. Nos. 29948–15, 9627–16, and 22148–16 (2019) would have addressed the issue, but it was settled immediately before trial.

§ 14.05 TAX GOVERNANCE AND TRANSPARENCY

(A) REPORTABLE TRANSACTIONS AND LISTED TRANSACTIONS

The United States also has been ahead of much of the rest of the world in requiring disclosure and reporting of tax advantaged transactions. As a general matter, the Sarbanes-Oxley Act of 2002 mandates that corporate officers certify companies' financial statements to ensure that they do not contain any misstatements of material fact or omit any material facts that would make the statements misleading.

More specifically related to tax matters, tax shelter regulations (Reg. § 1.6011–4) require that a transaction that is considered a reportable transaction must be specially disclosed on a taxpayer's return if (subject to some specified exceptions) it falls within any one of the following categories:

- Listed transactions;

- Confidential transactions;

- Transactions with contractual protections;

- Transactions generating tax losses exceeding certain stated amounts;

- Transactions resulting in a "significant" book-tax difference; and

- Transactions generating a tax credit if the underlying asset is held for less than 45 days.

A "listed transaction" is a transaction that is the same as or substantially similar to a transaction type that the IRS has determined to be a tax avoidance transaction and has designated as such in published guidance (*e.g.*, Notice 2009–59, 2009–2 C.B. 170). Confidential transactions are those offered under conditions of confidentiality for the benefit of "any person who makes or provides a statement, oral or written, (or for whose benefit a statement is made or provided) as to the potential tax consequences that may result from the transaction."

A transaction is deemed to have contractual protections if the taxpayer has obtained or been provided with contractual protection against the possibility that part or all of the intended tax consequences will not be sustained. For example, a fee contingent on achieving certain tax consequences constitutes a contractual protection.

A transaction is a "loss transaction" for this purpose if it results in, or is reasonably expected to result in, a specified level of loss under I.R.C. § 165 (*e.g.*, for corporations—$10 million in a single year/ $20 million in a combination of years). The "significant book-tax difference" category applies only to taxpayers that are either: (1) reporting companies under the Securities Exchange Act of 1934 (and related business entities); or (2) business entities with gross assets greater than or equal to $100 million (including assets of related business entities). A book-tax difference for a transaction will be considered "significant" only if it is, or is reasonably expected to be, more than $10 million on a gross basis in any taxable year. A transaction falls within the less than 45 day holding requirement category if it results in, or is reasonably expected to result in, a tax credit in excess of $250,000 and the asset giving rise to the credit is held by the taxpayer for less than 45 days.

Every "organizer and seller" (including a material advisor receiving a specified fee) of a "potentially abusive tax shelter" is required to maintain a list under I.R.C. § 6112. For this purpose, a "potentially abusive tax shelter" is:

1.   any transaction required to be registered as a tax shelter under I.R.C. § 6111; and

2.   "any transaction that a potential material advisor knows or has reason to know, at the time the transaction is entered into or an interest is acquired, meets one of the categories of a reportable transaction"—i.e., a transaction for which disclosure is required based on the above-mentioned six categories of transactions.

The lists must be furnished to the IRS when and if requested.

Other countries are belatedly following the U.S. government's lead. The BEPS action 12 report recommended that countries adopt mandatory disclosure regimes that included penalties to ensure compliance, and published model mandatory disclosure rules in 2018. The EU has now adopted these rules.

(B)   UNCERTAIN TAX POSITIONS (UTP)

Financial Accounting Standards Board (FASB) Interpretation No. 48, *Accounting for Uncertainty in Income Taxes—an interpretation of FASB Statement No. 109* (FIN 48 is now codified as Topic 740 of the Accounting Standards Codification) clarifies the accounting for uncertainty in tax positions. This Interpretation requires that a taxpayer in its financial statements recognizes the impact of a tax position if that position is more likely than not of being sustained on audit, based on the technical merits of the position.

However, taxpayers may have taken a position for tax purposes that it cannot "book" for financial purposes (*i.e.*, it creates a reserve for financial statement purposes). The difference between tax positions taken for financial statement purposes and for tax purposes—often referred to as "book-tax" differences—are reflected on Schedule M-3 of the corporate tax return (Form 1120) to provide the IRS with more efficient reporting and transparency between book and tax reporting.

The IRS Schedule UTP requires certain large business taxpayers to report their uncertain tax positions (UTPs) on their annual tax returns. It is the view of the IRS that preparation of Schedule UTP should flow naturally from the preparation of financial statements, listing out U.S. income tax positions for which a reserve has been established in audited financial statements, or those for which a decision not to reserve was made because of an expectation to litigate. The Schedule UTP essentially provides a roadmap for IRS examiners to positions taken by the taxpayer for tax purposes for which their auditors cannot get to "more likely than not" that the position is correct for financial statement purposes. By having taxpayers highlight their own uncertain tax positions, IRS examiners do not have to divine these positions from the rest of the return and can adjust audit activity accordingly.

(C) TRANSFER PRICING DOCUMENTATION

The BEPS Project (action 13), introduced transfer pricing documentation recommendations applicable to large multinational companies. These reporting requirements include a master file; a local file; and country-by-country reporting. More than 100 countries have adopted, or announced plans to adopt, some kind of country-by-country reporting requirements. *See* § 11.07(B).

U.S. multinational groups (with annual revenues in excess of $850 million) are required to comply with these requirements by providing information on Form 8975, which mandates that a filer list each entity in the group (both domestic and foreign), indicating each entity's tax jurisdiction (if any), country of organization and main business activity, and certain financial and employee information for each tax jurisdiction in which the group does business. T.D. 9773, Reg. § 1.6038–4. The financial information includes revenues, profits, income taxes paid and accrued, stated capital, accumulated earnings, and tangible assets other than cash.

Companies file the country-by-country report with the tax administration in which they are headquartered. Tax administrations are supposed to exchange this information automatically. Many jurisdictions are complying with the exchange requirement via the Multilateral Convention on Administrative Assistance in Tax Matters. The United States has opted instead to enter into bilateral competent authority agreements providing for the exchange of information. One open question about the volume of information now being provided is how tax authorities will use it. Another is whether these reports will ultimately be made public. There have been strong initiatives within a number of countries in the latter regard.

§ 14.06   GLOBAL DEVELOPMENTS

As you wrap up your initial study of U.S. international tax rules, hopefully you've come to realize that even this comprehensive review represents nothing more than a toe in the proverbial international tax waters, and that it's not possible to think about the U.S. international tax rules in isolation. Rather, they are the product of a continuous give and take between the United States and other countries in terms of seeking to attract investment and investors and cracking down on planning opportunities.

It's in this second aspect of the development of international tax rules that the OECD has come to take on a larger role over the past several years. The OECD is not itself a legislative body, and its reports are simply recommendations that other countries have made various levels of commitments to adopt. Moreover, members of Congress are notoriously reluctant to take direction and advice from international organizations, especially ones headquartered in other countries. Nonetheless, the BEPS project has been very influential in changing the conversation over the role of international tax rules to limit cross-border tax arbitrage, and evidence of its recommendations and reactions to the project are sprinkled throughout the TCJA.

As this book is going to press, the OECD is engaged in a new project that has morphed out of BEPS and its failure to address questions about how to appropriately tax cross-border profits in the digitalized economy. A project that began with limited scope has now evolved into one that is asking fundamental questions about how to allocate multinational companies' profits between and among nations. Whether this project will result in a wholesale rewrite of international tax rules and what the implications might be for U.S. international tax rules is uncertain at this time. But it's likely that this edition of International Taxation in a Nutshell won't be the last.

CHAPTER 15

TAX AND TRADE AND FOREIGN POLICY

§ 15.01 TAXES, TRADE AND TARIFFS

As the previous chapters of this book have shown, international tax rules have been subject to revision by Congress repeatedly throughout the past century to achieve various goals relating to U.S. and overseas investment. The history of the development and evolution of U.S. international tax rules is to some degree a reflection of shifting U.S. policy goals relating to overseas development, balance of payments, and the strength of the domestic economy. In this chapter, we'll consider some of the tools that Congress has, and has authorized the executive branch to use, through which U.S. international tax rules are used more explicitly to advance U.S. protectionist or expansionist goals, or to influence or deter other countries' or taxpayers behaviors.

Generally speaking, tax and trade have developed as separate disciplines over the past fifty years—you probably won't discuss the World Trade Organization in a tax course, and the Internal Revenue Code is unlikely to be required reading in any course on international trade. But the reality is that tariffs— which are the ultimate enforcement mechanism when trade disputes go awry—are simply another means for imposing a tax on cross-border trade in goods (or services). If tariffs haven't been part of the international tax curriculum, it's because tariffs have played an increasingly smaller role in cross-border trade over the past several decades.

That trend may be reversing; whether that reversal is a short-term or longer-term trend remains to be seen. But what it does make clear is that international tax practitioners can't just ignore the impact and interaction of trade disputes—including the consequences of tariffs—on the pricing of goods and services as they move cross-border. Below we include a brief overview of trade agreements that overlap with international tax. The remaining parts of this chapter discuss a number of provisions that were explicitly enacted into the Code to influence other countries' behaviors (behaviors that have nothing to do with taxation). Finally, we conclude with a brief mention of a provision that allows the President to retaliate against other countries' discriminatory taxes.

(A) BILATERAL INVESTMENT AGREEMENTS

Bilateral investment agreements (BITs) between two countries are designed to offer protection to the investors from one jurisdiction for their investments in another. While BITs trace their roots to earlier in the 20th century, they became prevalent starting in the 1960s. An important feature of investment treaties is the protection they provide for investors against government expropriation of their investments without adequate compensation. Under the expropriation clause that's standard in BITs, investors retain protection from expropriation via tax assessments. In recent years, some taxpayers have used investment agreements as the basis for bringing claims against foreign governments for aggressive assessment of taxes on overseas investors.

(B)   GATT AND GATS

The General Agreement on Trade in Services (GATS) entered into force in 1995. It extends to the services sector the principles of the General Agreement on Tariffs and Trade, first signed in 1947. GATS and GATT generally prohibit countries from discriminating against residents of other countries in the trade of goods and services. Tax measures cannot be applied in an arbitrary or unjustifiably discriminatory way between countries where like conditions prevail, or as a disguised way to restrict trade in services. Tax measures won't be considered inconsistent with the requirements of national treatment if differences in treatment are designed to ensure the "equitable or effective imposition or collection" of direct taxes. As an example of a recent proceeding in which a tax measure was found to violate international trade agreements, in 2016, a WTO Appellate Body ruled that a number of measures that Argentina had adopted against countries it considered non-cooperative for tax purposes were violations of its trade commitments. WT/DS453/R.

The European Union has throughout the years sought to use the U.S. commitments in its trade agreements to have U.S. tax rules it views as harmful overturned. There has been discussion of a number of TCJA provisions potentially violating GATT or

GATS, including the deduction for FDII under I.R.C. § 250.

(C) COMPETITION POLICY AND CROSS-BORDER TAX

Beginning in 2014, the EU competition office has initiated public investigations against some EU member states for violating the EU treaty and in particular its state aid doctrine by granting beneficial and allegedly illegal tax rulings to (primarily U.S.) multinationals. Adverse decisions have been delivered against some countries/companies but as of the time of this book's writing they remain under appeal. The EU investigations similarly illustrate the blurring of lines between tax rules and trade policy in the cross border area and demonstrate how tax lawyers have to consider the broader social and regulatory landscape at the same time as weighing in on the technical language of the Code and the regulations.

§ 15.02 OVERVIEW OF INTERNATIONAL BOYCOTT PROVISIONS

Since 1976, I.R.C. § 999 has penalized U.S. taxpayers for participation in certain international boycotts. While the provisions are broadly written, they were enacted in response to the Arab boycott of Israel. Where the boycott provisions are applicable to a specific operation, a U.S. taxpayer is not entitled to any otherwise applicable foreign tax credit for foreign income taxes imposed on income from the operation. In addition, if the participating entity is a controlled foreign corporation, income earned from the operation is taxed directly to the U.S. shareholders even if the subpart F provisions would not otherwise apply.

The operation of I.R.C. § 999 is set forth in Guidelines published by the IRS in question and answer form. They were first issued in 1976 and have been revised several times since then, although the last major revision was in 1978. 1978–1 C.B. 521. The citations that follow refer to questions in the Guidelines.

Not all boycotts trigger the tax penalties of I.R.C. § 999. Boycotts sanctioned by U.S. law or an Executive Order—such as the sanctions against Iran—are not penalized. I.R.C. § 999(b)(4)(A). Furthermore, not all or even most unsanctioned boycotts are subject to I.R.C. § 999. Restrictions on the import or export of goods from a specific country—a primary boycott—are not addressed by I.R.C. § 999. I.R.C. § 999(b)(4). The principle of national sovereignty permits any country the right to decide who its trading partners will be. So for example, the fact that Syria does not permit Israeli products to be imported or that Kuwait requires that its exported oil not be resold to Israel does not trigger I.R.C. § 999 for a U.S. seller or buyer. U.S. bank's conditioning the payment of a letter of credit on providing a certificate that the goods did not come from a boycotted nation also is not boycott cooperation. Guidelines H-31. However, capital is treated differently from goods and services so that an agreement not to use capital originating in a boycotted nation in the production of goods is boycott cooperation. Guidelines I-6.

It is secondary and tertiary boycotts that are addressed by I.R.C. § 999. A secondary boycott is where a country refuses to deal with a company because that company (or a related corporation) deals with a boycotted nation in other transactions even though no products of the boycotted nation are involved in the transaction at hand. A tertiary boycott is where a country refuses to deal with a U.S. company that does no business with the boycotted country but which has dealings with other companies that deal with the boycotted country.

Specifically, I.R.C. § 999(b)(3) provides that a taxpayer cooperates with an international boycott if the taxpayer agrees to refrain from: (a) doing business with a boycotted nation; (b) doing business with anyone who does business with a boycotted nation; (c) doing business with any company whose management consists of people of a particular nationality, race, or religion; (d) hiring people of a particular nationality, race, or religion; (e) shipping or insuring products bound for the boycotting nation if the shipper or insurer does not cooperate with the boycott. I.R.C. § 999(b)(3).

Even if a taxpayer does not participate in an international boycott, the taxpayer may have a reporting obligation under I.R.C. § 999(a). There is a duty to report to the IRS any request for participation in an international boycott if a taxpayer or any related person had "operations" related to a boycotting country, its companies, or nationals. A request to participate in a primary boycott need not be reported. The Secretary of the Treasury maintains a list of boycotting countries. As of July 1, 2015, the list includes: Iraq, Kuwait, Lebanon, Libya, Qatar, Saudi Arabia, Syria, United Arab Emirates, and Yemen.

(A) BOYCOTT PARTICIPATION

In order for there to be participation in a boycott, a taxpayer must "agree" to certain prescribed conduct as a condition of doing business with a boycotting country. I.R.C. § 999(b)(3). An agreement not connected with business in a boycotting country is not addressed by I.R.C. § 999. For example, if a company doing business in Greece agrees with a vessel charterer to avoid Israeli ports, there is no boycott participation because the agreement was not made as a condition of doing business in an Arab country. Guidelines H-27.

If a taxpayer is doing business with an Arab country, an agreement (either oral or written) can be specific or can be inferred from a general course of conduct. If there is no agreement but a company in fact complies with the Arab boycott by refusing to hire Jewish workers, such actual compliance is not by itself an agreement. However, such compliance when combined with other factors might present a course of conduct that constitutes an agreement. The other factors might include the termination or lessening of business relationships with blacklisted firms in the absence of compelling non-boycott reasons or the refusal to enter into such relationships when there are compelling reasons to do so. Guidelines H-3. Conversely, if the company enters into an agreement to boycott which the company regularly ignores, tax penalties nevertheless apply. Guidelines H-18.

Perhaps the most transparent distinction in the Guidelines is the difference between "apply" and "comply." A contract term providing that an Arab country's boycott laws "apply" does not make the contract an agreement to boycott, but a term that says a company will "comply" with the same laws does. Guidelines H-3 and H-4. It is true that an "apply" provision can be one factor in an overall course of conduct from which an agreement to boycott may be inferred although repeated use of the "apply" provision does not give rise to the inference.

(B)   EXAMPLES OF PENALIZED CONDUCT

(1)   Discriminatory Refusals to Do Business

As indicated above, a taxpayer is penalized if there is an agreement to refrain from doing business: (a) with a boycotted country (or in a boycotted country), its nationals, or companies; (b) with a U.S. company doing business with a boycotted country (or in a boycotted country), its nationals, or companies; (c) with companies whose ownership is comprised of individuals of a specified nationality, race, or religion.

With respect to the first category (*i.e.*, secondary boycotts), an agreement to refrain from doing some types of business in a boycotted country but not others is cooperation with the boycott. Guidelines H-

21. An agreement not to supply a boycotting country with goods produced or manufactured with capital originating in a boycotted country is also prohibited conduct. Guidelines I-6.

The tertiary boycotts that trigger I.R.C. § 999 are refusals to do business with U.S. persons that conduct business with a boycotted nation. Consequently, a refusal to do business with a foreign company because it conducts business with a boycotted country is not penalized. Guidelines J-2B and J-11. However, an agreement not to deal with blacklisted companies constitutes boycott cooperation if no U.S. companies are presently on the list because they could be added to the list in the future. Guidelines J-4.

The third refusal-to-do-business category applies if in order to do business in a boycotting country, the ownership or management of a company cannot consist of individuals of a specified nationality, race or religion. For example, compliance with a country's request that the leader of an underwriting syndicate exclude from the syndicate a particular company because of the religion of its directors would trigger I.R.C. § 999. Guidelines K-3. On the other hand, an agreement by an exporter of goods that the goods will not bear any mark symbolizing a particular religion or a particular boycotted country does not constitute boycott cooperation. Guidelines K-1.

(2) Discriminatory Hiring Practices

The manner in which a restriction is drafted often determines if a provision amounts to boycott participation or not. For example, a contract provision precluding employment within the boycotting country or abroad of individuals who are members of a particular religion or nationals of a boycotted nation is boycott cooperation. Guidelines L-1 and L-5. On the other hand, if the U.S. company conditions employment upon an individual's obtaining a visa from a boycotting country which is categorically unavailable, there is no boycott cooperation. Guidelines H-10 through 12.

(3) Discriminatory Shipping and Insurance Arrangements

An agreement not to use a blacklisted shipper or insurer generally is boycott cooperation, with some exceptions. Guidelines M-1 and M-7.

(C)   TAX EFFECT OF BOYCOTT PARTICIPATION

Once it has been determined that a U.S. person has cooperated with an international boycott, a presumption arises that all operations in the boycotting country involve cooperation with the boycott. In ascertaining what activities are affected, the term "operations" takes on great importance. I.R.C. § 999(b)(1). The term "operations" has been interpreted to include all forms of business activities including purchasing, leasing, licensing, banking, extracting, manufacturing, transporting, and services of any kind. Guidelines B-1.

Not only is there a presumption that if boycott cooperation is found, all activities in the boycotting country are tainted, but I.R.C. § 999(b)(1) also presumes that the operations of all related persons involve boycott cooperation. Generally, related corporations are those with more than a 50 percent common ownership link, including brother-sister corporations controlled by a common parent as well as parent-subsidiary corporations. I.R.C. § 993(a)(3). The application of the related persons rules is more complicated than indicated but the thrust of the rules is to prevent U.S. taxpayers from isolating the boycott cooperation activities in one corporation without contaminating other business activities carried on through other related corporations with the boycotting nation.

The presumptions that contaminate all dealings with the boycotting country by a boycott-cooperating U.S. person and its related parties can be overcome by showing that some of the operations in the boycotting countries are clearly separate and identifiable from the boycott operations in which the taxpayer cooperated. I.R.C. § 999(b)(2).

Once the extent of the boycott cooperation has been determined, there are two alternative methods for computing the loss of tax benefits: the international boycott factor method or ascertaining the taxes and income specifically attributable to the tainted income. Method election is annual.

The "international boycott factor" is defined as a fraction, the numerator of which reflects the foreign operations of a person (and related persons) in or related to the boycotting country with which that person (or related persons) cooperates during the taxable year. The denominator represents the entire foreign operations of the person (or related persons). I.R.C. § 999(c). More specifically, the numerator is the sum of: (a) purchases made from all boycotting countries associated in carrying out a particular international boycott; (b) sales made to or from all boycotting countries associated in carrying out a particular international boycott, and; (c) payroll paid or accrued for services performed in all boycotting countries associated in carrying out a particular international boycott. Reg. § 7.999–1(c)(2).

Recall that the presumption of cooperation extended to all operations in a boycotting country while the international boycott factor formula is more sweeping. Consequently, the I.R.C. § 999(b)(1) presumption is more important using the method that determines specifically attributable taxes and income.

When the international boycott factor has been determined, it is used in computing tax penalties. Under I.R.C. § 908, the foreign tax credit that would otherwise be allowed under I.R.C. § 901 is reduced by the product of that amount and the international boycott factor. For example, suppose the numerator of the international boycott factor fraction (*i.e.*, purchases, sales, and payroll in the boycotting country) is $200,000 and the denominator (*i.e.*, total foreign purchases, sales, and payroll) is $1 million. Assume further that X Corp. would normally have a foreign tax credit computed under I.R.C. § 901 of $30,000. Under I.R.C. § 908, the foreign tax credit is reduced by $6,000 ($200,000/$1 million × $30,000) to

$24,000. Oddly, foreign taxes which are not creditable because of I.R.C. § 908 may be deductible under I.R.C. § 164 or as a business expense under I.R.C. § 162. I.R.C. § 908(b).

To the extent that a CFC cooperates in an international boycott, income which would not otherwise be treated as subpart F income is treated as subpart F income. I.R.C. § 952(a)(3). As a result, the income from the boycotting country will be treated as if it were distributed to the U.S. shareholders as a dividend. The amount of the constructive dividend is equal to the product of the international boycott factor and the income of the CFC which would not otherwise be treated as a constructive distribution.

Under some circumstances, the application of the international boycott factor method results in a loss of substantial tax benefits even when most of the benefits are not related to boycott operation. This arises because the international boycott factor is multiplied by, in the case of the foreign tax credit, the worldwide foreign tax credit of the taxpayer, and in the case of a CFC, the worldwide income.

To avoid this broad reach, a taxpayer can elect to determine the boycott penalty by identifying the specific taxes or income attributable to the boycott operations. Under this method, a taxpayer loses the tax benefits specifically attributable to operations tainted by cooperation with the boycott. This "specifically attributable" method is particularly attractive where the boycott-related operations produce little income and insignificant foreign taxes but would produce a large international boycott factor because of heavy purchases, sales, or payroll activities.

§ 15.03   FOREIGN BRIBERY PROVISIONS

Deterring cooperation with an international boycott is not the only ethical engineering in which the Code engages. The Code also discourages the payment of certain bribes and kickbacks to a foreign government in a number of ways. First, such payments are not deductible under I.R.C. § 162(c)(1) to the extent the payments violate the Foreign Corrupt Practices Act of 1977. Second, earnings attributable to bribes and kickbacks paid by a CFC are treated as subpart F income which is directly taxed to U.S. shareholders. Furthermore, the payments do not decrease the E&P of the CFC. I.R.C. §§ 952(a)(4) and 964(a).

These restrictions apply only to certain types of bribes and kickbacks. On the one hand, a free market philosophy suggests that the United States should be indifferent to bribes paid to foreign government officials. After all, such payments are business expenses paid for business reasons. Indeed, the line between a bribe and a commission can be quite fuzzy. Moreover, because other companies from other nations may have less compunction about paying bribes or kickbacks, U.S. companies need to make such payments to compete in a global economy. On the other hand, there is a notion that the U.S. government should not subsidize corrupt conduct by providing tax benefits to offending companies even if payments are made abroad. The payment of a bribe or kickback is corrupt under U.S. standards even if the recipients are not offended by the payments and such payments are standard operating procedure elsewhere.

The uneasy compromise arising out of these conflicting goals perhaps lacks a theoretical basis. The Foreign Corrupt Practices Act makes it illegal to make payments to foreign government officials with the intent of influencing official action to obtain business. However, payments to foreign government employees to expedite ministerial action in the course of business—"grease payments" or more euphemistically "facilitating payments"—are not prohibited. Facilitating payments might include: payments for expediting shipments through customs, securing adequate police protection, obtaining required permits, or payment to keep an oil rig from being destroyed.

One could be cynical and view the distinction between illegal bribes and kickbacks and grease payments as a U.S. attempt to benefit low-level foreign government officials rather than high-level officials that decide with whom to do business. One would suspect that profit-maximizing high-level foreign officials use low level officials as conduits to funnel grease payments to the high level officials. It seems doubtful that the Foreign Corrupt Practices Act has been much of a deterrent in eliminating the payments of bribes and kickbacks. Indeed, over the years, Congress has weakened the Foreign Corrupt Practices Act by: lessening criminal penalties;

creating a good faith defense for reasonable expenses incurred for product promotion or to ensure contract performance; clarifying that payments which are legal in the recipient's country do not violate U.S. law, and; clarifying that payments made to expedite ministerial government actions (grease payments) are not violations.

§ 15.04   DISCRIMINATION
AND RETALIATION

In addition to the anti-boycott and anti-bribery rules, the foreign tax credit rules also deny a foreign tax credit more generally to those countries that the United States doesn't recognize or with respect to which it has severed relations. The following countries meet this description for 2018: Iran, Libya (subject to a waiver), North Korea, Sudan and Syria. I.R.C. § 901(j). Income from such countries is also treated as subpart F income under I.R.C. § 952(a)(5).

Just like the Code provides a mechanism for punishing taxpayers who engage in behavior that members of Congress have found objectionable as a moral or policy matter, it also provides a means for retaliating against countries that engage in behavior that is viewed as discriminating against U.S. persons. Section 891 says that whenever the President finds that, under the laws of any foreign country, citizens or corporations of the United States are being subjected to discriminatory or extraterritorial taxes, the President shall so proclaim. In such case, the rates of tax imposed by I.R.C. §§ 1, 3, 11, 801, 831, 852, 871, and 881 shall, for the taxable year during which such proclamation is made and for each taxable year thereafter, be doubled in the case of each citizen and corporation of such foreign country.

Section 891 has never been invoked by a U.S. President since its predecessor was originally enacted in 1934. But it has been discussed as a possible means for the U.S. to respond to gross revenue digital taxes being imposed by some other countries that primarily impact U.S. companies.

The United States has also launched an investigation under § 301 of the U.S. Trade Act of 1974 against these digital taxes, which could authorize the President to take all appropriate action, including retaliation, to obtain the removal of any act, policy, or practice of a foreign government that violates an international trade agreement or is unjustified, unreasonable, or discriminatory, and that burdens or restricts U.S. commerce.

INDEX

References are to Pages

INBOUND TRANSACTIONS
See also U.S. Activities of Foreign Taxpayers, this index
Definition, 17, 21
International tax-free non-outbound transactions, 512

INCOME SOURCE
See Source Rules, this index

INDIVIDUAL INCOME
U.S. activities of foreign taxpayers, 26

INFORMATION EXCHANGE AGREEMENTS (TIEA)
Treaty provisions, 172

INSURANCE INCOME
Controlled foreign corporations, 284

INTANGIBLE ASSETS
Definition, 483
International tax-free transactions, 480
Outbound transactions between related parties, deemed
    payments, 483–484
Source rules, 51
Transfer Pricing and, 401

INTERCOMPANY PRICING
Generally, 375
Advance pricing agreements, 416
Arm's length principle, 381, 387, 397
Controlled services transactions, 398
Cost-sharing agreements, 400
Methodologies overview, 375
Penalties, 412

INTEREST EXPENSE
Business interest limitation, 117
Deductibility, 102
Deduction allocation rules
    Foreign corporations, 105
    U.S. corporations, 355, 361
Foreign currency contracts, gain and loss treatment, 428